AMERICAN ENTERPRISE IN SOUTH AFRICA

AMERICAN ENTERPRISE IN SOUTH AFRICA

Historical Dimensions of Engagement and Disengagement

RICHARD W. HULL

NEW YORK UNIVERSITY PRESS
New York and London

Library of Congress Cataloging-in-Publication Data
Hull, Richard W., 1940–
American enterprise in South Africa : historical dimensions of
engagement and disengagement / Richard W. Hull.
p.   cm.
Bibliography: p.
Includes index.
ISBN 0-8147-3462-6 (alk. paper)
1. Investments, American—South Africa—History.   2. Corporations,
American—South Africa—History.   3. International business
enterprises—South Africa—History.   I. Title.
HG5851.A3H85   1990   89-12548
338.8'8973'068—dc20   CIP

Book design by Ken Venezio

This book is dedicated to

VINCENT P. CAROSSO,

KENAN PROFESSOR OF HISTORY,

NEW YORK UNIVERSITY,

a valued friend and colleague.

Contents

Illustrations

Tables

Preface and
Acknowledgments

This book is a history of nearly three centuries of American entrepreneurial involvement in South Africa, from the late seventeenth century to 1988. It focuses on the elements of change and continuity in the role of the American private sector in South Africa's development. Over the last twenty-five years a debate of increasing intensity has been raging in the United States over the question of U.S. presence in that racially torn country. Eloquent and impassioned arguments have been posited on the pros and cons of engagement and disengagement, of economic sanctions and trade embargoes, of cultural boycotts and assistance to organizations seeking to overthrow the white power structure and the apartheid institutions that sustain it.

Since the Sharpeville tragedy in 1960, there has been a great efflorescence of publications of uneven quality concerned with the recent history of South Africa. Many of them are rather unbalanced, aiming to promote a specific viewpoint. Perhaps one can argue that it is impossible to analyze South Africa's tumultuous history without risking criticism for being passionate and polemical, insensitive or racist, radical or revolutionary. But this book is not a history of apartheid, nor is it really an economic or social history of South Africa. Were it so, one could fault it for a multitude of omissions of historical facts and trends. Instead, the volume intends to provide an essential historical dimension to the current debate on America's presence in South Africa—a debate that hitherto has lacked depth as well as breadth and that has shed more heat than light on an enormously complex and multifaceted issue.

I believe this book is unique in several respects. To my knowledge, no one has published a work that focuses specifically on the full range of American activity in South Africa—missionary, social, cultural, business, and educational—from its very beginnings to the present day. And very few scholars have attempted to trace the role of American multinational corporations in South Africa from the last quarter of the nineteenth century. I am fully aware that such an undertaking is intellectually dangerous and potentially controversial. The intensive phase of my research, which spanned a decade and included libraries and archives in six countries and twenty-one cities, was akin to crossing a mine field or working within the eye of an anti-apartheid cyclone. It began in South Africa on June 16, 1976, and ended on April 18, 1986, on the Yale University campus amidst an anti-apartheid demonstration. My probings into corporate activities frequently generated mixed reactions of wonderment and suspicion from government officials, librarians, and executives in the United States as well as in South Africa.

This research has drawn upon a massive corpus of primary and secondary material, ranging from public documents to annual reports of key missionary societies, multinational corporations, and private philanthropies. The final product may be faulted as being more encyclopedic than analytical; and, indeed, one of my objectives has been to identify key individual and institutional actors, to place them chronologically in the South African drama, and to assess the nature of their activities. In that sense, this is a book for serious students of African studies and American business history, as well as a guide for journalists, corporate executives, directors of private philanthropies, government policymakers, and lay persons in search of a broad, nonpolemical perspective and concerned with the long view of things. Can it be argued that it is intellectually dishonest to cast judgments on the present state of affairs between the two countries without some comprehension of the history of our long involvement, especially in the pre-Sharpeville decades? While a moral consensus may have at last been reached on the inherent evil of apartheid, there still remains a significant divergence of opinion over the means to eradicate it.

There are limitations to sweeping surveys, to macrohistories, particularly if we attempt to compress so much over such a long period into a few hundred printed pages. The final product can be quite superficial. Certainly, this is not intended to be a definitive study, or the last word. But it does seem to fill a gap, and I hope that it will both be a pioneering work in its scope and help to set the debate in a wider historical context.

In this book I have suggested that America's involvement in South Africa extends very deeply into the past, long before Soweto, Sharpeville, or even the Second Boer War, and that it has been marked by cycles of engagement and disengagement, cycles affected as much by economic policies and events in the United States as by the actions and policies of Great Britain and South Africa.

Since entrepreneurship figures prominently in this book, it might be useful to define the term. It is a concept that is in a continual state of evolution. The French economist J. B. Say may have been the first to use the term in 1803. He defined *entrepreneurs* as people who strive to improve the productivity, or yield, of available resources. Over the years, entrepreneurs came to be regarded as individuals willing to take risks and to deal with uncertainties in hopes of maximizing a profitable return on their investment of time, techniques, money, and resources.

For the purposes of this study, I define *entrepreneur* as an individual, institution, or corporate entity that takes advantage of opportunities to develop new markets and new consumers for their ideas or products, to introduce technological or managerial innovations, or to improve methods of production or marketing. Entrepreneurs might also develop or reorganize an industry to enhance its performance. In other words, American entrepreneurs in South Africa exploited change as an opportunity to introduce new concepts, techniques, and services.

Not all entrepreneurs are capitalists, seeking to accumulate wealth exclusively for themselves or their organizations. Indeed, some may be altruistically motivated, anticipating that their enterprise may ultimately promote the happiness or well-being of their recipients. They are, however, all risk-takers, and they are not afraid to operate in an environment of uncertainty. In this study, entrepreneurs appear in many realms, including the social, religious, and educational as well as economic. They operate primarily in the private sector but also use government agencies to advance their ends. I concur with Peter Drucker that "the entrepreneur always searches for change, responds to it, and exploits it as an opportunity."[1] Entrepreneurs are in essence innovators. I also agree with Jules Backman that an entrepreneur sees a need and then brings together the manpower, materials, and capital required to meet it.[2]

It should become apparent that the entrepreneurial impulse has been a vitally important and heretofore underemphasized force impelling

Americans to South Africa. They went out to that corner of the world not to lay down permanent roots or to establish a colonial outpost, and not always to emplant doctrines of freedom and racial equality but to take advantage of opportunities for the advancement of themselves as well as South Africans, both black and white. They came as slavers and whalers, missionaries and gunrunners, pimps and prostitutes, educators and social workers, preachers and doctors, prospectors and engineers, moneylenders and merchants. They injected new technologies, fresh entrepreneurial ideas, and, ultimately, capital resources that were essential to the nation's economic growth but that also both contributed to and militated against the evolution of apartheid. Given their miniscule physical presence and the fact that America's trade with South Africa never amounted to more than 1 percent of its total foreign commerce, it is a wonder that they played such an enormously vital role in South Africa's economic development. Indeed, from an entrepreneurial perspective alone, Americans helped to establish one of the first high schools and hospitals for blacks and one of the earliest African newspapers. They laid the managerial foundations for the De Beers diamond monopoly, helped to rescue the gold mining industry, and provided start-up capital for Anglo-American, one of the world's largest corporations. They also became the chief suppliers, refiners, and distributors of petroleum and provided South Africa with the technology to achieve greater energy self-sufficiency through synfuels and nuclear-power generation. And among many other things, Americans played an important role in developing the modern shipping, computers, office equipment, fruit, and entertainment industries. Substantial numbers of South Africans moved their goods in American vehicles and aircraft, cultivated, enclosed, and irrigated fields with American farm equipment, fabricated much of their clothing on Singer sewing machines, organized their data with American information systems, fought wars against themselves and others with American military materiel, mined their ores with American drills, and looked at themselves through photographic film and cameras made by Eastman Kodak. In many complex and contradictory ways American enterprise helped to strengthen as well as to weaken the forces of apartheid.

Obviously, many other countries were as profoundly affected by the United States and its products. This study, however, examines the reasons behind the ebb and flow of the United States' entrepreneurial presence in a nation where its activities are presently under intense international scrutiny. The anti-apartheid legislation that has emerged from the U.S. Congress will have profound implications not only for America's relations with South Africa but for the conduct of American enterprise in the wider world economy for many years to come.

While the vast majority of works on South Africa are concerned with diplomatic or political history, this one concentrates on the activities of the private sector. It can, however, be placed within the context of a number of excellent recent historical works that may be less economic in orientation and more narrowly focused but are nevertheless extremely useful. For the early period, there is Alan Booth's *The United States Experience in South Africa, 1784–1870* (1976). John W. Cell compares segregation in late nineteenth-century South Africa and the United States in *The Highest Stage of White Supremacy* (1982), while Thomas J. Noer looks at the period from a diplomatic perspective in his *Briton, Boer and Yankee: The United States and South Africa, 1870–1914* (1978) and continues with that perspective in mid-century with *Black Liberation: The United States and White Rule in Africa, 1948–1968* (1985). More recent diplomatic relations between the two countries are examined by Christopher Coker in *The United States and South Africa, 1968–1985* (1986). More general works include George Fredrickson's *White Supremacy: A Comparative Study in American and South African History* (1981) and William Minter's *King Solomon's Mines Revisited: Western Interests and the Burdened History of Southern Africa* (1986). And finally, there is the sweeping *The United States and Africa* (1985) by Peter Duignan and L. H. Gann, who cover the entire continent.

Of the many individuals who have assisted me in one way or another, space allows me to name only a notable few. I first thought about writing this book after reading two engaging works: *Americans in Africa, 1865–1900* (1966) by Robert O. Collins, Clarence Clendenen, and Peter Duignan and *Stars and Stripes in Africa* (1968) by Eric Rosenthal. Further inspiration came from my dear friends and longtime colleagues, Professor Peter Hlaole 'Molotsi and Akwasi B. Assensoh. Helpful encouragement and guidance also came from Reon Meij and Terry Collins as well as from Professors Harvey Feinberg, Hunt Davis, Henry F. Jackson, and David Coplan. Special thanks are due to Len Battifarano and Cheetah Haysom and to Professors Vincent P. Carosso and Warren Dean who read various drafts of all or part of the manuscript. Their suggestions proved to be invaluable. I must also acknowledge with gratitude the financial support received from New York University. I alone, of course, am fully responsible for any errors of fact or interpretation that remain.

NOTES

Explanations of abbreviations used in the notes as well as full publication information for those works cited in abbreviated form can be found in the bibliography.

1. Peter F. Drucker, *Innovation and Entrepreneurship* (New York: Harper and Row, 1985), p. 28.
2. Jules Backman, ed., *Entrepreneurship and the Outlook for America* (New York: Free Press, 1983), pp. 8–13.

AMERICAN ENTERPRISE IN SOUTH AFRICA

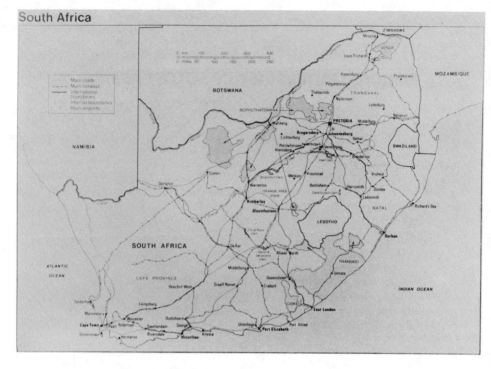

1. The Republic of South Africa, 1987. (Courtesy, *The Economist*)

ONE

Introduction: Early American Enterprise, 1680–1834

This chapter focuses on the origins and early development of American trade in the tempestuous waters and tranquil bays of southern Africa. It is a story of calculated courage mixed with reckless guile and of legitimate trade as well as brazen piracy. It is the beginning of a long history of Anglo-American competition for the riches of South Africa and its hinterlands. The chapter identifies the early American entrepreneurs and examines their motives as well as the nature of their commerce. What did they export, and what did they seek in return? What drew them to southern Africa, and what obstacles did they encounter? The chapter assesses the impact of the British occupation of the Cape and the American response. It reveals how the intrepid and opportunistic American entrepreneurs took advantage of conflicts not only between the British and the French but between the British and the local populations. The seafaring and peripatetic Americans, with their anticolonial bias, discovered that they could expand commercially and establish an extremely profitable niche in the trade without resorting to territorial conquest or even permanent settlement. Early American enterprise in South Africa was of an overwhelmingly commercial nature. But it reflects the dynamism, resilience, and dogged persistence of the Yankee captains in the face of overwhelming British naval superiority. While Britain possessed the naval power, the United States had the goods that were critical to the economic development of South Africa. The Americans acting as individuals, were almost always able to evade the web of official British and United States trade restrictions. Periods of retreat, or disengagement, were usually followed by eras of robust advance and deeper involvement.

THE PROFITS OF PIRACY

American involvement in southern Africa reaches far back into history, at least to 1680, with the arrival in Massachusetts of slave cargoes from the northwest coast of Madagascar. The slave trade in Madagascar was already of some importance, not only to neighboring Mauritius but also to the Cape and India. Along the northeast coast of Madagascar freebooting North American pirates and their middlemen established a number of small fiefdoms, including Libertalia and the island state of Sainte Marie. They garnered handsome profits preying on Arab dhows bound for the Persian Gulf as well as on European maritime traffic passing between the East Indies and the Cape of Good Hope. Pirates took on supplies in Cape Town or at an anchorage just to the north in Saldanha Bay, where the deep, cold waters offered excellent anchorage and an abundance of fish. Perhaps even earlier, occasional traders from British North America sold or bartered Madagascar slaves to officials of the Verenigde Oostindische Compagnie (VOC), or Dutch East India Company, at their castle in Cape Town. Certainly, captains of many nationalities called at Cape Town to sell small portions of cargo in order to have their ships repaired or to obtain provisions for their destinations in the East, in Europe, or in the Americas. Some slaves were sold as a hedge against possible losses of cargo in transit to the Americas. Almost from the time of the base's establishment in 1652, Cape Town was well integrated into the VOC's vast overseas mercantile empire.[1]

Slavery at the Cape was introduced to support the company and later to provide labor for the small, nonplantation agriculture of the white burghers. In the early years, however, Americans must have found it difficult to exchange slaves because company officials preferred to acquire them from their own fleets. It was only after the emergence of independent white burghers that opportunities for slave exchange improved.[2] In this early period southern Africa was a region for only the most audacious and daring of American entrepreneurs since English mercantilist policies severely limited their freedom of trade. Parliament's Navigation Acts of 1651, 1660, and 1663 established the ground rules for colonial participation in world trade.[3] Entrepreneurs in the British colonies were required to transport their goods in either English or colonial ships. Certain items, such as dyestuffs made from American flora and fauna, could be exported only to England or to other English colonies. The few American imports that trickled into Cape Town consisted mainly of ship masts, tobacco, cotton, and dyewoods and first had to be shipped to England for taxation before their reexportation to southern Africa. In other words, key products flowing between North America and southern Africa had to be marketed through the British mercantilist network. For example, cargoes from ports in the western Indian Ocean had to land on the South Atlantic island of St. Helena to obtain clearance from the English East India Company before proceeding to New York and elsewhere. The Navigation Acts further discouraged free trade by forbidding foreign merchants and trading companies from dealing directly with the English colonies. To make matters worse, a law passed in 1699 made it illegal to export colonial wool, yarn, and finished wood products to any foreign possession. Naval supplies were added to the enumerated list under the Navigation Acts in 1705. These laws effectively closed the British Empire to the Dutch. By the same token, they made trade with the Dutch possessions extremely risky and less attractive. It is therefore not surprising that, slaving aside, comparatively little direct trade existed between British North America and the Cape.[4]

The Dutch East India Company station at Cape Town was practically off limits for American entrepreneurs. Consequently, smuggling became common and adventuresome Yankees slipped into Cape Town's harbor with desperately needed supplies of tar, resin, and pitch used in the repair of ships. The ship chandlering trade of the Cape had already become quite substantial, and Cape businessmen and company agents looked to British North America for vital supplies.

American slavers and pirates encountered a different set of trade barriers that forced numbers of them to shift their operations to southeast Africa and to the Indian Ocean. For decades American pirates in the Caribbean had preyed on Spanish vessels laden with valuable ores and coinage from the mines and mints of the New World. Specie (metallic currency) was in short supply in British America, thanks in part to the Currency Act of 1764, which severely limited colonial money supply. But illlegal sourcing in the Caribbean dramatically declined after British men-of-war began convoying the Spanish ships. In the West Indies and along the coast of West Africa pirates interested in other booty had to contend with Royal West African Company, which had enjoyed an official monopoly among the Anglophone traders since its charter by the English Crown in 1672.[5]

The North American colonies, chronically short of specie looked to every source, legitimate or otherwise. Slavers from New York and Narragansett Bay eagerly furnished pirates with supplies in return for specie and gold that had been plundered from ships en route to India. In the last two decades of the seventeenth century pirates of the western Indian Ocean were a major source of specie and figured prominently in the strength of the colonial economies of North America.

For a brief spell opportunities improved for American pirates after Parliament's refusal in 1694 to renew the East India Company's trade monopoly beyond the Cape of Good Hope. Wealthy New York merchants and landowners, notably Frederick Philipse, his son Adolphus, and Stephen DeLancey, took full advantage. Late in the 1690s the senior Philipse, who by then had become New York's largest slave importer, boasted of profits exceeding several thousand pounds on single voyages between the Hudson Valley and Madagascar and Mozambique. Slaves who were sold to Americans in southeast Africa for less than £2 commanded £30 or more in New York. The Philipses and other New York merchants also shipped rum, purchased locally for about two shillings a gallon, and sold it to pirates in the Indian Ocean for upwards of sixty shillings.[6]

The lucrative flow of slaves and specie substantially diminished after the East India Act of 1698 reimposed tight restrictions on trade east of the Cape of Good Hope. In the summer of that year the English company secured a new charter, conferring on it a monopoly of trade in waters off Mozambique and Madagascar. For years, the English East India Company had complained that piracy in the Indian Ocean was disrupting commercial intercourse with India and depriving the stockholders of potential profits. The Royal Navy now put teeth into the new act by making more energetic efforts to reduce piracy on the high seas. Captain William Kidd, of Bahamian origin, was just one of many North Americans who were sent out to combat piracy, only to be lured into the occupation by the enormous profits. Kidd was eventually captured, returned to New York, and hanged in 1701. Meanwhile, New York merchants had already begun to reduce their involvement after the English courts confiscated a heavily loaded ship owned by Philipse. For the moment the risks of business loss and public ridicule outweighed the profits.[7]

YANKEES IN SEARCH OF SPERMACETI

Late in the eighteenth century American skippers began to recognize that the waters off southern Africa in the Mozambique Channel offered a bounty as lucrative as ivory and slaves: whales. Many homes of colonial America were illuminated by whale oil, and a substantial whaling industry had already emerged in the ports of New England. However, by the 1750s whales had practically disappeared from the American coast as a result of extensive and unregulated killing. For most whalers, the price differential between whale and vegetable oil no longer merited the expense and hazards of offshore whaling, so many abandoned the trade. The most intrepid ones, especially those of Nantucket Island, where whaling was as much a social institution as an economic one, began to venture thousands of miles away from home in search of treasured spermaceti, a white, waxy substance found in the head of the sperm whale. Such mammals were in great abundance in the Mozambique Channel, and their contents fetched handsome prices in North American ports. Even whale oil of a lesser quality could be sold to leather tanners and paint manufacturers. By the 1780s whalers from Nantucket, New Bedford, New London, Newport, and Salem were utilizing Cape Town and Walvis (whalefish) Bay as provisioning bases for their operations along the Namibian coast and in the Mozambique Channel. The incentive to whale in southern Africa increased in 1787, after markets in France were opened to American whale oil. Fortunes were built on whale oil and so, to a degree, were the opulent Greek-revival clapboard mansions erected in the seaports of New England by ship owners, captains, and merchants. The profits and risks of whaling were as astonishing as the meager wages and inhumane conditions suffered by the ships' crews. Mortality rates on board were exceedingly high, and alcoholism was pervasive.[8]

REVOLUTION AND COMMERCE

For decades Americans had played a large and disproportionate role in world trade, whether in slaves or in other commodities. New England, endowed with seemingly limitless timber resources, became a preeminent supplier of wood for the construction of ships and warehouses. By the onset of the Revolution in 1775, more than a third of British-registered ship tonnage was constructed in the North American colonies, much of it in small, independently owned shipyards from Maine to New York.[9]

American commercial activity in southern Africa suffered during the early years of the Revolution. The British blockade of North American ports greatly reduced maritime activity, and the volume of wartime overseas trade reached a nadir early in 1777. The directors of the Dutch East India Company in Amsterdam warned their officials in Cape Town not to offer assistance to American vessels. The officials, however, had profited from trading with the Yankees and tended not to enforce the directive. Indeed, American captains en route to Madagascar and Mauritius continued to drop anchor at Table Bay. Cape Town was an important refreshment and ship repair center and provided a port where captains and crews of all friendly nations could obtain fresh water, meat, and citrus fruits. Yet in those turbulent times, the Cape exported precious little to the American colonies other than wine. The colony was more an entrepôt than a center of production for export. Thus, from early times Americans valued the Cape more for its strategic location and commercial utility than for its human or natural resources. Nevertheless, the vineyards of Henrik Cloete produced an inexpensive and tolerably good Constantia wine that in the late eighteenth century found a place on many American ships and in the bawdy seaside taverns of New England.

American trade outside the British possessions rebounded dramatically after 1778. Privateering emerged as a major enterprise, revitalizing the American colonies' fragile wartime economy and weakening the fiber of British shipping. Indeed, over the course of the war, the British lost two thousand vessels.[10]

TARGETS OF OPPORTUNITY

With the restoration of peace and British recognition of American independence in 1783, the sea lanes were reopened. The American economy had come through the Revolution surprisingly well and appeared fundamentally stronger than it had been on the eve of the conflict. The wartime import famine had stimulated, not weakened, indigenous enterprise. Perhaps through the trauma and challenge of war Americans had become more willing to take risks and to venture into new markets in order to survive and, if fortunate, to prosper.

The postwar decade experienced a steady increase in American exports of wheat, flour, and maize. Between 1772 and 1792 shipments almost doubled in volume to the African region, especially to the North African principalities and to small traders in southern Africa.[11] Free at last from the straightjacket of mercantilist restrictions, American entrepreneurs eagerly looked for new opportunities to trade. They took full advantage of this new freedom to operate directly in non-British markets, though perhaps more out of necessity than choice, considering that U.S. ships were banned from the British West Indies after 1783. The colonial possessions of France and the Netherlands were now viewed as particularly attractive targets of opportunity.

American commerce waxed in the Indian Ocean and south Atlantic as whaling and other commercial activities rebounded vigorously after a near suspension during the war. Elias H. Derby, a merchant from Salem, Massachusetts, pioneered in the trade to India. Derby's voyage in the *Empress of China* from New York to Canton in 1784 fired the United States' curiosity and launched the fledgling new republic into the great Far Eastern trade. On Derby's initiative, many Salem entrepreneurs became active in the Indian Ocean, and from 1786 their vessels appeared frequently at Cape Town's wharves. The port became an important provisioning point for ships owned by Derby and his associates trading in the Indian Ocean and in the Far East.[12]

Cape Town was fast becoming more than a mere victualling port for passing ships. Exports from the United States alone climbed from $46,582 in 1792 to $91,531 a year later. Since 1788 trade had been sufficient to merit a special "American Wharf" at Cape Town. It was becoming clear to all mariners and merchants that the small Cape settlement was developing into a full-fledged colonial economy. A small but active local entrepreneurial class had emerged and looked for new commercial opportunities. They found Americans eager to buy local hides, ostrich feathers, Constantia wines, and Dutch East India Company imports from Asia. The Capetonians purchased lumber, mainly pine board, from the forests of northern New England, slave-grown Virginia tobacco, and winter wheat harvested on small family farms in Massachusetts and New York.[13]

THE LION AND THE EAGLE

The era of the Napoleonic Wars in Europe provided further opportunities for American overseas trade. Ship builders and ship owners reflected upon those years of European conflict as their golden age. For a breathtaking moment, the young and diminutive United States commanded the enviable position of great neutral shipper for the world. Initially, the United States was negatively affected by the outbreak of hostilities, and in 1794 exports to the Cape fell dramatically to $4,376.[14] Then, in September 1795, shortly after France overran Holland, the British seizure of Cape Town ended almost 143 years of Dutch East India Company rule. The first British governor regarded the Cape as the master link of connection between the Western and Eastern worlds. The passage to India had to be free of enemy threats, and thus the Cape was viewed by British military strategists as the "Gilbraltar" of the Indian Ocean. It was not long before the British had established a huge garrison at Cape Town. Starved of critical supplies as a result of the wars in Europe, the garrison had little choice but to encourage American smugglers.[15]

Though the U.S. presence in that part of the world was growing, there was little impulse in government to establish a colony, as Congress made clear in 1796, when it flatly rejected a request by several U.S. naval officers to create a colony along the Natal coast in South Africa. The United States wanted to expand trade but it was loath to forge an overseas territorial empire. The British, however, remained unconvinced of America's aims in southern Africa, and for decades afterwards they looked suspiciously on U.S. commercial activities in the region.[16]

FORMALIZING THE RELATIONSHIP

Nevertheless, the volume of American trade with the Cape colony became large enough to justify the opening of a consulate at Cape Town in 1799. It was one of the first to be established overseas and clearly attested to the importance the United States attached to this small though busy seaport. Annual exports to the Cape had reached $183,569, largely reflecting substantial wheat shipments from Philadelphia. Between 1795 and 1800 no less than 135 American vessels called at Cape Town. American entrepreneurs were exporting increasing volumes of wooden planks and pine boards, spermaceti candles, and cattle and horses from New England. Philadelphia's trade with the Cape had shown especially robust growth. Clearly, the United States needed an official to protect and promote the interests of American merchants and mariners along the coast of southern Africa. Not surprisingly, it was a Philadelphian, the prosperous John Elmslie, who was despatched to Cape Town and opened the first U.S. consulate in Africa south of the Sahara.[17]

What kind of colony greeted Mr. Elmslie as he opened the doors of the new U.S. Consulate? It was an intensely patriarchal, caste-like, highly stratified, and racially segregated society of slaveowners. The British garrison aside, its white population of nearly 22,000 consisted overwhelmingly of conservative, Dutch-descended Calvinists with a mixture of French Huguenots and Germans. A few hundred cosmopolitan and prosperous freeburgher families lived in Cape Town or on expansive estates in nearby valleys amid a larger white population of impoverished Boers, or poor tenant-farmers, some of whom had already begun to disperse, or trek, eastward and northward in search of land. The ancestors of most of these whites had at one time been in the employ of the Dutch East India Company. Toiling under the white farmers were approximately 26,000 ethnically diverse slaves, mainly of Angolan and Mozambican origin. In Cape Town itself were also a sprinkling of Muslim craftsmen of predominantly Malaysian provenance. The indigenous populations of Khoikhoi and San, whom I will discuss later, had already been dispossessed of much of their ancestral lands. Khoi, slaves, and a few whites over the century had genetically merged to produce a racially mixed population known as Cape coloreds. They numbered in the thousands, and though many of them were westernized, Christian, and spoke the language of the whites, they suffered social discrimination and were derisively referred to as Bastaards. Out on the eastern frontier, the Cape populations confronted the numerically superior Bantu-speaking populations, particularly the Xhosa, who were also dispersing. The whites feared them and derisively referred to them as kaffirs. These racial and ethnic groups competed violently for land and cattle, occasionally cooperating and forming alliances but more often stealing one another's cattle and destroying crops and homes. The company officials in Cape Town had attempted to maintain security and to reduce interracial friction through territorial segregation and a racially discriminatory and Draconian penal code. But economic imperatives inexorably drew the various populations together, often with implosive force. The young American consul seemed undaunted by the turmoil on the frontier and the political uncertainty of newly imposed British rule in Cape Town and the colony. The prospect of local profit and the crucial position of Cape Town along the new route to the Indies sufficed to justify an official United States presence.

Peace between England and France was briefly restored between 1801 and 1803, and the sea lanes were reopened between the Cape and the British Isles. Consequently, after 1801 the British garrison at Cape Town was reduced and became less needful of American imports. Internally, trade at the Cape was liberated from the stifling company monopolies of the Dutch past. Externally, the remote colony was gradually brought into the system of British imperial preferences. In December 1801 a proclamation allowed duty-free access for goods manufactured in Britain or Ireland and transported to the Cape from British ports in British hulls, but all other manufactures, even if carried in British ships, were required to pay a 10 percent duty.[18]

The proclamation may have reflected English concerns over the explosive growth of American trade in the East. Even though it became effective in July 1802, Cape imports from the United States in that year alone soared to an astonishing $240,286. As John Barrow, a contemporary observer, noted, "Americans, for some years past, have been establishing a very considerable carrying trade from the eastward on the ruins of the Dutch commerce, and have acquired no small portion of the India and China trade." He added that "Americans sell lumber at the Cape and in payment they are glad to get bills on India for hard money, which they carry to China to purchase goods."[19] Cape businessmen paid for American goods in Indian currency. The Americans then sailed on to the East, laden with an easily convertible currency and often with Cape goods taken on consignment. On the return voyage, some ships carried foodstuffs and calcutta cloth from India, Chinese porcelain, herbs and tea, and other exotic items. Some of these goods were exchanged in Table Bay for Cape products and marine repair services.[20]

The new restrictions did not bode well for nationals of countries outside the British Empire, especially for Americans, who were already reeling under their most severe economic depression since independence. Underlying their economic malaise was the reduced demand by foreigners for American exports.

A measure of free trade returned to the Cape between 1803 and 1806. In that brief interlude, Britain transferred the Cape colony to the Batavian Republic, a regime governed from the Netherlands. Company rule, notorious for its corruption, monopolistic practices, and mismanagement and verging on bankruptcy, was not restored. To the delight of local merchants, the new Dutch authorities, who were distrustful of British and French imperial designs and were only too anxious to diversify their trade in the direction of the United States, followed a relatively liberal trade policy with the Americans. The local economy prospered, and American exports soared again, reaching a dramatic peak of $473,345.[21] The volume of trade was actually greater if one considers that specie had always been chronically in short supply and a fair amount of trade had to be conducted by barter.

From 1805 Americans at home were in the floodtide of prosperity. Agriculture dominated the economy, and fully two-thirds of its produce found overseas markets, with a considerable portion of the foodstuffs destined for northern and southern Africa. Cape demands for imported food were escalating. By 1806 its population had expanded to approximately twenty-six thousand whites, thirty thousand slaves, and more than twenty thousand Khoi servants.[22] It should be noted that the Dutch East Company had always forbidden the enslavement of indigenous populations. The light-skinned Khoi and San ethnic groups had preceded the Dutch at the Cape by many centuries and therefore could not be placed in human bondage. The San, or bushmen, were, however, often hunted down like game, and the Khoi, who possessed valuable cattle, interacted economically with the white aliens. Eventually their ranks were decimated by European diseases for which they had no natural immunities. The white settlers encroached on their lands, and by the opening of the nineteenth century the once-proud Khoi, or "Men of Men," had become vagrants and clients on the lands of their ancestors.

THROUGH BLOCKADES AND EMBARGOES: THE PROFITS AND PITFALLS OF NEUTRALITY

War resumed between England and France, rekindling concerns that Napoleon's navy might attempt to seize the Cape and interdict British shipping. Those fears were allayed in January 1806, after the outgunned Batavian garrison at Cape Town readily surrendered to an English fleet. The second British occupation was more explicitly aimed at safeguarding Great Britain's lucrative trade with India. This time, the British were determined that their rule would be permanent. The Cape colony could no longer be entrusted to a foreign government unable to withstand an attack from a nation hostile to British maritime interests.

Anglo-American relations steadily deteriorated in the early years of the nineteenth century, especially when Great Britain reopened the issue of American neutrality after the war resumed against Napoleon in May 1803. In 1805, the British reimposed the old Rule of 1756, permitting neutrals, notably the United States, to ship only goods normally carried in peacetime. This rule, also known as the Essex Decision, was countered by Napoleon's Berlin Decree, which implemented a strategy of blockading Britain by sea.[23]

Many American ships were subsequently boarded and searched by the British navy and harassed by the French. Neutrality may have reaped handsome profits, but it also invited greater risks. Foreign commerce became so difficult and dangerous that in retaliation President Thomas Jefferson asked Congress to counter with the Embargo Act of 1807. The act, effective from December, closed American ports to foreign ships and barred American vessels from trading in overseas ports. United States consulates were closed, including the one in Cape Town.

The effect of the Embargo Act on trade with the Cape Colony was immediate and catastrophic. U.S. products, including vital naval stores, cotton, and flour, were bottled up in American warehouses. The economic strangulation in the United States forced hundreds of businesses into bankruptcy. In 1808 U.S. exports to the Cape fell to $12,390.[24] Worldwide, American commerce went into such a tailspin that in 1809 President James Madison repealed the legislation. The superseding Non-Importation Act of 1809 partially reopened trade by allowing commerce with all countries except England and France.

The United States profited from its position as a neutral in the wars between England and France. Increasing tension with Great Britain, however, forced the United States in 1812 to abandon neutrality and to declare war on its former master. Hostilities between the United States and Great Britain dragged on from June 1812 to the first quarter of 1815. Commerce was interrupted again as the British blockaded nearly the entire American coastline. Exports to the Cape and to almost everywhere fell drastically. After the war, however, trade with the Cape colony resumed with vigor.

MONEY AND BANKING: BUILDING FOR PERMANENCE

The Napoleonic Wars had made Britain appreciate the vital strategic importance of the Cape of Good Hope for the preservation of hegemony in India. The British were now intent on establishing a permanent position at the Cape and began to implement programs for developing the local economy in order to make the colony financially self-supporting.

The Dutch formally and permanently ceded the Cape colony to Great Britain after the signing of a treaty at the London Convention of August 1814. In December the Treaty of Ghent ended the war between Britain and the United States. Peace returned to the high seas, and the period 1807 to 1819 witnessed rapid economic growth for the Cape.

After the Napoleonic Wars the British authorities instituted a series of fiscal reforms to set the colony on a firmer financial footing and to integrate it more fully into the imperial system. Great Britain had determined the monetary practices of the colony since the reoccupation in 1806. But for economic development to accelerate, the economy first had to be more thoroughly monetized in order to link it to the metropolis; a nonmonetized economy could not be integrated into the capitalist world.

Only in Cape Town did currency circulate freely. Under Dutch company rule, coins of many nations had circulated in an unregulated, almost chaotic manner. Moreover, the Cape had historically suffered from a chronic drainage of coins due, perhaps, to the persistent negative balance of foreign trade and the high incidence of illegal trading with passing ships by private Cape Town merchants. In the face of these problems, the Dutch company regularly purchased currencies, and from early company days, the coin of choice had been the Mexican-minted Spanish dollar because of its high silver content.

For decades Americans had taken advantage of the chronic shortage of specie, and well into the early 1830s ship captains carried coinage to the Cape. In fact, a considerable quantity of mainly Mexican-minted "American" coinage flowed out to numerous countries. This erratic and uncontrolled flow of specie contributed to a degree of monetary instability in the United States as well as at the Cape. Some American traders brought coins to Table Bay; others acquired Indian Ocean cowries in Cape Town markets and sold them in West Africa. Americans found an especially good market for cowries in the port of Whydah, where agents of the king of Dahomey bought them for the royal treasury.

Until 1825 the Cape suffered from having an inconvertible currency and a floating exchange rate. In that year the British Treasury made sterling coinage legal tender. The grossly inflated and unstable Rix dollar, now convertible into the far stronger sterling, soon disappeared. The old burgher families were deeply angered by the conversion process because since the British occupation in 1806 the Rix dollar had fallen by more than a third in value. Many of these old Cape Dutch families thus suffered considerable financial losses in the conversion process.[25]

With the ascendancy of British currency came the introduction of a modern credit system and the emergence of modern banks. Before 1808 the Cape had only one, the Lombard Bank, which was also the only bank anywhere in sub-Saharan Africa. Established in 1793 to assist in the introduction and circulation of paper currency,[26] it was, however, essentially a mortgage institution and pawnbroker, not a bank of deposit. The currency it issued never gained wide acceptance, depreciating steadily instead, even before the British occupation. Clearly, the Cape needed an institution capable of providing short-term credit without borrowers having to mortgage fixed assets. Consequently, in 1808 the British government set up a Discount Bank as a subsidiary of the Lombard Bank. This new state institution acted as a commercial bank and issued legal-tender paper money. The establishment of the state Discount

Bank and the monetary reforms of 1825 greatly stimulated British investment in the Cape's economy and more fully integrated it into the British capitalist system. Inevitably, private enterprise flowered as British capital trickled into the Cape.

THE TIDES OF TARIFFS

Much of the early foreign investment flowed into the vineyards, which rapidly developed into a major export industry. With British capital, Cape wine growers planted nine million new vines between 1811 and 1819, spurred on after a substantial tariff concession was granted in 1813 for Cape wines entering British markets. By 1822, 10 percent of all wine consumed in the British Isles came from Cape vineyards.[27] Britain's gain was the United States' loss, for wine exports to the United States fell dramatically after the American tariff of 1828. Conversely, American wheat exports to the Cape declined substantially when the military garrison at the Cape was reduced to 2,400 men in 1817.

Official tariff policies created enormous difficulties and frustrations for Americans and South Africans anxious to penetrate each other's markets. The Tariff Act of 1816 placed the United States on a protectionist course that continued for nearly two decades. And after about 1814 British tariff and nontariff barriers practically closed Cape Town to American traders. With British authority entrenched at the Cape, every effort was made to place British nationals in an advantageous position. English shippers and merchants gained an early lead because of their financial ties with British institutions in the metropolis. A British Order in Council of 1820 permitted American trade at the Cape but placed high duties on their goods. As in the past, Americans circumvented the restrictions by smuggling; and in the 1820s trade actually increased.[28]

Nearly a century and a half had elapsed since Americans first competed for the trade of southern Africa. Their presence was highly irregular and almost totally opportunistic. Only a handful of Yankees were attracted enough to take up permanent residence, and fewer still displayed any inclination to establish an enterprise or to make a direct investment. However, all this began to change quite dramatically in the 1830s.

NOTES

1. George E. Brooks, *Yankee Traders, Old Coasters, and African Middlemen* (Boston, 1970), pp. 9–16. See also Femme Gaastra, "The Shifting Balance of Trade of the Dutch East India Company," in Leonard Blusse and Femme Gaastra, eds., *Companies and Trade* (Leiden, 1981), pp. 47–69.

2. M. Whiting Spilhaus, *South Africa in the Making, 1652 to 1806.* See also Robert Ross, *Cape of Torments: Slavery and Resistance in South Africa* (London, 1983); Victor De Kock, *Those in Bondage: An Account of the Life of the Slave at the Cape in the Days of the Dutch East India Company* (Pretoria, 1963), pp. 71–77; Nigel Worden, *Slavery in Dutch South Africa* (London, 1985).

3. John J. McCusker and Russell R. Menard, *The Economy of British America, 1607–1789* (Chapel Hill, N.C., 1985), p. 47; Edward J. Perkins, *The Economy of Colonial America* (New York, 1980), p. 18.

4. James A. Henretta and Gregory H. Nobles, *Evolution and Revolution: American Society, 1600–1820* (Lexington, Mass., 1987), p. 31. See also James C. Armstrong, "The Slaves, 1652–1795," in Richard Elphick and Hermann Giliomee, eds., *The Shaping of South African Society, 1652–1820* (Cape Town, 1979); John G. B. Hutchins, *The American Maritime Industries and Public Policy, 1789–1914* (Cambridge, Mass., 1941), p. 244.

5. Charles Johnson, *General History of Pirates* (London, 1724). See also Edwin J. Perkins, *The Economy of Colonial America* (New York, 1980); John W. McElroy, "Seafaring in Early New England," *New England Quarterly* 8 (June 1935): 331–32.

6. Gary Nash, *The Urban Crucible: The Northern Seaports and the Origins of the American Revolution* (Cambridge, Mass., 1986), p. 42. For information on Philipse and the slave trade see Jacob Judd, "Frederick Philipse and the Madagascar Trade," *The New York Historical Society Quarterly* 55, 4 (October 1971): 354–74.

7. Johnson, *History of Pirates,* p. 18. See also Robert C. Ritchie, *Captain Kidd and the War Against the Pirates* (Cambridge, Mass., 1986).

8. See Alexander Starbuck, *History of the American Whale Fishery.* See also Edouard Stackpole, *Whales and Destiny: The Rivalry Between America, Britain, and France for Control of the Southern Whale Fishery, 1785–1825;* Stackpole, *The Sea Hunters: New England Whalemen During Two Centuries, 1635–1835* (New York, 1953).

9. Roy A. Foulke, *The Sinews of American Commerce* (New York, 1941).

10. Anna Cornelia Clauder, *American Commerce as Affected by the Wars of the French Revolution and Napoleon, 1793–1812* (Philadelphia, 1932). See also Jonathan Hughes, *American Economic History* (Glenview, Ill.,

1985); McCusker and Menard, *Economy of British America,* p. 362; Samuel Eliot Morison, *The Maritime History of Massachusetts, 1783–1860* (Boston, 1921).

11. Gordon C. Bjork, *Stagnation and Growth in the American Economy, 1784–1792* (New York, 1985).

12. Alan R. Booth, *The United States Experience in South Africa, 1784–1870,* p. 36. For greater detail, see The Papers of Elias H. Derby, Essex Institute, Salem, Mass.

13. Leonard Guelke, "The White Settlers, 1652–1780," in Elphick and Giliomee, eds., *South African Society,* pp. 41–67.

14. U.S. Documents, 4th Cong., 2nd sess., House Miscellaneous Document no. 44, 1795 (NAW). George McCall Theal, ed., *Records of the Cape Colony, 1793–1827* (London, 1897), vol. 1. Brookes, *Yankee Traders.*

15. Vincent Harlow, "The British Occupations, 1795–1806," in E. A. Walker, ed., *Cambridge History of the British Empire* (Cambridge, Eng., 1936), vol. 8. See also Eric Rosenthal, *Stars and Stripes in Africa* (Johannesburg, 1968).

16. Eric Rosenthal, ed., *Cape Directory, 1800.* See also Clarence C. Clendenen and Peter Duignan, *Americans in Black Africa up to 1865,* p. 27.

17. U.S. Department of State, *Consular List: Cape Town, 1800.* (Washington, D.C., 1802) (SAL). See also Booth, *U.S. Experience,* p. 19.

18. William M. Freund, "The Cape Under the Transitional Governments, 1795–1814," in Elphick and Giliomee, eds., *South African Society,* pp. 211–14.

19. John Barrow, *An Account of Travels into the Interior of South Africa* (London, 1804), 2:181.

20. Consul Elmslie to James Madison, Secretary of State, Report on Conditions, March 14, 1803, Letters from the American Consuls at the Cape of Good Hope, 1799–1870 (Washington, D.C., 1800) (NAW). See also Booth, *U.S. Experience,* p. 21.

21. Ibid., p. 21.

22. Consul Elmslie to James Madison, Secretary of State, Report, March 19, 1806, Letters from American Consuls (SAL). See also Richard Elphick and Robert Shell, "Intergroup Relations, 1652–1795," in Elphick and Giliomee, eds., *South African Society,* pp. 116–67.

23. Robert G. Albion and Jennie B. Pope, *Sea Lanes in Wartime: The American Experience, 1775–1942* (New York, 1942). See also Myron H. Luke, "The Port of New York, 1800–1810: The Foreign Trade and Business Community," Ph.D. dissertation (New York University, 1950).

24. Walter B. Smith and Arthur H. Cole, *Fluctuations in American Business, 1790–1860* (New York, 1935). See also Booth, *U.S. Experience,* p. 38.

25. V. E. Solomon, "Money and Banking," in Francis L. Coleman, ed., *Economic History of South Africa,* p. 129. E. H. D. Arndt, *Banking and Currency Development in South Africa, 1652–1927* (Cape Town, 1928).

26. Brian Kantor, "The Rixdollar and the Foreign Exchange," *South African Journal of Economics* 31, 1 (March 1971): 69.
27. Timothy Pritkin, *A Statistical View of the Commerce of the United States of America*. See also Freund, "The Cape Under the Transition Governments," pp. 216–17.
28. Theal, ed., *Records,* 9:293–97. See also Rosenthal, *Cape Directory,* pp. 24–25.

TWO

Expanding Horizons, 1835–1885

This chapter traces the activities of a new generation of American entrepreneurs in South Africa, ranging from insurance salesmen and diamond diggers to missionaries, merchandisers, and shipping agents. It identifies a new set of entrepreneurial motives for penetrating South Africa and analyzes the economic and other transformations in both countries that led to their emergence. The chapter assesses the impact of finance capital and modern American mass production as well as advances in marine and telecommunications technologies. It also explores the changing nature of United States commerce with South Africa, its conduct as well as its content and the reasons for its ebb and flow.

For the first time American missionaries appear on the stage, pioneers among the Zulu, fostering individual initiative through the promotion of Christianity and private enterprise. But while the missionaries emphasized indigenous self-reliance by providing agricultural technology and educational opportunity, they also fatally allied themselves to the white power structure in Natal and gave crucial support to their nascent policies of separate racial development.

For American entrepreneurs South Africa became more than one of several stops on an extensive voyage of profit and adventure. It became a destination. Americans as residents embroiled themselves in internal South African politics and culture. And they quarrelled among themselves over the best approach to take in "civilizing" the Boers and the Bantu. In the early years many disengaged out of fear, frustration, and failure. Some Americans left forever; others returned and remained almost for a lifetime. In any event, many of them became acute observers of the South African scene and played an instrumental role in shaping popular American perceptions of South Africa. From the late 1860s the miners were lured by notions of Eldorado and quick riches. The missionaries and merchants, on the other hand, prized the country not for what it was but for what it might eventually become. They viewed its future with a measure of cautious optimism. Some of them envisioned a democratic, egalitarian, English-speaking republic incorporating the rugged individualism of the Boers, the financial resources of the British, the humanitarianism of the Bantu, and the technological ingenuity and entrepreneurial spirit of the Yankees.

Americans in this early period provided a critical base of experience and information that made possible other forms of penetration toward the end of the century. They established a reputation among white South Africans as useful innovators in the fledgling diamond industry and as purveyors of superior agricultural machinery. Even before the discovery of gold in 1886 on the Transvaal's Witwatersrand, the United States had become an important market for South Africa's raw materials. Thus, it should become evident that the years between 1835 and 1885 were ones of discovery, in which both intellectual and economic horizons expanded.

ISAAC CHASE: THE MASTER MERCHANDISER

The trade situation vastly improved for American entrepreneurs after 1830, when the United States was granted most-favored-nation status at the Cape and discriminatory port charges and anchorage fees were eliminated. In reciprocal fashion the United States Compromise Tariff Act of 1833 provided for a gradual and steady reduction of duties on goods of South African provenance. For half a decade afterward the Cape colony and the United States enjoyed unprecedented prosperity, no doubt stimulated in at least small measure by the liberalization in their trade policies.[1]

The year 1834 marked a turning point in American relations with South Africa. In the past American enterprise was overwhelmingly of an irregular nature, concerning itself almost exclusively with commercial activities related to offshore whaling and the victualling and repair of ships en route to distant ports. However, in the decade of the 1830s a new generation of American entrepreneurs arrived on the scene, holding a vision of South Africa as a land of enormous opportunity and an interest in establishing locally operated long-term ventures. This new era unfolded in 1834, when the American consulate was reopened after a hiatus of nearly three decades and Isaac Chase, a Bostonian business-man, prepared to take up the post. In those days consuls received an extremely modest salary and were expected to support themselves through consular fees, private trading, and business on their own account.

Consular relations were formally restored on Chase's arrival at Cape Town in June of that year. Chase, an astute entrepreneur, quickly rec-ognized the opportunities afforded by the Cape's robust economic growth, and before the end of the year he had established the first regular shipping service between the United States and South Africa. He also wasted no time in launching an aggressive trade promotion campaign through his family and associates in Boston. Over the years Chase stimulated some mild interest by authoring occasional articles in Bos-ton's *Morning Post* and circulating copies of *The South African Almanac and Directory,* which contained glowing and often exaggerated reports on the colony's business climate. He also initiated a number of local business ventures with the financial assistance of his brother in Boston, whose firm, Hezekiah Chase and Company, had amassed a modest fortune from a large whaling enterprise in Lynn, Massachusetts. In those days the whaling industry of New England demonstrated vigorous growth in response to demands for sperm oil as a machine lubricant. The spermaceti variety was valued for its tolerance of high temperatures. Southern Africa, particularly the Mozambique Channel and the Nami-bian coast, was still one of the best sources; and from the late 1830s Chase regularly sent ships to the Cape for trade and provisioning.[2] Though Chase's own business ventures were profitable, he had little luck in stimulating broad American interest in South Africa's potential. His brother hoped to corner the trade himself and shrouded his own trading operations in secrecy. Moreover, many Americans preferred to trade in East or West Africa, where they were less affected by discriminatory British trade practices.

But significantly, while his brother's ships plied the waters of southern Africa, Chase opened his own business offices in Cape Town and in Port Elizabeth in the eastern Cape. There he marketed a wide variety of American products, from bicycles and books to plows and reapers.

These were also the halcyon days for American whalers. In 1835 the U.S. frigate *Potomac* visited Table Bay in a show of support for whaling interests in southern African waters. U.S. whaling tonnage increased steadily, from 35,000 in 1820 to 190,000 in 1858. American merchants found many consumers of southern African spermaceti, including the entrepreneurs William Procter and James Gamble, who in 1837 established a candle factory in Cincinnati, Ohio.

Chase became quite influential in business circles at the Cape and worked successfully with the powerful Commercial Exchange in Cape Town, a kind of chamber of commerce, to secure reductions in duties on certain items. Additionally, he persuaded Washington to reduce the tariff on Cape wines. The energetic American consul also recognized opportunities in the field of marine insurance, an enterprise that was only in its infancy in the United States. By the time of his retirement as consul in 1847 Chase had become an agent for thirty-two American insurance companies. But he was not without competition. British houses dominated the field and not a few American firms, including the powerful Philadelphia Marine Assurance Company, appointed as their exclusive agents British firms such as John J. Irvine and Company.[3]

CAPITAL FORMATION AT THE CAPE

The 1830s were marked by prosperity and domestic capital formation at the Cape, which led to the emergence of locally controlled financial institutions. Slavery was abolished in 1835, and owners of the approximately thirty-six thousand slaves in the colony received financial compensation from the government. Some of the more enterprising former slaveholders then invested the monies in joint stock companies and other business ventures. The first South African insurance company was established in 1831, to compete with a handful of British life insurance firms. Then, in 1834, the South African Association for the Administration and Settlement of Estates was founded and enjoyed the distinction of being the world's first trust company. It later merged with Syfrets, a firm established in 1850 to serve as a professional arbitrator in disputes settled out of court. A year later the first local fire insurance company was formed. This was followed in 1837 by South Africa's first truly private bank, the Cape of Good Hope Savings Bank.[4] Interestingly, this joint stock company was started with local capital. In the succeeding year the Board of Executors was organized to care for the financial needs of widows and orphans and to administer estates. It evolved into a powerful financial institution and celebrated its one hundred and fiftieth anniversary in 1988. From the 1840s through the 1860s a few of these new financial institutions helped to underwrite the expansion of southern Africa's wool production. More will be said of that later.

Strong competition from British firms at Cape Town encouraged some Americans to trade farther up the coast and to look to independent African kingdoms for markets. American trade along the eastern coast of South Africa expanded with the growth of British imperial hegemony. The 1820 settlement of five thousand British immigrants in the eastern Cape marked the beginning of large-scale, white, English-speaking colonization of the coastal region. Partially as a result of this intrusion, the eastern Cape frontier and beyond became a theater of escalating turmoil and warfare.[5] Conflicts with the expanding Xhosa populations on the eastern Cape frontier and the Kaffir War of 1834–1835 made the area an attractive market for military supplies. In the early 1830s the brig *St. Michael* was one of scores of American vessels to land muskets, gunpowder, and knives along the Natal coast. Additionally, Americans sold arms at Port Natal to Dingane, the Zulu king, and to white migrants *(voortrekkers)* who had only recently left the Cape Colony in their covered wagons to escape color-blind British-imposed laws and institutions. Skippers also bartered guns and ammunition for local hippo tusks and hides of buffaloes and other animals. Eastward, in Lourenco Marques, American whalers of the Mozambique channel off-loaded wheat and exchanged beads, highly prized by local Africans, for wood and fruits rich in vitamin C. All along the southern coast Americans sold slave-grown tobacco from Virginia and Maryland's Chesapeake Bay and introduced Indian corn and mimosa gum. Many of these items were destined for the expanding Zulu empire, and thus from an early period Americans and Zulus entered into mutually advantageous relationships. Theirs was a special connection that endured well into the decade of the 1980s.

In 1842 the British seized Port Natal (later renamed Durban) and terminated the short-lived Boer Republic of Natalia. According to David Welsh, the British feared that "the Boers might eventually establish friendly relations with foreign powers who might use Natal as a port from which to disrupt British lines of communication with India."[6] The Natal region was then annexed to the Cape colony and opened up to white, mainly English-speaking immigrants. In 1856 Natal was detached from the Cape and established as a separate British crown colony. North of the Drakensberg mountains, on the high veld, the Boers were allowed to establish their own landlocked semiautonomous republics governed by constitutions that totally excluded Africans from the political process.

Americans viewed the British official presence in southern Africa as a two-edged sword. On the one hand it instilled a greater sense of security among the whites and their allies and led to the rapid economic development of the new colony and to greater opportunities for business enterprise. On the other it resulted in the extension of Britain's imperial system of exclusive trade preferences.

FINANCING AMERICAN TRADE

For decades after the Revolution Americans continued to rely on English merchant bankers to finance their trading operations throughout the world. The use of travelers' and commercial letters of credit and bills of exchange often financed trade with southern Africa, and this practice greatly facilitated trade in commodities by making credit easily available to growers, manufacturers, and shippers. When the bills fell due, they were settled in money or with other bills of exchange.

In the early nineteenth century American exports to southern Africa were financed predominantly on the London money market. The London House of Baring Brothers and Company gained a near monopoly with North American traders and merchants. They and other smaller import/export commission merchants bought and sold merchandise as well as bills of exchange. By 1830 Baring had become the chief lender in the United States of credit on commission. The company negotiated insurance and assembled freight on behalf of shipowners. Americans conducting business in South Africa could operate exchange accounts on the basis of credit financed by Baring. Much of the grain, for example, that was exported to southern Africa in the 1830s was arranged through American agents of Baring.[7]

In New York City and elsewhere in the 1840s commission houses gradually replaced the more general all-purpose merchants. The commission merchants sold directly to buyers or on consignment. Competition in trade financing intensified in the 1840s and Brown Brothers and Company, founded in New York in 1826, emerged as a major rival to the House of Baring. Brown Brothers issued travelers' letters of credit that were highly valued by American importers of African goods. In North America in the 1840s Brown Brothers grew rapidly after introducing the innovative "documentary bill" as an instrument for financing the overseas marketing of American produce. By 1848 the company had supplanted the Baring as the leading issuer of commercial letters of credit in the American market, with branch offices and agencies in Baltimore, Philadelphia, Boston, Charleston, New Orleans, Mobile, and Savannah. It was not long, however, before Peabody and Company, another Anglo-American merchant banking house, became a formidable competitor. Peabody took an immediate interest in the American trade with southern Africa, and in 1870 it became the first American firm of its kind to open an office in South Africa. Competing for business was Lee, Higginson and Company, founded in Boston in 1848. In the 1850s, it played a significant role in financing New England merchants and shippers operating in African waters.[8]

In the 1850s Baring Brothers made little effort to modernize or to seek new clients. Instead, it tried futilely to remain competitive by reducing commission rates. Business steadied but their profit margins weakened; and by the commencement of the Civil War the company was scaling down its American operations. The Baring retrenchment was a mixed blessing. In the postwar era American capital looked westward, and traders involved with Africa found it more difficult to finance their operations through Great Britain.[9]

THE LURE OF WOOL AND HIDES

From the late 1830s American merchants were increasingly attracted to South Africa by the growing opportunities for trade in wool and hides. Woolen and leather exports from South Africa greatly increased after 1836, when Port Elizabeth was given permission to trade directly with foreign ports. The seaport had already become an important exporter of fleece; the 1846 repeal of the archaic Navigation Acts provided an added stimulus. Its scope for international trade widened further in 1853, when the Cape colony was given a constitution and internal self-government under a bicameral parliament. The era of direct legislation for internal affairs by London had ended, and with this reform came more freedom to determine trade policies. Consequently, in 1855 the new parliament passed the Cape Customs Tariff Act, equalizing rates on British and American imports and enhancing the Americans' competitive position. The environment improved further a year later, when for the first time South Africa's coastal trade was officially opened to non-British nations.[10]

These opportunities roughly coincided with the dramatic expansion of the factory system in the United States and with the emergence of large-scale industrial development, especially in New England and in the Middle Atlantic states. From 1846 woolen manufacturing output advanced rapidly in New Jersey, Connecticut, and Massachusetts. Major technological changes were occurring in the manufacture of leather goods, particularly shoes. Mechanized shoemaking in New England led to a substantial fall in retail prices and to explosive manufacturers' demands for leather hides. As early as the mid-1840s, the United States had become the top buyer of Cape hides and skins, making the American trade with the colony second only to the United Kingdom.[11]

Wool farming at the Cape expanded rapidly in the period 1850 to 1869, partly in response to breathtaking American advances in the mass-manufacture of woolens that created seemingly insatiable consumer demands for woolen products. Moreover, white Cape farmers were switching to sheep raising in the face of chronic labor shortages and sagging wine exports. By 1855 wool outstripped in value all other exports combined, and Cape wool had become prominent in American markets. By 1861 it amounted to nearly a quarter of all American wool imports and was valued at more than a million U.S. dollars.[12]

The rise in woolen exports could not have occurred at a more advantageous moment for South Africa. A phylloxera outbreak in the 1860s practically devastated the Cape vineyards and sent wine exports plummeting. It must also be recalled that Cape wines could no longer compete favorably with French wines in British markets after the Anglo-French commercial treaty of 1860. The Cape wine industry would probably have collapsed completely were it not for introduction in 1873 of disease-resistant American varieties.[13]

Trade was brisk between the Cape and the United States in the 1850s.

The decade opened with the colony importing £40,000 worth of goods from the United States and exporting £20,000. Within seven years the respective trade figures had shifted to the Cape's favor after soaring to £144,000 and £182,000. Chief imports from the United States included flour from western New York state and southeastern Pennsylvania,[14] as well as timber when, in the 1850s, the great Douglas fir forests began to open up along the Pacific coast of Oregon and Washington and timber was carried down to the port of San Francisco and shipped to various regions of the world, including the Cape.

Much of the increase in trade may be credited to the entrepreneurial efforts of Consul Chase and Gideon Holmes, an American merchant. Holmes had been active in commerce with the Cape since 1836; and in 1847 he succeeded Chase as consul in Cape Town. Holmes began his South African business career as an agent for whalemen of New Bedford and New London. In Cape Town he built repair shops and served as an agent for Boston and New York underwriters. By the mid-1850s Holmes had formed his own company and was shipping more than two hundred thousand skins annually to Boston. His firm, G. S. Holmes and Company, became one of the earliest, if not the first, American enterprises to base operations in South Africa.[15]

The dramatic increase in bilateral trade justified the opening of U.S. consular agencies at Port Elizabeth and Durban in 1851 and in East London six years later. American mobilization as a result of the outbreak of the Civil War in April 1861 stimulated American commerce to an unprecedented degree. Large purchases were made of Cape wool and Natal cotton for the manufacture of military uniforms. Hides were bought for the fabrication of boots and saddles. Within three years wool exports to the United States had soared to $3 million, amounting to more than a third of America's wool imports. At the onset of the Civil War Americans were purchasing nearly 20 percent of South Africa's wool and 35 percent of its hides and skins. The weight of wool exported to the United States exceeded that sent to the British Isles by nearly two million pounds. By 1864 nearly 25 percent of total Cape exports were destined for the United States, which emerged from the war as the Cape's largest customer in overall trade. In terms of imports, however, the United States ranked fourth, just behind Brazil.[16]

During the war years Port Elizabeth served as the major harbor for American trade in southern Africa. Between June and September 1863 alone thirty-seven ships cleared for Boston and thirty-one for New York. They were laden with sheep and goat skins, hides, wool, aloes, and other agricultural goods. Nevertheless, wool remained king in the commerce with the United States.

With the growth of trade export commission houses began to proliferate in coastal ports. Many of them no longer confined their business to executing orders in the Cape for foreign importers but also bought and sold on their own account and acted as agents for American manufacturers. A fair amount of trade was expedited by J. C. Hess, a U.S. consul, who worked with the trading agencies of Mackie Dunn and Company and Dunnell, Ebden and Company. J. B. Ebden, a principal in the latter firm, was a member of the legislative council at the Cape and wielded considerable influence on questions of trade.

THE RISE AND FALL OF THE CLIPPER SHIPS

For a decade after 1845 American commerce with southern Africa greatly benefited from the introduction of clipper ships, the fastest vessels at sea and therefore excellent long-distance carriers. Traveling time fell between Cape Town and New York. However, the narrow-beamed hull of the clipper ships prevented them from carrying large cargoes. From the mid-1850s the British gained an enormous advantage with their new screw-driven, iron-hulled steamships, which demonstrated greater strength and durability and could transport goods at lower costs. The Americans, unable to compete with the larger, more efficient British iron industry, soon lost their short-lived competitive edge. Another blow to the American merchant marine came in 1858 with the termination of government subsidies. The British, on the other hand, increased the subsidization of their own steamship lines.

The demise of the sailing ship brought about a corresponding decline in the United States' merchant marine. Overseas trade with southern Africa and elsewhere continued, but goods moved increasingly in British, not American, hulls. American ship owners were unable to buy British iron-hulled and steel-hulled ships because of federal regulations. Shipbuilders from Maine to Philadelphia and elsewhere kept constant pressure on Congress not to renege. Consequently, the high cost of ship construction in the United States and the expense of operating under the

American flag forced various investors and traders to sail under foreign flags. In painful reality, British ships were cheaper and less costly to operate. Moreover, Britain's abolition of the Navigation Acts in 1849 enabled American-owned ships to carry British registry. Naturally, American businessmen cultivated a preference for British carriers. In New York Henderson and Brothers abandoned their American clients and became agents for the Union Steamship Company's Royal Mail Steamers. The dominance of a few, select British shipping concerns was made even more secure in 1883, after the establishment of the exclusive South African (Shipping) Conference. Thus, with the demise of the clipper ship and the loss of government support went the United States' hopes of dominating the sea lanes of southern Africa and, indeed, those in the world beyond.[17]

THE CHALLENGE OF THE IMPERIAL BANKS

American entrepreneurs found themselves at an additional disadvantage as a result of Britain's widening control over South Africa's financial institutions. At first the prosperity of the 1850s spawned a number of locally controlled financial institutions. By 1856 there were seventeen local banks in the Cape colony, two in the Orange Free State, and one in Natal. Six years later Cape Town alone boasted twenty-eight privately owned banks, which were essentially "unit" discount banks, without branch operations and owned and operated primarily by major local business figures. Most of the institutions issued their own banknotes that were convertible into gold on demand.[18]

In the 1860s private banking in the Cape and Natal fell under the hegemony of large overseas imperial institutions. Indeed, a new era in South Africa banking history opened in 1861, when the London and South African Bank opened a branch in Cape Town. This was followed in 1862 by the establishment of the externally financed Standard Bank of British South Africa. A keen rivalry developed between the two banks, which soon overshadowed the local institutions and led to their merger in 1877. The imperial banks, joined by a third, the Bank of Africa in 1864, were highly capitalized and could lend on more favorable terms and provide wider services than the local institutions.

These banks established a network of branches which competed effectively with the weaker local banks. They soon dominated the financial life of the Cape and Natal, but initially enjoyed less success in expanding into the Afrikaner republics. In 1868 the Standard Bank failed to secure a charter in the Orange Free State; and in 1877, the Afrikaner republic established its own national bank. This was followed in 1888 by the Netherlands Bank and Credit Association, based in Pretoria and chartered by the King of the Netherlands mainly with Dutch capital. In the Cape and Natal, however, British entrepreneurs gained an enormous advantage over Americans and other foreigners by obtaining easier and faster access to capital. It was no secret that the imperial banks were biased towards citizens of the Empire, especially those domiciled in the British Isles.[19]

THE GREAT AMERICAN RETREAT

American commercial activity in sub-Saharan Africa fell dramatically after the Civil War. The era of the clipper ships had passed, and the U.S. merchant marine emerged from the conflict severely weakened. Confederate cruisers had destroyed nearly 11,000 tons of Union shipping. Moreover, insurance rates during the war had reached such heights that an additional 752,000 tons were sold to foreign merchants. The U.S. share of South African exports fell from more than 24 percent in 1864 to less than 3 percent three years later. U.S. capital investment dropped from a historic peak of $1.25 million in 1863 to about $1 million in 1867.[20]

Several reasons can be offered for the decline in trade. The American wool industry collapsed after the war, and merchant bankers in the United States and Great Britain shortened credit. Changes in U.S. tariffs in the 1860s effectively closed the American market to South Africa's grease wools. The American economic depression of 1857 brought renewed demands for protection and led to the Morrill Tariff of 1861. The tariffs of 1862 and 1864, though aimed at raising money for the war effort, proved to be even more protectionist. Levels were raised to 47 percent, the highest in the nation's history, and remained in the forties until World War I.[21]

American protectionism during the war years had little effect on trade with the Cape because South African goods were needed for military purposes. But shortly after the war, in 1867, American wool growers convinced Congress to place a duty of nearly 60 percent on wool imports. In respect to British southern Africa, it did not take much to move the legislators. Washington had been angry with the Cape for its strong Confederate sympathies during the war. British-built Confederate ships preyed on northern vessels along the coast of southern Africa and reputedly captured at least fourteen—mostly the work of the *Alabama,* which battled in Table Bay with the *U.S.S. Kearsarge* and the barque *Sea Bridge.* Though the Cape's constitution forbade it from conducting foreign affairs, the government did not prevent the Confederate sale of American prizes to local entrepreneurs.

The *Alabama* issue left a bitter legacy of American indignation against Great Britain and the Cape colony. Prior to 1861 Anglo-American relations had been moving steadily towards freer trade and economic cooperation. But the Civil War left the inheritance of the *Alabama* court claims. The Americans asserted that in 1862 the British had allowed the *Alabama* to clear from Liverpool and thus enabled the Confederate ship to launch its destructive campaign against American commerce. After the war the Americans demanded heavy compensation. The British balked, and the issue dragged on for a decade, generating mutual hostility.[22]

The weakening American demand for wool and hides surely contributed to economic problems at the Cape in the late 1860s. An American commercial agent in Cape Town complained that "truly, the United States tariff on wool has been the destruction of American navigations in these waters."[23] From the mid-1860s most trade between South Africa and the United States was transferred progressively to British firms.

The demise of U.S. whaling industries also impacted on U.S. activity in southern Africa. By the mid-1850s the whale populations in the Mozambique Channel had been largely devastated, and with the growing scarcity of spermaceti, oil prices in the United States soared. The crisis, however, was not of great duration. Edwin Drake struck oil in Titusville, Pennsylvania, in 1859 and put an end to the need for whale oil as an industrial lubricant and illuminant. The discovery of cheap petroleum sounded the death knell for the whaling industry. Moreover, there was a weakening demand for spermaceti candles as Americans switched to kerosene and natural gas to illuminate their homes and factories. And, finally, after the Civil War the United States directed its entrepreneurial energies, financial resources, and commercial sights inward, toward the development of its own domestic markets and national infrastructure.

In 1865 the economies of the Cape and Natal slid into deep depression. Economic conditions in the interior Afrikaner polities of the Orange Free State and the South African Republic (Transvaal) were even worse and approached bankruptcy. All of these economies were still overwhelmingly agrarian. As late as 1867 South Africa's agricultural goods were 93.8 percent of total exports, and minerals amounted to a paltry 2.5 percent. Wool still represented more than 80 percent of the value of raw goods exports.[24] There were very few secondary industries and no extractive operations other than a small copper mining complex in the northwest Cape. I have already indicated the crisis facing the wool and hide industries and the near-collapse of the vineyards. In the jaundiced eyes of American entrepreneurs South Africa's future looked rather grim. The stagnant economy was seemingly going nowhere, and whites were beginning to emigrate to other British possessions, particularly to Australia and New Zealand.

ALL THAT GLITTERS: THRESHOLDS OF CHANGE

South Africa's economies began to recover just as commerce with the United States reached a low point for the decade. A mineral revolution of breathtaking proportions was triggered by the discovery of diamonds in the Cape colony in 1867. Diamond discoveries between 1867 and 1870 radically transformed the Cape's economy and quickly reversed the economic decline. More than anything, they stimulated markets in the interior as well as overseas. The opening of the diamond mines attracted trade, immigrants, and foreign capital, all mainly of British provenance, although more than a thousand American miners were lured to the diamond fields. Some came with innovative ideas and techniques for improving production. Jerome Babe of Louisiana, for example, developed a new device for sorting diamondiferous gravel, which vastly improved efficiency and raised profit margins.[25]

Diamond production greatly increased after 1871 with the opening of the De Beers and Kimberley pipes. Within a year South Africa had surpassed Brazil as the world's largest producer of diamonds. The Cape colony's economy now acquired an enormously strong leg, assuring local whites of greater political leverage. In 1872 a new constitution was promulgated, giving the locally elected legislature virtual control over the executive branch.

By 1878 diamonds had displaced wool as the principal export of the Cape colony. Most of these sparkling stones were destined for England, though from the beginning, diamonds also found ready markets in the United States, arriving via Boston and New York by 1870.[26] In 1873 gold in appreciable quantities was discovered in the eastern Transvaal, but not enough to lift fully the impoverished republic out of its financial problems. Indeed, the Transvaal had approached bankruptcy by 1877, when it was occupied by the British and proclaimed a crown colony.

From the early 1870s trade between the United States and the colonies of South Africa began to recover, albeit slowly at first. By 1872 South Africa was still importing less from the Americans than in 1857, but its exports to the United States had jumped nearly five-fold, to £824,000, largely as the result of diamond exports from the Cape and the Orange Free State.[27]

For the first time the United States was beginning to take note of the economic potential of lands beyond the Orange River. Diplomatic relations had been established with the two Afrikaner republics in October 1870, and their desire to expand trade with the Americans was given legal substance upon the conclusion in December 1871 of the Treaty of Friendship, Commerce, and Extradition. The document was finally ratified by Congress in 1872, the year in which the Orange Free State opened a consulate in Philadelphia.[28]

This was not the most auspicious time to expand trade. After the Panic of 1873, the American economy slipped into a recession that lingered for nearly five years, with banks closing, prices collapsing, and many factories shutting down. Clearly, the Afrikaners had an extremely difficult challenge before them in their efforts to generate bilateral trade. Diplomatic and other official missions were sent to the United States in 1876 to address organizations such as the American Geographical Society in New York and chambers of commerce and other trade organizations in key American cities. Such a trade and investment mission from South Africa was unprecedented. And indeed, few if any countries beyond Europe had ever dared to venture so far afield to promote their own countries before foreign business audiences. Unfortunately, this extraordinarily bold venture into the world beyond Africa's veld did little to weaken the popular American perception of Afrikaners as provincial, inward-looking Boers. It does, however, furnish readers today with a glimpse of the lengths an ultraconservative, insular, rural population will go in order to meet perceived threats to its survival.

The work of the delegation may have borne some fruit. By 1877, U.S. trade with the colonies of South Africa had reached $629,000 in exports and $900,500 in imports. The growth of trade with Natal and the Afrikaner republics, though small, showed new strength, exports to the three states growing from £3000 in 1860 to £131,000 in 1880.[29] This modest growth, however, paled in the face of the avalanche advance of the British. By 1880 Natal alone was taking more than £2 million in British imports.

Trade with South Africa was a small fraction of the United States' total overseas commerce. Historically, it never exceeded 1 percent of U.S. foreign commerce. When the United States emerged from its recession in the late 1870s, private investment gravitated to domestic railroad development. Most eyes were cast towards the Pacific, not in the uncertain direction of the British-dominated South Atlantic.

Diplomatic recognition of the Transvaal lapsed in 1877, when the ailing Afrikaner republic was annexed by the British and proclaimed a crown colony. The annexation, however, stimulated an awakening of Afrikaner nationalism. Self-government was restored in 1881, after the unprepared British were defeated by the Afrikaners in the First Boer War. Nevertheless, diplomatic relations with the reconstituted South African Republic were not resumed; and in 1884 the Americans rejected a proposed commercial treaty with the Transvaalers out of concern that it would anger the British, endanger relations with the Cape, and risk losing access to the sea ports.

The economies of the United States and the Cape colony were recovering by 1879, as was American interest in trade. In that year the State Department sent a naval expedition to Asia and Africa to explore opportunities for trade expansion. Commodore Robert W. Schufeldt and the *U.S.S. Ticonderoga* visited several African ports, including Cape Town. Schufeldt lamented the lack of American business interest in South Africa but pointed to the enormous potential for trade and investment. He was persuaded, however, that the four colonies comprising South Africa would only achieve their greatest economic potential if they were united under British rule.[30] The British were of course delighted by his position, which remained a fixed point in American policy towards South Africa until the end of the Second Boer War in 1902. It was a pragmatic policy assessment. The industrializing United States had begun to invest heavily in the British Isles and would not jeopardize future opportunities by siding with the landlocked Afrikaner republics. At the time of Schufeldt's visit the Cape's economy was steaming ahead. With the exception of a few interruptions, it showed robust growth through the First Boer War.

In the final two decades of the nineteenth century South Africa was drawn more deeply into the British imperial orbit. A telegraph cable had been completed between Aden and South Africa via Zanzibar and Mozambique. And in 1885 South Africa was linked with Europe by a cable running down the west coast of Africa—a connection that indirectly benefited the Americans as well because a transatlantic cable already operated between the United States and the British Isles. Finally, on the eve of the Second Boer War in 1899, a telegraphic submarine cable directly linked the Cape with Great Britain. South Africa was henceforth only minutes, rather than weeks, distant from the metropolis.[31]

New financial connections were also drawing South Africa and the metropolis into a tighter embrace. Four years earlier, the Cape became more closely linked monetarily when it was placed on the British gold standard. The colony now had a currency that enjoyed the stability, strength, and convertibility of the pound sterling.

From 1866 to 1875 the United States ran an unfavorable balance of trade with most countries. Thereafter, until 1894, the trade picture became generally more favorable. Overall, after the mid-1870s the balance of trade shifted in favor of exports. For years later merchandise exports to most countries exceeded imports by a growing margin. Mass production lowered the prices of American manufacturers, and the price levels for its manufactured exports declined more than those of equivalent items produced in Great Britain or Europe. Thus, even though export volumes steadily increased, the dollar value grew less swiftly. In both respects, America's export trade with South Africa continued to rise and reached a record high in 1881.[32]

Diamond prices began to sag a year later, and the South African economy lost steam. Between 1882 and 1886 the South African states suffered their most severe economic depression of the nineteenth century. Imports fell by more than half, while the export sector also showed signs of extreme weakness. Matters were not helped by a recession in the United States, which lasted from 1883 to 1885.

FINANCE CAPITALISTS AND THE EMERGENCE OF CORPORATE GIANTS

The 1860s and 1870s witnessed a spectacular rise in investment banking in the United States. Investment bankers were primarily middlemen, bringing entrepreneurs searching for funds into contact with investors and providing letters of credit for merchants engaged in foreign commerce. However, the growth of personal savings and business investment after the Civil War led to the emergence in the 1870s and 1880s of the modern corporation. A national market for stocks and bonds began to develop, and finance capitalists became part of the business landscape. Investment banking houses were established to specialize in underwriting governments, railroads, and a range of corporate securities and commercial enterprises.

Most of these houses were founded by well-established Protestant New England entrepreneurs or German-Jewish immigrants. Much sought-after foreign capital was obtained by setting up branches in Great Britain and on the continent. Since most trade with South Africa at that time was financed in sterling, a London connection of some sort was almost essential. J. and W. Seligman, one of the most active houses dealing in American-African trade, began in New York in 1862 and opened an office in London two years later. From its early beginnings the House of Seligman was active in expediting the wool trade with South Africa. Kidder, Peabody and Company became a close competitor after it established links with the renowned London concern of Baring and Brothers in 1878. Nevertheless, the giant in investment banking was the Drexel Morgan partnership, which enjoyed unrivalled access to the London money markets through its affiliate, J. S. Morgan and Company. As Vincent Carosso has noted, these houses were highly diversified banking institutions, dealing in gold and specie and foreign exchange as well as in the issuance of commercial and travelers' letters of credit.[33]

There were no South African banks in the United States; consequently, few if any South African firms established branch operations or distributorships. To expedite trade, mainly imports, from the United States, the Standard Bank in the 1880s designated local agents and correspondents, particularly Warren and Company of Boston, Howland and Aspinwall in New York, and the Nevada Bank of San Francisco for West Coast business. Because no American banks engaged agents in South Africa, American entrepreneurs found themselves at a considerable disadvantage in conducting their business.

By the late 1870s America was shipping a higher volume of raw products to the Cape colony and Natal. Wheat and lumber were becoming particularly valuable exports. The vast wheat region on the Great Plains of the Midwest came into full production just as the labor force in South Africa's mines exploded in numbers. By 1874, less than eight years since the first diamond field opened, more than ten thousand diggers were employed in Kimberley alone. The demand for foodstuffs could not be met locally, and thus opportunities abounded for American grain exporters. In the lumber section the Timber and Stone Act of 1878 resulted in the transfer of vast timberlands to the private sector in Oregon, Washington, and California. Huge lumber companies emerged, and wood output soared. South Africa, with few forests, desperately needed American lumber for its mining operations as well as for the construction of railroad rolling stock.[34]

In the 1870s and 1880s the United States benefited enormously from the emergence of corporate giants. Already by 1860 the country was the second ranking industrial nation, producing about 20 percent of the world's output. American multinational corporations had just begun to emerge after the Civil War. In the decade of the 1870s the process of factory mechanization led to a smaller number of firms and to larger corporate entities. The era of corporate mergers had opened, and industry grew spectacularly in scale. From 1879 horizontal combinations developed in enterprises that produced the traditional consumer staples. Industries began to standardize and systematize their manufacturing processes, and the unit price of goods fell dramatically. Concurrently, major technological advances were achieved in nearly every phase of the American economy. All this put American manufacturers in a far better competitive position in overseas markets.[35] Chapter 4 will reveal how these benefits became evident to South African consumers in the 1880s and 1890s.

FROM RAW MATERIALS TO MACHINES:
A CHANGING TRADE LANDSCAPE

The nature of the United States' exported products began to change with the inexorable march of industrialization. Formerly, raw items, mainly agricultural and arboreal, made up the bulk of American exports to South Africa. In the future, it became industrial machinery and mass-produced durable consumer goods. The Singer sewing machine became one of the first household products to enter the South African market. In 1851 Isaac Singer patented in the United States an improved sewing machine and began to mass produce it. By 1867 his company had become the world's largest manufacturer of sewing machines. An office was opened in London, which distributed machines to an outlet in Cape Town that was established in 1877. Eventually, the machines destined for South Africa were manufactured in Singer plants in the British Isles. More will be said of that later.[36]

American arms manufacturers also penetrated the South Africa market at an early date. In 1851 Samuel Colt of Hartford, Connecticut, opened a factory in England for the manufacture of his patented revolver, thereby becoming the first exporter of American arms technology. Other Americans pioneered in the development of repeating rifles, which Smith and Wesson began manufacturing in 1855, followed by Winchester twelve years later. Very quickly, these weapons found their way into South African markets. In 1871 the British purchased a number of American-made .45 caliber Gatling guns for use in their wars against the Zulu. But the Remington Arms Company was the first of the American arms manufacturers to establish an agency in South Africa.[37]

American entrepreneurs also pioneered in the early development and export of agricultural implements. In 1851 several English manufacturers bought licenses to build the famous Obed Hussey reaper. Within a few years the machine was well-known to white South African farmers, thanks to G. S. Holmes and Company of Cape Town. Reapers and other agricultural implements manufactured by Cyrus McCormick also found their way onto South African farms. The first mechanized reaper, designed and constructed in the United States by McCormick, was demonstrated in the Orange Free State in 1852. Farmers in the eastern Cape wheat belt were soon hiring them for their harvesting.[38] In 1877 the first agricultural show in South Africa was held in the Cape colony, and McCormick's reapers, binders, and harvesters won prizes for their outstanding performance. White South African farms were soon enclosed by American-made barbed wire, a product patented by two Illinois farmers in 1874. Within a decade it had become a feature of the South African landscape.[39]

The United States also achieved an early lead in the marketing of petroleum products. The kerosene industry had been expanding rapidly since 1859, when a method was devised for extracting kerosene from petroleum less expensively than from coal. John D. Rockefeller, a pioneer in the industry, established Standard Oil Company of Ohio in 1869 and embarked on a strategy of relentless domestic expansion. Almost overnight, Standard Oil became the leading producer of kerosene, and by 1878 it owned or leased 90 percent of America's petroleum-refining capacity. Overproduction of kerosene in the 1870s encouraged Standard Oil to develop markets overseas, including South Africa. By the early 1880s cans of Standard Oil kerosene were being distributed throughout the Cape colony.[40] In the last quarter of the nineteenth century, Singer, Remington, and Standard Oil became highly visible and widely respected brand names in South Africa and had much to do with drawing the attention of South African consumers to American industrial products.

EARLY MISSIONARY ENTERPRISE: THE EVANGELISTIC IMPULSE

Mission stations were among the earliest manifestations of American enterprise in southern Africa. But missionary endeavors had to be supported largely through local initiatives. Consequently, missionaries had little choice but to develop entrepreneurial skills in order to generate enough business to sustain their religious and educational activities. Missionaries became entrepreneurs, launching business ventures, introducing new products and technologies, exploring new markets, and mobilizing human and material resources. In the process, they introduced new combinations and organizational techniques that disturbed the prevailing social, cultural, and economic equilibrium. It is no wonder that many Africans viewed them as both innovators and creative destroyers. American missionaries were strong believers in the Protestant work ethic, and they imposed on their converts concepts of personal freedom and individual financial gain. The mission station became simultaneously a school for entrepreneurship and a center for Christian proselytization.

Missionary movements became a prominent feature of the American religious landscape in the early years of the nineteenth century. They followed by approximately a decade the establishment of missionary societies among Protestant churches in the British Isles. In the New England states, Congregationalism assumed an early leading role in the unfolding Evangelical movement. Religious revivalism in America, the so-called Great Awakening,[41] aroused a spirit of humanitarianism and a concern for the physical as well as the spiritual welfare of the poor and the oppressed. Not surprisingly, the missionary impulse was intimately connected with the movement to abolish slavery and the slave trade. From the turn of the century pastors preached on the need for evangelizing Africa, arguing that the present generation must atone for the sins of their slave-holding fathers and that the souls of fallen African slave-trading savages must be saved through Christian conversion.

In seemingly paradoxical fashion abolitionism reinforced the primacy of capitalist values and institutions, particularly the notion of free wage labor, while questioning the idea that the church and state should not under any circumstances interfere with the forces of the marketplace or tamper with the sanctity of private ownership of property. Some abolitionists argued that only the state (Congress) could end slavery and the slave trade.

In examining the British scene, David Brion Davis suggests that "slavery stood in direct opposition to the virtues inculcated by the market."[42] The same may be said for the United States. In the minds of many merchant-philanthropists and pastors the ideologies of the free market and laissez-faire private enterprise would never acquire a sound moral standing until slavery and the slave trade were abolished.

The American missionary movement in southern Africa can be traced to the founding of the American Board of Commissioners for Foreign Missions in 1810. Based in Boston, the American Board was interdenominational and assumed responsibility for coordinating the overseas activities of the Congregational, Presbyterian, and Dutch Reformed churches. By cutting across denominational barriers, the Board was able to develop great organizational strength and enormous influence.[43] Indeed, in the first half of the nineteenth century it was the American missionary effort's principal organizational arm for the "promotion and spread of the Gospel in Heathen Lands."

The American Board, a comparatively rich and powerful organization, drew its initial support from well-educated upper middle-class families, many of whom had business interests. In the African field its missionaries demanded of themselves and their converts personal freedom and individual enterprise. The organization was drawn into Africa through the activities and ideals of the London Missionary Society (LMS), which had begun operating at the Cape in 1799. The LMS, like the American Board, was nondenominational in orientation and outlook but Congregational in spirit and practice. Subsequently, the LMS sought to improve its stature in the colony by upgrading the credentials of its dynamic superintendent, John Philip, who arrived in 1819. A doctorate from Columbia University in New York was purchased for him that year, followed months later by a theological degree from Princeton.[44] Even in those days American universities freely granted degrees to luminaries seeking to enhance their professional status.

The American Board leadership may have first learned of LMS activities in South Africa through the writings of Reverend William Brown. In 1820 he published in Philadelphia a work that outlined in part the LMS missionary programs at the Cape from 1798 to 1811. At about the time that Brown's book came out, an American Board missionary from Ceylon recuperated briefly in Cape Town. He may have been the first American missionary to visit southern Africa and probably provided Dr. Philip with his first exposure to the American Board. Philip himself became known to the Board through his 1828 book, *Researches in South Africa*, which surveyed the potential for missionary enterprise in the colony and its hinterlands. Later, American evangelicals drew additional inspiration from T. Fowell Buxton's *The African Slave Trade and its Remedy*, which eloquently maintained that slavery and the slave trade could only be ended by inculcating in Africans the superior benefits of legitimate trade. Buxton proposed that indigenous agriculture be encouraged, reasoning that outlawing the slave trade would not of itself end the institution of slavery. Buxton anticipated that eventually agricultural production would rest entirely with African managers and be free of

European control. He envisioned a series of inland missionary stations, serving as centers of production, trade, and progressive Western influence.[45]

By the early 1830s the Evangelical Revival had gained adherents among eminent figures in American commerce and industry. The Board's energetic secretary general, Rufus Anderson, called for the establishment of "self-supporting, self-extending, and self-governing autonomous organizations." The Board's objectives overseas were not simply to make conversions to Christianity but to train the converts in practical matters and then to leave them to their own devices.[46]

A RENDEZVOUS WITH THE ZULU

Anderson's impassioned calls fell on the ears of many young Americans. The early missionaries of the American Board were drawn from enterprising farm families in the Midwest and merchant families of New England, deeply imbued with concepts of self-reliance and rugged individualism.

On the advice of Dr. John Philip, the American Board in 1834 decided to establish an American Mission in South Africa. Philip's lengthy and enthusiastic response to an American student's request for information on missionary prospects there had been published in the *Missionary Herald*, the Board's official organ. The Board was already active overseas but it was not thought appropriate to expand into southern Africa. Further correspondence with Philip led in 1835 to the despatch of the first American missionaries. Philip, who had recently completed an extensive tour beyond the colony's frontier, suggested that the Board begin its work among the Zulu. American merchants had already been trading occasionally at Port Natal (Durban) and had sold a variety of goods, including blades, gun powder, muskets, and salt, to the agents of local Zulu leaders.

Thus, in February 1835, after a two-months' voyage from Boston, two parties of Americans and their spouses arrived at Cape Town. Aldin Grout and George Champion, missionaries, and Newton Adams, a physician, were instructed to work with the coastal Zulu. Daniel Lindley and Henry Venable, missionaries, and Alexander Wilson, another physician, would operate far beyond the Vaal River among the Ndebele. In March 1836 Reverend Champion, a graduate of Yale University and Andover Theological Seminary, established the first school ever sponsored by an American missionary in Africa. He made exhaustive investigations of the physical environment and in 1836 published an essay in the *American Journal of Science* on the topography and geology of the Cape colony.[47] Meanwhile, in 1837 Dr. Adams founded a school at Umlazi and enrolled fifty Africans. Lindley, a son of the first president of Ohio University, by then had established the American Zulu Mission in Natal. The Zulu king, Dingane, welcomed the Americans as entrepreneurs who might stimulate trade and teach him and his advisors how to read and write, and it was not long before several of Dingane's young men and women were studying in Champion's school.

Hostilities between Dingane and the expanding Afrikaner voortrekkers led to the murder of several Zulu Christian converts and to the assassination in 1838 of Piet Retief, a major Boer leader. The voortrekkers and the Africans were both land-hungry pastoralists, raiding each others' cattle and encroaching on each others' pastures. Other sedentary, loosely knit agricultural groups found themselves caught in the deadly crossfire, losing their ancestral lands and often their lives. The violence escalated, and the frightened American missionaries decided to abandon their missionary stations. Wilson, Grout, the Champions, and the Venables returned to the United States. Lindley stayed on and between 1841 and 1847 served as a preacher to the Boers in their trekking across the Drakensberg mountains.[48] Lindley was convinced that race relations would never improve until the Boers became better educated in Christian principles. He may have been the first American to call for a strategy of "constructive engagement" as a means of reforming the strong-willed and independent Afrikaners. The Boers, who had embarked on the Great Trek out of the Cape colony in the late 1830s, did not succeed in attracting a single *predikant,* or preacher, from among their own population. Lindley, who had failed to baptize a single Zulu, obliged and became the first minister to the voortrekkers, baptizing 819 of them and preaching the virtues of cultural toleration and republican government to their parents. But young Lindley discovered that providing religious instruction was a far easier matter than changing Boer attitudes and behavior towards the Africans.

LAYING THE FOUNDATIONS OF APARTHEID?

Eventually, the disillusioned Lindley returned to his work among the Zulu, this time with more success. The American Board had been persuaded by Dr. Philip to resume its operations, and the Board decided to increase the scope of its activities. Lindley baptized his first Zulu in 1846; three years later he and Mr. and Mrs. James Dube, two young Zulu converts, became charter founding members of the American Board's Inanda Church.[49] Lindley's activities among the Boers and the Zulu and his acquaintance with leaders in both communities soon came to the attention of British-born Theophilus Shepstone, whose tenure as Secretary for Native Affairs in Natal colony extended from 1845 to 1875. British immigration into Natal was accelerating, and the colonial authorities were anxious to effect an orderly redistribution of land among the Boers, the new immigrants, and the indigenous populations. Lindley and the American Board were anxious to expand their own landholdings. It was therefore not surprising that Lindley accepted an offer to serve on the newly formed Locations (Land) Commission. The commission had already begun creating African Locations, or reserves, near the white town of Pietermaritzburg. Lindley accepted the concept of racially segregated locations, supporting Shepstone's contention that without reserves Africans would eventually lose all their lands to the expanding and encroaching white farmers. Objectives do not always match results, and the Native Secretary's scheme ultimately deprived the Zulu of much of their most fertile lands.[50]

Shepstone was the architect of African segregation in Natal, and many scholars today maintain that his system became the prototype of modern apartheid in South Africa. In any case, it seems obvious that his policy of racial segregation was utilized as the key instrument for the maintenance of white supremacy. Lindley's cooperation paid big dividends for the American Board, when Sir George Grey, the colonial governor, agreed to grant five hundred acres to each American Board mission station. In the process, between 1855 and 1856, the Natal authorities distributed several thousand acres to the American missionaries, bringing their total land area to 6,288 acres.[51]

THE BIBLE AND THE PLOW: DEVELOPING COMMERCIAL AGRICULTURE AMONG THE AFRICANS

From the mid-nineteenth century British and American missionaries in much of Africa fell under the spell of Dr. David Livingstone, who seemed to epitomize the ideal missionary. Livingstone, a Scottish medical missionary in southern Africa, echoed the earlier thoughts of Buxton and the abolitionists, intoning in his *Missionary Travels And Researches in South Africa,* "Sending the Gospel to the heathen must include much more than . . . a man going about with a Bible under his arm. The promotion of commerce ought to be specially attended to, as this, more speedily than anything else, demolishes the sense of isolation which heathenism engenders, and makes tribes feel themselves mutually dependent on and mutually beneficial to each other."[52]

American missionaries yearned to transform Natal into a self-reliant colony of African peasant farmers, producing for a world market, including the United States. Some anticipated that eventually Zululand would emerge as a modern Christian democratic republic, with representative institutions similar to those in the United States and with a leadership embracing capitalistic enterprise. To achieve these objectives, American Board missionaries encouraged African peasant production and promoted crop diversification. They sought to foster cash-crop, export-oriented production on lands leased to enterprising Africans by the missionary stations. In return, the Zulu were urged to renounce their pastoral ways, which some missionaries associated with such seemingly savage practices as bride-price and polygyny, and to take up the plow and become sedentary farmers.

Reverend Lindley concerned himself with the overall development of Natal and believed that coal and cotton could become key elements in the colony's growth. He was not convinced, however, that economic development could be initiated under African leadership. In this he and American missionaries Grout and Adams differed. From 1844 the two had become salaried government missionaries and received an annual Natal government grant to build and operate missionary schools. Grout wrote sympathetically and optimistically of the Zulu converts and expressed the conviction that missionary stations must introduce Africans to modern agricultural technology, especially the plow. Grout himself was quite knowledgeable in modern farming techniques and undertook numerous experiments in growing cash crops. By this time per capita consumption of sugar in the industrial centers of United States and Western Europe was soaring, and the soil and climate of Natal proved ideal for sugar cultivation. At the Umvoti station on the Natal coast, Aldin Grout secured from Shepstone in 1859 a grant to establish an experimental sugar cane plantation.[53] For the next two decades it operated with moderate success. Africans grew the cane, which was processed in the mission-run, government-funded mill. Two additional mills were built, at Amanzimtoti and Ifumi, both on African initiative. Indeed, the Amanzimtoti Mill and Growers' Cooperative were entirely under African management. Within a few years sugar had become a highly successful crop in Natal. But it was not long before the whites, with greater access to capital, began to establish their own, expansive, and more mechanized operations. Soon, the whites were able to produce cheaper cane and cheaper sugar, and the sugar industry eventually became almost exclusively the preserve of white Natalian farmers and millers.[54]

Dr. Adams shared Grout's interest in developing commercial agriculture among the Africans. The first cotton seeds from the United States were introduced by Adams and planted in the missionary garden at Umlazi. During the American Civil War the American missionaries and their African associates obtained money from the government's Native Reserve Fund to establish a training school to teach Africans the cultivation of cotton. Initially, the project was a great success, largely because wartime military demands for cotton were enormous. Moreover, the British, deprived of their traditional markets in the American south, looked desperately for other sources. But after the war exports from the United States resumed, cotton prices weakened, and by 1875 cotton was no longer regarded by Natalians as a commercially profitable crop. Missionary enthusiasm waned, the school was closed down, and South Africa did not see another expansion of cotton cultivation for the remainder of the century.[55]

The missionaries and Africans had only mixed success with other cash crops. Zulu farmers were encouraged to grow such new crops as arrowroot and pecans in addition to sugar. However, after the harvests were taken in, the Board missionaries made little effort to help the farmers to market their produce. Thus, in the end the inexperienced farmers suffered under intense competition from their white neighbors and from price fluctuations that together acted as powerful disincentives. The American missionaries also attempted to introduce new agricultural technologies. In the 1870s the Mfengu Africans in the Ciskei were becoming prosperous farmers on their own initiative, thanks in part to their purchase of American farm implements, especially plows. By 1875 they were selling a substantial amount of agricultural produce to miners in the interior. Reverend Hyman Wilder was impressed and introduced to the Zulu a variety of American-made farm implements, including Eagle plows, Hussey reapers, and spades and augurs. All these noble efforts resulted in a moderate expansion of acreage under cultivation. Nevertheless, the American Board, with its strong emphasis on self-reliance, often too quickly terminated its involvement and doomed the projects. Moreover, African farmers received insufficient financial assistance, and the missionaries themselves usually lacked the managerial skills and experience necessary to develop successful training programs.

Between the late 1860s and the late 1880s African peasant cultivators in Natal struggled to compete effectively with the white settler farmers and planters. Natal administrative and legislative measures were usually biased in favor of white business interests and tended to stifle peasant enterprise. Moreover, white farming in the region was expanding and steadily encroaching on Zulu lands. Whites saw African cash-crop production as a threat to their own economic interests. In 1877 the British annexed most of coastal Zululand and two years later divided it into thirteen separate territories under thirteen mutually antagonistic chiefs. The remaining portions of Zululand were annexed just a decade later. By then all the missionary and African sugar mills were idle, including the project at Umvoti started in 1859 by the American missionary, Aldin Grout. To Board leaders in Boston Africa was low on the list of priorities. The bulk of its physical and financial resources were directed towards the Far East and elsewhere.

Despite half-hearted support from home, missionary activity grew explosively in Natal from the mid-nineteenth century. By 1851 the American Board missionaries had established a chain of twelve mission stations extending along the South African coast northward from Umthwalumi to Maphumulo.[56] It has already been noted that in 1856 considerable acreage for the so-called "Mission Reserves" was acquired from the Natal government. In turn, the land was not sold or granted to

African farmers but rather set aside in trust. Thus, Africans, beholden to the well-meaning but excessively paternalistic missionaries, could not freely launch their own experiments.

The American missionaries encouraged a certain amount of entrepreneurship in the field of journalism. In 1861 they imported into Natal one of the first printing presses in the colony for African use and worked with their Zulu converts to produce a religious newspaper, published in the vernacular. In a sense, then, Americans helped to lay the foundations of black journalism in South Africa.

Government land grants enabled the American missionaries to expand their operations, and by 1864 the Board had established twenty-one Mission Reserves.[57] A year later the Amanzimtoti Institute, founded in 1853 to train Africans as teachers, was revived and expanded under the direction of Reverend Ireland. The Board had received a £100 grant from the government's new Native Reserve Fund and a £100 gift from several white merchants in nearby Durban. In support of the African population the Natal government annually made a fixed grant of £5,000 from the Native Reserve Fund. The monies, however, were raised from direct taxes levied on the local African population, while the allocation did not increase with the growth in tax revenues, which by 1865 exceeded £10,000 annually. Consequently, Africans rarely benefited equitably or fully from economic growth.[58]

EDUCATIONAL ENTERPRISE

It is often forgotten today that Americans were in the forefront of early educational enterprise in South Africa. In 1869 the first school for African women, Inanda Seminary, was established in Natal by the the American Board. Mary K. Edwards, an American educator, was appointed principal and remained at Inanda until her death in 1928.[59] Its counterpart, the Inanda Station School for Boys, was led by a Zulu, Reverend John Dube, after the retirement of Lindley in 1873. The Board had begun to ordain African pastors in 1870, and control over missionary education as well as the churches gradually passed to the indigenous Christian leadership.

By the early 1880s a new class of Westernized literate Africans, called the *kholwa,* had begun to emerge in Natal. Kholwa literally meant "believer," and a large percentage of them were products of the American missionary schools. Tragically, the kholwa found themselves caught between the local white population, who feared them as a potential economic force, and the traditional African elites, who saw them as a threat to their power and to their traditional social and cultural institutions.

By the 1870s the American Board sent a few Zulu converts each year to the United States for further studies. Most of them were enrolled in segregated schools, mainly in the South. White and black church denominations over the years had established their own educational institutions for blacks, including Lincoln University, established in Pennsylvania in 1854 by the Presbyterian Church; Wilberforce University in Ohio, founded by the African Methodist Episcopal Church two years later; Hampton Institute and Fisk University, opened in 1868; and Tuskegee Institute, which was patterned after Hampton and started in 1881 by Booker T. Washington, the conservative black American educator.

Among the most successful of the early students from South Africa was Ira Adams Nembula. Baptized by Dr. Newton Adams, who, it must be recalled, was one of the first American Board missionaries in South Africa, Nembula was sent to the United States in 1882 to assist in the translation of the Bible into Zulu. A year later the work was published by the American Bible Society, and Nembula entered the University of Michigan Medical School. He earned an M.D. degree in 1887, returned to South Africa, and served as a physician in Zululand until his untimely death in 1896. Dr. Nembula was the first Zulu, and possibly the first black South African, to obtain a doctorate in medicine.[60]

The American Board was not alone among American missionary organizations to penetrate South Africa before the mid-nineteenth century. Mormons of the Church of Jesus Christ of Latter-Day Saints began their work in the Cape colony in 1853 and within two years had established a church with 176 white members. However, as fervent believers in the divine mission of the white race, they had little interest in working among Africans, and their South African membership remained rather static for the balance of the century.[61]

Americans also played an early role in establishing secular schools for whites. In 1874 the Huguenot Seminary for Girls was founded near Cape Town with funds contributed by Dr. Andrew Murray, a local philanthropist. Its curriculum and organization were modeled after Mount Holyoke College in Massachusetts. The school, under an American principal trained as a Presbyterian mininster, prepared students for careers in teaching and missionary work.[62]

American missionaries were the first to introduce the American public to the cultures of South Africa. Lewis Grout, one of the most acute observers, immersed himself in Zulu culture and in 1859 published the *Grammar of the Zulu Language,* a 432-page text that for more than a decade served as the most authoritative work on the subject. In the face of Natal government assertions that the Zulu had no legal rights to the land, Grout undertook an exhaustive oral history in order to legitimate their ancestral claim to their lands.

Grout was not the only American who developed an expertise in Zulu civilization. James C. Bryant, a graduate of Amherst College in Massachusetts and a Congregational missionary, arrived at the American Board's Amanzimtoti station in 1847. Two years later he published a remarkably accurate and unbiased essay on the Zulu in the influential *Journal of the American Oriental Society.* In 1866 the Board sent out Reverend William Taylor to tour the various missions in the eastern Cape. Upon his return, he published in New York his *Christian Adventures in South Africa,* which attracted wide readership in Protestant church circles.[63]

As the decade of the 1880s unfolded, the European scramble for Africa greatly accelerated. Suddenly, vast territories were conquered by imperialist armies and millions of Africans found themselves exposed to the full force of Western institutions. Great new opportunities for Christian proselytization were recognized, and in 1883 the American Board in Boston decided to extend its operations northward, out of the colony of Natal. Three hundred thousand dollars of a recent bequest of one million was earmarked for the ambitious undertaking. In 1884 C. W. Wilcox of the American Board called upon several Zulu pastors in Natal and three black American educators, Nancy Jones and the Reverend Mr. and Mrs. Owsley, to help him establish a temporary base at Inhambane on the coast of Portuguese Mozambique. It was hoped that Inhambane would serve as the missionaries' gateway to central Africa. The Americans, all recent graduates of Fisk University in the United States, became the first black Americans despatched by the board to southern Africa.[64] This East Central African Mission, an offshoot of the Zulu mission in Natal, became the vanguard for missionary enterprises in the vast reaches of Africa between the Limpopo and Zambesi rivers. A new era of American enterprise was about to unfold in southern Africa.

CONCLUSION

Americans and South Africans are often astonished upon discovering that for centuries, not decades, their two countries have been bound together intimately and inextricably in both mutually advantageous and disadvantageous relationships. They are also surprised to learn that the affiliations have been profoundly affected by a long history of intermittent economic sanctions and embargoes as well as by spasms of domestic racial and ethnic turmoil. On the United States' part the relationships from the very start have been characterized by certain degrees of ambivalence and inconsistency.

The quest for a "constructive engagement" with South Africans did not begin with U.S. Under Secretary of State Chester Crocker in the early 1980s. Since the first missions, Americans have fitfully debated with each other their objectives in South Africa and the best means of achieving them. Reverend Daniel Lindley epitomized this ambivalence, working initially with the Zulu, then with the Boers in hopes of tempering their racial fears and hostilities, then returning to the Zulu in frustration, and ultimately collaborating with the English-speaking Natalians in establishing Native Reserves, a forerunner of modern apartheid.

This first phase of American involvement, to 1885, belonged to the Yankee ship captains, enterprising consuls, missionaries, and, towards the end, the diamond prospectors. Though Southern Africa was at the margins of the expanding capitalist world economy, Americans were there, eager to do business, legitimate and otherwise. One of the very first U.S. consulates anywhere was opened in Cape Town in 1799, clearly attesting to the importance of that harbor to America's expanding international trade.

From the beginning much of the export trade was financed through London and conducted indirectly on British terms via English seaports. In this and subsequent periods, there was more often than not an imbalance in the bilateral trade in the United States' favor. In this early period the United States became chief supplier of a surprisingly wide range of essential goods, including marine stores and foodstuffs. Indeed, South

Africa depended heavily on the Yankees for an awesome array of American forest and agricultural products, particularly wood. Americans, on the other hand, were less interested in imports from South Africa, which were comparatively few and nonessential, than in Cape Town and Port Elizabeth as refreshment and victualing ports for passing ships. Missionaries and traders alike viewed South Africa in the wider context of activities in the South Atlantic and Indian Ocean. In those days their commercial interests were primarily maritime.

American consuls were moderately successful in developing their own businesses in trade, marine insurance, and the like but encountered less success in convincing fellow citizens of the country's commercial opportunities. Despite the rhetoric of free trade, both the British and the Americans devised trade policies that discouraged American enterprise. The U.S. merchant marine, the envy of the world from the late eighteenth to the mid-nineteenth century, became a victim in the last half century of benign government neglect, an indifferent public that redirected its developmental priorities inwardly, and to the technological advance of British shipping. Moreover, British commercial and financial dominance at the Cape pushed the Americans eastward to Port Elizabeth and farther along the Natal coast. They took advantage of the burgeoning export trade in wool and hides and became a major trading partner on the eve of the American Civil War.

In this early period Americans, though numerically small, played a surprisingly important entrepreneurial role, introducing new varieties of commercial crops and new agricultural and industrial machinery to blacks as well as to whites. They became key adjuvants for the Zulu and through modern education introduced them to notions of Judeo-Christian individualism and capitalist enterprise. A special relationship developed between the Americans and the Zulu, one that has endured to the present. In this early era the United States viewed South Africa through a missionary-held Zulu prism; and Americans developed a set of images of South Africans that remained remarkably constant through history.

A new era opened for American entrepreneurial involvement with the discoveries of huge gold deposits along the Transvaal's Witwatersrand and with the emergence of multinational corporations and mass production in the United States. From 1886 to 1902 American entrepreneurial relations with the South Africans deepened and were transformed in many fascinating ways. Innovative and unique American products pioneered new markets in a South Africa that suddenly found itself economically transformed by diamonds and gold. Onto the stage came a fresh cast of actors with a new set of objectives and strategies. At the close of the American Civil War it looked as though the United States would completely disengage from South Africa. Instead, it turned out to be another loaded pause. The United States was poised for a reengagement on a massive and totally unprecedented scale.

NOTES

1. Sidney Mendelssohn, ed., *Mendelssohn's South African Bibliography to The Year 1925*, p. 25. See also T. R. H. Davenport, "The Consolidation of a New Society," in Monica Wilson and Leonard Thompson, eds., *The Oxford History of South Africa* (New York, 1969) 1: 272–311.
2. René F. Immelman, *Men of Good Hope: The Story of the Cape Town Chamber of Commerce, 1804–1954* (Cape Town, 1955), pp. 129, 139–40.
3. Alan R. Booth, *The United States in South Africa*, p. 90.
4. "A Banking Legacy," *Financial Mail*, June 6, 1986, p.7. See also Eric A. Walker, *A History of Southern Africa* (London, 1968), p. 156.
5. Robert Ross, "Capitalism, Expansion, and Incorporation on the Southern African Frontier," in Howard Lamar and Leonard Thompson, eds., *The Frontier in History: North America and Southern Africa Compared*, pp. 209–35.
6. David Welsh, *The Roots of Segregation: Native Policy in Natal, 1845–1910*, p. 78.
7. Ralph W. Hidy, *The House of Baring in American Trade and Finance, 1763–1861* (Cambridge, Mass., 1949). See also Philip Ziegler, *The Sixth Great Power: Barings, 1762–1929* (New York, 1988).
8. Edward C. Bursk, Donald T. Clark, and Ralph W. Hidy, eds., *The World of Business*. See also Kevin Danaher, *The Political Economy of U.S. Policy Towards South Africa*, p. 33; David Francis Bacon, *Wanderings on the Seas and Shores of Africa* (New York, 1843), passim.
9. C. G. W. Schumann, "Aspects of Economic Development in South Africa," in Marcelle Kooy, ed., *Studies in Economics and Economic History*. See also U.S. Department of State Despatches, Consuls in Cape Town (1799–1853), Doc. no. 205, Yale University Archives, Reel 1, RG 59, T 191 (YUL).
10. T. Hall to Daniel Webster, Consul Despatch, January 2, 1851, Yale University Archives, Reel 1, RG 59 T191 (YUL); U.S. Consulate, Cape Town Despatches, 3rd ser. (SAL); C. W. De Kiewiet, *A History of South Africa: Social and Economic*, p. 11.

11. Booth, *U.S. Experience,* pp. 90–96. See also Chester W. Wright, *Wool-Growing and the Tariff: A Study in the Economic History of the United States* (Boston, 1910); Blanche E. Hazard, *The Organization of the Boot and Shoe Industry in Massachusetts Before 1875* (Cambridge, Mass., 1921); Eric Hobsbawm, *The Age of Capital: 1848–1875* (New York, 1975), ch. 1.
12. Wright, *Wool-Growing,* p. 119.
13. Peter Duignan and L. H. Gann, *The United States and Africa,* p. 197.
14. Edward Chester, *Clash of Titans: Africa and U.S. Foreign Policy,* chs. 2–3.
15. *The Cape Argus,* July 2, 1970. p. 1 (SAL). See also Booth, *U.S. Experience,* pp. 90–93.
16. Henry G. Aubrey, *U.S. Imports and World Trade* (Oxford, 1957).
17. Robert Greenhalgh Albion, *Seaports South of the Sahara,* p. 101.
18. *Cape of Good Hope Blue Book, 1865,* Reel 1/4424; (SAL) *Colony of Natal Blue Book, 1865,* Reel 4/4426 (SAL). See also E. H. D. Arndt, *Banking and Currency Development in South Africa, 1652–1927* (Cape Town, 1928), pp. 144–45.
19. Peter Wickins, *Africa, 1880–1980: An Economic History* (London, 1986), p. 38. See also Charles A. Jones, *International Business in the Nineteenth Century* (New York, 1987), p. 167; J. A. Henry, *The First Hundred Years of the Standard Bank* (London, 1963).
20. See William Fleming, *Alagoa Bay: Trade and Statistics (1868);* Anonymous, *Alagoa Bay Trade and the Trade Statistics of Port Elizabeth, 1864.* See also Francis L. Coleman, ed., *Economic History of South Africa.*
21. C. Joseph Pusateri, *A History of American Business* (Arlington Heights, Ill., 1984), p. 210.
22. See Maureen M. Bullen, "British Policy Towards a Settlement with America, 1865–1872," M.A. thesis (University of London, 1956).
23. Eric Rosenthal, *Stars and Stripes in Africa* (Johannesburg, 1968), p. 167.
24. D. Hobart Houghton and Jenifer Dagut, eds., *Source Material on the South African Economy, 1860–1970,* 1:45–66.
25. Patrick Manning, "Notes Towards A History of American Technical Assistance in Southern Africa, 1870–1950," unpublished manuscript (California Institute of Technology, n. d.), p. 5. See also Rosenthal, *Stars and Stripes,* p. 60; Mendelssohn, ed., *Mendelssohn's South African Bibliography,* pp. 44.
26. Benjamin S. Pray and Company papers, Baker Library, Harvard University, File LA 1/5/70S. See also Francis Wilson, "Farming: 1866–1966," in Wilson and Thompson, eds., *Oxford History of South Africa,* 2:113–16.
27. D. M. Goodfellow, *A Modern Economic History of South Africa.* See also F. V. Meyer, *Britain's Colonies in World Trade* (New York, 1948).
28. Charles I. Bevans, comp., *Treaties and Other International Agreements of the United States, 1776–1949,* 10:610; "Commercial Relations of the

United States With Foreign Countries, 1855–1902," Special Agents Series no. 199, vol. 20 (Washington, D.C., 1904). See also Thomas J. Noer, *Briton, Boer and Yankee: The United States and South Africa, 1870–1914* (Kent, Ohio, 1978), passim.

29. D. Hobart Houghton, *The South African Economy*, pp. 60–66.
30. Russell Warren Howe, *Along the Afric Shore: A Historical Review of Two Centuries of U.S.–African Relations.* See also Robert W. Schufeldt *Report on Commerce and Navigation*, Library of Congress, box 23/116/79 (Washington, D.C., 1879) (NAW).
31. Daniel R. Headrick, *The Tools of Empire: Technology and European Imperialism in the Nineteenth Century* (New York, 1981), pp. 157–64.
32. Ralph Gray and John M. Peterson, *Economic Development of the United States* (Homewood, Ill., 1974); T. Nicol Jenkin, *Report on the General Trades of South Africa* (London, 1902), p. 15.
33. Vincent P. Carosso, *More Than A Century of Investment Banking: The Kidder, Peabody and Company Story* (New York, 1978), p. 17; Vincent P. Carosso, *The Morgans: Private International Bankers, 1854–1913*, p. 174; Emily Rosenberg, *Spreading the American Dream: American Economic and Cultural Expansion, 1890–1945.*
34. Ralph H. Blodgett, *Our Expanding Economy* (New York, 1955), p. 37; *Commercial Directory and Guide to the Eastern Province of the Cape of Good Hope*, 1881, 968.75 T(05) (SAL).
35. C. Joseph Pusateri, *A History of American Business*, p. 177.
36. Robert Bruce Davies, *Peacefully Working To Conquer The World: Singer Sewing Machines in Foreign Markets, 1854–1920*, p. 219.
37. Headrick, *Tools of Empire*, p. 101.
38. Alex Groner, *American Business and Industry* (New York, 1972), pp. 119–20.
39. John G. Glover, ed., *The Development of American Industries*, p. 222.
40. Ralph W. Hidy and Muriel E. Hidy, *History of the Standard Oil Company (New Jersey) : Pioneering in Big Business, 1882–1911.* See also Pusateri, *American Business*, p. 199.
41. Norman Etherington, *Preachers, Peasants and Politics in Southeast Africa, 1835–1880.* See also Richard Elphick, "Africans and the Christian Campaign in Southern Africa," pp. 270–308; Oliver Elsbree, "The Rise of the Missionary Spirit in New England, 1790–1815," *New England Quarterly* 1 (July 1928); 291–97; John A. Andrew, *Rebuilding the Christian Commonwealth: New England Congregationalists and Foreign Missions, 1800–1830* (Lexington, Ky., 1976), passim.
42. David Brion Davis, "Reflections on Abolitionism," *American Historical Review* 92, 4 (October 1987); 803. See also David Brion Davis, *Slavery and Human Progress* (New York, 1984), passim.
43. "Frederick Brainerd Bridgman," The American Board.
44. Andrew Ross, *John Philip (1775–1851)*, p. 61.

45. For Buxton, see Philip D. Curtin, *The Image of Africa: British Ideas and Action 1780–1850* (Madison, Wisc., 1964), pp. 434–38. See also Bruce C. Hawthorn, "Industrialism and the Foreign Missionary Movement in New England," Ph.D dissertation (Boston University, 1953).

46. Rufus Anderson, *Memorial Volume of the First Fifty Years of the American Board of Commissioners for Foreign Mission,* 5th ed. (Boston, 1862).

47. Alan R. Booth, ed., *Journal of the Reverend George Champion,* p. xii. See also D. J. Kotze, ed., *Letters of the American Missionaries, 1835–1838.*

48. E. W. Smith, *The Life and Times of Daniel Lindley, 1801–1880.* See also Graham Mackeurton, *Cradle Days of Natal, 1492–1845.*

49. See Edgar Brookes and Colin DeB. Webb, *A History of Natal.* See also John Bird, ed., *The Annals of Natal, 1495–1848,* 2:372.

50. Joseph Tracy, *History of the American Board of Commissioners for Foreign Missions.* See also Welsh, *The Roots of Segregation,* pp. 31–51.

51. Ibid., p. 47. See also J. Du Plessis. *A History of Christian Missions in South Africa.*

52. David Livingstone, *Missionary Travels and Researches in South Africa* (New York, 1858), p. 132.

53. Peter Richardson, "The Natal Sugar Industry in the 19th Century," in Bill Albert and Adrian Graves, eds., *Crisis and Change in the International Sugar Economy, 1860–1914.* See also Eric Rosenthal, comp. *Southern African Dictionary of National Biography,* p. 152.

54. John Robinson, *Notes on Natal: An Old Colonist's Book for New Settlers* (Durban, 1872), p. 97. See also Colin Bundy, *The Rise and Fall of the South African Peasantry* (London, 1979), p. 78.

55. See B. J. T. Leverton, *The Natal Cotton Industry, 1845–1875: A Study in Failure* (Pretoria, 1963). See also George McCall Theal, *History of South Africa 1795–1872* (Cape Town 1964) 3:251; Robert James Mann, *The Colony of Natal* (London, 1859).

56. Horton Davies and H. W. Shepard, eds., *South African Missions, 1800–1950.* See also Oscar D. Dhlomo, "A Survey of Some Aspects of the Educational Activities of the American Board of Commissioners for Foreign Missions in Natal as Reflected in the History of Amanzimtoti, 1835–1956."

57. For an excellent discussion of the Mission Reserves, see Welsh, *Roots of Segregation,* pp. 250–51, 282–84.

58. See Etherington, *Preachers,* pp. 75–199.

59. Agnes Wood, *Shine Where You Are: A History of Inanda Seminary: 1869–1969.*

60. For an excellent discussion of the *kholwa* see Normal Alan Etherington, "The Rise of the Kholwa in Southeast Africa: African Christian Communities in Natal, Pondoland, and Zululand, 1835–1880," Ph.D dissertation (Yale University, 1971). For the American Board see "Bridgman," p. 66.

On Nembula see Arthur F. Christofersen, *Adventuring with God: The Story of the American Board Mission in South Africa*, p. 164.

61. Lawrence E. Cummins, "The Saints in South Africa," *Ensign* 3 (March 1973); 44–78. See also Farrell R. Monson, "History of the South African Missions of the Church of Jesus Christ of Latter-Day Saints, 1853–1970," M.A. thesis (Brigham Young University, 1971). See also personal correspondence of Grant Allen Anderson, Historical Department, Church of Jesus Christ of Latter-Day Saints, Salt Lake City, June 16, 1986.

62. Rosenthal, *Stars and Stripes*, p. 175.

63. Walter Lee Williams, "Black American Attitudes Toward Africa: The Missionary Movement, 1877–1900," Ph.D. dissertation (University of North Carolina, 1974); Lewis Grout, *Zulu-land: Or, Life Among the Zulu* (Philadelphia, 1864).

64. Historical Note, Rhodesia Mission (1893–), NAZ file, UN-3 series. Josiah Tyler, *Forty Years Among the Zulus*, p. 261. Charles Robert Lord, "The Birth of a Mission: Background and Early History of the Rhodesia Mission," manuscript, 1971, pp. 4–7 (NAZ). Christofersen, *Adventuring*, p. 120.

THREE

The American Rediscovery of South Africa, 1886–1902

In this period of rapid economic transformation American entrepreneurs confronted new challenges, discovered new opportunities, and assumed strikingly different roles on the domestic landscape. The United States was fast emerging as the world's premier industrial economy, as the preeminent mass producer and mass marketer of goods essential for economic development and material prosperity. Its inventive capacity was best exemplified by the avalanche of patents and trademarks in the last two decades of the century, an advance that made American products extremely attractive to South Africans but threatening to British competitors.

Beyond the Orange River, Americans discovered new markets for the consumption of U.S.-produced consumer and capital goods. This chapter examines the critical role private Americans played in South Africa's transition from an agrarian economy to a mining giant. They became enmeshed in local politics, helping to devise and implement schemes for British imperialist expansion. As engineering and management consultants to local governments and to the fledgling extractive industries, some of them garnered personal fortunes and exercised enormous influence, vastly disproportionate to their numbers. The missionaries, on the other hand, Africanized their leadership and greatly expanded the size and scope of their educational enterprises. In the process they became a vanguard for Cecil Rhodes's expansion into Central Africa.

This was a time when middle-class entrepreneurial black Americans discovered South Africa, and through cultural exchange they helped reshape indigenous Africans' image of themselves and their vision of the future. This was also a moment of discovery for the American mass media, as they responded to the highly dramatic events leading up to and including the Second Boer War. Nevertheless, the discovery of diamonds and gold beyond the Orange River was the crucial event of this period.

THE MINING REVOLUTION

The discovery and exploitation of diamonds in Kimberley in the late 1860s and gold on the Witwatersrand in 1886 led to an economic transformation in southern Africa of monumental proportions. Formerly, the economies of southern Africa were grossly underdeveloped and essentially agricultural. The landlocked Afrikaner republics of the Orange Free State and Transvaal were practically bankrupt, and the only areas of real importance to the world were the British colonies of the Cape and Natal, valued for their geographical position along the vital shipping lanes to the Far East, the Americas, and Europe. The coastal economies staggered under the collapse of world wool prices, costly and chronic frontier wars with the indigenous populations, and devastating periodic droughts.

The mineral revolution of the last quarter of the nineteenth century led to a dramatic expansion of commercial agriculture and provided foundations for the emergence in the early twentieth century of a modern industrial economy. Fabulous profits generated by the extractive industries led to the rapid accumulation of an enormous amount of capital, much of it flowing into the development of agriculture, transportation, and secondary industry. Trunk railroad lines were built to connect the centers of mineral extraction in the interior with the burgeoning seaports of Cape Town, Port Elizabeth, East London, and Durban. The emerging urban industrial complex on the rich Witwatersrand, or Rand, was connected by rail to the Cape in 1892, to Mozambique's Delagoa Bay in 1894, and to Natal a year later.[1] In less than two decades the interior of South Africa was drawn completely and inexorably into the capitalist world economy.

In 1884 the South African Republic (S.A.R.), or Transvaal, was barely solvent. Six years later its revenues had surpassed Natal's and came close to matching the Cape's. By 1898 the South African Republic had become the world's largest producer of gold, accounting for nearly 28 percent of output.[2] The Transvaal's economy rose like an awakening giant. This former backwater, now with newly acquired purchasing power, diversified its sources of trade in order to reduce its humiliating economic dependence on the British. The reorientation provided considerable opportunity for two industrial giants, the United States and Imperial Germany, to compete with Great Britain for the booming South African trade.

From the 1870s scions of the international mining community invaded the two Afrikaner republics. They posed simultaneously as economic adjuvants and political and cultural threats. The labor-intensive mining operations impelled a swelling stream of whites from North America, the British Isles, and Australia as well as black Africans from diverse ethnic backgrounds and geographical areas. Extremely heterogeneous urban agglomerations suddenly emerged out of the stark landscape of the high veld. By 1871 Kimberley, nonexistent a decade earlier, boasted a population of over fifty thousand blacks and whites, making it the second largest city in South Africa, behind only Cape Town.[3] Even more spectacularly, Johannesburg rose from a desolate Transvaal farm in 1886 to a sprawling metropolis of 102,000 barely six years later. Their demands for consumer goods, especially foodstuffs, and the insatiable need for mining experts and heavy machinery caused a dramatic inflation in producer prices and wages, making South Africa an extremely attractive market for both capital investment, consumer goods, and skilled manpower. The opportunities for American entrepreneurship seemed unlimited.

Initially, African and European farmers competed quite successfully in furnishing urban markets with staples. They quickly adopted new farming techniques and cash crops. In some regions African peasants' output per acre exceeded that of their white neighbors.[4] But Africans continued to lose their most arable land to European encroachment and found themselves being pushed onto overcrowded native reserves. State revenues from customs duties and taxes on mining profits were used to subsidize secondary rail lines to white farming areas, and financial institutions made capital more readily available to white farmers. Consequently, Africans encountered difficulty in acquiring imported technology and their competitive position steadily deteriorated. Moreover, both white and black farmers had to compete with cheap imported food, much of it from the United States. For the African the death knell was sounded in 1896–1897, when drought and a devastating rinderpest epidemic drastically reduced their own yields and boosted imports of American food, especially wheat. In addition, the new railway line from Cape Town to Kimberley enabled importers of American grains to undercut the African farmers in neighboring Basutoland, who for more than a decade had prospered on their own exports of food to the hungry miners.

The incorporation of marginal farmers into the colonial economy as miners and hired farm hands was partially the result of these new developments. Patterns of labor migrancy became more apparent as the position of small farmers weakened. The frontiers in the United States and in South Africa were fast closing. In South Africa the last "frontier wars" between 1871 and 1887 and the incorporation of the remnants of Zululand into Natal colony gave further impetus to the creation of a landless African peasantry.

From 1874 the diamond mining operations were subjected to a process of rapid amalgamation. Cecil Rhodes, the British-born entrepreneur, entered into a bitter struggle with other magnates for possession of the claims of thousands of small diggers on the overcrowded diamond fields. It had become painfully evident at an early stage that diamond supplies had to be controlled if the industry was to remain profitable. In 1880 Rhodes formed the De Beers Company and accelerated his purchase of claims.[5] Until then much of the diamond expansion resulted from reinvestment of profits and modest investments by businessmen and bankers from the Cape and Kimberley. In the early 1880s competition on the crowded diamond fields intensified and threatened to ruin the industry. In desperation Rhodes turned to the European merchant bankers N. M. Rothschild and Sons, who were already active diamond-share speculators. He secured a £1 million loan that enabled him to gain control of the prized Kimberley Mine.[6] By 1885 De Beers commanded a capital of £841,550. Over the next five years the British-based recapitalization scheme enabled Rhodes to buy out his biggest rivals and achieve a near monopoly over diamond production. By this ruthless process he pooled his holdings into a vast new entity, De Beers Consolidated Mines, which was created in 1888 and endowed with a charter allowing it to engage in any business enterprise anywhere in southern Africa. Within two years De Beers' assets had grown to an astonishing £14 million.[7] It was not long before all the companies on the diamond fields were absorbed by the De Beers giant.[8]

Through Rhodes's energy, cunning, and ingenuity South Africa's diamond industry was transformed into a formidable monopoly that for the next century controlled the world's diamond markets, dominated the trade, and eventually influenced demand. It can be argued that without such an expansive monopoly the diamond industry would have collapsed either through uncontrolled overproduction or sharp and unpredictable fluctuations in prices. In any case, De Beers eventually became the largest corporation on the entire African continent and one of the greatest mining enterprises in the world.[9]

The gold industry on the Witwatersrand, or "white waters reef," underwent a similar process of amalgamation. In 1886 vast gold-bearing deposits were discovered in the Transvaal, stretching nearly forty miles in an east-west direction along the desolate high veld. Rhodes saw another great opportunity, and in 1887, only a year after the discovery, this consummate capitalist created the Gold Fields Company and floated its first shares in London.[10] But the gold mining boom between 1886 and 1889 was followed by a sudden and unexpected recession as Transvaal shares on the London Stock Exchange lost more than half their value.[11] Miners and investors were shocked to discover that the surface gold deposits were not extensive and would soon be depleted.

As the industry tottered on the brink of collapse, John Hays Hammond, an American engineer in Rhodes' employ, suggested that the subterranean deposits, though of lower grade, were enormous and might be worked to depths approaching five thousand feet. The articulate Hammond convinced Rhodes of the great potential of the Witwatersrand deep-level areas and won his endorsement of an experimental but enormously expensive shaft-sinking procedure that the American had learned of during his mining experience in the western United States.[12] Still, the commercially viable exploitation of the Rand's ores, which were of uniformly low grade, would have been impossible without the recent discovery of the MacArthur-Forrest cyanide process, which was introduced to the Randlords, or magnates of the Rand, in 1890 by Hennen Jennings, an American who at the time served as chief consulting engineer to H. Eckstein and Company in Johannesburg.[13] Quite literally, the process saved the Transvaal's gold industry by permitting a 90 percent recovery of gold from the raw ore. Thus, the Rand ores became extremely cost-effective. But the process could only become viable through the acquisition of new, extremely costly equipment. Hammond knew this and urged Rhodes to seek funds overseas. Until then, a substantial proportion of the capital requirements for gold extraction were generated from within South Africa, from small banks and individual investors whose profits had come from diamonds and farming. Now, the industry needed enormous new infusions of capital that only overseas British investors could furnish. Rhodes looked again to his homeland for capital, this time to buy up the claims of undercapitalized miners who were facing bankruptcy and to purchase state-of-the art mining technology.

By the end of 1890 he had transformed his small firm into the Consolidated Gold Fields of South Africa.[14] But Rhodes was not without competition. Between 1890 and 1895 five other large mining houses were formed by other British capitalists in South Africa. At the pinnacle stood Wernher Beit and Company, with Consolidated Gold Fields a close second. Collectively, six firms now controlled the extraction of gold on the Rand.[15] In the merger process, smaller houses and minor partners, such as the American entrepreneur H. J. King of S. Neumann and Company, a London firm, were leveraged out of existence. King and other American capitalists failed to attract investors in the United States, where fortunes were being made in domestic manufacturing and transportation. American investors were looking for less risky enterprises closer to home. The six new companies possessed the capital, mostly London-based, to make the transition after the mid-1890s to deep-level underground mining on a massive scale.[16]

AMERICAN EXPERTISE AND TECHNOLOGY

American expertise and technology, not finance capital, played a crucial role in the early development of the diamond and gold industries in South Africa. Indeed, American mining engineers and technicians provided much of the knowledge that laid the essential foundations of South Africa's enormously profitable extractive industries. Historians maintain that they transmitted to white South Africans the art of deep-level mining. This is not surprising, for by the late nineteenth century the United States enjoyed a global reputation for its mining technology. It was second to none in the world of mining in terms of output, cost-effectiveness, and expertise. Graduates of the Columbia and Colorado Schools of Mines and the University of Pennsylvania School of Metallurgy took phenomenally high-paying jobs in various parts of the world and rapidly rose to positions of great influence. Other American mining experts gained skills from practical experience in the mines of Wyoming, Arizona, Colorado, Montana, and elsewhere in the Americas. By 1896 several dozen American mining consultants worked in South Africa. Indeed, nearly half the mines were managed by American engineers.[17]

The first American to manage a South African diamond mining company was Gardner Fred Williams, a Michigan engineer who in 1884 was attracted to the early gold discoveries in the eastern Transvaal. His real expertise lay in the extraction of quartzite-impregnated ores, and three years later Rhodes lured him into becoming general manager of De Beers, a position he held for nearly two decades. During his tenure Williams introduced a vastly improved subterranean mining system and made significant technological advances in diamond extraction.[18]

Williams was not alone among the great American innovators and inventors of the Rand. Major Louis Irving Seymour, who joined De Beers in 1891 as chief mechanical engineer, invented a self-winding engine that revolutionized South Africa's mining operations by making them vastly more efficient and cost-effective.[19] George Labram, who arrived in Kimberley in about 1894 to oversee the erection of a huge American-made washing plant, stayed on and designed an efficient grease table for sorting diamonds. Charles Butters from California came to South Africa as a specialist in the treatment of refractory ores, and he designed and built the first chlorination furnace and then invented the Butters Filter, which was widely used in the country's gold mines. The ingenuity of these and other Americans was responsible for substantially increasing the industry's productive capacity and profitability.[20]

American engineers made an even bigger mark in the gold industry. And no American in South Africa in the nineteenth century wielded as much political and professional influence as John Hays Hammond. Already a highly respected mining engineer in the United States, Hammond became second only to Rhodes in the management of Consolidated Gold Fields of South Africa. He was convinced of the enormous potential of deep-level mining and correctly predicted that before 1900 the Witwatersrand would be producing gold in excess of £20 million annually. To assist in the development of deep-level shaft-sinking, Hammond hired scores of Americans, including William Russel Quinan, a leading American dynamite expert. Enormous quantities of dynamite were of course needed to reach down to such great depths, and Quinan built up a local explosives industry that by the turn of the century had become one of South Africa's largest manufacturing concerns.[21]

The capital to underwrite this enormous undertaking on the Witwatersrand would not have been forthcoming without concrete evidence that the reef was indeed worth exploiting. Hammond's recommendations to Rhodes were supported by evidence furnished by American engineers. In a report published in early 1893 Hamilton Smith became the first person to scientifically reveal the true potential of the Rand gold resources. Smith, who had wide experience in Nevada silver mining, was hired by the Rothschild interests in Europe to study the Rand in hopes of confirming Hammond's assertions, and, indeed, Smith's exhaustive studies did much to sway the Rothschilds into vastly increasing their Witwatersrand investments. Three years later Dr. George F. Becker, chief of the prestigious United States Geological Survey, visited South Africa and produced a report on the practicality of mining to depths of four thousand feet. Becker's extensive geological surveys of the Witwatersrand fields became an indispensable guide to the auriferous seams. The Smith and Becker findings provided the crucial evidence that Rhodes needed to convince the directors of Consolidated Gold Fields to fund the deep-level operations.[22]

Not all Americans worked in the private sector, or, for that matter, for British capitalists. Indeed, a few engineers held advisory positions in the local governments, notably Ethelbert Woodford, who in 1887, after a decade of work in South Africa, became chief mining engineer for the South African Republic. Woodford authored a comprehensive mining code that remained the centerpiece of the industry for more than half a century.[23] His counterpart in the government of the Cape colony was the American engineer, William H. Hall, who also provided important ideas in regard to mine safety codes.[24]

Other Americans went into the mining business as private entrepreneurs. Jerome Babe from Los Angeles developed a small though successful diamond brokerage business. B. Chafee Warriner became a manager and shareholder of the famous Bonanza mine in the mid-1890s. He later organized Crown Mines, which became the largest single gold property in South Africa before the turn of the century. By 1899 there were many other imaginative entrepreneurs among the several thousand Americans north of the Orange River who over the last two decades had built up, and often lost, small fortunes. Most of them were prospectors or in businesses connected to the extractive industries. Generally, they came to South Africa with an extraordinary amount of skill and ambition but very little capital.

It must be emphasized that in those days it was an almost impossible task to convince businessmen in the United States to make capital investments in Africa. Consequently, enterprising Americans with ambitions in Africa had to seek funds in Europe. Colonel Edward McMurdo, with European backing and under a Portuguese concession, had constructed a railway line between Lourenco-Marques in Portuguese Mozambique and the Transvaal border. But in 1889 the Portuguese colonial authorities had seized the nearly completed line out of fear that the British-financed enterprise might lead to an eventual British seizure of the colony's hinterland. McMurdo and his creditors appealed to President Grover Cleveland, who submitted it to international arbitration. The case dragged on for another decade until the courts finally ruled against the Portuguese. By then, however, McMurdo was financially ruined. Meanwhile, George Washington Williams, a black American representative of Collis P. Huntington, the American railroad magnate, visited Natal and the South African Republic in 1890. Like most other black American visitors in those days Williams was accorded all the privileges of a white person, including accommodations in first-class hotels and a private meeting with the Transvaal's vice president.[25] The Afrikaners were desperately seeking capital to develop a transportation infrastructure independent of the British. Nevertheless, Williams was unable to convince Huntington to invest his money in South African railroads. The McMurdo affair did much to discourage American investment in areas of political turmoil.[26]

American entrepreneurs were also involved in the early development of Johannesburg's municipal transportation system. By 1892 the city had become clotted with people and private vehicles.[27] Recognizing the need for mass transportation, H. J. King and his partners in a local mining concern secured a controlling interest in the newly formed Johannesburg City and Suburban Tramway Company in 1889. Failing to garner American support, they obtained European capital and opened a horse-drawn system two years later. Then in 1896 William Keller, a Californian, assembled a syndicate of thirty investors from the United States and fought unsuccessfully for a government concession from the Transvaal to develop an electric tramway in Johannesburg. The Volksraad (parliament) narrowly defeated the proposal in the face of enormous pressure from European investors who owned shares in the existing City and Suburban Tramway Company. Clearly, American investors did not have the influence enjoyed by their European counterparts.[28]

Americans assumed early and formative positions of leadership in professional organizations connected with the mining industry. In 1894 Charles Butters was elected president of the Chemical and Metallurgical Society of South Africa, and Joseph Storey Curtis, a geologist known as the father of scientific gold-mining in South Africa, became vice president of the powerful Chamber of Mines a year later. Three years earlier Curtis had founded the South African Association of Engineers and Architects, whose first president was the American engineer Hennen Jennings. As a young professional in America, Curtis had won wide recognition for his work with the United States Geological Survey. But as an executive in the Chamber of Mines he made an enormous impact. The Chamber, formed in 1889, enjoyed the membership of nearly all the leading mining-finance houses on the Rand. Indeed, the Chamber of Mines was the representative and consultative body of the Transvaal's gold-mining industry and played a crucial role in setting wage rates for black as well as white miners. During Curtis's tenure the Chamber supported the formation of the Native Labour Department, which was charged with ensuring an adequate labor supply. In 1895 the Chamber persuaded the South African Republic's Volksraad to legislate a pass system to facilitate the ethnic identification of black workers and to control their mobility for security reasons. In doing so, it helped to lay the foundations of the modern system of apartheid. Thus, with government cooperation, the predominantly English-speaking Chamber of Mines achieved centralized control over African labor recruitment and worked to reduce competition among the mining companies over wages and working conditions. Policies laid down in that formative period set the stage for gross racial discrimination in the extractive industries throughout the next century.[29]

The United States' influence also extended into the field of agriculture. The possibilities of developing a vast export-oriented citrus industry were recognized in 1892 with the first experiments in transporting fresh fruit to England under refrigeration. Rhodes was keenly interested in developing the industry, and in 1895 as Cape prime minister he appointed Dr. Charles P. Lounsbury of New York as the government's first entomologist. Lounsbury developed an import policy to control the entrance into the country of insects such as the kind that led to the devastating phylloxera that had nearly finished the wine industry two decades before.[30] Rhodes was persuaded by a visiting California fruit-grower, H. E. V. Pickstone, to purchase many of the ruined vineyards and to transform them into citrus groves. Pickstone directed the operation, and with the assistance of a few other Californian horticulturalists, he developed the estates for Rhodes and laid the foundations of South Africa's modern fruit industry. Numerous varieties were introduced from the United States and were among the country's first citrus exports in 1903. The Rhodes Fruit Farm was transformed into one of the most progressive agricultural enterprises in the country. Within a few decades South Africa became one of the world's largest fruit exporters.[31]

The transition after the mid-1890s to more labor-intensive deep-level mining gave fresh impetus to overseas immigration. Numerous immigrant organizations sprang up on the Rand, including the American Society, which emerged in 1895 to acclimatize recent arrivals and to assist them in finding employment or in establishing enterprises. By then more than two thousand Americans worked in the Transvaal alone. By contrast, very few Americans resided in the Cape colony, possibly because business opportunities were more limited. In a census of 1890, only 249 Cape residents claimed the United States as their birthplace.[32] Unlike their counterparts north of the Orange River, they tended to develop families and to put down permanent roots.

South Africa's new wealth attracted some of the brightest and most resourceful entrepreneurs. Not all of them, however, had noble intentions. Substantial opportunities for prostitution and pimping were provided by the multitude of male miners without families. By the mid-1890s, a number of pimps, prostitutes, and so-called "white slavers," expelled from New York City's lower East Side in a major police sweep, had emigrated to the Rand via London. Most of them were Russian and Polish-born Jews, who came to be known in Johannesburg as the "Bowery Boys." Charles Van Onselen asserts that they were the largest and best organized syndicate of white slavers on the Rand between 1897 and

1899.[33] Joe Silver, the notorious "King of the Pimps," founded the American Club as an association of Polish-American Jewish pimps. Their presence on the Rand was as tenuous as that of the profit-seeking miners. With the onset of War in 1899, these motley groups fled the Transvaal and moved their operations to coastal cities or out of the country altogether.

Other Americans pioneered in social work, though with limited success. Settlement houses in the United States in the late nineteenth century represented a new approach to the problem of social services for the urban poor. Under a plan spearheaded by Jane Addams and others, social workers established refuges in the midst of urban slums. The idea caught on, and in the 1890s scores of settlement houses, including Hull House in Chicago, were established in northern and western cities of the United States. The approach was transmitted to South Africa by American Board missionary Mary K. Edwards, principal of the Inanda Women's Seminary, who opened a hostel in Durban in 1895 for young girls in transit and in need of lodgings. Unfortunately, Edwards was unable to secure external funding, and the hostel closed four years later. More successful was the American branch of the Salvation Army, which opened an office in South Africa in 1883. Its earliest efforts were directed at reducing prostitution in the mining cities, particularly Kimberley. Eight years later it expanded its work into rural Zululand and Rhodesia.

PENETRATING SOUTH AFRICA: CREATING NEW MARKETS FOR NEW PRODUCTS

South Africa's mining revolution unfolded almost concurrently with the American revolution in industrial techniques and corporate organization. The enormous amount of capital that accumulated in the United States from the 1870s fueled the expansion in scale of companies and facilitated the development of new techniques and products that proved cheaper and often more cost-effective than those manufactured in other industrialized countries. American industrialization was based primarily on the highly mechanized production of standardized items for domestic and overseas consumer markets that were huge and rapidly expanding. By the turn of the century the United States' achievements in industrial production had far outstripped Britain's. Its corporations gained an early lead in products such as business machines, electrical equipment, and mining machinery.[34]

As a result of enormous advances in technology Americans held superior patents to key consumer and capital goods. Their patents and trademarks were of great importance in opening up and monopolizing South Africa's markets for a broad range of goods. By the onset of the Second Boer War Americans had gained control over markets for almost every new product, including vehicles, office equipment, oil, cameras, and cigarettes. The United States could offer unique products that found ready consumers in South Africa.[35]

The growth in American exports to South Africa in the late nineteenth century was in part the result of the increasing strength of its manufacturers, whose products were sought by South African consumers because of superior patents, technologies, and marketing skills. At the turn of the century American companies were scrambling to register their patents and trademarks in South Africa and elsewhere in an effort to establish market positions more effectively. Indeed, American manufacturers were impelled to establish British-based production facilities in order to prevent local imitators from preempting their products and markets. In South Africa their success was visibly revealed in 1898 in the dazzling array of products displayed by over a hundred American exhibitors at the Grahamstown Industrial Exhibition.[36] At the time American entrepreneurs based their operations on several key principles, including mass production at low cost, international distribution, and extensive and aggressive advertising.

Almost from the discovery of gold on the Witwatersrand, the United States was an important supplier of stores and equipment for the extractive industries. As a result of deep-level mining the method of mineral extraction changed dramatically. Picks and shovels gave way to highly mechanized forms of exploitation. Williams and Hammond, the pioneers of deep-level mining, placed in operation huge hauling, pumping, and washing machines.[37] They also illuminated the mines with electric lighting and moved miners down the shafts in Otis elevators. The U.S.-based Otis Elevator Company, scarcely five years old, began selling electric lifts to South African mining companies in the mid-1890s.

Through the efforts of Hammond and Williams, the United States was the largest supplier of heavy equipment to South Africa's mines in the

1890s.[38] U.S. products moved easily into South Africa as a result of a liberal Cape tariff (1889) that reduced duties on heavy machinery and mining tools and Transvaal tariff policies enabling American agricultural, railway, and mining equipment to enter duty free.[39] As early as 1887 thirty-three wagons reached Johannesburg loaded with American batteries and crushing mills supplied by Fraser and Chalmers of Chicago. Fraser and Chalmers, a household word among miners, was established in the United States in the 1860s to manufacture heavy equipment. In the early 1890s, the firm entered into a joint venture in England with two large South African mining groups, Wernher and Beit and Company and Rand Mines, thus adding a British dimension to its operations. By 1893, the firm was supplying over 40 percent of the mining equipment on the Rand; and at the beginning of the Boer War, its Johannesburg agency was doing over a million dollars worth of business.[40]

Another U.S.-based firm that took advantage of this burgeoning demand was the Ingersoll Rock Drill Company, which at the time was one of the world's largest manufacturers of rock drills and compressed air machinery. In 1890 a merger with a fellow giant, the Sergeant Drill Company, resulted in the creation of the mammoth Ingersoll-Sergeant Company. W. R. Grace acquired the business in 1894 and expanded it into an aggressive multinational corporation, eventually known as Ingersoll-Rand. By the Second Boer War in 1899 Ingersoll products were well-known to Rand miners and competed successfully with British counterparts.[41]

South Africa's extractive industries required a wide array of electrical equipment to illuminate mines and to run machinery. Here, too, Americans played an important role. In 1895, only three years after its formation, the General Electric Company began selling generators to mining firms on the Witwatersrand.[42] General Electric, born out of a merger between Edison General Electric and Thomson-Houston Electric, went multinational and established worldwide distribution networks, including a sales and distribution operation in South Africa. Business was so profitable that in 1898, GE formed a subsidiary in South Africa, called South African General Electric.[43] In doing so, General Electric became one of the first American companies to make a direct investment in South Africa. Westinghouse, its major competitor, was formed in 1886 and also cast its eyes upon the booming Transvaal economy. Rhodes's

British South Africa Company, impressed by Westinghouse equipment displayed at the 1893 Chicago World's Fair, placed a huge order for generators for his newly formed Victoria Falls Power Company.[44]

To fuel infrastructural development, the various South African colonies imported enormous quantities of American timber, iron, and steel. Wood was shipped from Oregon through the San Francisco firm of Pope and Talbot.[45] Hardwoods were needed in the mines and for railway ties, while softer varieties were used in the construction of railway rolling stock. It must be remembered that southern Africa, with few timberlands of its own, had relied heavily on lumber from the forests of North America since the late eighteenth century. From the 1890s the United States began producing enormous quantities of iron and steel and exporting in great bulk. The United States Steel Corporation, established in 1897 out of a merger of the Carnegie Steel Company and the Illinois Steel Company, immediately began shipping girders and heavy rails to South Africa's transportation companies.[46] American firms also became major vendors of metal piping. In 1899 a number of large pipe-manufacturing firms combined into a vast new entity, the National Tube Company. It, too, went multinational and within a few years had become a major supplier to South Africa of hydraulic equipment for the mines and of pipes for agricultural irrigation schemes.[47]

The United States also became a major provider of foodstuffs, especially wheat, corn, and oats as well as a range of dairy products, including cheese and ice cream. As I have already noted, for a brief moment in the late nineteenth century American farm products nearly monopolized the markets of the Rand, often at the expense of local producers, particularly African commercial farmers.[48]

The commercialization of agriculture in South Africa followed the discoveries of diamonds and gold. Farming became more market-oriented and land prices soared. South Africa's agricultural revolution of the late nineteenth century was driven by rising prices for foodstuffs. In response, Americans became major providers of a wide range of agricultural implements and hardware. Citrus-packing machinery arrived from the Skinner Machinery Company of Dunedin, Florida. In the vineyards of the Cape farmers cultivated with American Planet Jr. plows, while Boers in the Orange Free State used McCormick reapers, harrows, and cultivators to expand their output. In Johannesburg stores advertised American-made coal stoves, emery boards, axes, and hammers. And nearly all commercial farmers used American-made barbed wire in their fields. Along the coast of Natal and the Cape fishermen wore American-made Cape Ann rain gear and lit their way with kerosene lamps manufactured in the United States.[49]

The robust trade figures gave visible testimony to the huge South African demand for American equipment. As early as 1892 the United States had pulled ahead as South Africa's second most important supplier of imports. By 1898 it directly imported $13.4 million worth of U.S. manufactures and was the Americans' third biggest non-Western market, behind only Brazil and Japan. The figures would have been even more impressive had they included trade with the Transvaal via the ports of Mozambique. American exports of hardware into the Cape colony alone jumped from £9,717 in 1887 to £94,905 in 1901.[50] By the mid-1890s Lloyds and Company had become the largest U.S. exporter to South Africa of agricultural machinery and implements, with offices in Philadelphia, London, and Cape Town.[51]

American penetration of the tobacco and beverage sectors was also extensive, though short-lived. The huge American Tobacco Company trust swept into South Africa in the 1890s with ambitious plans to build a plant in Johannesburg. However, the project was abruptly abandoned in 1895 in the face of high duties on cigarettes. Business prospects dimmed further in 1902, when thirteen independent British companies were amalgamated into the Imperial Tobacco Company in order to compete effectively with the American Tobacco Company and to prevent it from monopolizing markets in the British Empire. The huge British tobacco conglomerate became so competitive that by the end of 1902 American Tobacco had begun to prepare for a complete withdrawal from South Africa.[52]

Late in the nineteenth century great strides were being made in the United States in the field of beer-brewing technology. This was not lost upon foreigners, and in the 1890s South African Breweries outfitted their new plant in Johannesburg with state-of-the-art equipment designed and built in New York. In 1897 the immensely profitable South African Breweries became the first industrial company listed on the new Johannesburg Stock Exchange.[53]

Americans did less well in the equally profitable field of pharmaceuticals. The United States had become an important source for South African consumers, but the "American Pharmacy" in Johannesburg, the major direct importer of American drugs and chemicals, was unable to snatch from the larger British and German firms a dominant position in the burgeoning market. Not until the post–World War II era did the United States achieve a dominant position in pharmaceuticals. More will be said of this in chapter 5.

Substantial progress was, however, achieved in the export of vehicles to South Africa. American stage coaches, most of which were manufactured by Abbot-Downing of Concord, New Hampshire, and by the LaPorte Carriage Company of Indiana, had enjoyed considerable popularity since the opening of the Kimberley Mine in the 1860s. As early as 1897 American wagons and carriages far outsold British competitors. In that year Americans marketed $358,000 worth of wheeled vehicles, nearly three times the value of their British counterparts.[54]

Petroleum products were one of America's most vital and profitable export items to South Africa. Here, too, an early lead was maintained. By 1870 Standard Oil of Ohio had established itself as the world's largest oil manufacturing firm. Nine years later the gargantuan Standard Oil Trust was created to achieve a monopoly of oil refining. Plans were then laid to establish distributing businesses overseas by forming subsidiaries.[55] By 1886 the Standard Oil complex of companies controlled more than 90 percent of the American petroleum business and was well along the road to becoming the nation's premier company in overseas markets. American petroleum products ranked fourth in the total value of U.S. overseas exports. Kerosene, alone, accounted for more than 80 percent of the value of pretroleum exports. By then, America had become the top supplier to South Africa, contributing nearly half a million imperial gallons annually, mostly through the burgeoning Natal port of Durban. Kerosene was the chief petroleum export to South Africa before the turn of the century. Much of it, shipped and distributed in five-gallon tin cans, was destined for the Rand, mainly for use in illumination and industrial machinery.[56]

Standard Oil absorbed many smaller American firms, including the Vacuum Oil Company, which had developed a superior lubricating oil from a petroleum base. In 1890 expansion slowed, though only temporarily, when the U.S. Supreme Court splintered the mammoth trust into twenty companies. Nevertheless, Standard Oil of New York maintained its operations in South Africa and used its monopoly of American kerosene to build a formidable marketing network throughout the region.

Especially active was the Vacuum Oil Company, an American spin-off that was incorporated as a subsidiary in South Africa in 1897 and marketed Mobil oil out of a depot in Cape Town. By 1899 nearly all the petroleum products marketed in South Africa were of American provenance.

Americans also became leading small arms exporters. The Colt Patent Arms plant in Hartford, Connecticut, by then one of the largest producers of small arms in the world, advertised regularly in *The Cape Argus* newspaper.[57] Mining companies purchased obsolescent guns and sold them to Africans, who traditionally hunted, as an incentive for employment. However, one weapon unavailable to Africans was the machine gun. An American inventor, Hiram Maxim, developed the world's first machine gun and began manufacturing it in England for the British government. It was used with deadly effectiveness against the Zulu in the 1880s and in the war against the Ndebele of Matabeleland in 1893.

The phenomenal growth of business in South Africa created a substantial demand for office equipment. Remington, already a big name in arms even in South African markets, diversified into typewriters and established an agency in Cape Town. The Burroughs Adding Machine Company, founded in 1886, opened a London office a decade later and started selling mechanical office machines in various parts of the British Empire, including South Africa.[58] The National Cash Register Company, a major competitor, was organized in 1899 and went international immediately with a London office to handle sales in the British realm. By 1903 South Africa ranked fifth as an importer of American cash registers. In 1890 Singer began to form national sales companies worldwide, and in South Africa a partnership with a local distributor was established in 1901. Singer was already the leading seller of sewing machines, possibly the best known American product in the country.

South Africa proved to be an excellent market for American cameras and film. George Eastman's Eastman Company of Rochester, New York, held the patents on inexpensive portable cameras and photo-finishing processes that enabled the company to move quickly into overseas markets. In 1888 Eastman came out with his first "Kodak," a small, simple to operate, lightweight box camera that transformed photography into a popular pastime. The company began to manufacture abroad in 1891 from a plant in England, and by the late 1890s a distribution network had been established in South Africa, serviced by its British subsidiary.

2. Singer in South Africa, ca. 1892. The caption to this advertising card read, "This is a fertile, well-watered country of South Africa, on the Indian Ocean, and forms a part of the region known as Kafraria. The native Zulus are a fine warlike people of the Bantu stock, speaking the Bantu language. The language extends over more than half of Africa and is one of great beauty and flexibility. The Zulu bids fair to be as forward in civilization as he has been in war. Our group represents the Zulus after less than a century of civilization. Worth wins everywhere. Our agent at Cape Town supplies both the European and native inhabitants of Zululand, the Transvaal, and Orange Free State with thousands of Singer machines." (Library of Congress)

Kodak cameras and film became an immediate success. Even before the close of the Second Boer War, *Kodak* was the equivalent of *camera* in South Africa.[59]

It should be recalled that insurance firms were among the first U.S. businesses in South Africa. In the early nineteenth century they came in as marine underwriters. But in the 1890s the exploitation of the deep levels on the Witwatersrand and its attendant safety hazards stimulated a mushrooming interest in life insurance, which became popular when the economy reached a stage at which risks and losses could no longer be easily sustained by individuals and their families. Life insurance in

South Africa as well as in the United States developed on a large scale when people moved into industrial and commercial enterprises. For their future security urban workers now had to rely more on wages than on the decaying dynamics of the extended family.

Agents were despatched from New York by such emerging American giants as New York Life Insurance Company, the Mutual Life Insurance Company, and the Equitable Life Assurance Society of New York. Equitable was the first to enter South Africa when, in 1887, J. Bryant Lindley, a descendant of Reverend Lindley of missionary fame, received an agency contract to develop business in South Africa, Mauritius, Madagascar, and Reunion. Mutual Life followed with an office in Cape Town in 1890 and quickly became the largest of the three American firms. Within a decade it had established branches in Durban, Port Elizabeth, Johannesburg, and in the southern Rhodesian town of Bulawayo. Mutual did more than sell insurance policies; it became entrepreneurial, erecting office buildings in Cape Town and other South African cities and purchasing Orange Free State bonds in the years immediately preceding the Second Boer War. New York Life, also based in Cape Town, opened agencies in Kimberley, Port Elizabeth, Durban, and Bulawayo. Significantly, Equitable, Mutual, and New York Life were among the first American firms to use South Africa as a base for regional business.[60]

THE BRITISH CHALLENGE: FINANCE AND SHIPPING

It must be recalled that in the first half of the nineteenth century a large proportion of U.S. trade with South Africa was financed through the American offices of British financial institutions. Trade was conducted almost entirely by use of foreign currency bills, usually drawn on London-based banks through commercial letters of credit. Only rarely did traders use American commercial credits involving the drawing of dollar drafts on American banks. But the flow of Americans to South Africa in the last quarter of the nineteenth century and the growing volume of capital-goods exports put greater pressure on American finance houses to expand their role. J. and W. Seligman of New York and Kidder,

Peabody and Company of Boston gradually increased their volume of letters of credit to American businessmen; and the American Express Company in the 1890s introduced its innovative travelers' checks, which soon supplanted letters of credit for tourists and other visitors. American Express checks could be negotiated outside a bank and at any time, an obvious convenience to Americans engaged in overseas business.[61]

By 1900 New York City had forged ahead of Boston and Philadelphia to become the preeminent financial and mercantile center of the United States. J. P. Morgan and Company and Kuhn, Loeb and Company had by then built up an extensive foreign exchange and underwriting business, stealing the lead in investment banking from Boston's two giants, Lee, Higginson and Kidder, Peabody. American investment houses at this time were capitalizing a wide variety of American industries and contributing to their expansion and transformation into modern transnational corporations.[62] Financing overseas ventures, however, remained extremely problematic. The federal government forbade American national banks from establishing overseas branches upon which customers could draw drafts in sterling. Moreover, the strict Cape Banking Law of 1891, ironically modeled after the U.S. Banking Act of 1864, made the penetration of non-British banking institutions into South Africa extremely difficult.[63]

Not surprisingly, London remained the center of finance for the industrialized countries of the world. The British strove to maintain that preeminence by accumulating gold from ore-rich regions under their control. By 1890 gold had become the basis of international payments among the leading industrialized countries. As a result of new discoveries in Australia, Canada, and especially South Africa, the increased output of gold enabled Britain to enlarge its money reserves considerably and to guide the expansion of international trade. Large gold reserves reduced problems of liquidity and allowed trade and industry to expand with relative protection from the constraints of cash shortages and paper currency inflation. Under the gold standard adjustments in the exchange rates occurred only rarely, when for budgetary reasons a government was forced to reduce the gold content of its currency.

In the late nineteenth century gold entered the trade and investment picture as a decisive and crucial factor. This was nowhere more visible than in the United States, which was undergoing enormous industrial and trade expansion. But during this period American industry grew faster than the supply of gold. Indeed, from 1866 to 1880 there was almost no increase in the amount of gold currency in circulation. A decade later, the supply grew modestly, though not enough to provide the currency needed by the fledgling business community. For the next three years Americans redeemed greenbacks and treasury notes for gold, which they hoarded or sent overseas. Consequently, between 1890 and 1894 the net gold reserve of the United States fell from $190 million to less than $65 million.[64] The financial panic of 1893 in the United States was partially caused by the withdrawal of gold by foreign investors who were selling their American securities. Certainly by March 1893 the American public had begun to question whether the U.S. Treasury would be able to continue gold payments and maintain the dollar's covertibility.

The gold drain caused a severe loss of confidence in the soundness of the dollar. A crisis loomed, and in February 1895 the government persuaded the House of Morgan to form a syndicate to purchase a large issue of U.S. bonds for London gold that was mainly of South African provenance. Since the early 1880s South African gold had helped Britain to reduce its own liquidity problems without resorting to excessive inflation. The United States now attempted to use gold for the same purpose. As the business historian Vincent Carosso noted, the bond sale was a spectacular success.[65] Confidence in the nation's credit condition was restored, and henceforth the United States became a major purchaser of foreign gold, much of it mined in South Africa and purchased on the London market.

American gold stocks began to rebuild, and the economy recovered as a result of overseas mineral sourcing and the Klondike discoveries in Alaska. By 1900 the situation had improved enough for Congress to pass the Gold Standard Act, which defined the American dollar solely in terms of gold and in effect put currency on the gold standard. The British made certain, however, that gold would continue to be purchased from London rather than directly from South Africa. Between 1897 and 1904 $1 billion of new foreign investment flowed into the United States, contributing substantially to the net inflow of gold.[66] Indirectly, South Africa had begun to figure prominently in world monetary affairs. Gold production in the Transvaal soared, exceeding U.S. output in 1895. By the end of 1898, South Africa had become the world's largest producer.[67]

In light of these developments it is not surprising that trade with South Africa grew vigorously in the decade after 1893. Exports surged from $2 million in 1892 to $14 million in 1896 and to more than $20 million by the turn of the century. The Americans and the Germans were beginning to make significant inroads into Britain's traditional export markets. The United States had become second only to Great Britain in exports to the Transvaal. Much to the dismay of the British at the Cape and in Natal, the Americans were beginning to ship through Lourenco-Marques in neighboring Portuguese Mozambique, thus depriving the British colonies of their full share of customs revenue.[68]

This growth in trade led to the expansion of the United States' official presence. Although the United States had established diplomatic links with the Transvaal in 1870, it was not until 1891 that an American consulate opened its doors, and then only in Johannesburg. In 1898 a second consulate was opened in Pretoria, mainly to keep abreast of political events.[69] Obviously, the United States had not developed an official policy toward South Africa but instead continued to view the region through an essentially British perspective, as will be further discussed later.

South Africa's export trade to the United States did not grow commensurately, possibly because the McKinley Tariff of 1890 raised import duties to almost 50 percent. The Dingley Act of 1897 raised them higher still. Moreover, South Africa's economies were still overwhelmingly of an agrarian and mineral-extractive nature.

Surprisingly little U.S.-South African trade was carried in American ships, considering that at the opening of the Second Boer War the United States stood second among nations exporting directly to South Africa. The cost of operating a thousand-ton American vessel averaged $1,250, as opposed to $800 for a British counterpart, and consequently, only 7 percent of American goods exported to South Africa were carried by American flagships.[70] Americans also had to contend with a monopolistic British-controlled shipping conference, formed in the South African trade in 1883, that assured British dominance of the conference lines for years. A deferred rebate system, which entitled shippers to a delayed refund of part of the freight charges, provided they agreed to avoid nonconference ships in the interim, followed three years later.[71]

Regular steamship service between the United States and South Africa was inaugurated in 1893, when Donald Currie's British-based Castle Company combined its Clan Line with Bucknalls to create the American and African Line. Naturally, it was a British-owned enterprise. Gone were the days of the swift-moving American clipper ships. The age of steam, iron, and steel initially belonged to the British, not the Americans.[72] In 1900 the Castle Line merged with its main rival to become the Union-Castle Mail Steamship Company. Currie's establishment of regular steamship services between Europe and South Africa provided a maritime foundation for the growth of British trade and investment in the region.

THE IMPERIAL FACTOR: BANKING

Investment in South Africa by American companies without British connections was inhibited by the British bias of South Africa's banking system. Before the discovery of diamonds and gold South Africa's twenty-three small, autonomous banks led a precarious financial existence. In 1860, for example, their total capital resources barely amounted to £1.3 million and their notes issue had not reached £400,000.[73] Restrictive and deeply conservative banking regulations in the Orange Free State and Transvaal confined nearly all commercial banking activity to the British colonies of Natal and the Cape.

In chapter 2 I briefly examined the advent of London-based imperial banks in the 1860s and 1870s. Their modest growth was sharply affected in the late 1880s by an over-extension of credit in the Transvaal share boom, which led to a banking crisis in 1889 and to the collapse of most of the locally based, or colonial, banks. This was followed by a process of rapid concentration and consolidation. Banking in all but the South African Republic (Transvaal) fell almost completely under the control of three private imperial banks, which had already imposed English practices in the Cape and Natal. In 1891 the last of the local banks was taken over, this time by an imperial newcomer, the African Banking Corporation of Britain. Nevertheless, the British-based Standard Bank had already achieved a preeminent position, with seventy-two branches scattered throughout the two British colonies and the Orange Free State. The Transvaal, however, continued to resist the

British intrusion and tried to counterbalance it in 1890 by chartering the National Bank of the South African Republic with capitalization from the Deutsche Bank and a consortium of French financial interests.[74]

Outside the Transvaal the imperial banks with their innovative branch operations were in a superior position to provide an enormous pool of funds for long- and short-term lending to local ventures on terms better than those offered by the failing local financial institutions. Enjoying overseas connections, the huge imperial banks could also more completely dominate the financing of commodity trade. All this did not augur well for Americans and other non-British citizens, including Africans and poor white Afrikaners. Because their services were directed primarily at British expatriate interests, the imperial banks showed little inclination to cooperate with small local lenders or depositors or with people lacking financial resources in Europe or in the British Isles.[75]

IMPERIALIST STRATEGIES: RHODES AND HIS AMERICAN COLLABORATORS

Cecil Rhodes and the British at the Cape and in London began to view the Transvaal in an entirely different light after the Witwatersrand gold discoveries. Earlier, in 1877, the British had taken over the near-bankrupt Transvaal government as a first step in an effort to achieve a federation of the white colonies and states of South Africa.[76] But the Boers resisted, and after a short war in 1881 the British returned self-government to the Afrikaners. A protracted war against the Boers was not worth the cost. In 1884 the London Convention allowed the Transvaal Afrikaners to revive the name "South African Republic" (S.A.R.). Nevertheless, Britain retained an ambiguously defined "suzerainty" over the Afrikaners, including the right of veto over foreign relations. Then came the great gold discoveries and the fear that some day control over the economic and political destiny of southern Africa might no longer rest with the Cape colony but with the Afrikaners of the Transvaal.

Rhodes grew impatient with the South African Republic and he decided to leap-frog over it in an effort at eventual encirclement. He also expected to find a "second Rand" north of the Limpopo River. In 1867 a German-American, Adam Renders, had been the first white man to visit the ruined city of Great Zimbabwe and to return with visions of enormous gold deposits in the region. His accounts persuaded another American, Jerome Babe, to obtain the first mining concession ever held by a white in what later became the Rhodesias. Such reports and speculation were enough to convince Rhodes to push forward.

The cost of expansion across the Limpopo was borne by him alone and not by a still-hesitant British treasury in London. In 1888 one of Rhodes's agents, C. E. Rudd, obtained a concession from Lobengula, the ruler of Matabeleland, for exclusive mineral exploitation. A year later, this monopolistic Rudd Concession enabled Rhodes to secure a royal charter for his newly formed British South Africa Company. The charter vested Rhodes's private company with powers approaching those of a sovereign state.[77]

With the assistance of Maurice Heany, a former officer in the U.S. Army, Rhodes assembled a group of white immigrant-settlers to serve the expected miners and to attract future investors. They were lured into the scheme with promises of land and mining claims in an African nation, Matabeleland, that was still politically independent. A road was cut by American and British employees of the company, and in 1890 a "pioneer column" of miners, farmers, and traders marched into Mashonaland, a territory claimed by Lobengula and his Ndebele people by right of previous conquest. An important member of the Pioneer Column was William Harvey Brown, an American naturalist, who, after the wars was rewarded by Rhodes with 30,000 acres. The enterprising American established a number of profitable ranches and farms and parlayed his economic power into politics after he became mayor of Salisbury, Rhodesia's capital.[78]

King Lobengula, faced with the prospect of permanent land-hungry white settlers and not underground miners, felt betrayed. The result was the first Matabele War in 1893 and Lobengula's untimely death. Rhodes then made his own claim to Matabeleland by right of conquest.[79]

After the war Rhodes's American advisor, John Hays Hammond, conducted a geological survey of the region and concluded that the quartzite reefs of Matabeleland and Mashonaland were not in the final analysis a second Witwatersrand. Another American, Frederick Russell Burnham, came back with more encouraging news from north of the Zambezi, where his team discovered major copper deposits in what came to be called the Copperbelt of Northern Rhodesia.[80]

Disappointed by Hammond's report, Rhodes turned to the exploitation of the other resources of Matabeleland and Mashonaland. Many frustrated "pioneers" either left or sought compensation by looting African cattle and destroying vast herds of wild game to make way for white farms. In 1896–1897 the Ndebele and Shona—the latter being the original inhabitants of the region—challenged the settlers and the British South Africa Company in another futile war, or series of uprisings, which they called the "Chimurenga." It took the combined forces of the company police and British troops to crush the rebellion. Consequently, what is today the Republic of Zimbabwe came under the rule of the British South Africa Company. The northward expansion of the South African Republic was effectively blocked, but at the cost of tens of thousands of pounds sterling, thousands of lives, and generations of racial mistrust.[81]

Rhodes had already concluded that British economic dominance in the Transvaal could only be assured by transferring political control, via an expansion of the franchise, to the non-Afrikaner white immigrant community, called the Uitlanders, or outsiders. By 1895 the Uitlanders represented more than half the Transvaal's white population and contributed in excess of five-sixths of its taxation.[82] Between 1886 and 1895 South Africa's overseas trade and domestic railway mileage had almost doubled and its population had tripled. The value of total gold output in South Africa had risen to $42.5 million, which was more than the output of the United States.[83] To many observers the center of economic and political gravity seemed to be shifting from the Cape to the Transvaal. And as the Transvaal's economy boomed, its anti-imperialist Afrikaner government under Paul Kruger became more self-assertive.

To Rhodes's increasing frustration the Transvaal refused to join a tariff or railway union on imperial terms. Moreover, the Transvaal began construction of a railway line eastward to Portuguese Delagoa Bay, a line that threatened to divert trade from the British seaports of the Cape and Natal. Since at least the 1840s it had been British policy to check Afrikaner territorial expansion and to prevent any portion of the southern coast from falling under their control.

By the end of 1894 Rhodes as Cape prime minister and Kruger as president of the South African Republic had reached an impasse over the franchise issue.[84] It seemed that a change in regime could only be achieved by military means. Rhodes's imperial plan called for the extension of British hegemony and Anglo-Saxon institutions and capitalism from

Cape Town to Cairo, Egypt. A politically independent S.A.R. was viewed as an obstacle in this grand scheme. Clearly, Rhodes yearned for a politically and economically consolidated southern Africa firmly within the imperial system but under the control of local British loyalists. Kruger, on the other hand, believed in a united South African republic under Afrikaner hegemony and pursuing an economic policy free of British control.

By the early 1890s it had become clear to all that a major aim of British imperial strategy was the encirclement and elimination of Afrikaner power and the absorption of the Afrikaner republics into a political federation of South African states run by local South Africans but under British hegemony. The South African Republic had become the wealthiest and most powerful state in southern Africa, and there was growing concern that Kruger would seek foreign alliances and develop an independent railways and tariffs policy that would economically cripple the once-supreme Cape colony. Rhodes and the British had succeeded in blocking the South African Republic's northward expansion by occupying Matabeleland and establishing a colony and protectorate over Bechuanaland. Conventions in 1891 among the Portuguese, British, and Germans established the frontiers of modern Zimbabwe, Zambia, Mozambique, and Malawi. Any southward expansion of the Transvaal toward the coast was precluded by the conquest and annexation of Zululand in 1887 and Tongaland eight years later.[85]

In South West Africa the situation was less certain. The Germans had declared a protectorate over Angra Pequeña on the Namibian coast but British annexation of Bechuanaland seemed to foreclose a railway connection from there to the Transvaal. Rhodes's efforts to buy Delagoa Bay in Mozambique from the Portuguese, however, were frustrated by German opposition. Germany had become a major trade partner of the South African Republic and was especially interested in importing gold. In 1894 the South African Republic completed its railway line to the bay and obtained an independent access to the sea. The Republic was at last free to shift its trade from the Cape and deprive the colony of a major source of revenue. Rhodes and his associates stewed in the face of Transvaal manipulation of the rates on all rail traffic within its boundaries.

Also, in 1892 the deep-level mines on the Rand were coming into operation and the Republic was enjoying an unprecedented boom. The deep levels assured the Afrikaners of a long-term future for the extractive industries. At the same time Rhodes, who was prime minister of the Cape colony, was losing the support of the Cape Afrikaner Bond, which comprised key Afrikaans-speaking political and economic leaders. Thus, Rhodes and his associates, including his American consultant, John Hays Hammond, conspired to stage a coup d'état against the Kruger regime, hoping to install a regime dominated by the immigrant mining community of Uitlanders.[86]

The Americans were divided over the issue. Hammond and other key advisors to Rhodes supported an overthrow and favored a covert military operation. Most of the American miners or prospectors concurred. Such a regime, they reasoned, would be more efficient and more compliant and might work more closely with the mining magnates, or Randlords. An efficient British bureaucracy might be better equipped to attract British trade and capital investment, to render gold mining the dominant economic force in the Transvaal, and to make mining capitalism the supreme mode of production in southern Africa.

Others, who either worked for the S.A.R. government or were of Irish background and harbored anti-English sentiments, were more inclined to push for peaceful reforms. Nor did everyone in the English-speaking population favor military intervention. Many of the London-based gold mining concerns preferred an Afrikaner-controlled regime to political instability. G. F. Hollis, the U.S. consul-general at Cape Town, was pro-Boer and wanted greater trade with the Transvaalers. Some American entrepreneurs saw the Boers as able to undermine British supremacy in southern Africa and thus create an opportunity for Americans.[87]

The majority of American traders did not care whether goods flowed through the Cape or Mozambique. Yet most American miners on the Rand—many of them in Rhodes's employ—supported the Reform Committee, which had been pressuring the S.A.R. for voting rights and were strongly anti-Kruger. Ten of the sixty-three committee members were Americans. Hammond was deeply involved in the committee's work and authored many of the reports critical of Kruger's government. In a poll in December 1895 495 of 500 Americans supported an armed uprising against the Kruger regime. Already, 150 American miners had organized the George Washington Corps, which vowed to support any insurrection by the Uitlanders.[88] Gardner Williams, American consul at Kimberley and an executive with Rhodes's De Beers concern, had al-

3. John Hays Hammond, ca. 1908. (Library of Congress)

ready begun to oversee the smuggling of guns and ammunition from Kimberley to the Reform Committee in Johannesburg. The arms, many of Colt manufacture, were shipped clandestinely in Standard Oil drums. Rhodes in the meantime had secretly obtained the tacit approval for a raid from Joseph Chamberlain, the British colonial secretary. In mid-December 1895 President Cleveland had informed the U.S. Congress of his support of Venezuela's boundary dispute with British Guiana. Chamberlain saw a certain urgency in resolving the South African issue before dealing with the Americans over Latin American problems.[89]

In late December 1895 a raid was launched from British Bechuanaland under the leadership of Rhodes's closest associate, Dr. Leander Starr Jameson, and with police from Rhodes's own British South Africa Company. The Jameson Raid, as it was called, ended in disaster. The Reform Committee and Washington Corps failed to mobilize the other Uitlanders, and within days the Transvaal police had arrested the raiders, including Hammond and other private Americans. The Kruger government charged them with high treason. Rhodes was humiliated and resigned as Cape prime minister. Any hope of a continuing alliance with the Afrikaner Bond was finished. Rhodes had to pay the South African Republic a $100,000 fine for the release of Hammond, Jameson, and their gang.[90] Officially, the United States remained neutral over the Jameson Raid and refused to pay the fine or to indemnify Rhodes for doing so.

THE UNITED STATES AND THE CRISIS OF BRITISH IMPERIAL SUPREMACY

The Jameson Raid of 1895 revived the crisis of British imperial supremacy in southern Africa. It turned Afrikaners throughout South Africa even more fervently against the British and transformed Afrikaner nationalism, hitherto rather weak and unfocused, into a more cohesive and aggressive pan–South African movement. The raid also destroyed any lingering trust between Kruger and the British Colonial Office. And in the ensuing years the S.A.R., in self-defense, engaged in an ambitious rearmament program that only heightened British fears. Anglo-Afrikaner tension rapidly escalated after the arrival in May 1897 of Sir Alfred Milner as governor of the Cape colony and high commissioner of South

Africa. Milner, a fervent believer in worldwide Anglo-Saxon unity, was convinced that Afrikanerdom had to give way. Armed with an aggressive diplomacy against the South African Republic, the archimperialist set southern Africa on a course that could only lead to war.

The mining industry on the Rand slumped abruptly after the raid and remained depressed until late 1898. The British were now more convinced than ever that their long-term imperial interests in southern Africa were threatened by the continuing political independence of the Republic. Nevertheless, in the years after the Jameson Raid, the Transvaal made substantial political concessions in the face of growing British demands as well as initiating economic and administrative reforms and significantly broadening the franchise to include more Uitlanders. The South African Republic did not object to Uitlander domination of the extractive industries as long as the mining magnates recognized Afrikaner political hegemony. The Afrikaners lacked the expertise to exploit the mines and grudgingly settled for foreign control in return for the right of taxation. Most of the Randlords, with the exception of Rhodes, Hammond, and a handful of others, generally opposed war. They believed that through constant external pressure the Transvaal Afrikaners would eventually initiate the necessary economic and political reforms.

But the South African Republic's search for greater political independence presented a challenge to the British imperialists. According to scholars Ronald Robinson and John Gallagher, Britain expressed concern that the Republic's growing power and wealth would eventually draw all the states of South Africa out of the British Empire and transform them into a united South African Republic under Afrikaner control.[91] Britain reasoned that such an eventuality would jeopardize its free access to the gold deposits and threaten the strategic sea route to India, the jewel in the British Crown. After failing to topple Kruger's regime through diplomacy and military raids by third parties, the British were prepared to risk an all-out war.

Before 1895 the American reading public knew very little, and cared even less, about South Africa. Rarely did stories appear in the papers, and the few missionary publications that covered the region concerned themselves more with African heathenism and the urgency of Christian proselytization. The dramatic Jameson Raid changed all this. Here was a story that made excellent copy. Overnight South Africa became a hunting ground for American writers and journalists in search of a good story. Moreover, John Hays Hammond, with his connections to the American news media and the business community, made sure that his arrrest was brought to wide attention. From the start American opinion was sharply divided over the Jameson Raid. In 1896 Mark Twain on a world tour made a brief visit to South Africa, and in his subsequent book, *Following the Equator: A Journey Around the World* (1899), he expressed sympathy for the grievances of the Uitlanders. Hammond, in a spirited series in the influential *North American Review*, echoed that view but went a step further by calling for an end to the Kruger regime. The famous American journalist Poultney Bigelow also visited South Africa in 1896 and wrote a ten-part series in *Harpers New Monthly.* Bigelow had a lengthy interview with Kruger and described him as a political anachronism. In the series and in a book that followed, entitled *A White Man's Africa* (1898), Bigelow argued that "all the races must unite to form a white man's Africa." He concluded that in the long term American economic interests in the region would be better served by British rule. Occasional editorials in the *New York Times* intoned that the Boers stood in the way of full economic development in South Africa. Articles in 1896 in the *National Geographic* and in *Scientific American* addressed themselves to the economic potential of southern Africa and urged the American business community to become more involved.[92] It must be noted that many of these pieces were written amid a rising tide of jingoism in the United States that preceded the Spanish-American War.

American diplomats in South Africa were also deeply divided. The consuls in Cape Town and Durban were pro-British, while the consuls in Pretoria and Lourenco-Marques tended to sympathize with the Afrikaners.[93] There were also deep divisions among the American expatriate population, though the overwhelming majority seemed to favor British supremacy.

President Kruger's landslide reelection in March 1898 only strengthened High Commissioner Milner's resolve to destroy the Afrikaner republics. Perhaps to buy time, the South African Republic followed a conciliatory policy, agreeing to broaden the Uitlander franchise, but on the condition that the British recognize the republic's sovereign status. Milner and Chamberlain refused. In September 1899 Kruger asked the United States, through the Orange Free State consul in New York, to mediate the franchise dispute. A petition was sent to Congress with the signatures of 104 representatives and scores of prominent American educators and state supreme court judges. President McKinley and the majority in Congress were unmoved for fear of endangering Anglo-American relations, which were already tense over the Venezuela issue in South America. Less than a year earlier the United States, in its own burst of imperialist fervor, had taken Cuba, Puerto Rico, Guam, and the Philippines and had annexed the independent nation of Hawaii. The United States was also preparing for war against Filipino insurgents who were struggling for an independent Philippines. Since the British had provided diplomatic cover for the Americans in Central America and the Caribbean, should not the United States do the same for the British in southern Africa? In light of that question it is not surprising that the United States opted for neutrality though it was no secret that McKinley, a Republican, and his administration harbored strong pro-British sentiments. Secretary of State Hay confided that "the fight of England is the fight of civilization and progress and all of our interests are bound up in her success."[94] Most American journalists, missionaries, and businessmen had long argued that America's long-term interests would be best advanced through a unified South Africa under British rule. Looking to the postwar era, most Americans expected that by remaining neutral officially they would curry British favor while capitalizing on Afrikaner enmity toward their British conquerors.

The Second Boer War, or South African War as many called it, erupted in October 1899. The gold mines soon closed down and remained inactive until 1901. The New York Stock Exchange momentarily suffered losses on fears that the Boers might sabotage the idled mining equipment.[95] Though the American public continued to be split in its loyalties in the early months, opinion began to turn as the war dragged on and news of British atrocities against the Boers appeared in the American media. Initially, the business community in the United States favored the British and raised over $200,000 to commission a hospital ship.[96] Numerous articles suggesting that a British victory would benefit everyone appeared in the highly respected *North American Review*. Alfred Thayer Mahan, the celebrated American naval historian and strategist, wrote several articles and a book supporting the British and was the first American to advance the notion that South Africa was of great strategic importance to the British Empire and its allies.[97] But the economic argument continued to be pushed vigorously. D. A. Willey in a September 1900 article in *Arena* magazine suggested that "The United States has almost as much interest in the result of the war in South Africa as Great Britain . . . from a purely commercial standpoint." He added optimistically that "a market will be opened to the manufactures of the United States that is almost limitless."[98]

The black American community tended to support the British, believing that their seemingly more liberal attitudes towards black South Africans would lead to postwar reforms. In Congress both the House and the Senate committees on foreign affairs were also biased toward the British.[99]

In December 1899 the pro-Boer American consul in Pretoria was replaced by the son of Secretary of State Hay. James Stowe, the consul-general in Cape Town, was pro-British, while his counterpart in Portuguese Lorenco-Marques expressed sympathy for the Afrikaners. Stowe predicted confidently that after the war "higher civilization will prevail, new mines will be developed, new industries inaugurated, and all men will be equal under the law."[100] By then the American community in the S.A.R. had dwindled to a few hundred. Many had left for the gold strikes of Alaska's Klondike. Hammond sailed for New York in December to lobby for British support. This abrupt exodus brought to a conclusion the second phase of American entrepreneurial involvement in South Africa.

The news media seemingly enjoyed considerable control over the minds of its American readers. The conflict impelled a host of American newspapers and magazines to send correspondents to the front. Among them was Howard Clemens for the *New York World,* John T. McCutcheon for the *Chicago Record,* who interviewed President Kruger in the Transvaal, and Richard Smith and George Denny, who covered the war for the newly formed Associated Press, then based in Illinois.[101] It is no wonder that the British occupation of Pretoria on May 31, 1900, captured the headlines of the major American newspapers. But in the spring of 1900 American opinion began to shift more massively towards the Afrikaners as news of fresh British atrocities flowed across the pages of major newspapers. By midsummer most Americans had done an about-face and had become overwhelmingly pro-Boer. Joseph Pulitzer, who published the influential *New York World* and *St. Louis Post-Dispatch,* came out in support of Kruger and attacked the war as a crude product of English jingoism.[102]

4. An anti-British cartoon that appeared in Hearst publications in the United States, 1902. (Library of Congress)

In the summer of 1900 a Transvaal delegation visited the United States and sparked the formation of pro-Boer lobbies in major American cities, the most influential of them being the Transvaal League of Chicago and Philadelphia's Boer Legislative Committee. Sympathy for the Boers also came from leaders in the Dutch Reformed Church and from the Irish-American and German-American communities. Especially outspoken was the Ancient Order of Hibernians. The Holland Society, which was comprised of descendants of early Dutch families in New York and New Jersey, also leaned towards the Boers. Andrew Carnegie, a founder of the Anti-Imperialist League, was outraged by the British conduct of the war and supported a mass pro-Boer rally in New York.[103] Many organizations contributed to the Boer Relief Fund. The war had become a heated domestic issue, and in 1900 the Democratic platform came out in favor of the Boers. Theodore Roosevelt, who assumed office in September 1900, admired the Afrikaners but viewed their struggle against the mighty British as a lost cause. Thus, he refused to move from neutrality, and Kruger was not granted asylum at the U.S. consulate in Lourenço-Marques after his flight from Pretoria.

Some U.S. citizens became physically involved in the conflict. Irish-Americans sailed to South Africa under the guise of Red Cross nurses only to join Boer commando units as sharpshooters. The famed Irish Brigade was essentially an American volunteer unit under the leadership of John Blake, a West Point graduate. The so-called American Scouting Corps served as Boer advance units in the field. Many of them had long previous experience as U.S. government scouts in the wars against the Native Americans.[104] In 1901 the U.S. War Department sent a team of observers to the war front. The group reported that 150 American citizens were fighting with Boer commando units and another 150 were associated with "independent organizations."[105]

Other American volunteers were equally explicit in their support for the British. Horatio L. Scott, a black American who fought against the Boers, published his recollections, *The Truth of Africa* (1902), after the war. Naively, he extolled the British as friends and potential allies of black South Africans. Like most Americans Scott viewed racial discrimination and injustice in South Africa as purely a product of Afrikaner-inspired institutions and practices. It was widely believed in the United States that once the Afrikaners were removed from power, the forces of liberalism and multiracialism would lead to freedom and democracy for all, regardless of race.

The United States reaped great trade benefits from the war. South Africa ran an extremely unfavorable trade balance during the conflict, in part the result of huge imports of military supplies and also because of the near-cessation of gold production in the Transvaal. Indeed, American direct exports to South Africa jumped from $16 million in 1899 to over $20 million in 1900.[106] Much of it was the result of an enormous increase in South Africa-destined military exports to Great Britain during the war years. Exports to the Transvaal almost ceased after the imposition of a British blockade off the Mozambique coast from the beginning of 1900.[107]

The Second Boer War was extremely costly to the British government and was unpopular in many sectors of the population. To avoid imposing new taxes, the British cabinet decided in 1900 to make a public bond offering to help finance the war and to replenish the treasury's gold reserves. From the opening of the conflict gold exports from the Transvaal had dwindled. Consequently the British raised an initial £300 million National War Loan and asked Morgan Grenfell in London to sell a portion of the issue in the United States, bestowing on J.P. Morgan enhanced prestige and future access to a stronger client base. The New York House of Morgan was then named the Bank of England's exclusive American agent. To everyone's surprise, the loan, which amounted to $12 million, was greatly oversubscribed.[108] Much of the success can be attributed to the participation of America's major insurance companies, particularly Mutual, Equitable, and New York Life.

The Morgan interests organized another war loan in 1902. Altogether, nearly $150 million of British government bonds were floated in the New York market in support of the war.[109] From the perspective of American enterprise in South Africa the war loan represented a turning point: For the first time American capital was mobilized in support of political objectives in South Africa, and in the decades ahead private American capital would play an increasingly important role in the economic and political development of southern Africa.

The Boers lost the war and peace was restored in May 1902. It was a conflict that left nearly 53,000 dead and cost the British taxpayer more than £222 million.[110] In the immediate postwar era American trade with

South Africa soared and reached an all-time high of $31 million in 1903. Between 1902 and 1903 South Africa imported more American goods than any other non-European nation, excepting Canada and Mexico.[111] For a moment South Africa had become the United States' third largest export market. But Great Britain did not intend for the United States to steal away its markets. The open door soon began to close. In *The American Invaders* (1902) F. A. McKenzie complained that "America had acquired almost every new industry created during the past fifteen years" and warned of "armies of American entrepreneurs conquering British markets."[112]

SOUTH AFRICANS DISCOVER THE UNITED STATES: RELIGIOUS AND CULTURAL CROSSCURRENTS

Missionary societies were among the earliest American enterprises to create transnational networks for communication and development. From headquarters in Boston, months away and thousands of miles distant, missionary schools, churches, and farms in Natal received equipment, personnel, and policy directives. In the 1880s and early 1890s the American Board's activities greatly increased through funds from the Otis bequest and after 1888 from rental income on lands leased to African farmers on the Mission Reserves. By 1895 the American Board had accumulated 150,000 acres in Natal from the colonial government.[113] Most of the land was under cultivation by the Zulu. Nevertheless, the introduction of rents led Africans to view the Americans as landlords, and as a result a certain degree of tension developed between the two. To the consternation of the Natal colonial authorities the kholwa, or "believers," bridling under the Board's policy of charging rent, agitated for private ownership of property on the basis of individual tenure. The Board had always intended to withdraw altogether from South Africa after the African Christian congregations had achieved a momentum of their own. And after 1894 the American Board in the United States was no longer called upon for any grants towards the support of congregations or their staff. All this was in keeping with the original Board philosophy of establishing self-supporting, self-propagating missionary enterprises.

Church membership soared as leadership in the American Zulu Mis-

sion was progressively Africanized. The Americans had become concerned over the growth of Christian independent churches, as expressed
in Ethiopianism, and hoped that an acceleration of the indigenization
process would prevent schisms. In 1890–1891 the Board opened churches
in the cities of Durban and Johannesburg to meet the needs of Zulu
migrants to the urban areas. They broadened the scope of their activities
and gave greater responsibility to the membership. After a hiatus of
nearly sixty years the Board resumed medical missionary enterprise with
the appointment of Dr. Burt W. Bridgman in 1892 as head of a new
medical department at the Amanzimtoti mission station, while in 1898
Dr. James B. McCord established a Zulu hospital in Durban,[114] the first
modern medical facility for Africans in South African history.

By 1895 a small nucleus of Zulu pastors, farmers, and petty traders
had begun to emerge on and near the Mission Reserves. It has already
been noted that the Board's educational endeavors contributed greatly
to the emergence of the kholwa. This new middle class of Westernized,
literate, Christian converts became champions of the Protestant work
ethic and enthusiastically espoused notions of private capitalist enterprise. They were ardent followers of Booker T. Washington, the black
American educator and philosopher who placed strong emphasis on
rural self-sufficiency.[115] Over the years American missionaries had done
much to foster this independence through their encouragement of agrarian enterprise. Africans who settled on the mission lands were encouraged to become peasant farmers, being taught the use of plows and
urged to grow cash crops and to purchase American-made wagons and
implements.

Industrialization, Western education, and urbanization contributed
greatly to the rise of independent African churches. They spread like a
brush fire in the 1890s through sprawling African ghettos on the Witwatersrand and elsewhere. Black American missionaries played a vital
role in this development. In 1892 in Pretoria Reverend Mangena Mokone broke away from the white-controlled Wesleyans (Methodists) and
organized the first Ethiopian church in South Africa.[116] The ancient
kingdom of Ethiopia, with its Coptic Christian Church and its glorious
history of successful resistance of first Islamic and ultimately European
imperialist conquest, became a powerful symbol for the independence of
Africans from European control. Educated Africans everywhere developed a strong sense of hope and expectancy from the Old Testament

prophecy that "Ethiopia shall soon stretch out her arms unto God." Thomas Karis contends that Ethiopianism rejected the liberal assumptions of a common nonracial society.[117] It also rejected the color bar in white-controlled churches. Whites in South Africa viewed Ethiopianism as a threat, largely because it tended to be interethnic and pan-African in its appeal and organization. The separatist church movement was also a reflection of the growing literacy among Africans. People gained an ability to read the Bible for themselves and to challenge missionary interpretations. The publication of the scriptures in vernacular languages was a crucial step toward religious separatism, or independency.

In 1895 Reverend Mokone learned of the African Methodist Epsicopal Church (AME) in the United States through his niece, Charlotte Manye, who was a student at the AME's Wilberforce University in Ohio. Subsequently, Mokone wrote to Bishop Henry McNeal Turner of the U.S.-based African Methodist Episcopal Church and proposed a merger with the American organization. Turner, an ardent emigrationist who espoused back-to-Africa movements, had recently returned from a tour of Sierra Leone and Liberia and was convinced that it was the manifest destiny of black Americans to redeem Africa from "barbaristic animism." At the time Turner edited *Voice of Missions,* an organ of the AME church that enjoyed a circulation in Africa as well as in the black American community.[118]

Black American interest in Africa was spurred on by the Congress on Africa that met in Chicago in August 1893 under the sponsorship of the American Missionary Association. Over a hundred papers were read by missionaries, explorers, and other self-proclaimed authorities on Africa. This was followed by the Atlanta, Georgia, Conference on Africa, held in 1895 in conjunction with the Cotton States and International Exposition and under the sponsorship of the Stewart Missionary Foundation and the Gammon Theological Seminary. The white-run Stewart Foundation aimed at encouraging black American involvement in missionary endeavors. The conference addressed itself to the issue of the "heathen" condition on the "dark" continent and to the need for Christian redemption.[119] In some respects the patronizing black American image of Africa and Africans differed little from that of their white counterparts.

In Atlanta the AME authorities voted to accept Mokone and his South African followers into membership. And in 1896 the invitation was enthusiastically accepted at a conference of independent churches in Pretoria. Within months Pastor James M. Dwane was despatched to the United States to expedite the amalgamation. Dwane was well received and accomplished his mission. In 1898 Turner reciprocated with a visit to South Africa in order to ordain sixty-five local mininsters, who would preside over a church membership that already exceeded seven thousand in the Transvaal alone.[120] Turner viewed southern Africa as holding enormous potential for black American missionaries. While in South Africa the black American bishop was granted an audience with high ranking Afrikaner government officials, including Presidents M. T. Steyn and Paul Kruger of the Orange Free State and Transvaal, respectively.[121] In Cape Town Turner opened the first AME conference and consecrated Dwane as vicar-bishop. Soon afterward, the South African pastor returned to the United States in an unsuccessful effort to raise funds in the black community and to seek a promotion for himself to full bishop over the South African sister churches. During his visit he complained of excessive paternalism and domination by the American leadership and urged his hosts to devolve more responsibility on their sister congregations in South Africa.

His appeal apparently fell on deaf ears. In frustration and anger Dwane returned to South Africa in 1899 and split from the AME altogether. The organization in South Africa was clearly in trouble, and in 1900 Levi Jenkins Coppins was sent out as bishop in an effort to mend walls and to shepherd the disparate Ethiopian churches back into the AME fold. But the AME leadership in the United States was strongly biased against Ethiopianism, and consequently, many of the South African churches were rejected or themselves refused to have anything to do with the Americans. Nevertheless, Coppins was successful in raising nearly $22,000 from AME congregations in the United States for the establishment of the Bethel Institute, a multiracial, predominantly religious school that was opened in February 1902 amid great hopes that it would someday evolve into a degree-granting college. Though it had an overwhelming black student body, it did boast of a few whites and also offered courses in a variety of languages, including English and Afrikaans. Coppins' wife, another energetic educational entrepreneur, became involved with Wilberforce Institute, which had been established under AME auspices near Johannesburg in 1897, and opened the Fanny

Coppins Girls' Hall as a kind of sister institution. By the turn of the century Wilberforce had gained a reputation as the Tuskegee of South Africa.[122]

The National Baptist Convention, another black American organization, was also in the forefront of evangelical pan-African activity in southern Africa. Its members established a base in Cape Town in 1894 but unlike the AME, missionaries from the Convention chose not to affiliate with indigenous churches. In the late 1890s they did, however, send a number of black South African students to the United States for higher education.[123]

Church separatism was not a phenomenon confined to blacks. Many small, newly established white American fundamentalist evangelicial churches flooded southern Africa in the late nineteenth and early twentieth centuries. The Seventh Day Adventists arrived in 1887 and were followed four years later by the General Missionary Board of the Free Methodist Church of North America. They were complemented in 1892 by the Scandinavian-oriented Evangelical Alliance Mission.[124]

In chapter 2 I note that in the last decade of the nineteenth century American missionary organizations began to expand northward into African territories between the Limpopo and Zambezi rivers. They were attracted, in part, by generous offers of land recently conquered by Cecil Rhodes. Overseas church organizations were promised three thousand acres per missionary family. In 1895 Rhodes transferred nearly ten thousand acres of prime land along the Rhodesian-Mozambican frontier to the American Board. This Mount Selinda tract became the nucleus of the Board's activities in Rhodesia.[125]

The Seventh-Day Adventists moved into Mashonaland in 1894, and in 1897 the American Methodist Epsiscopal Church received 2,300 acres from Rhodes to establish a model farm at Umtali, also in Mashona country. The United Methodists arrived with their own staff at about the same time. In 1898 the Brethren in Christ Church started work in the Matopo Hills, approximately thirty miles south of Bulawayo, the former capital of the conquered African nation of Matabeleland. And, finally, the Pilgrim's Holiness Church was drawn into Rhodesia in 1900. The American organizations were joined by scores of British counterparts who were also attracted by Rhodes's incentives.[126] Initially, many of these missionary stations were branches of operations based in South Africa.

By the twilight of the nineteenth century the American Board's high school was well underway in South Africa and pressures from its graduates were mounting for more advanced studies abroad. It should be recalled that Ira Adams Nembula was the first to go to the United States under Board sponsorship, and upon his return Dr. Nembula may have been the first black in South Africa to register as a surgeon.

Upon Nembula's return to South Africa in 1887 the Board sent John Langalibelele Dube to Oberlin College in Ohio. Dube came from a distinguished kholwa family. His father had been baptized and trained by Reverend Lindley, who, like Adams, was with the first American missionary team to South Africa. The senior Dube assumed a high position in the Board's educational system and became a prosperous entrepreneur, accumulating a modest fortune in land, trade, and transportation. His son may have been the first black South African to study in the United States under private family support.[127]

During his five years of academic studies in the United States the young South African fell under the influence of the philosophy of Booker T. Washington and the Tuskegee model of vocational education and self-help. He returned to South Africa in 1892 but then went back to the United States for theological studies in Brooklyn. There, he came into contact with the newly formed Pratt Institute, founded by the industrialist and philanthropist Charles Pratt with profits from his Astral Oil Company. Pratt Institute began as a school for applied knowledge and practical industrial education, its early programs stressing mechanical drawing, nursing, and sewing. In an interview with the *New York Herald* Dube expressed his goal of establishing a school so that "oxen instead of women could labor in the fields."[128] He returned to South Africa much impressed by these American educational models, and in 1901 he founded the Christian African Industrial School at Ohlange. Not surprisingly, it was a coeducational institution based on Washington's Tuskegee model. Dube's institution was the first high school in South Africa founded by a professionally trained African educator. A major champion of practical education, Dube became known as the "Booker T. Washington of South Africa." With strong entrepreneurial inclinations, Dube also set up a Bantu Business League, modeled after the National Negro Business League in the United States, to provide training and incentives to Africans interested in forming their own businesses.

5. John Langalibelele Dube, ca. 1905. (Courtesy, Oberlin College Archives)

6. The Christian African Industrial School at Ohlange, South Africa, ca. 1910. (Courtesy, Oberlin College Archives)

Booker T. Washington's philosophy was not embraced by all black South Africans studying in the United States. Perhaps the most prominent of those who followed another orientation was Charlotte Manye Maxeke. After touring the United States with a black South African choir, Maxeke persuaded the African Methodist Episcopal Church to sponsor her at the AME's Wilberforce University in Ohio. During her studies there (1895–1901) she fell under the influence of W. E. B. Du Bois and Hallie C. Brown, the black American feminist. After becoming the first black South African woman to earn a university degree, she returned to her country to pursue a career in education.

Maxeke became an early advocate of mass-based political activism. She held the conviction that the major emphasis in education should be on preparing Africans for political leadership and for the professions. Following that line, she established several schools, including Wilberforce Institute, which were free of white missionary domination. Wilberforce became the leading African secondary school in the Transvaal. Maxeke also advocated mass resistance through education as well as labor and community organizations. Along with Dube and Isaka Pixley Seme, who earned a B.A. from Columbia College in New York, she played a critical role in founding the African National Congress in 1912.[129] These early leaders drew much of their inspiration from the Afro-American Niagara Movement, which had led to the formation in America of the National Association for the Advancement of Colored People (NAACP), one of the first mass black political organizations in the United States.

At the turn of the century the AME church was also keenly interested in bringing South Africans to the United States for an education. By 1900 eleven were registered at Wilberforce alone. Most of them had graduated from the sister institution in South Africa. After the Boer War these ties began to loosen and by the 1920s there were few, if any, South African students under AME sponsorship in the United States.

The last decade of the nineteenth century was a time of cultural as well as religious contact between blacks of the United States and South Africa. In 1875 the racially segregated Fisk University in Tennessee organized a student choir, the Jubilee Singers, in a fund-raising effort. "Negro" spirituals and work songs were sung to a diverse audience, first in North America and ultimately in England, Germany, and other European countries. After seven years on tour the choir had raised over $150,000 in support of their alma mater. The idea caught on, and in 1887 McAdoo's American Jubilee Singers visited South Africa on their world tour and introduced black American minstrelsy to the country's music halls. They were immensely popular among whites as well as blacks, and within a few years minstrel and variety entertainment became a part of black South Africa's cultural landscape.

Two white South Africans subsequently organized the African Native Choir, modeled after McAdoo's group, and took it on a tour of Great Britain and the United States in the early 1890s. This may have been the first international venture involving black South African performing artists. However, the choir ran into financial problems in the United States and broke up. Some of its members, notably Charlotte Manye, remained briefly to complete their education at black educational institutions. In 1900 another American group, the Loudin Jubilee Singers, toured South Africa, and they, too, made an indelible impression. These and successive American groups gave impetus to many amateur and professional minstrel companies in black South Africa in the early twentieth century. The anthropologist David Coplan suggests that the black American companies introduced an awareness of commercial potential for African performers. Popular American culture also filtered into the missionary schools, where students organized American-style string bands.[130]

In this period South Africa was also exposed for the first time to American plays and theatrical performers. One of the most successful runs was *Belle of New York,* which won rave reviews after its 1900 opening at Cape Town's prestigious and segregated Opera House. Three years later W. C. Fields, the American comedian, undertook a successful tour of empire theaters in Cape Town, Johannesburg, and elsewhere, his performances doing much to generate South African enthusiasm for American vaudeville. South Africans were also exposed to waves of American literature after Mark Twain toured South Africa in 1896 and introduced his books to South African readers.

CONCLUSION

Many lay persons mark the post–World War II period as the comencement of American entrepreneurial initiative in sub-Saharan Africa. Yet, in the twilight years of the nineteenth century in South Africa a few dozen American experts found themselves in great demand and in positions that allowed them to exert considerable influence over the country's destiny. The locus of American entrepreneurial activity shifted to the interior, specifically to the areas of mineral extraction at Kimberley and on the Rand. For the first time American entrepreneurs played pivotal economic roles, as mining engineers, geologists, entomologists, mechanical innovators and inventors, authors of seminal mining codes, and leaders of powerful professional societies. Cecil Rhodes, more than any other South African, recognized the value of an American connection and used it to great advantage in the development of his many capitalist enterprises. As never before Americans became embroiled in the domestic politics of their employers, and under Rhodes some of them helped to design, supply, and direct imperialist plots aimed at overthrowing governments, black as well as white. From the mid-1890s, in a dramatic new departure, we see Americans as well-paid mercenaries, propagandists, and correspondents. And in the South African War, Americans in the United States found themselves for the first time as third-party financiers of a major conflict in sub-Saharan Africa.

This was also a new era of missionary enterprise. In some instances American missionary organizations entered into Rhodes's imperial calculations north of the Limpopo River, receiving recently conquered lands in return for the right to establish schools, farms, and hospitals. In South Africa the American Board missionaries expanded their physical plants and speeded the process of Africanization in their churches and school faculties. This was also an exciting moment when Afro-Americans and black South Africans discovered each other, when the latter began to flow into the United States in search of educational opportunity and the former into South Africa to give strength to religious independence. For the first time we see a process of intellectual and cultural crossfertilization.

This period witnessed breathtaking industrial expansion and modernization in the United States, a process that in South Africa was reflected in a phenomenal expansion of imports of American patented manufactured goods, particularly to the Afrikaner-controlled South African Republic. Advanced American mining technology and state-of-the-art heavy industrial machinery rendered South Africa's extractive industries more cost-effective and thus more competitive in world markets. American experts played a crucial role in convincing local and European financiers of the enormous potential of the region's mineral resources and in so doing attracted the finance capital necessary for their exploitation. But it must be remembered that it was not American capital. The United States remained second fiddle to the British, their former colonial masters and major trading partners. London's great financial houses, the expanding British-based imperial banks in Africa, and the British shipping monopolies served as powerful disincentives to U.S. direct investment. It was the missionary societies, the greatest transnationals of all, that held fixed assets in land and physical plants. What counted more for Americans were markets for their manufactures, not the headaches and expense of formal colonial empire.

The high drama of the Jameson Raid and the Second Boer War beckoned American writers to South Africa and generated enormous public interest and curiosity back home. It also created deep divisions of opinion, even though by 1900 most Americans sympathized with the Afrikaner underdogs. Significantly, the United States government ran against the popular tide and maintained official neutrality. Unofficially, it threw its support behind the British. The government and the emergent multinational corporations viewed the crisis in the context of endangerment of Anglo-American economic relations at a time when the multinationals were setting up manufacturing subsidiaries in Great Britain in hopes of breaking into the vast imperial system.

Moreover, it was widely held in the international business community that the British were far better equipped to unify and to economically develop South Africa than the Afrikaners, who were relatively poor, rurally based, and seemingly less business-oriented. Additionally, many missionary organizations, especially the Afro-American controlled AME, were convinced that the English-speaking whites were more liberal and thus more likely to establish a multiracial democracy in the postwar era. Thus, in the final analysis, the United States chose to play the British card, offering the Boers little more than their sympathy and token support. Chapter 4 will reveal the unexpected consequences of that fateful decision.

NOTES

1. C. W. De Kiewiet, *A History of South Africa: Social and Economic*, p. 125. See also J. Longland, ed., *Longland's Johannesburg and District Directory, 1899*, p. 11.
2. B. R. Mitchell, comp., *International Historical Statistics*, p. 93. See also Francis L. Coleman, ed., *Economic History of South Africa*, p. 179.
3. Department of Statistics, *Statistical Register: Cape of Good Hope* (Cape Town, 1872) (SAL); *Cape of Good Hope Census*, 1875, G. 42-1876 (SAL), p. 294.
4. Correspondance on Encouragement to Natives to Engage in Agriculture (SAL/C.8-81). See also R. C. Germond, *Chronicles of Basutoland* (Lesotho, 1967), p. 470; Colin Bundy, *The Rise and Fall of the South African Peasantry* (London, 1979).
5. Hedley A. Chilvers, *The Story of De Beers* (London, 1939), pp. 263–64.
6. Ibid., p. 67.
7. *Report on the The Diamond Fields*, Cape of Good Hope Parliamentary Papers (CGHPP), 1890, G. 11 (SAL). See also U.S. Bureau of Manufactures, "*Report on the The Diamond Fields*," no.134/A, November 1891 (Washington, D.C., 1891), pp. 395–99.

8. *The Diamond Fields Mail,* Vol.10, December 16, 1898, p. 4 (SAL). See also Apollon Davidson, *Cecil Rhodes and His Time* (Moscow, 1984), p. 83. See also De Beers, *First Annual Report,* July 1889 (SAL). W. J. De Kock, ed., *Dictionary of South African Biography,* 2:785. Geoffrey Wheatcroft, *The Randlords* (London, 1985).

9. S. H. Frankel, *Capital Investment in South Africa: Its Course and Effects,* p. 67.

10. Enid De Waal, "The Part Played by the Americans on the Witswatersrand During the Period 1886–1899," M.A. essay (University of South Africa, 1971). See also Clement Tsehloane Keto, "American Involvement in South Africa, 1870–1915: The Role of Americans in the Creation of Modern South Africa," p. 95; *Goldman's Atlas of the Witwatersrand and Other Gold Fields.*

11. See R. V. Kubicek, *Economic Imperialism in Theory and Practice: The Case of South African Gold Mining Finance, 1886–1914* (Durham, N.C., 1979). See also *The Gold Fields: 1887–1937* (London, 1937); Fred Jeppe, *Jeppe's Transvaal Almanack and Directory* (Pretoria, 1889).

12. A. P. Cartwright, *Golden Age: The Story of the Industrialization of South Africa and the Role Played by Corner House Group of Companies, 1910–1967,* p. 5.

13. De Kock, *Dictionary,* 2:114. Enid De Waal, "American Black Residents and Visitors in the South African Republic," p. 16. See also Patrick Manning, "Draft: Notes Toward a History of American Technical Assistance in Southern Africa from 1870–1950" (California Institute of Technology, n.d.), p. 4.

14. J. G. Lockhart and C. M. Woodhouse, *Cecil Rhodes: The Colossus of Southern Africa* (New York, 1963).

15. Cartwright, *Golden Age,* p. 99.

16. John Hays Hammond, Private Papers, box 259/13 (YUL). See also "Revolt of the Uitlanders," *National Geographic Magazine* 7, 11 (November 1896), p. 365; John Hays Hammond, *The Autobiography of John Hays Hammond,* 2:211–14. See also Charles Van Onselen, *Studies in the Social and Economic History of the Witwatersrand, 1866–1914,* 1:9.

17. Alex Groner, *American Business and Industry* (New York, 1972), p. 210. See also Peter Duignan and L. H. Gann, *The United States and Africa,* pp. 154–55.

18. William H. Worger, *South Africa's City of Diamonds: Mine Workers and Monopoly Capitalism in Kimberley, 1867–1895* (New Haven, 1987), p. 248; Gardner Williams, *The Diamond Mines of South Africa.* Robert I. Rotberg, *The Founder: Cecil Rhodes and the Pursuit of Power* (New York, 1988), p. 201.

19. Myra Goldstein, "The Genesis of Modern American Relations with South Africa, 1895–1914," Ph.D. dissertation (State University of New York, Buffalo, 1972), p. 38.

20. David Harris, *Pioneer, Soldier, and Politician* (London, 1931), p. 198.
21. Duignan and Gann, *The United States and Africa*, p. 156. Anon., *Gold Fields*, p. 14. See also Papers of John Hays Hammond, box 11 (YUL).
22. Eric Rosenthal, *Gold, Gold, Gold: The Johannesburg Gold Rush*, p.204; Goldstein, "Genesis," p. 43.
23. Manning, "Draft," p. 10. See also "The United States and South Africa," Backgrounder Pamphlet Series 4 (May 1979), South African Embassy (Washington, D.C., 1979), p. 4.
24. U.S. Department of State, Consular Reports, Special Agents Series vol. 48, no. 218 (November 1898), p. 458 (NAW).
25. Goldstein, "Genesis," p. 40. See also John Hope Franklin, *George Washington Williams*, p. 182; Enid De Waal, "American Black Residents and Visitors."
26. Malcolm McIlwraith, "The Delagoa Bay Arbitration," *Fortnightly Review* 74 (1900):413–23. See also Clarence Clendenen, Robert Collins, and Peter Duignan, *Americans in Africa, 1865–1900*, pp. 106–108.
27. Longland, ed., *Longland's Johannesburg and District Directory, 1896*. For labor recruitment see Worger, *City of Diamonds*, p. 77.
28. Stanley W. Hollis, "American Trade with Natal."
29. De Waal, "Americans," p. 83. See also A. M. Fransman, "Capital Accumulation in South Africa," in Martin Fransman, ed., *Industry and Accumulation in Africa* (London, 1982), p. 236.
30. *State of the Union: Economic, Financial, and Statistical Yearbook for the Union of South Africa, 1958*, p. 194.
31. Clark W. Powell, *Citrus* (Johannesburg, 1908). See also R. A. Davis, *Citrus Growing in South Africa* (Cape Town, 1924), p. 77; U.S. Bureau of Manufactures, "Viticulture in Cape Colony," Reports from the Consuls, no. 27 (January 1897) (Washington, D.C., 1897), pp. 42–46.
32. Department of Statistics, *Statistical Register of the Cape of Good Hope, 1899* (SAL). Eric Rosenthal, *Stars and Stripes in Africa* (Johannesburg, 1968), p. 72. See also Enid de Waal, "American Technology in South Africa Gold Mining before 1899."
33. Charles Van Onselen, *Studies in the Social and Economic History of the Witswatersrand, 1886–1914*, 2:122.
34. John H. Dunning, *American Investments in British Manufacturing Industry*, p. 32.
35. Alfred Chandler, "The Beginnings of Big Business in American Industry."
36. C. Joseph Pusateri, *A History of American Business* (Arlington Heights, Ill., 1984), p. 198.
37. Ibid., p. 200. See also Ralph Gray and John M. Peterson, *Economic Development of the United States* (Homewood, Ill., 1974), p. 467.
38. Ralph W. Hidy and Muriel E. Hidy, *History of the Standard Oil Company (New Jersey): Pioneering in Big Business, 1882–1911*, p. 128. See also

U.S. Bureau of Manufactures, "South African Progress," Reports from the Consuls, no. 117 (June 1890) (Washington, D.C., 1890), pp. 256–67.

39. James R. Beniger, *The Control Revolution: Technological and Economic Origins of the Information Society*, p. 349.

40. William H. Becker, "American Manufactureres and Foreign Markets, 1870–1900," *Business History Review* 47 (Winter 1973):46. See also "British Merchants Alarmed by American Inroads, " *The New York Times*, March 22, 1899, p. 3.

41. U.S. Department of State, Consular Reports, vol. 59 no. 223, April 1899, (Washington, D.C., 1900), pp. 673–75 (NAW). See also George Koether, *Ingersoll-Rand: The Building of Men, Machines, and a Company*, p. 7.

42. General Electric, *Update on South Africa* (Schnectady, N.Y., November 1984), p. 1.

43. "South Africa," *The Investor* (Schnectady, N.Y., November 1987), p. 6. See also *Journal of Commerce* 20, 16,907 (May 31, 1949), p. 81.

44. Harold G. Passer, *The Electrical Manufacturers, 1875–1900* (Cambridge, Mass., 1953), p. 206.

45. Macrum to Hill, July 22, 1899 (no. 49) U.S. Dept. of State, Miscellaneous Letters Received and Sent, 1899 (Washington, D.C., 1900). See also Rosenthal, *Stars and Stripes*, p. 211.

46. Victor S. Clark, *History of Manufactures in the United States 1893–1928* 3:118.

47. Ibid., p. 129. See also Keto, "American Involvement," p. 44.

48. *The South African Agriculturalists's Almanac for 1893*, p. 24.

49. U.S. Department of State, *Report on General Trades of South Africa, 1902*, (Washington, D.C., 1902), p. 83 (NAW).

50. Ibid., p. 65. See also Hidy and Hidy, *Standard Oil*, p. 219.

51. U.S. Department of State, "Report from the Field," Consular Reports on Commerce and Manufacturing Special Agents Series no. 207 (Washington, D.C., September–December 1900), p. 155.

52. F. A. McKenzie, *The American Invaders*, p. 71; Robert Porter, "Origins of the American Tobacco Company," *Business History Review* 43 (Spring 1985): 59–76.

53. *The Cape Argus*, January 2, 1891, p. 3 (SAL); U.S. Department of State, "Report from the Field," Consular Reports on Commerce and Manufacturing, p. 155.

54. J. Longland, ed., *Longland's Johannesburg and District Directory, 1897*, p. 11.

55. John M. Stopford and John H. Dunning, *The World Directory of Multinational Enterprises, 1982–83*, 2:67.

56. Hidy and Hidy, *Standard Oil*, p. 227.

57. *Cape Argus*, January 2, l891, p. 3 (SAL).

58. "South Africa," *Scientific American*, June 20, 1896, p. 19; Keto, "American Involvement," p. 391.

59. Michel Auer, *The Illustrated History of the Camera* (Boston, 1975).
60. R. Carlyle Buley, *The Equitable Life Assurance Society of the United States* (New York, 1959), p. 44.
61. Alden Hatch, *American Express: A Century of Service*, p. 89. See also Peter Z. Grossman, *American Express: The Unofficial History of the People Who Built the Great Financial Empire* (New York, 1987), p. 101.
62. Groner, *American Business*, p. 181. See also Gray and Peterson, *Economic Development*, p. 164.
63. A. G. Kenwood and A. L. Lougheed, *The Growth of the International Economy, 1820–1980*, p. 47.
64. Rosenthal, *Gold, Gold*, p. 253. See also V. E. Solomon, "Money and Banking," in F. Coleman, ed., *Economic History of South Africa*, p. 147.
65. Vincent P. Carosso, *The Morgans: Private International Bankers, 1854–1913*, pp. 311–13.
66. Milton Friedman and Anna J. Schwartz, *A Monetary History of the United States, 1867–1960* (Princeton, 1963).
67. Jean Jacques van Helten, "Empire and High Finance: South Africa and the International Gold Standard, 1890–1914," *Journal of African History* 23, 4, (1982):530. See also Rosenthal, *Gold, Gold*, p. 253.
68. U.S. Bureau of Foreign and Domestic Commerce. Consular Reports, Special Agents Series no. 225 (Washington, D.C., 1924.). See also Thomas J. Noer, *Briton, Boer and Yankee: The United States and South Africa, 1870–1914* (Kent, Ohio, 1978), p. 186; Stanley W. Hollis, "American Trade with Natal," U.S. Bureau of Manufacturers. *Reports from the Consuls*, no. 141 June, 1892 (Washington, D.C., 1892) (YUL).
69. U.S. Department of State, Despatches from Consuls in Pretoria, 1898–1906. RG57 T 660 reel 1 (YUL).
70. Marischal Murray *Union-Castle Chronicle, 1853–1953* (New York: Longmans-Green, 1953), p. 301.
71. Ibid., p. 344.
72. Ibid., p. 360.
73. C. G. W. Schumann, "Aspects of Economic Development in South Africa," in Marcelle Kooy, ed., *Studies in Economics and Economic History*, p. 91. See also V. E. Solomon, "Money and Banking," p. 147.
74. C. G. W. Schumann, *Structural Changes and Business Cycles in South Africa, 1806–1936*, p. 38.
75. Frankel, *Capital Investment*, p. 66.
76. Ronald Robinson and John Gallagher, *Africa and the Victorians* (New York, 1961), p. 63.
77. House of Commons, Parliamentary Papers, 1888, C.5363, "Further Correspondance Respecting Affairs of Adjacent Territories" (London, 1889) (RH). See also Stanlake Samkange, *Origins of Rhodesia* (New York, 1969), p. 69.
78. William Harvey Brown, *On the South African Frontier: The Adventures*

and *Observations of an American in Mashonaland and Matabeleland*, p. 40.

79. House of Commons, Parliamentary Papers, 1893, C 7171, "Correspondence Relating to the British South Africa Company in Matabeleland" (London, 1894) (RH).

80. Frederick Russell Burnham, *Scouting on Four Continents* (Garden City, N.Y., 1928). See also De Kock, ed., *Dictionary*, 2:287. Rotberg, *The Founder*, p. 514.

81. I. Phimister, "Rhodes, Rhodesia, and the Rand," *Journal of Southern African Studies* 1 (1974):17.

82. "The Revolt of the Uitlanders," *National Geographic* 7, 11 (November 1896). Hansard, Cape of Good Hope, 4th ser., 12, 139 (Cape Town, 1895).

83. "Restive Uitlanders," *The New York Times*, February 17, 1896, p. 6. "Raid in the Transvaal," *Economist*, June 11, 1895, p. 782.

84. John Flint, *Cecil Rhodes* (Boston, 1974), p. 157.

85. Robinson and Gallagher, *Africa and the Victorians*, p. 428.

86. Robinson to Chamberlain, November 4, 1895, in J. L. Garvin, *The Life of Joseph Chamberlain* (London, 1932), 3:59–62. See also E. M. Drus, "The Question of Imperial Complicity in the Jameson Raid," *English Historical Review* 62 (October 1953): 592–93.

87. U.S. Department of State, Despatches from the U.S. Consuls in Cape Town, RG 59 T 191, reel 2 (1900) (YUL). See also U.S. Department of State. Despatches from U.S. Consuls in Pretoria. RG 57 T 660 reels 1 and 2 (1898–1906) (NAW).

88. U.S. Department of State, Papers Relating to the Foreign Relations of the United States, Protection of American Citizens in the Transvaal (Washington, D.C., 1897), pp. 562–81. See also Eric A. Walker, *A History of Southern Africa* (London, 1968), pp. 454–58.

89. Ferguson, *American Diplomacy*, p. 28. See also David Healy, *U.S. Expansionism: The Imperialist Urge in the 1890s.* (Madison, Wi., 1970), pp. 25–29; Walter LaFeber, *The New Empire: An Interpretation of American Expansion, 1860–1898* (Ithaca, N.Y., 1963), pp. 242–83.

90. See: John Hays Hammond, *The Autobiography of John Hays Hammond*, 1:85–86. See also Flint, *Rhodes*, p. 179; Jean Van der Poel, *The Jameson Raid* (Cape Town, 1951), pp. 16–20; Drus, "The Question of Imperial Complicity," pp. 592–93.

91. Robinson and Gallagher, *Africa and the Victorians*, p. 412.

92. Mark Twain, *Following the Equator: A Journey Around the World* (New York, 1899); Poultney Bigelow, *A White Man's Africa*: Sidney Mendelssohn, ed., *Mendelssohn's South African Bibliography to the Year 1925*: "Africa Since 1888," *National Geographic* 7, 5 (May 1896); "South Africa," *Scientific American*, June 20, 1896.

93. Ferguson, *American Diplomacy*, p. 35. Hay to White, September 24, 1899,

in William Thayer, *The Life and Letters of John Hay* (Boston, 1915), 2:221.

94. Walter LaFeber, *The New Empire*, p. 38. See also Noer, *Briton, Boer and Yankee*, p. 17.
95. "Trouble on the Veld," *Wall Street Journal*, October 21, 1899, p. 1.
96. Edward Chester, *Clash of Titans: Africa and U.S. Foreign Policy*, p. 123. Duignan and Gann, *United States and Africa*, p. 160. See also Henry Houghton Beck, *History of South Africa and the Boer-British War* (Philadelphia, 1900), pp. 430–31.
97. Alfred Thayer Mahan, *The War in South Africa* (New York, 1900).
98. Day Allen Willey, "American Interests in Africa," *Arena* 25 (September 1900):293–98.
99. Willard B. Gatewood, "Black Americans and the Boer War." See also Sylvia Jacobs, *The African Nexus: Black American Perspectives on the European Partitioning of Africa, 1880–1920*, p. 130.
100. Quoted in Noer, *Briton, Boer*, p.86. See also J. P. Fitzpatrick, *The Transvaal from Within* (New York, 1899).
101. Robert W. Desmond, *The Information Process: World News Reporting to the Twentieth Century* (Iowa City, 1978), p. 413.
102. Donald C. Seitz, *Joseph Pulitzer: His Life and Letters*, p. 250.
103. See *New York Times*, August 30, 1900, p. 16. See also Paul Kruger, *Memoirs of Paul Kruger*.
104. J. Y. F. Blake, *A West Pointer with the Boers*. See also Chester, *Clash of Titans*, p. 157; De Kock, *Dictionary*, 3:71; Richard Harding Davis, *With Boer Armies in South Africa*.
105. U.S. Department of War. Reports on Military Operations, July 1901, no. 33 (Washington, D.C., 1901), p. 322 (NAW). See also Papers of Burnham, box 3 (HIL); "Boer War: Horse Shipments," 57th Cong., 1st Sess., House of Representatives Document no. 568, 1902 (NAW).
106. "Commerce and Navigation," vol. 2, 57th Cong., 1st Sess., House of Representatives Document no. 568., 1902, p. 320 (NAW).
107. U.S. Bureau of Foreign Commerce, The Foreign Commerce and Navigation of the United States for the Year ending June 30, 1911, p. 33 (NAW).
108. Carosso, *Investment Banking in America*, pp. 80–81.
109. Ibid., p. 81.
110. U.S. Department of State, Commerce, Manufactures. Consular Reports, vol. 57, (January–April 1900) (NAW).
111. U.S. Department of State, *Commercial Relations of the U.S. with Foreign Countries, 1855–1902*, vol. 47 (1903) (DOC). See also "Statistics on the South Africa, British, and American Trade," *Scientific American* Supplement no. 1407, December 20, 1902, pp. 225–48; T. Nicol Jenkin, *Report on the General Trades of South Africa, 1865–1900*.
112. F. A. McKenzie, *The American Invaders* (London, Richards, 1902).
113. American Board Missions, Annual Reports of the Missions to the Board in

Boston, 1848–1897, vol. 41 a/3/41 (NAD). See also David Welsh, *The Roots of Segregation: Native Policy in Natal, 1845–1910*, p. 45; J. Du Plessis, *A History of Christian Missionaries in South Africa*, p. 303.

114. Arthur F. Christofersen, *Adventuring with God: The Story of the American Board Mission in South Africa*, p. 116.

115. Louis R. Harlan and Raymond W. Smock, eds., *The Booker T. Washington Papers* (Urbana, Ill., 1977), 4: 1901–1902. See also Charles Robert Lord, "The Birth of a Mission: Background and Early History of the Rhodesia Mission of the Amerrican Board," ms. box 971 s/44 (ZNA). Du Plessis, *Christian Missions*, p. 44.

116. Imanuel Geiss, *The Pan-African Movement* (New York, 1972) p. 144, See also K. M. MacKenzie, *The Robe and the Sword: The Methodist Church and the Rise of American Imperialism, 1865–1900*.

117. Thomas Karis and Gwendolen Carter, eds., *From Protest to Challenge: Documents of African Politics in South Africa, 1882–1964*, 1:8.

118. Walter Lee Williams, "Black American Attitudes Towards Africa: The Missionary Movement, 1877–1900," Ph.D dissertation (University of North Carolina, 1974), p. 224; Jacobs, *Nexus*, p. 178.

119. J. M. Chirenje, *Ethiopianism and Afro-Americans in Southern Africa, 1883–1916*, p.277. See also Michael McCarthy, *Dark Continent: Africa as Seen By Americans*.

120. Jacobs, *Nexus*, p. 178; De Waal, "Americans," p. 38.

121. H. M. Turner, "My Trip to South Africa," *AME Church Review.* (April 1899):809–12. See also John W. Cell, *The Highest Stage of White Supremacy: The Origins of Segregation in South Africa and the United States*, pp. 38–44; Duignan and Gann, *United States and Africa*, p. 165.

122. Williams, "Black American Attitudes," p. 100. See also "The South African College," *Voice of Missions*, October 1, 1901, p. 2; L. J. Coppin, "The Progress of Our Work in South Africa," *Voice of Missions*, November 1, 1902; Chirenje, *Ethiopianism*, p. 98.

123. Clendenen, Collins, and Duignan, *Americans in Africa, 1865–1900.* For information on the National Baptist Convention, see Lewis G. Jordan, *Up the Ladder in Foreign Missions* (Nashville, 1901), pp. 18–23.

124. Peter Duignan, *Handbook of American Resources for African Studies*, pp. 70–77; G. P. Groves, *The Planting of Christianity in Africa*, 2:98.

125. Mt. Selinda Mission, Advance of the Rhodesian Mission, no. 1, 1938, s/ AD 804 (NAZ).

126. See Duignan, *Handbook*, passim; Groves, *Planting*, 2:98. See also Edwin W. Smith, *The Way of the White Fields in Rhodesia: A Survey of Christian Enterprise in Northern and Southern Rhodesia* (London, 1928), pp. 69–146.

127. Shula Marks, *The Ambiguities of Dependence in South Africa*; Sheridan Johns, in Karis and Carter, eds., *From Protest to Challenge*, 3:8.

128. See Karis and Carter, eds., *Protest to Challenge*, 4:24–26; Shula Marks, "The Ambiguities of Dependence: John L. Dube of Natal," *Journal of*

Southern African Studies 1 (April 1975): 162–180. See also R. Hunt Davis, "John L. Dube: A South African Exponent of Booker T. Washington," *Journal of African Studies* 2 (Winter 1975): 497–528; Louis R. Harlan, *Booker T. Washington: The Wizard of Tuskeegee, 1901–1915* (New York, 1983), p. 273.

129. Julia Wells, "Charlotte Manye Maxeke," Unpublished manuscript (n.d.).
130. Franklin, *Williams,* p. 344. "The Jubilee Singers," *Imvo Zabantsundu* (South Africa) October 16, 1890 (SAL). See also David Coplan, *In Township Tonight: South Africa's Black City Music and Theater,* p. 39.

FOUR

New Dimensions in American Penetration, 1903–1929

In the early twentieth century South Africa became a voracious consumer of American products, manufactured either in the United States or in Canada, Great Britain, or South Africa by a subsidiary or under license. In the 1920s U.S. government agencies became active promoters of American enterprise abroad, subsidizing private shipping, encouraging international banking, and opening trade sections in their embassies. For the first time, private U.S. citizens played a role in launching new South African-based companies and reinvigorating old ones. Indeed, for South Africa, the era of U.S. direct and portfolio investments had begun. South Africa was valued not only as a market for manufactures and a source of diamonds and gold but as a vital supplier of industrial base minerals. Moreover, despite British resistance South Africa became a springboard for the expansion of American mining enterprise and investment into South West Africa and the British Rhodesias.

No longer did South Africans look to Americans primarily for their expertise in mineral exploitation. They now sought their advice in such fields as education, library science, social work, and monetary reform. South Africa in the 1920s and 1930s was a fertile field for American philanthropic enterprise, spearheaded by the Carnegie and Phelps-Stokes foundations. American philanthropists and missionaries intensified their interest in the human condition and developed a concern for the social implications of urbanization and industrialization for blacks and whites. However, as will become evident, in doing so, they catapulted themselves into controversies of international dimensions and far-reaching consequences. Less controversial, though of greater impact, was the

American entertainment industry. Truly, the American invasion of South Africa had begun, and Britain and South Africa viewed it as a challenge and an opportunity as well as a threat. This chapter examines the invasion, its nature, impact, and consequences.

STEMMING THE AMERICAN INVASION

After the Second Boer War South Africa slipped into an economic depression that lasted until 1909. Agriculture in the defeated Afrikaner republics (now British colonies) had been devastated, and large segments of the Boer population were destitute, demoralized, and uprooted. The condition of the African population was even worse. Imperial Britain, now fully in control, sought to integrate more completely the economies of the former Afrikaner republics with the British coastal colonies of Natal and the Cape. Under the authoritarian and rabidly anglophilic leadership of Alfred Milner, the governor general, policies that drew the entire southern African region, including Portuguese Mozambique, into the imperial network of trade and investment were unilaterally implemented.

Great Britain had become alarmed by the growth of American economic influence in the Transvaal in the decade before the war. Cecil Rhodes, though no friend of the Transvaal political leadership, had done more than anyone in the 1890s to tap American expertise and to take advantage of American mining technology. But after Rhodes's death in 1902 first De Beers and then other mining firms declined to renew the contracts of American engineers and managers. The American presence in South Africa's extractive industries receded almost as quickly as it had appeared, its position taken by British citizens, some Germans, and other nationals.

The United States' suddenly diminished role in South Africa was perhaps most visible in the lucrative field of life insurance. The withdrawal, however, was more the result of events in the United States than elsewhere. In New York the 1905 Armstrong investigation into the life insurance industry came on the heels of a nationwide campaign against trusts and big business in general. The investigation and the legislation of 1906 changed profoundly the operations of American life insurance companies.[1] Henceforth, they had to restrict their operations to life insurance and abandon other entrepreneurial activities. Consequently, their real estate investments in South Africa and elsewhere, which in some cases had turned a handsome profit, had to be liquidated. A major incentive for expanding in South Africa had thus been lost, and the companies began to scale back their operations. Moreover, their major customers had been American miners, most of whom left South Africa on the eve of the Boer War and did not return.

The American disinvestment provided a great opportunity for the development of local South African insurance enterprise. Since 1894 I. W. Schlesinger, an American entrepreneur, had represented the Mutual and Equitable Insurance companies of New York in Johannesburg. A decade later he established his own insurance firm, the American Life Assurance Society, which soon began to fill the vacuum left by the retreating American companies. Already by 1905 Schlesinger had purchased the Robinson South African Bank and converted it into the Colonial Banking and Trust Company, which specialized in small loans to fledgling locally owned businesses. Thus the future of South Africa's insurance industry passed to local entrepreneurs, not least among them Schlesinger.[2]

U.S. direct investments in South Africa had always been negligible, in large measure because the British had historically discouraged American involvement in the imperial dominions. Nevertheless, as I have indicated in chapter 3 by the turn of the century many American products were invading British markets worldwide. And from the eve of the Boer War Great Britain had become acutely aware of the need to achieve a more favorable balance in its trade. In response greater efforts were made to reduce direct imports from the United States.

In the first two decades of the twentieth century the merging American multinational corporations (MNCs) began to devote more energy to improving their marketing and distribution networks. Singer Manufacturing Company, one of America's earliest modern MNCs, became a leader in such endeavors when in 1904 it organized the Singer Sewing Machine Company as its marketing arm with the objective of purchasing from the parent firm all sewing machine thread and needles and retailing them through its own sales and marketing networks overseas. Most of the American MNCs were under the control of their American parents, although some did eventually break away. The Westinghouse Electric Company, for example, which had organized a British subsidiary in

1899, sold its holdings in 1917 to a British syndicate. As a result, Westinghouse (U.K.) became an independent company, competing actively in world markets against its parent. General Electric and a few others followed a similar course.[3]

The merger movement in America, which gained so much momentum in the 1890s, had climaxed by 1903. In that tumultuous period mergers had been most successful and most apparent in modern metals, machinery, petroleum, and chemical groups. Industrial concentration in the United States was most pronounced in the base metals industries whose production had been transformed by high-volume techniques. But high-volume production could only be achieved by heavy capital investment and large operating expenditures and through extensive purchasing networks for the acquisition of raw materials. Substantial distributing facilities were also needed to market the manufactured products. Thus, large multinational corporations emerged in fields of production that were technologically complex and where largeness in scale offered economic advantages.[4]

In this early period American MNCs were not prepared to establish manufacturing subsidiaries in South Africa. Consumer demand there was still too weak, British resistance too strong. Consequently, attention continued to be given to the search for markets for finished goods and to the development of more efficient distribution networks. American products were sold primarily through local agencies by means of contracts or licensing agreements.

Even though American entrepreneurs were not manufacturing in South Africa, by 1903 at least forty U.S. corporations were conducting business there—twelve of them in Johannesburg alone. Most of them had maintained agencies in Cape Town long before the war. And, as I discussed in chapter 3, their products enjoyed a prominent position in the marketplace and had already won wide consumer recognition. Many South Africans illuminated their homes with Dietz lamps filled with Standard Oil kerosene. Singer practically monopolized the sewing machine market as Kodak did for film and cameras. In offices of business and government the Remington had become the preferred typewriter, Burroughs adding machines were in great demand, and "National" became almost synonymous with cash registers in most large retail establishments. Armour tinned meats were a popular item in many grocery stores. American products also continued to sell well in the extractive industries. In 1905 in the United States the Ingersoll Rock Drill Company, which was already doing a brisk business on the Witwatersrand, combined with the Rand Drill Company to form the mighty Ingersoll-Rand. Overnight, it became the leading name in the world for drilling equipment.[5]

Mining technology in the United States was already advancing at a breathtaking speed. Inexpensive but clumsy hand drills were rapidly replaced after the Boer War by Ingersoll-Rand's light jack-hammer, which could cut more easily and quickly into the gold-impregnated hard quartz rock of the Witwatersrand. Not surprisingly, Ingersoll-Rand drills immediately found their way into practically every South African gold mine and were used alongside mining equipment powered by General Electric motors.[6]

The century unfolded on a note of optimism that U.S.–South African trade would expand rapidly. In 1905 the Standard Bank of South Africa confidently opened an agency in New York to service the expected flood of merchants.[7] This was the first South African bank in history to enter the American financial scene. Chapter 5 will reveal the extent to which the bankers' expectations were fulfilled.

In the wake of the South African War the British searched for new sources of local revenue to finance postwar economic reconstruction. In the process they sought to make the economy less sensitive to forces outside the imperial system. Concern was expressed over the growing vulnerability of South Africa to economic fluctuations in the United States. For example, by 1903 America owned half of the world's diamonds and had become the chief ultimate purchaser of South African output. A distressingly high correlation had developed between business cycles in the United States and the health of the local diamond industry. When the American economy was in recession, diamond exports weakened. The British used this volatility equation to argue for greater imperial control over the volume and direction of South Africa's trade in general.[8]

Clearly, the tariff system had to be recast to protect British trade as well as to raise local revenue. Traditionally, customs duties were quite moderate and fell rather equally on all imports. However, in 1903 protectionist momentum began to build after the formation of a customs union of the four South African colonies and the British possessions of Basutoland, Bechuanaland, Swaziland, and the Rhodesias. The action held enormous promise for an integrated market throughout southern

Africa. Three years later the British raised local tariffs and reduced transport costs between the British Isles and South Africa in hopes of reducing import volume from the United States. All internal customs dues were abolished and a 10 percent ad valorem duty was imposed on imports. Significantly, British firms could receive a 25 percent rebate, the so-called Imperial Preference, if they shipped from Cape Town or Durban rather than from Portuguese Mozambique. This extremely advantageous Imperial Preference was available only to enterprises in the United Kingdom and in the colonies and dominions. The Customs Convention of 1908 raised tariffs even higher, while retaining the Preference for imports from Great Britain and its possessions.[9]

The Imperial Preference presented an enormous and dangerous challenge to the United States, and it became an important factor in America's corporate expansion into Canada, a British dominion. Since 1904 U.S. coporations were able to take advantage of a preferential tariff that had been extended into Canada by a South African Customs Union Convention. Surely, American entrepreneurs had to find new and more imaginative ways of retaining their recently achieved competititve position in the potentially lucrative markets of the British Empire. Consequently, between 1904 and 1910 numerous American companies established export-oriented factories in Canada; and in the decades following, many American products destined for South Africa were manufactured by U.S.-owned subsidiaries in Canada and exported in whole or part from Canadian ports.

Initially, American entrepreneurs were hurt by the double impact of protectionism and the postwar South African depression. Exports to South Africa plunged ominously from a record high of nearly $31 million in 1903 to a low of about $7.7 million in 1907.[10] Agriculture was the export item most affected by the British Imperial Preference, with Australian wheat growers, for example, now able to undersell their American competitors.

American trade with South Africa was further constrained by a weak, uncompetitive merchant marine. In 1905 the British government had restructured the steamship monopoly and in doing so reduced shipping costs between South African ports and England to levels comparable to those between South Africa and ports along the United States' eastern seaboard. To make matters worse, the powerful Union-Castle companies merged in 1900 and, it must be recalled, assumed control of the American-African Line. This and other lines were members of the British-controlled United States–South African Outward Conference, which dictated rates, pooling arrangements, and rebates.[11] Union-Castle not only enjoyed an annual government subsidiary but also was given berthing priority for its mail ships in South African ports. This made the line popular with passengers as well as with shippers.[12] Thus, American shippers outside the Conference operated under a severe handicap.

Even though by 1909 every major South African port was serviced by regular direct shipping from the United States, less than 10 percent of that trade was conducted in ships of American registry.[13] Before 1912 American shipowners could not secure U.S.' registry for vessels built overseas. This was especially unfortunate because construction costs tended to be lower in other countries.

All these constraints had the effect of weakening America's competitive position and slowing its penetration of South African markets. In the game for South Africa the British had won another important round.

RESTORING THE AMERICAN CONNECTION: ENERGY AND TRANSPORTATION

In May 1910 the South Africa Act became operational, transforming the four colonies into constituent provinces within a Union of South Africa. South Africa was now a formal British dominion, with an administration under a locally elected prime minister. In a deal between the local white population and London Africans were denied direct participation in the new central government. The all-white general elections of 1910 had brought into power a predominantly English-speaking regime under the leadership of Louis Botha, a former Boer War general who was willing to collaborate fully with the British. Botha's power was based on a loose coalition of Afrikaner and English-speaking political parties.[14]

With a large measure of local control restored, the Union government began to seek ways of expanding trade with countries beyond Great Britain and the Empire. In this they were remarkably successful, for over the next three and a half decades the rate of increase in their trade outside the Empire more than doubled the rate within it. And in comparison with the other dominions South Africa's foreign trade grew at a considerably faster pace. A new receptivity to American products developed at a time when U.S. MNCs were accumulating more capital to expand their operations overseas. As a result of antitrust action in the United States courts, many MNCs went public and greatly increased their capital resources by selling stock. They began to expand their marketing networks in a South African economy that historically had never been so fully integrated. In many respects the Union's first Customs Tariff Act (1914) was a victory for the free traders in that it repealed the separate tariffs in force in the four provinces.[15]

American expansion into South African markets in the early twentieth century was greatest and most visible in the energy and transportation sectors. It must be recalled that Standard Oil products were already selling widely in South Africa and that the Rockefeller organization had gained an almost virtual monopoly over the kerosene market. By 1910 annual exports of Standard Oil products to South Africa had reached 14.2 million gallons, nearly all of it kerosene.[16] Standard Oil had gained control of the oil industry through vertical combination—through a process, in other words, of control over nearly all the stages of production and distribution: from the extraction of crude, through refining, to transportation, and finally to retailing to consumers at filling stations. Even though the mammoth Standard Oil Trust had been splintered by the courts in the early 1890s, New Jersey legislation enabled Rockefeller to reorganize his vast oil empire into a holding company in 1899. Competing firms were then absorbed through outright merger. In 1911 the huge enterprise was again broken up, a victim of a new wave of antitrust legislation. Its products were henceforth distributed in South Africa by Standard Oil of New York (later called Mobil) and Standard Oil of California.[17] In the same year a newcomer entered the South African field. The Texas Company (Texaco), which had been formed in the United States in 1902, began to market four key products: Unicorn and Tower Parafin (for cooking stoves), Motor Spirit gasoline, and so-called Lubricating Oil.[18] The three companies collectively enjoyed a near monopoly over the supply and distribution of petroleum products in the country. To stem threats from British competitors, the Standard Oil firms had to develop bulk distribution and make improvements in the quality of its packaging.[19]

Nevertheless, competition intensified in the 1920s as motor vehicle sales boomed and the demand for gasoline skyrocketed. Royal Dutch-Shell, the huge Anglo-Dutch group of companies, began to take up the market share. In 1922 Texaco started to build its own filling stations, and in 1928 California Standard Oil in the United States formed an export corporation in order to handle the foreign distribution of its products more expeditiously. Meanwhile, in South Africa oil consumption increased along with a dependency on petroleum products. Throughout the century South Africa has been engaged in a futile search for indigenous reserves of petroleum. In the early decades nearly all of South Africa's petroleum was sourced by firms owned or controlled by Americans and refined in the United States. Thus, from the very start oil dependency was South Africa's Achilles' heel and America's golden spur. U.S. petroleum companies became the new vanguard for American trade with South Africa, just as the Yankee whaling enterprises spearheaded American trade a century earlier.

Motor vehicles were naturally the handmaidens of petroleum; and it must be remembered that American companies had been selling vehicles in South Africa since the late nineteenth century. The introduction of assembly-line techniques in vehicular manufacturing enabled the American companies to mass produce vehicles at lower cost. It was not long before the vehicular industry in the United States assumed an oligopolistic structure.[20] It achieved enormous growth rates and rapidly gained domination in world markets. In 1908 General Motors was formed in the United States upon the acquisition of the Cadillac, Oakland, and Oldsmobile companies.[21] The products of those firms were already well known in South Africa. For example, as early as 1903 advertisements for Olds cars appeared regularly in the *Natal Mercury,* a widely read newspaper. Between 1910 and 1920 more than thirty firms came under the General Motors Holding Company, including Chevrolet in 1918.[22] The General Motors Export Company was founded in 1911 to sell and ship GM products overseas, and sales representatives were soon established in scores of foreign countries, including South Africa.

From an early period South Africa became a major market for American autos; and by 1915 the country stood in fifth place among all foreign buyers of American vehicles.[23] In the same year Prime Minister Botha and his South African party were returned to power, thanks to the support of the mainly English-speaking Unionist party. Though Botha had always been receptive to the import of American vehicles, Jan Smuts, his successor, was even more so. GM gained higher product recognition and prestige in 1919, when Smuts, the new prime minister, bought a Cadillac and set a precedent for the use of that model for ministerial cars.[24] By then General Motors had become one of the world's largest multinational corporations and the largest manufacturer of motor vehicles. Quite simply, the British were outgunned from the start. Their vehicles may have been better built, but they were more expensive and technologically inferior. General Motors did not begin to assemble overseas until 1923, when it opened a plant in Denmark. Two years later it absorbed the British Vauxhall Company, and in 1929 it acquired the German Opel firm.[25]

Ford vehicles also penetrated the South African market with great success and at an early date. Henry Ford's Model T appeared in Cape Town in 1908 and became an immediate success. From 1912 most Fords were marketed through a huge dealership in Kimberley owned by Harold G. Holmes, whose ancestors, it must be recalled from chapter 2, originated in America. In Southern Rhodesia Ford sales were handled by Duly and Son, another locally owned firm.[26]

Ford first entered South Africa through Canada. When the Ford Motor Company was set up there by a Canadian in 1904, a 51 percent equity was retained by the Detroit parent in exchange for all Ford rights and processes in South Africa, Canada, New Zealand, and the other British dominions.[27] Consequently, most, though not all, Fords destined for South Africa were of Canadian manufacture.

American entrepreneurs also made deep inroads into the farm equipment and tractor market. In 1902 International Harvester was formed out of a merger of the McCormick Harvesting Machine Company, which started manufacturing reapers in 1834, and the McCormick and Deering Harvester Company, makers of a broad range of agricultural equipment. International Harvester opened its first Canadian plant in 1902, and within half a decade its products were well known among South Africa's white farming community.[28] In 1913 the first McCormick tractor was displayed at an agricultural fair in the Transvaal. Sales were brisk from the start, and in 1927 the high sales volume warranted the formation of an autonomous subsidiary. Another early and successful entrant was the J. I. Case Threshing Machine Company, which began marketing its products in South Africa in 1917. By then American-owned firms were selling more farm machinery in South Africa than their British competitors. Indeed, more than half of the country's farm machinery was of North American provenance.[29]

Trucks and autos required rubber tires; and American firms were quick to establish distribution networks. Firestone started selling in 1915, with Goodyear Tire and Rubber Company following less than a year later. In early 1919 Goodyear opened large depots in Cape Town and Johannesburg. Yet neither company was able to approach the sales volume of Dunlop, the giant Great Britain tire manufacturer.[30]

A SHIFTING BALANCE: THE IMPACT OF THE WAR ON TRADE AND FINANCE

From a global perspective American trade and investment showed steady growth despite the protectionist policies of Great Britain and other industrialized nations. The value of total American exports soared from an extremely modest $800 million in 1895 to $2.3 billion in 1914—an increase of more than 240 percent.[31] The growth rate for manufactures alone was nearly 500 percent; and between 1897 and 1914 American direct investment abroad more than quadrupled, from $634 million to $2.6 billion.[32]

The figures for South Africa were no less impressive. By 1913 U.S. exports to that country had rebounded to $14 million, and amounted to 9.5 percent of the total value of South Africa's imports.[33] The balance of direct trade had already become grossly distorted in the United States' favor. In 1911, for example, South Africa exported only $2.2 million in goods to the United States, representing a paltry .9 percent of its total exports.[34] But the figures are a bit misleading because they mask the surging volume of mineral exports shipped to the United States via third parties. Significantly, throughout much of the twentieth century the trade statistics fail to include diamond and gold shipments to London that were ultimately reexported to the United States, often through Canadian ports. Before World War II practically all U.S. diamond imports originated in South Africa. Most uncut diamonds were reexported through London, and cut stones came in chiefly from Belgium and the Netherlands. It would therefore be difficult indeed to overestimate the enormous volume of South African exports to the United States.

World War I profoundly affected the nature of American–South African economic relationships. During the war years South Africa encountered severe problems in obtaining critical supplies from Great Britain and the Western European allies. The Union of South Africa therefore had to develop local substitutes and to rely more heavily on the United States.[35] Dislocations of war gave American vehicles a special entry into South African markets; and in the war period autos and trucks rose to first place among total U.S. exports to South Africa.[36]

Undisputably, the war years changed the balance and volume of trade between the two countries. By 1917, 17 percent of South Africa's imports came from the United States, and at least 21 percent of its exports were destined for American markets. The United States' share of South Africa's total trade climbed from 5 percent in 1913 to 16 percent in 1918, a gain for more than 300 percent.[37] Undoubtedly, the growth would have been even greater if more ships had been available. Of even more significance was the vast increase in the value and volume of South Africa's trade with the United States. During the war years South Africa increased its shipments of wool and hides, while it purchased not only more American vehicles but more kerosene, lubricating oils, mining equipment, electrical goods, and agricultural machinery. The country's merchandise exports to the United States surged from $2.2 million in 1911 to $13.4 million in 1923. And this did not include gold or diamond exports.[38] Trade was so brisk that several New York export commission houses opened offices in Cape Town and Johannesburg.

The war had also sparked local secondary industry, particularly light manufacturing. Between 1915 and 1919 the number of South African manufacturing concerns rose by 45 percent, and the net value of local manufacturing jumped 53 percent.[39] The most impressive growth came in the textile, leather goods, furniture, and dairy processing industries, which will be further discussed later.

The postwar era witnessed a steady increase in the United States' share of the world export trade in manufactures. Yet while the country advanced enormously in the export of engineering products and transportation-related equipment, its exports of raw materials and foodstuffs declined proportionately. On the other hand, the United States was becoming a large purchaser of base metals for industrial use, and in that regard American entrepreneurs had begun to take an interest in the mineral potential of lands north of the Limpopo River. During the war the United States moved into a close second place to Great Britain in trade with Southern Rhodesia.[40]

Inevitably, American eyes now looked across the Zambezi River to the British Protectorate of Northern Rhodesia and to South West Africa. As a result of the war the operations of many German mining firms in southern Africa were liquidated and their assets were sold off to foreign interests. I will later discuss how this provided unprecedented opportunities for American MNCs.

The United States emerged from World War I as an international creditor. Great Britain and the European allies were forced to liquidate a substantial portion of their investments in the United States in order to meet the costs of the war. They also found themselves borrowing heavily in American money markets and liquidating their dollar securities to help pay for American goods. From 1914 to April 1917, when the United States entered the conflict, the New York market was the only major source of credit to the British and their allies. Thus, the outbreak of war and the closing of the London market made New York City for the first time in history the center of world finance. The war had indeed eroded the old structures of international finance and trade, and in the process, the United States was transformed from a net capital importer into a net capital exporter. This extraordinary shift created many new opportunities for American banks, multinational corporations, and shipping concerns.[41]

MOVING THE GOODS: GOVERNMENT STRATEGIES FOR TRADE PROMOTION

The government had already begun to think about ways of expanding foreign trade. As early as 1909, under the Taft administration, Congress voted to study means of providing incentives for trade expansion.[42] In 1912 pressure from the Commerce Department and its allies in the business community resulted in the transferral of responsibility for trade promotion from the State Department to the Department of Commerce. Congress was also pressured into establishing a Bureau of Foreign and Domestic Commerce within the Commerce Department.[43] On its own initiative the private sector in the same year established the United States Chamber of Commerce, while a year later the American Manufacturers' Export Association was set up. These and other emergent trade association movements began to push for stronger government support of foreign commerce. They argued that it was in the national interest for foreign commerce to expand into areas of strategic importance. And in the 1920s there were numerous discoveries in southern Africa of minerals that during the war were considered by the Allied Powers to be of great strategic value.[44]

The first major government move came in the form of the Federal Reserve Act of 1913, which allowed American banks to grant short-term credit for financing trade and commerce and permitted national banks to establish foreign branches. Previously, banks incorporated under federal law and most state banks could not maintain offices outside the country or accept foreign drafts or bills of exchange. Access to foreign markets could only be gained through foreign correspondent banks. Private banks and trust companies had historically enjoyed more freedom in their activities, but few had ventured far beyond America's shores. There had never been an American bank in South Africa, and much American trade with that country had to be financed through such private mercantile firms as J. and W. Seligman, a New York importer that had established a banking house in London in the 1860s.[45]

In 1916 the Wilson administration provided new momentum for international commerce by releasing a two-volume document entitled *Cooperation in the Export Trade*. The report waxed enthusiastically about untapped overseas markets and called for more government initiative in promoting foreign trade and banking.[46] The outbreak of war in 1914 had given strong incentive to expand overseas banking services into the vacuum created by interruptions of traditional British channels of financing.

In a first big step to promote postwar trade Congress in 1918 passed the Webb Pomerene Act, which permitted the formation of business combinations and export associations for the purpose of engaging in the export trade. The legislation was followed in 1919 by the Edge Act, which was designed to assist in the financing of exports. The Edge Act was an amendment to the Federal Reserve Act and authorized national banks to buy shares in corporations engaged in making foreign investments. It also allowed commercial banks to establish federally chartered corporations for the purpose of engaging in international banking.[47] This opened the way to large investment trusts. Congress correctly anticipated that the Edge Act would marshall substantial amounts of American capital, increase American lending abroad, and better enable foreigners to purchase American exports. Commercial banks now had the green light to create overseas corporations to engage in a wide variety of activities that antitrust legislation prohibited within the United States. Thus, banking corporations were free to reorganize themselves to participate fully in international trade. The Edge Act also enabled American manufacturers to discount their foreign assets and to use the proceeds to expand their businesses.

BANKS: A CAUTIOUS ENTRANCE

American banks were still hesitant to move into South Africa, despite congressional incentives and encouragement from Jan Smuts, who in 1919, upon the death of Louis Botha, became prime minister of the Union. American trade with Africa was showing steady growth. Indeed, total trade with Africa grew from $30 million in 1900 to $150 million at the conclusion of World War I.[48] But the United States' official presence in South Africa was still extremely modest, with businessmen served by only seven consulates staffed by ten individuals.[49] Clearly, the United States government was not yet prepared to provide adequate resources within the host countries to promote American enterprise.

In 1920 the United States opened a Trade Commissioner's office in Johannesburg and indicated its intention to increase its support of bilateral trade.[50] In the same year the private U.S. Chamber of Commerce established an office in Johannesburg. The National City Bank of New York was particularly pleased by these developments. After the war the Standard Oil complex had cooperated with the bank in an effort to develop an integrated global trade and financial system independent of the British. National City had become one of the largest commercial banks in the United States. J. P. Morgan and Company, the United States' preeminent private banking partnership, and the Chase National Bank of New York did not share National's desire to challenge British banking in its own dominions. Their connections with British banking counterparts were simply too important and lucrative to be endangered by bold forays into the hallowed overseas preserves of British banking institutions. Any potential business in Africa was not worth the risk.

Banking in South Africa was undergoing a process of centralization at this time. The number of commercial banks in the country had been reduced from thirty in the 1890s to seven at the time of the creation of the Union of South Africa in 1910. By 1920 further consolidations had reduced the number to five.[51] The extent of concentration in banking in South Africa was possibly greater than in any non-Communist country in the world. By late 1920 most banking in the Union was in the hands of the two huge imperial institutions: the National Bank of South Africa and the Standard Bank. The Netherlands Bank of South Africa, registered in Amsterdam, was a weak third. Standard and National had achieved this dominance by establishing branches and buying out the old local district banks.[52]

After a thorough study of the economic situation in South Africa, the National City Bank of New York opened a branch in Cape Town in January 1920 and incorporated it under the National City Bank of New York, South Africa Branch.[53] The bank had been most impressed by the explosive growth of American auto exports to the Union and anticipated a surge of direct investment. Their optimism was not entirely unfounded. In South Africa auto imports had jumped from 218,000 vehicles in 1914 to a breathtaking 3.1 million in 1920.

The South Africans were also optimistic. The National Bank of South Africa, a totally unrelated bank, opened a branch in New York City in 1921.[54] It should be recalled that the Standard Bank had been doing business in New York since 1905. But these events could not have occurred at a less propitious moment. New York State banking law did not allow the two South African banks to conduct a general business, including the acceptance of deposits. In retaliation South Africa passed a law making the same limitations applicable to any American bank in the country.[55] These bold ventures into each other's financial turf had, in short, gotten off to a bad start. And the going would get tougher.

South Africa's banking system was in a state of enormous upheaval and transformation as the economy moved into the decade of the 1920s. To deal with this problem, the Reserve Bank was created in 1920 as a privately owned institution. By 1922 it was acting as South Africa's central bank, with the right to issue its own banknotes, a privilege that soon became exclusive. Within a short time it also became the custodian of the nation's gold and foreign reserves. Moreover, it gained the right to maintain credit lines with foreign financial institutions, which could be used to top up the country's foreign reserves in times when the balance of payments was in deficit. Significantly, the Reserve Bank was allowed to make gold swap arrangements with foreign institutions, by which gold was sold spot and repurchased forward in order to gain temporary access to foreign currency.[56]

THE RISING TIDE OF TRADE PROTECTIONISM

The Currency and Banking Act of 1920 required National City Bank to subscribe to the capital of the new Reserve Bank.[57] This and the creation of the Reserve Bank itself occurred when both countries had just slipped into an economic recession. In the summer of 1920 the boom in the United States peaked and commodity prices plunged. A severe world-wide recession quickly set in. South African imports from the United States fell from 18.4 million sterling in 1920 to 5.8 million sterling in 1922.[58] World gold prices had also fallen, and labor turmoil in the mines was escalating as mineowners sought to cut labor costs. Already in 1920 the mines were jolted by a series of crippling strikes by Africans, who complained that their wages were progressively falling behind those of their white counterparts. Then, in 1922, the government brutally crushed a massive strike by white miners. The workers feared unemployment in the wake of a cost-cutting decision by the powerful Chamber of Mines to eliminate the color bar in all semiskilled positions.

The recession in the United States fueled the fires of protectionism. In 1921 the Emergency Tariff Act raised duties on a broad range of goods. Then, the Fordney-McCumber Act of 1922 raised them higher, thereby substantially reducing imports from South Africa.[59] This was no blow to the Americans because, excluding diamonds and gold, South African imports still consisted mainly of such items as ostrich feathers, sheep skins, mohair, and wool. Wool, however, was an important earner of foreign exchange for South Africa, and since the opening of World War I the Americans were buying an increasing volume of wool direct from the Union as opposed to reexports from Great Britain.[60]

The Fordney-McCumber Act enraged South Africa. It was not long before South Africa and a host of other countries erected retaliatory trade barriers. Undoubtedly, these events had a moderating effect on American–South African trade even though U.S. exports continued to climb. National City Bank of New York had problems with the Soviet Union and faced massive defaults on loans to Cuban planters. All these obstacles seemed to converge, and in response National City Bank decided to close several of its less profitable branches, including the one in South Africa.[61]

The abrupt disinvestment came as a great blow to I. W. Schlesinger and to a host of other American entrepreneurs in South Africa who in the early 1920s had formed a branch of the Rotary Club and an American Chamber of Commerce. They had anticipated a great surge in American direct investment on the entrance of the big American banks.[62] The American Trade Commissioner lamented that "There are lots of American companies that have branches in South Africa operating as sales organisations but none that have factories or industrial plants."[63]

British capital, by contrast, was undeterred, if not greatly relieved by the turn of events. In 1926 the local National Bank of South Africa, not to be confused with the New York bank, was absorbed by the London-based Barclays Bank, D.C.O. (Dominion, Colonial, and Overseas),[64] a move that represented a great victory for imperial banking. Consequently, the scope of British financial interests in South Africa expanded considerably.

In 1924 the Afrikaner-dominated National party, supported by Afrikaner farmers and workers, came to power in coalition with the Labour party, which represented the interests of the mainly English-speaking white mineworkers. Under Prime Minister J. B. Hertzog the South African political scene became more conservative and nationalistic.[65] Economically, this translated into greater trade protectionism. Hertzog was anxious to make the economy more self-reliant by protecting and nurturing local infant industries and by encouraging the growth of government-owned corporations, or parastatals, that required huge amounts of capital. These actions came on the heels of dire predictions by the Chamber of Mines that the gold-mining industry would end within forty years or sooner. As early as 1918 fear was expressed that the low-grade mines would eventually have to be shut down for lack of profitability. For decades the big mining houses had discouraged manufacturing for fear it would draw labor from the mines and put pressure on wages. But now the Chamber of Mines forecasts provided compelling reasons for a massive economic restructuring.

Henceforth, South Africa would encourage import-replacement investment as an alternative source of growth. In 1925 Parliament passed a Customs Tariff and Excise Duties Amendment Act that made provision for preference as a fundamental factor in general tariff policy.[66] The legislation marked the introduction of the first genuinely protective customs tariff in twentieth century South African history. It was designed to protect industry rather than to raise revenue and gave protection primarily to the consumer goods sector. The capital goods sector, on the other hand, received relatively little protection.

From this time on, South Africa's protectionist policies had the effect of reducing imports as a percentage of total supply. Undeniably, South Africa's manufacturing sector had been expanding steadily since union in 1910. However, before the Hertzog administration, manufacturing contributed to only 12 percent of national income. In the years ahead, protectionist policies and import substitution would stimulate local manufacturing output.

The Americans were worried by this trend. In 1926 16.7 percent of South Africa's total imports were from the United States while 47.6 percent came from Great Britain.[67] The American automotive industry had made considerable headway in South Africa—indeed, by the end of World War I, the Americans had cornered approximately 80 percent of the country's motor car business.[68] But all vehicles and spare parts were made outside of the Union.

Clearly, the policies of the Hertzog administration presented the Americans with a new challenge. Under the new protectionist legislation American imports were destined to be costlier and possibly less competitive. Thus, with the United States' export position threatened, there was little choice but to establish local manufacturing subsidiaries in order to maintain or expand market share. Americans reasoned that if they did not do this, the British or some other power would. And the labor costs were such in South Africa that products could be manufactured there less expensively than in the industrialized world. The larger American MNCs quickly recognized that through direct investment they could avoid the high tariffs and also be closer to markets and materials. Some American MNCs, notably Ford, which in 1923 had opened its first plant in South Africa, had begun to see the advantages of manufacturing within South Africa,[69] as will be further discussed later.

MOVING UNDER THE AMERICAN FLAG

If the United States hoped to significantly expand the scope and profitability of its trade with southern Africa, and with the rest of the world for that matter, it would first have to develop a larger, more modern merchant marine of its own. It must be remembered that before 1912 American shipowners could not secure U.S. registry for ships built abroad, where costs tended to be lower. Not surprisingly, since the 1870s the United States was heavily dependent on foreign flag services. Indeed, on the eve of World War I, less than 5 percent of the merchant shipping tonnage in the world was American.[70] But the devastations of the war provided Americans with a great opportunity. During the war they carried a large portion of Britain's tonnage with southern Africa because so much of the British merchant marine had been damaged, destroyed, or diverted by German submarines. Afterward, the U.S. merchant marine was still small and inefficient. Only the American Australasian Line operated regular berth service to southern Africa. The small line had been formed by four American merchant companies: H. W. Peabody, Mailler and Quereau, R. W. Cameron, and Arkyll and Douglas, the last having been at the time one of the top export agents and financial risk underwriters for Americans trading with South Africa. Though based in New York, the company maintained South African offices in Port Elizabeth, Johannesburg, and Cape Town,[71] and it also kept offices at the port of Montreal through which a considerable volume of trade between South Africa and the United States passed. Ford vehicles manufactured in the United States as well as in Canada were shipped from Montreal. As recently as 1919 only twenty-six U.S.-registered ships entered South Africa's harbors as opposed to 867 British vessels.[72] Yet the United States was South Africa's second largest trade partner. Clearly, not enough ships existed to meet demand; and to make matters worse, American-Australasian's only steamer to southern Africa sank in 1920. The situation was deplorable and required government intervention.

The Merchant Marine Act of 1920 represented a real turning point in American maritime history. It gave considerable power to the U.S. Shipping Board, a newly created federal regulatory agency, instructing the Board to place vessels on essential trade routes and to find private-sector buyers willing to assume responsibility once things were in place. Government vessels under the Shipping Board were subsequently sold to private companies. In this way the Board disposed many moth-balled wartime cargo ships, but with the proviso that buyers had to maintain scheduled line service on designated routes for at least five years.[73] In 1922 the Board established its own service between New York and the Portuguese port of Beira in Mozambique with a stopover in Cape Town. A year later it relinquished management of the route to the A. H. Bull and Mallory Line, which was renamed the American–South African Line. It was purchased in 1925 by James A. Farrell, Jr., president of the U.S. Steel Corporation, who incorporated it with five ships and eventually transformed it into the famous Farrell Line.[74] Four years later a group of businessmen in San Francisco formed the South African Dispatch Line and began to offer direct service to South Africa from the West Coast.

There were some good economic reasons for American entrepreneurs to consider expanding into African waters. By the mid-1920s the newer ships in transoceanic transportation were powered by diesel engines that were faster and more cost-effective in terms of fuel consumption and servicing. Sailing time between New York and Cape Town was reduced from a rough average of thirty days at the turn of the century to seventeen by 1926—a dramatic reduction from the nearly three-months' time normally logged by sailing vessels as recently as the mid-1890s. In addition large bulky items were now being transported between the two continents: machinery and vehicles from the United States and base metals from Africa.

American commerce with South Africa in the years after 1922 moved increasingly under the national flag. This was in part the result of a variety of government support programs. Government subsidization took a dramatic step forward with the passage of the Jones-White Act of 1928, which increased payments on routes considered economically essential or in the national interest. The act also offered new incentives for domestic shipbuilding and provided for mail subsidies.[75]

Government subsidies played a large role in rebuilding the U.S. merchant marine after 1928. The expansion of the merchant marine stimulated trade with South Africa by enabling American businesses to import heavy mineral ores in ships of United States registry. Thus, the ores of southern Africa could be transported to the United States at a reasonably economical cost. On the other hand, South African protectionism en-

7. Advertisement for the New York–based Mutual Life Insurance Company, 1914. *Source:* W. J. Laite, ed., *Laite's Commercial Blue Book for South Africa,* p. xiv.

couraged American entrepreneurs to engage in manufacturing within the Union in order to remain competitive.

SETTING UP IN SOUTH AFRICA: THE AUTOMOTIVE INDUSTRY LEADS THE WAY

The United States first entered the manufacturing field in South Africa through the automotive industry. In 1923 the Ford Motor Company of Canada set up and incorporated Ford of South Africa, with a capitalization of $960,000.[76] In the same year Ford opened an assembly plant in Port Elizabeth, where an American consulate had been established eighteen years earlier. In many respects this move represented a great turning point in South African economic history. It was the first vehicle assembly line in the country and Ford was the first American-controlled MNC to make the move from an essentially branch operation in South Africa to on-site manufacturing. The Port Elizabeth facility became the distribution point for all of Africa south of the equator as well as Kenya and the British colony of the Gold Coast in West Africa.[77] However, not until after South Africa's swing towards protectionism, from the mid-1920s, were components manufactured in the country. Formerly, all parts were made in the United States or Canada and exported to overseas plants for final assembly.

In response to Hertzog's protectionist policies other American com-

8. General Motors assembly plant, Port Elizabeth, ca. 1928. (National Archives)

panies followed Ford's lead. In 1926 the General Motors Corporation, which had just surged past Ford in world vehicle output, established a wholly owned subsidiary in the country and incorporated it as General Motors, South Africa. A year later, it began assembly operations in Port Elizabeth, and within months of opening it was producing Chevrolets, Oldsmobiles, Pontiacs, and Buicks.[78] The demand by whites for vehicles was enormous, and by 1927 South Africa had become the United States' third largest foreign market for its automobiles. By 1930, 96 percent of all autos registered in the Union were manufactured by American firms. Consumer demand for agricultural equipment was also booming, and in 1927 International Harvester Company opened an assembly plant in Durban.[79] Its competitor, the Caterpillar Company, began marketing its products in 1926 through a local dealership.[80] A series of protectionist laws followed, requiring two-thirds of each vehicle to be of local origin. In this way the automotive industry became a powerful engine for the expansion of the manufacturing sector and the growth of white working-class employment.

The increase in bilateral trade, especially in South African imports, partially resulted from policies of the Hertzog government. It should be recalled that the Nationalists had always been antagonistic to British foreign trade and investment. They struggled to limit British influence in every sphere of life and to develop economic policies that would reduce their reliance on Great Britain. The Nationalists' restrictionist trade practices and their search for new, non-British markets provided an important stimulus to American direct investment. Under Hertzog trade beyond the British orbit accelerated, with the United States providing a rising share of South Africa's imports.

Hertzog and the Nationalists encouraged the state to play a larger role in the manufacturing and agricultural sectors. The government became a major stimulus in the expansion of the iron and steel industry, utilities, and transportation through the capitalization of vast, recently created, parastatals. By 1930 the state-owned Electricity Supply Commission (ESCOM) was supplying nearly 30 percent of South Africa's power.[81] The expansion and modernization of such key industries gave further encouragement to American MNCs to launch manufacturing operations within the country rather than to export and face high tariffs.

The South African economy responded impressively to the new development and trade strategies. Between 1922 and 1929 the growth rate averaged 7.6 percent a year, largely because of great advances in secondary industry.[82] As demand for American products in the late 1920s grew faster than for those of British manufacture, American manufacturers of pharmaceuticals, cosmetics, and toiletries began to take a serious look at South Africa's potential. Merck, the drug manufacturer, began marketing from Johannesburg in 1917. The Colgate-Palmolive Company decided to establish subsidiaries worldwide and in 1929 set up a wholly owned subsidiary in South Africa.[83] Within a few years it had captured nearly 30 percent of the local market for soaps, detergents, and toothpaste. The Gillette Company began operations in South Africa in 1930 with the establishment of a wholly owned subsidiary, which was essentially a marketing operation with a small manufacturing plant. Gillette, founded in the United States in 1901, already dominated the American market in shaving products and in the 1920s had begun to give attention to overseas markets.[84]

THE AMERICAN ASCENDANCY: SEEKING POWER THROUGH GOLD

After World War I New York City emerged as the preeminent international financial center. Formerly, most international transactions were centralized in London, with payments by transfer of bank balances held by English financial houses. International investment banking in the United States had grown moderately, but after the war New York rapidly began to assume functions that had hitherto been the preserve of London, Berlin, and Paris. This assertion of financial responsibility and control was partly a consequence of the United States' accumulation of gold, which, in terms of holdings as a proportion of the world's gold stock, grew from 14 percent in 1897 to 24 percent in 1913 to 44 percent by the end of 1923.[85] By comparison, Britain's had only risen from 3 percent to 9 percent. Over the years the United States had been steadily accumulating gold. From the California discoveries in 1848 to nearly the turn of the century the United States was the world's leading gold producer. But after 1905 South Africa had pushed ahead to the top.[86] In the process the South African economy became heavily dependent upon gold exports as a key earner of foreign exchange. Indeed, by the early

1920s two-thirds of the value of its total exports derived from gold and diamonds.[87]

During World War I the allies had to import enormous quantities of material from the United States and paid for much of it by selling their American securities. This only accelerated the transfer of gold reserves from Great Britain and the European continent to the United States. The gold that consequently accumulated was used to establish an enormous credit structure the Americans used to expand their foreign trade in the 1920s. It should be remembered that financially the war had strengthened the United States relative to Great Britain. When the conflict ended, the United States found itself with a huge foreign trade surplus and unprecedented gold reserves. The British entered the postwar era owing the Americans more than $4.7 billion.[88] Not surprisingly, the United States returned to the gold standard in 1919 and began to develop an aggressive gold diplomacy.

The United States thus found itself in the financial cockpit and sought ways to build an economic order based on a global, market-regulated gold standard. Washington reasoned that only then could the United States maintain economic predominance and hope to control inflationary pressures within the United States. Gold-rich South Africa was viewed as an essential factor in this grand strategy.

Monetarily, South Africa had been closely linked to Great Britain since the early nineteenth century. From 1825 monetary assets in South Africa were convertible into coin or sterling bills. But after the establishment of the autonomous Union government in 1910 the South Africans looked for ways to reduce their dependence on British sterling and to achieve more control over their own fiscal and monetary policies. We have seen that the Reserve Bank was created in 1920 and endowed with a monopoly right to issue currency. From 1922 coins were no longer minted exclusively in London, and foreign exchange rates were no longer always quoted via official sources in London.[89]

The prewar gold standard was in many respects a British sterling exchange standard that gave the United Kingdom a competitive edge. Both the United States and South Africa were anxious to deprive London of its control over foreign exchange transactions. When the United States returned to the gold standard in 1919, it brought pressure on the South Africans to do the same. In late 1924 South Africa invited the American–Netherlands Commission, led by Edwin W. Kemmerer, to investigate the fiscal status of the Union and to advise whether it should return to the gold standard. The Princeton professor and internationally respected financial wizard became the first American to advise South Africa about financial matters. Kemmerer was anxious to establish a direct New York–Johannesburg financial link, thus bypassing London altogether. He reasoned that the United States could expand its trade with the South Africans if it were more clearly linked to the dollar and urged South Africa to return to the gold standard and deposit its gold funds in New York City rather than in London, anticipating that this would eventually lead South Africa into denominating its currency in dollars.[90]

Kemmerer's suggestions were well received by the Afrikaners, but the English-speaking South African bankers, who still dominated the country's economy, were worried. They, and Churchill in London, wanted to unify the British realm under a gold standard set in the United Kingdom. But Hertzog was adamant, and in May 1925, South Africa returned to the gold standard. At the time the United States was the only major country that maintained parity with gold. Thus, South Africa's commodity value of gold was to be determined by the banking policy of the United States. Fortunately for the British, their pound had risen sufficiently against the U.S. dollar to allow them to return to the gold standard, which they did in July 1925. Perhaps the British acted defensively, in reaction to South Africa's decision to return to gold. In any event the Americans continued to accumulate gold in the 1920s; and by 1931 their stock had reached its highest level in history, amounting to 40 percent of the world's monetary gold reserves.[91]

THE LURE OF AMERICAN CAPITAL: SECURING FINANCE WITHOUT LOSING CONTROL

After World War I investors and entrepreneurs in Great Britain and South Africa realized that their southern African operations could not be substantially expanded without American capital. It took no expertise to grasp that the United States had become the primary source of investment capital. And Ernest Oppenheimer, the South African mining magnate, looked for capital to develop his recently acquired gold fields in the so-called Far East Rand. Oppenheimer was already deeply into diamond extraction, and in 1914 one of his key advisers, the American engineer Alpheus F. Williams, had drawn up a comprehensive survey of the South West Africa deposits.[92] De Beers, under Oppenheimer control, acquired the fields after the government seizure of German assets. Clearly, capital was needed for that operation as well.

Investor interest in South African mining was awakened in the final months of the war, for new capital was desperately needed to expand the ailing and antiquated gold mining industry. The London-based Consolidated Mines Selection (CMS) dominated the gold sector and would normally have been in a position to obtain the necessary finance. However, CMS was unable to raise funds because of its prewar ties to Germany. Oppenheimer saw this as a great opportunity, and he became the first South African to look to the United States as a source of capital.[93] He turned to his old friend, W. L. Honnold, a prominent American mining engineer who once served as the manager in Johannesburg of Consolidated's operations. Through Honnold, Oppenheimer was introduced to Herbert Hoover, who had also been involved in South African mining before the war, and it was through Hoover, in turn, that Oppenheimer was introduced to W. Boyce Thompson, an Arizona tycoon who controlled the enormously successful Newmont Mining Company. Thompson was receptive and involved his own bankers, J. P. Morgan and Company, and Morgan's merchant banker in London, Morgan Grenfell.[94] C. H. Sabin of Guaranty Trust Company in New York represented the Morgan interests in the negotiations.

The outcome was the formation in September 1917 of the Anglo-American Corporation. Of the initial £1 million of capital, a quarter was subscribed by the Morgans, a quarter by Newmont Mining Company, and the remaining half by Oppenheimer and his associates.[95] Sabin and Thompson were subsequently given seats on Anglo-American's first board.[96] In addition, a committee was set up in London and New York to work with the central board, with the New York committee chaired by Honnold and a seat given to T. W. Lamont, a prominent American financier, Morgan partner, and friend of Jan Smuts, who had powerful political connections in London and Pretoria.

The arrangement was of historic importance because it was the first participation of American capital in South Africa's gold-mining industry. Indeed, never before had American capital been employed on the Rand, through a formal arrangement. And as Duncan Innes put it, Anglo-

American became the institutional form through which American capital was channelled into the exploitation of South Africa's mineral resources.[97]

THE LURE OF AFRICA'S BASE METALS: ANGLO-AMERICAN RIVALRY

In the prewar period the United States had not taken much interest in the minerals of southern Africa other than gold and diamonds. However, this changed during the war, when American companies started to buy modest amounts of asbestos, fluorspar, and corundum. It was not long before South Africa became the third largest producer in the world of high-grade asbestos.[98] And the United States became an important customer.

The 1920s were marked by the United States' growing awareness of the enormous mineral potential of southern Africa. Soon the United States became the principal source of capital to develop the region's new mineral reserves. Indeed, U.S. foreign investments in southern Africa more than doubled between 1919 and 1928, with substantial gains recorded in mining, manufacturing, and petroleum. However, with the exception of the petroleum and automotive sectors, most equity holdings were not large enough to exert a controlling interest.

When American mining and chemical companies expanded after the war, they tended, as Alfred Chandler put it, to integrate backwards in order to assure themselves of basic raw materials. In the process the primary metals firms sought to gain control over present and potential supplies of ore.[99] Armed with enormous capital resources, modern technology, and an expanding merchant marine, Americans saw southern Africa as ripe for exploitation.

Since mining engineers discovered fabulous lodes of strategic metals in postwar southern Africa, the region was no longer prized for its gold and diamonds alone. Platinum became only one of the many new ores found in commercially exploitable quantity. For the United States and the industrializing West platinum was basic for the production of electrical equipment, magnetos, and munitions. And near the war's end the United States had begun to develop plans to ensure sufficient mineral supplies, including platinum, in the event of a national emergency. Before the war the United States had had to source platinum almost exclusively from Imperial Russia and Colombia. Indeed, the Russians had led the world in platinum production since the great discoveries of 1822 in the Ural Mountains. But now with Russia under Marxist rule a steady flow of this critical mineral could no longer be assured.[100] New sources had to be found, and to the great relief of the United States, they were forthcoming from a region of the world firmly under Western capitalist control. Platinum was not entirely unknown to South Africans. It had been discovered in small quantities on the Witwatersrand in 1892, though it was not until 1923 and early 1924 that commercially exploitable lodes were found in the Bushveld complex of the eastern and western Transvaal.[101]

The United States was also grossly deficient in manganese, an ore that is added to steel to improve its strength, hardness, and ductility. Again, South Africa came to its rescue with the discovery of huge high-quality deposits of the mineral at Postmasburg in 1925. Shipments of the ore to the United States began in 1929 and rose steadily in volume.[102]

American capital poured into South Africa in the late 1920s as speculators made portfolio investments in substantial amounts of Rand Mines Limited stock and in more than $5.7 million of Oppenheimer's De Beers Consolidated.[103] After the war Anglo-American, through its De Beers subsidiary, acquired the confiscated German diamond interests in South West Africa with capital furnished by J. P. Morgan and Guggenheim Brothers.[104] The American participation was no surprise, considering that since the 1890s the United States had been the world's largest purchasers of precious diamonds. But it was German technology that contributed so much to the diamond industry. During the war Germans developed cemented-carbide cutting tools that revolutionized the drilling business. Americans acquired the technology in the postwar years and quickly became important buyers of industrial diamonds for drill bits and grinding wheels.

Copper was also of enormous importance to American industry. During World War I, 80 percent of the world's copper was refined in the United States, which was already far and away the largest consumer of the ore.[105] Copper demands expanded enormously from the 1860s, after telegraph came into wide commercial use. By the 1920s huge amounts of copper were going into the production of tubes, electrical wire, telephones, and electrical motors and generators for motor vehicles, trolleys, and locomotives. The United States had become the great clearinghouse for world copper. By the 1920s American mining concerns were importing most of the world's copper output and refining it on the eastern seaboard. Large portions of the copper were subsequently reexported overseas, mainly to Western Europe. In the industrialized countries the copper market was exploding as a result of the electrification of industries. On the eve of the war two-thirds of European copper consumption was supplied by American-owned enterprises. And yet most of the ore was sourced in the European colonial possessions and British dominions.[106]

American firms were the best organized to play a dominant role. In the late nineteenth century the American copper producers and refiners underwent a process of merger and consolidation that climaxed in the early 1900s. Phelps-Dodge was incorporated in 1908, the huge Anaconda Copper Mining Company emerging two years later. Kennecott came onto the stage in 1915.[107] By 1930 Phelps-Dodge owned a majority interest in Nichols Copper Company, which had been refining its copper for many years. Thus, in the early twentieth century control of copper refining became concentrated in the hands of a very few American companies. The Guggenheim interests alone controlled 45 percent of American output before the Great Depression of the 1930s.[108]

The American Smelting and Refining Company (ASARCO) gained a dominant position in the world of copper refining. It was a huge trust, established with William Rockefeller's capital and designed to compete with the Guggenheim interests. But the Guggenheims acquired controlling equity in ASARCO in 1901.[109] Daniel Guggenheim then hired John Hays Hammond in 1903 for $250,000 a year.[110] We should recall that Hammond had only recently left South Africa, where he had worked closely with Cecil Rhodes and his mining interests. It was Hammond who opened the Guggenheims' eyes to the enormous possibilities of southern Africa. New technologies now made the copper ores of that part of the world commercially exploitable. Most noteworthy was a process developed in 1911 to extract the ore from copper sulphides, which made it possible to work the extremely deep ores of Southern Africa far more profitably than oxide deposits lying near the surface. And it was the discovery by American mining engineers of a vast zone of sulphide copper in Northern Rhodesia that triggered the great boom in southern African output. By 1920 the United States had emerged as the world leader in financing copper exploitation and in the technology of copper production. It had also become the chief producer.

In the process of this struggle for world dominance American firms sought to gain complete control over the pricing structure. Thus, between 1919 and 1923 the major American copper producers operated a cartel, called Copper Exporters, for the purpose of restricting output in hopes of maintaining high prices.[111] Its members accounted for over 90 percent of world production.

Quite naturally, the British saw this as a direct threat to their own interests so they worked to break the monopoly by developing the enormous copper sulphide deposits of Northern Rhodesia. Ironically, American mining engineers were hired to do the job. While British copper interests took immediate steps to open up the deposits for full exploitation, J. P. Morgan and Company and Anaconda were seeking to buy a dominant interest in Union Minière.[112] The Belgian-controlled company was one of the world's largest producers of copper, much of its success being due to P. K. Hoerner, an American who was closely associated with the Guggenheim interests and who had previously served as Union Minière's director-general. Union Minière's major operations were in the Katanga region of the Belgian Congo, which by the early 1920s was one of the world's major copper mining areas. The company was the only serious threat to American control of world copper prices. But in 1923 the Belgians, fearing American domination, refused to budge despite pressure from the Guggenheim group. The resistance was understandable for by that time Guggenheim's ASARCO and the Nichols Copper Company were between them refining in their American plants nearly half of Katanga's copper output.

With the Belgians balking, American attention shifted to southern Africa, particularly to the British Rhodesias. Since the late nineteenth century the British South Africa Company (BSAC) held mineral rights to all of Northern Rhodesia. Before 1912 the Company had given prospecting licenses to a large number of small concerns. But it soon became evident that the extensive exploitation of the ores required outlays of capital and technology that were far beyond the resouces of small companies. Henceforth, mining rights were transferred only to large, highly capitalized firms.[113]

Southern Rhodesia presented a different situation. There BSAC had acquired its mining rights through the Rudd Concession, granted in

1888 by King Lobengula of Matabeleland.[114] As a result, Cecil Rhodes and his company gained a monopoly over the mining of minerals. A year later Rhodes secured for his company a royal charter from the British Crown.[115] Henceforth, the pace of mining quickened, and by 1917, there were over 150 mining companies under license from the BSAC.[116]

In the 1920s American eyes shifted to the Rhodesias, especially to Northern Rhodesia, the scene of discoveries of rich copper sulphide deposits. With American technology the Northern Rhodesian deposits could be mined far more profitably than the oxide copper deposits of neighboring Katanga in the Belgian Congo. In 1921 P. K. Hoerner, who had by then left Union Minière, befriended the American engineer, Alfred Beatty and together they secured a concession.[117] A year later the British South Africa Company amended its mining laws to permit the granting of concessions to large multinational corporations. The Rhodesias were now open to American capital and technology; both flowed in vigorously. Deep test-drilling on the Copperbelt revealed immense deposits of sulphide ores. Consequently, full-scale exploitation of Northern Rhodesia's Copperbelt could begin in earnest. Between 1922 and 1926 the BSAC granted six huge concessions, among them the fabulously rich Nkana concession, which was sold in 1926 to Selection Trust.[118]

The once-touted copper cartel could no longer be sustained, especially after the Guggenheim interests withdrew. But it was no matter because by 1926 75 percent of the world's copper production was under American corporate control. American companies were in a position to influence prices and to make their own production decisions without having to resort to a formal cartel structure.

The groundwork for the exploitation of Northern Rhodesia's Copperbelt was laid by Alfred Beatty. Like so many of the American mining engineers in southern Africa, he was a graduate of the Columbia School of Mines in New York. Beatty, who began his career as an assistant to John Hays Hammond, was one of the first to recognize the rich potential of Northern Rhodesia. In 1914 he formed and largely financed Selection Trust. Six years later he entered the British protectorate of Northern Rhodesia by acquiring an interest in the Bwana Mkubwa Company. Over the next three years Beatty bought up other concessions. Roan Antelope Copper Mines was incorporated in 1927 and staffed mostly by American engineers. A year later he established the Consolidated African Selection Trust. A huge holding company was organized, called Rhodesian Selection Trust, to administer all his Northern Rhodesian interests. Much of the capital for this came from Solomon R. Guggenheim's American Smelting (ASARCO).[119]

ASARCO then tried to buy into Nchanga, the next largest concession. The British, alarmed by what they saw as an American invasion, sought ways to prevent the copperfields from falling completely under American control. In South Africa Ernest Oppenheimer shared this concern, and as a counterweight he formed Rhodesia Anglo-American (RAA) and in a preclusive move purchased the Nchanga concession. RAA subsequently acquired an interest in the Beatty group. Though it was under Oppenheimer's control, RAA was partially owned by Newmont Mining of New York and the American Mayflower Associates. Indeed, Newmont participated in the formation of Rhodesia Anglo-American in 1928 by supplying it with capital and engineering expertise.[120] It was in that year that rich copper deposits were found along the upper Kafue River, in a region that became known as the Northern Rhodesian Copperbelt.

Before the end of the 1920s the exploitation of Northern Rhodesian copper was almost completely under the domination of two companies: the Rhodesian Selection Trust (RST), almost exclusively American-capitalized, and Rhodesia Anglo-American, financed mainly from South Africa and Great Britain but with minority American interests. American capital had been paramount in the Rhodesian Selection Trust since 1927, when the American Metal Company and the Phelps-Dodge Corporation of New York acquired a large interest in RST's newly formed Roan Antelope Copper Mines.[121]

American Metal had an interesting history of its own. It was formed in 1887 by a group of financiers associated with firms in Germany, the United Kingdom, and the United States. But its autonomy as an American firm was established as a consequence of World War I. American Metal gained access to the Copperbelt by acquiring a 43 percent ownership of Rhodesian Selection Trust. It was primarily through American Metal Company that American investors by 1929 secured a substantial, though not majority, interest in the exploitation of Northern Rhodesian copper deposits.[122]

Oppenheimer, whose loyalty to the British Crown was unquestioned, took further measures to limit American control. As Myra Wilkins, the business historian, put it: the British "wanted American capital, but not the capitalists."[123] Business interests in South Africa welcomed American capital for the development of the mining industry but sought to limit American control. Certainly, in the case of Oppenheimer this was quite true. He had already bought up most American interests in the Anglo-American Corporation, and in 1930 he forced a merger of the three major mining companies on the Copperbelt into a new entity, the Rhokana Corporation. Rhokana was under the control of Oppenheimer-dominated Rhodesia Anglo-American. Thus, by 1930 Rhodesia Anglo-American and Belgian-controlled Union Minière of Katanga were the two leading suppliers of copper to the world. Neither one of them, however, was able to secure a commanding position in the refining and ultimate marketing of the product.

By the 1920s Americans had also begun to take an interest in chromium, an ore that is added to steel to give it resistance to corrosion. The resultant stainless steel was in great demand by manufacturers of kitchen equipment, motor vehicle bumpers, surgical instruments, and household flatware. Between 1827 and 1880 the United States ranked first in world chromite output. But production declined steadily, and other countries began to develop their own deposits.[124] Abundant reserves were found in Southern Rhodesia after World War I. By 1922 it had achieved first place in world output and for decades continued to be the largest producer by a wide margin. On the other hand, by 1930 the United States, in the face of an explosive domestic demand for chrome, had become entirely dependent on external sourcing. At the time Southern Rhodesia accounted for over half of the world's production of chrome and was fast becoming a key source for American enterprises.[125] The Americans were also in search of vanadium, an ore whose value lies in its ability to improve the resiliency of steel and to act as a catalyst in the production of sulfuric acid. Since commercially exploitable vanadium reserves in the United States are practically nonexistent, in 1926 two American firms, the Vanadium Corporation of America and the Mutual Chemical Company, formed a joint venture to mine both chrome and vanadium in Southern Rhodesia.

Americans also began to penetrate South Africa's mining sector after World War I, though local South African and imperial interests were more successful in containing this sector. Union Carbide was one of the earliest American corporations to become directly involved when it commenced operations in 1929. American portfolio investment in South African mining companies grew steadily in the early twentieth century because of the high rate of return on capital invested. Much of that capital, however, flowed indirectly to South Africa via firms headquartered in London.

HELPING THE FARMERS

Yankee ingenuity in South Africa extended beyond the fields of mining and manufacturing. In the decades after the Second Boer War Americans played a major role in reinvigorating the South African wine industry. French Huguenots had introduced viticulture to the Cape in about 1688, but by the late nineteenth century the industry was stagnant and wine exports were in full decline. Then, in 1918, through the advice of Californian experts, nearly five thousand wine growers of the Cape were organized into a body called the Cooperative Wine Growers Association of South Africa (KWV).[126] New, more disease-resistant vines had already been imported from the United States, and now more aggressive and imaginative marketing and distributing techniques were introduced by the Americans. William C. Winshaw of Tennessee played an important role in launching the highly successful Stellenbosch Farmers' Winery in the early 1920s. An added incentive for rejuvenating the wine industry was provided by the British, who in 1925 granted a hefty 50 percent preference to Empire wines of the heavy type. This enabled the KWV to enter the export field on very competitive terms. Subsequently, South African's wine industry demonstrated steady growth even though Americans invested little if any capital of their own.

American contributions to agribusiness were not limited to viticulture. In the last chapter I assessed the role played by Pickstone and Lounsbury in laying the foundations of South Africa's fruit industry. In 1925 a Fruit Export Board was established by the government, and in the following year some American experts helped to launch the Citrus and Subtropical Fruit Research Institute in the Transvaal.[127] In the 1930s exports of citrus and deciduous fruits mushroomed and were second only to wool in the agricultural export sector.

Experimentation in African peasant agriculture also occurred at Amanzimtoti in Natal, under the auspices of the American Board of Commissioners for Foreign Missions (AB). In 1920 a three-year agricultural course for training "native demonstrators" and local African farmers was instituted but met with only moderate success. Two years later the Board terminated a short-lived experiment in combining academic high school curricula with courses in agriculture. The predominantly Zulu student body showed little interest in pursuing rural careers. On the other hand, the academic program proved enormously successful. By 1925 a year after the opening of a high school department, the Aman-zimotti school could boast of over two hundred students above Standard VI (last grade in high school) and an active teacher-training program. Clearly, the Board's American Zulu Mission was still the leader in the field of African education in South Africa.

AMERICAN DIPLOMACY: FOLLOWING THE LEADERS

In the early decades of the twentieth century the American flag seemed to follow private American expertise and capital into southern Africa rather than the reverse. Consulates were not opened in Port Elizabeth and Durban until 1905 and 1906, respectively. Then, shortly after the unification of South Africa in 1910, the United States reestablished a vice consul and consul in the four South African provinces, basing them in Cape Town, Port Elizabeth, Durban, and Bloemfontein.[128]

Though the United States and South Africa cooperated on the economic front during World War I, they differed on their visions of a postwar Africa. The United States refused to become a League of Nations mandatory power over any former German colonies, and it opposed South Africa's bid to annex former German South West Africa. South West Africa thus became a class C League mandate under firm South African tutelage.[129] Nevertheless, the United States did not object to South Africa's exploitation of the colony's resources. Indeed, as we have seen, Americans did not hesitate to invest in mining companies operating in Southwest Africa.

Americans in the private sector as well as in diplomatic service in South Africa seemed oblivious to the spate of racially segregationist laws emerging from the new Union government. No apparent opposition was voiced against the Mines and Works Act of 1911, which made it a criminal offense for Africans to strike and excluded them from skilled industrial jobs by entrenching the principle of job reservation on a racially differentiated basis. Nor is there any evidence of American objections to the Land Act of 1913, which had the effect of dislodging African laborers from the rural areas and forcing them into the mines and industry. Apparently, no voices were raised against the Natives (Urban Areas) Act of 1923, which provided for residential segregation and influx control in urban areas throughout the country. And there appears to be no record of dissent over the Industrial Conciliation Act of 1924, which restricted the use of new collective bargaining machinery to whites and coloreds (mixed race) only and did not permit blacks to use it. Generally, whites in the business sector welcomed these discriminatory laws because they reduced the power of black competition in the labor market and rendered African workers more coercible.[130] The major objective of U.S. officials was to promote trade and investment. This sentiment was best revealed in a 1921 communiqué from the consul in Cape Town, indicating that "There are splendid openings here . . . for energetic men with sufficient capital to finance the undertaking and employ the large forces of cheap native labor found in most parts. . . . American capital could be put to splendid use here in the interests of American trade."[131]

After the National party came to power in South Africa in 1924, J. B. Hertzog, the new Afrikaner prime minister, brought increasing pressure on Britain for greater local autonomy. South Africa was allowed to establish its own department of external affairs in 1927. In response, the status of the American consulate in Pretoria was raised to consulate-general.[132] Two years later formal diplomatic relations between South Africa and the United States were established and legations were opened in Washington and Cape Town respectively. The South African legation was headed by the Afrikaner envoy, Eric Louw. Ralph Totten, the American consul in Cape Town, was elevated to minister resident and placed in charge of the Cape Town legation, which was transferred to Pretoria in 1930.[133]

AFRICAN EDUCATION: THE MISSIONARIES

The American Board missionaries in Natal emerged from the Boer War in a financially weak condition. Their operations had never received sufficient support from Boston, and since the 1840s their activities had been funded largely by income drawn from the so-called Mission Reserves, which were lands taken from the vanquished Africans by the Natal government and given to the missionaries. The latter in turn helped set up their Christian converts as tenant farmers and small entre-preneurs. But the missionaries had never been comfortable as landlords and administrators, and they drew resentment from those who worked the soil. Consequently, the Mission Reserves Act of 1903 transferred the administration of the lands to the white Natal government. In return, the Board henceforth received half of the annual revenues from the reserves. Africans could remain on the land but only as tenants. The peasants felt deeply betrayed by this deal because it ignored their long-standing pleas for full ownership.[134] In the following years the American Board followed a kind of apology policy, redoubling its efforts in the realm of education and health care.

It should be recalled that in the late nineteenth century American missionary societies had begun to recognize the need to do more than simply convert Africans to Christianity. Missionary leaders saw that they had to serve broad educational purposes as well and that the process had to occur in both South Africa and the United States. In the last chapter we found that scions of the emerging middle-class rural elites in Natal and in Pondoland in the Transkei were being sent to the United States for higher education. Between 1896 and 1924 at least twenty-two South African students attended Lincoln University in Pennsylvania. Scores more studied in other, mainly church affiliated and racially segre-gated schools.[135] Politically, they gained much from their American experience. In 1912 Charlotte Manye Maxeke, along with John Dube and Isaka P. Seme, who earned his B.A. from Columbia College in New York, played critical roles in founding the African National Congress.[136]

Growing numbers of Africans also gained admission to American-operated schools in South Africa. The American Board continued to lead in the field of African education, especially in Natal province, its historic base. By 1909 the American Zulu Mission consisted of four teacher-training institutes with 466 pupils. In addition it ran seventy-four pri-mary schools attended by 3,566 pupils who were instructed by 108 African educators. No other missionary operation in southern Africa could compare with the American Zulu Mission in terms of size and impact upon African education. The American Board also opened a number of small hospitals that served primarily as nursing institutions. In Durban in 1909 Board physician Dr. James McCord erected a hospital that soon boasted a School of Nursing and a Medical Trainees Program. It was the only institution of its kind in South Africa.[137] At Chikore, in Southern Rhodesia, the American Board started a small clinic in 1904, and in 1912 it opened a teaching hospital at its mission station at Mount Selinda near the Mozambique border, which by the late 1920s had become one of the most progressive teaching hospitals for Africans south of the Zambezi River.

American missionaries were also among the first to recognize and call attention to the deplorable conditions of the recently urbanized Africans. In the early 1920s Dr. Frederick Bridgman of the American Board pioneered in the social welfare dimension of missionary enterprise in South Africa. He was instrumental in establishing the Durban Native Affairs Reform Association, which was the first African welfare organization in the country. On the eve of World War I, Dr. Bridgman became intensely interested in urbanized Africans and their inadequate housing. Shortly after the war he conducted the first nationwide study of living conditions in the urban ghettos. Through extensive lectures and political lobbying Bridgman's pleadings resulted in the first government-supported African urban housing program.[138]

AFRICAN EDUCATION: THE PHILANTHROPISTS

After World War I several missionary societies in the United States took a hard look at their educational programs to determine their relevancy to changing conditions in Africa. The board of the powerful American Baptist Missionary Society in Boston led the way in 1919 by calling upon the newly formed Phelps-Stokes Fund to undertake a massive study of education in the colonies. The fund itself was incorporated in 1911 from a bequest of Caroline Phelps Stokes. Stokes was a granddaughter of Reverend Daniel Lindley, who, it will be recalled, was one of the first American missionaries in South Africa. Her other grandfather, Anson G. Phelps, served as president of the American Colonization Society of New York and was a founder of the American Board.[139] The Phelps family had made its fortune in international trade and mining and already enjoyed a reputation for private philanthropy. The family was intimately connected to the huge Phelps-Dodge Corporation, which from the 1920s played a major role in developing the extractive industries of the Rhodesias. By the time of Caroline Stokes's bequest charitable giving in the United States had become systematized and institutionalized. The country had entered a new era, one of incorporated philanthropic foundations established by fortunes garnered by the captains of finance and industry. As we shall see, these foundations became a new and extremely effective instrument for American penetration of Africa at a time when the federal government's interests and energies were directed primarily to other parts of the globe. Significantly, the Phelps-Stokes Fund was the first U.S. foundation to devote itself specifically to the improvement of education among blacks in the United States and Africa.

In 1919 the Fund's trustees decided to sponsor a massive survey of educational conditions and opportunities for Africans in order to make recommendations to American missionary societies and colonial governments on the type of education most beneficial to Africans and most appropriate to economic development. Chosen to lead the massive study was Welsh-born Jesse Jones, who in 1914 had completed an exhaustive study of black education in the United States. Jones selected James K. Aggrey, an American-educated Ghanaian, as his codirector for the African project. Aggrey was strongly under the influence of the Tuskegee-Hampton model of "practical" education. Jones, on the other hand, was impressed by the ideas of Dr. Charles T. Loram, a white South African educator who had studied at Yale University. Loram's book *Education of the South African Native* (1917) stressed the adaptation of education to the "special needs" of Africans, as defined by the white community.[140] Jones was also influenced by the Jeanes method of rural education, which involved the assignment of mentor-teachers to rural schools where they would work alongside local instructors and attempt to initiate changes through actual demonstrations. 'Learning by Doing' was a catch phrase in the Jeanes concept of education. The Jeanes method also aimed at linking rural schools with their surrounding community.[141] This program for the improvement of schools in rural southern black communities grew out of the Jeanes Fund, established in 1907 by Anna T. Jeanes, a Philadelphia Quaker. Jones believed that the Jeanes approach could be applied to the colonial African scene. Like so many black and white Americans of his day, Jones viewed the problems and prospects of blacks in Africa through an American prism.

Between 1920 and 1921 the Phelps-Stokes Fund sent a fact-finding commission to numerous colonies in sub-Saharan Africa, including South

Africa and the Rhodesias, to evaluate schools, faculty, and curricula. Aggrey and Jones visited a number of African schools and conferred with educators, superintendents, and colonial administrators. The resulting survey, published in 1922 as *Education in Africa,* was the first comprehensive study of the subject. While shying away from a broadside against colonialism, it did offer mild criticism of the lack of emphasis on agricultural education. The commission expressed the need to develop in Africa a genuine appreciation of rural life and values, and it suggested that teachers had to inculcate in African students a sense of responsibility to the surrounding community and its social and economic development. Teachers also had to emphasize character development and instill in their students moral, religious, and ethical dimensions. The Phelps-Stokes report further called for more education in the areas of health, hygiene, soil conservation, gardening, and handicrafts. Aggrey and Jones were convinced that "agricultural education" was in many respects more vital to Africa's future than any other kind and that neglect of it was one of the most grievous failures of missionaries and governments. The report was also one of the first of its kind to give attention to the need for community development as a component of education. Although the commissioners felt that for the near future the greatest emphasis must remain on primary education, they did lament the neglect of higher education by the colonial regimes. Nevertheless, the study's major thrust was in the direction of nonliterary, practical education as a first step in the advancement of Africans.[142]

The Phelps-Stokes commission returned to Africa in 1924 and examined schools in South Africa, the Rhodesias, Nyasaland, and colonial possessions in East Africa. The second tour was financed in part by Rockefeller money, via the Laura Spelman Rockefeller Memorial, and the newly created International Education Board, of which Anson Phelps Stokes was a trustee. Here was a prime example of a relatively poor foundation with bright ideas obtaining research and operational funds from a big "brother." From an early period private foundations developed interlocking directorates and collaborated with each other on a broad range of projects.

The second commission recommended an integration of health and hygiene into all the disciplines, including mathematics. It also suggested that more attention be given to the physical sciences and that extension programs had to be developed to serve the wider community. More forcefully than in the first report, the commissioners criticized the colonial neglect of food-crop cultivation, and they implied that if measures were not taken soon to increase the output and variety of food crops, Africa could ultimately become a food-deficit region. The report commented that "one of the most unfortunate results of the education . . . has been the depreciation of agriculture in Native opinion."[143] Farmers, they argued, must be accorded a higher status and must receive incentives or else future generations of leaders will abandon agriculture and gravitate to the urban centers. Colonial schools, the report suggested, should place less stress on books and more on "learning by doing." The Phelps-Stokes reports represented one of the earliest attempts to address the problem of food production in Africa. Moreover, the second report may have been the first educational study to identify the historic place of women in agriculture. At a time when political leadership in Africa was primarily in the hands of men, it called upon colonial governments to give more attention to the education of women and to recognize their key role in agriculture.

The Phelps-Stokes recommendations were strongly influenced by Samuel Chapman Armstrong, whose educational ideas were put into practice at Hampton Institute from its founding as a school for blacks in 1869. They also reflected the thoughts of Booker T. Washington, the Afro-American educator who in 1881 founded Tuskegee Institute.[144] Both schools were established to provide Southern blacks with a practical, vocationally oriented education. Aggrey, like many American missionary-educated intellectuals in Africa, was deeply impressed with the Hampton-Tuskegee model, and through his visits to Africa with the Phelps-Stokes commission he became its major promoter.[145] Indeed, the Phelps-Stokes commission acted as both a fact-gathering body and a champion in Africa of the Hampton-Tuskegee-Jeanes concept of education. Aggrey, an extremely eloquent spokesman, drew huge audiences in the United States as well as in Africa until his untimely death in the late 1920s.

Historically, the Phelp-Stokes reports constituted the first comprehensive statement of education policy for British Africa. And they resulted in greater colonial government involvement in and support for African education. The Phelps-Stokes Fund remained in the forefront of educational planning in southern Africa until the postwar years. A few— perhaps too few—of their suggestions became basic educational practice. But from the first report the foundation's findings and recommendations drew intense criticism from the Afro-American community. Marcus Garvey, W. E. B. Du Bois, and the black historian Carter Woodson accused Jones of trying to create an obedient, docile, fundamentally conservative black underclass. Many Afro-Americans argued vehemently that the commission's integrity was compromised by the inclusion of Dr. Loram, the white South African educator who was known for his support of racially segregated education. Before the war Loram had studied at Columbia Teachers College in New York and made many friends in the United States. His appointment as the official representative of the Phelps-Stokes Fund in South Africa in 1924 only gave more fuel to the critics.[146]

The Phelps-Stokes approach aimed at avoiding the alienation of educated Africans from their own people and the wider community. Jones spoke rather contemptuously of politically conscious urban Africans, and he predicted that an urban-dominated leadership might result in the neglect of agriculture.[147] On the other hand, Du Bois believed that the reports' emphasis on agro-industrial education was a cynical move to keep blacks down on the farm and to hold them in a subservient position. Du Bois was convinced that Jones really wanted to introduce the southern American system of education into Africa, a system based on caste and with an excessive emphasis on vocational training. Victor Murray, a prominent British educator, agreed, and in a scathing attack on the Phelps-Stokes approach he maintained that "differentiation without equality means the permanent inferiority of the black man."[148]

Criticism persisted well into the century. In the 1970s Edward Berman wrote that the ideas of Aggrey, Jones, and Loram, if fully implemented, would have retarded the process toward black leadership and therefore would have meant that the mass of Africans would be relegated to a caste from which there would be no escape. He accused Jones of attempting to "anesthetize the African . . . from political consciousness through a curriculum which would perpetuate his subordinate status." Berman argued that the Phelps-Stokes reports represented an Africanization of the Tuskegee philosophy and were the educational equivalent of the British administrative policy of "indirect rule."[149]

Unrelenting criticism and colonial-government reluctance to spend sufficient funds meant that the reports' recommendations were nowhere fully implemented. Nevertheless, they did have considerable influence.

Northern and Southern Rhodesia operated two Jeanes schools, respectively, and British Nyasaland and Portuguese Mozambique each had one. None, however, received enough funding to fully implement the ambitious programs. Most observers, then and later, seemed to have overlooked the reports' prescient remarks concerning agriculture. Julius Nyerere of Tanzania attempted to employ the Jeanes approach in his Ujamaa schools, but as in the colonial past, there were never enough funds or expertise to ensure their success. Not until the mid-1980s did African educators begin to redirect their curricula towards agriculture and vocational education. In South Africa the Phelps-Stokes call for greater government involvement in education served as a cruel rationalization in the 1950s and early 1960s for a state takeover of missionary and other forms of private education.

The work of the Carnegie Corporation was considerably less controversial and more profound in its impact. The foundation was chartered in 1911 with a huge endowment from Andrew Carnegie, the steel magnate. Its interest in South Africa began in 1927 with a visit by James Betram of the Carnegie Corporation and Frederick P. Keppel, a prominent American educator. A year later, the Carnegie Corporation launched a five-year $500,000 program for projects in British Africa. Concurrently, the foundation dispatched Milton J. Ferguson to Anglophone Africa to survey the libraries of Kenya, Southern Rhodesia, and South Africa.[150] Ferguson had already gained national prominence as state librarian of California. On tour, he discovered that South Africa had no school for training librarians and had done little to make books in the vernacular available to Africans. Ferguson developed a plan for a nationwide public library system and recommended the establishment of a free public library network open to everyone. He stopped short, however, of suggesting a racially integrated system. Loram, who in 1927 had become Carnegie Corporation's representative in South Africa, cautioned against it for fear of alienating Hertzog's Afrikaner-dominated government. Loram's advice was regrettable because, of the $63,500 in matching money subsequently granted to South Africa for library development, only $17,500 was earmarked for African resources. Ferguson's plan was also introduced to Southern Rhodesia and Kenya. But there, too, a grossly disproportionate amount of funds was committed to the white settlers' needs.

The Carnegie Corporation, an advocate of the Tuskegee model of education, became a chief source of funding for Phelps-Stokes Fund programs in Africa. In 1928, in pursuit of its own goal of seeking closer cultural unity among English-speaking peoples, it established a Travel Grants program, under which colonial officials and professionals from South Africa and other parts of the Anglophonic world were brought to the United States to meet their American counterparts and to give public addresses. Unfortunately, the overwhelming majority of the speakers from South Africa, including Jan Smuts, were sympathetic to colonialism. Thus, what could have been a multiracial forum for the exchange of views on African development became a platform for speakers who were usually advocates of white supremacy.

Nevertheless, the Carnegie Corporation was the first American foundation to recognize the need for interracial dialogue in South Africa. In 1929 it cofunded with Phelps-Stokes the South African Committee on Race Relations.[151] This liberal, multiracial organization evolved into the South African Institute for Race Relations and served as an important forum for moderate whites and blacks. C. T. Loram, the driving force behind its creation, dominated the committee in its early formative years and ensured that it would not engage in political lobbying or become an organ aimed at direct attacks on government policies.

LOOKING AT THE HUMAN CONDITION

American scholars from the early 1920s had begun to engage in serious research on South Africa's social and economic problems. In 1925 sociologist Edward A. Ross, who had recently visited Portuguese Mozambique, published a scathing critique on forced labor conditions and on the system of South African labor recruitment. Three years later the Harvard scholar Raymond Leslie Buell came out with *The Native Problem in Africa,* the first modern study of the plight of black Africans under white economic domination. Over a fifteen-month period in 1925–1926 he conducted field research in South Africa, the Rhodesias, Mozambique, and numerous colonies in East and West Africa. Buell looked into such problems as labor migrancy and urban housing and addressed the gross neglect of agriculture. He assessed the impact of modernization and westernization on Africans and offered practical solutions that might be implemented by the various white regimes. The outcome was a massive, scholarly, well-written, and penetrating analysis, but one that lamentably had little impact in white-ruled Africa or in the United States.[152]

Of greater social impact within South Africa was the American branch of the Young Men's Christian Association (YMCA), which had been operating for some years in Johannesburg. In 1922 the Y sent out a young black American, Max Yergan, to oversee its activities. Over the next fourteen years Yergan transformed the rather staid Y into a more progressive and socially activist organization committed to the idea of moral regeneration through social engineering. Yergan, an intellectual, was one of the first to promote the so-called New Negro, or Harlem Renaissance, schools of thought.[153] During Yergan's tenure the Y worked closely with the American Board missionaries; and in 1924 Dr. Ray Phillips, a Board social worker-cum-missionary, opened the Bantu Men's Social Centre within the YMCA facilities near Johannesburg. The interracial and multiethnic Social Centre offered athletic, educational, and cultural activities for urban African workers. Phillips went on and played an instrumental role in the establishment of the Jan Hofmeyr School of Social Work.[154]

THE NEW AMERICAN INVASIONS: MOVIES AND TOURISM

In many respects American enterprise made its deepest penetration of South Africa through the film industry. It became the key communicator of American popular culture to a country whose masses were only vaguely knowledgeable of the United States. Through the energies of I. W. Schlesinger, the American-born South African entrepreneur, the United States achieved an early and permanent lead in the field of film distribution in southern Africa. In 1910 three major theater owners in Cape Town began buying Edison's film releases from his London office. Three years later Schlesinger purchased the huge Empire Theatre in Johannesburg and established a centralized organization for the distribution of films on a nationwide basis. Eight film exchanges in South Africa were merged into the African Film Trust, a new entity under Schlesinger's control.[155] The Trust was a vertically integrated company, allied with African Film Productions, which distributed newsreels, and the African Theatres Trust, which consisted of a number of financially troubled theaters of the rapidly passing vaudeville era. Schlesinger bought his films in London or New York, showed them in his own theaters, and then rented them out to other houses. South Africans preferred American films because they were longer, had popular stars, and engaged in lavish cinematography.

Six years later Schlesinger was instrumental in introducing William Fox's Movietone News. Largely through Schlesinger's efforts American films by 1925 comprised approximately 90 percent of all motion pictures shown in southern Africa. The British became concerned by this new American invasion and a Quota Law in 1926 set limits on the volume of film imports from the United States. Nevertheless, the Schlesinger family interests continued to dominate the film distribution business in southern Africa for decades. In fact, the Schlesingers became a major world force in the film distribution industry when, in 1929, I. W. secured nearly all the major sound film patents in Great Britain and on the European continent and his brother in New York gained control of a company that held key sound patents in North America.[156]

In the 1920s I. W. Schlesinger also sponsored South Africa's first chain of privately owned radio stations, and in 1930 he formed the African Broadcasting Company. But within a decade the government established a state-owned broadcasting firm, and the pioneering Schlesinger era of South African radio ended abruptly.

The American tourist invasion of South Africa in the 1920s was short though spectacular. Indeed, Yankee tourism was slow in developing, perhaps because of the great time and cost involved in reaching the Cape from North American ports. Moreover, the South African government did not begin to promote tourism until the National Parks Act in 1926. The Kruger National Park, established in 1898, was then greatly expanded and equipped for visitors.[157] Gradually, other parks were added to the Union and provincial systems.

In the United States tours to South Africa were first promoted by the American Express Company. The first cruise tour sailed for Cape Town from New York in May 1928 and stopped over in Great Britain in order to fill the ship with enough passengers to ensure the voyage's profitability. The ambitious luxury tour lasted three months and included South Africa's so-called Big Game Country, which featured Kruger National Park. The extensive itinerary made it an expensive trip, not very profitable for American Express, and certainly beyond the reach of all but the wealthiest Americans. The era of American tourism to southern Africa would not open for another three decades.[158]

THE IMPACT OF MARCUS GARVEY

The pan-African ideas of Marcus Garvey and his New York-based Universal Negro Improvement Association (UNIA) swept through South Africa's black intelligentsia with explosive force in the postwar years. Indeed, Garveyism developed into a potent expression of early black consciousness, especially in the Cape province. South Africans attended Garvey's First International Convention of the Negro Peoples of the World, held in New York City in 1920, and his call of "Africa for Africans" drew an enthusiastic response from a number of African National Congress members, even though very few Congress leaders actually became Garveyites. Nevertheless, by mid-decade at least half a dozen UNIA branches had been established in South Africa and Southwest Africa. Black South Africans occasionally contributed articles to Garvey's journal, *Negro World,* which circulated in Cape Town. In Buffalo, New York, Dr. Theodore Kakaza, a South African expatriate physician, organized a UNIA chapter that became an important, though short-lived, bridge between adherents in North America and South Africa. Initially, government authorities in South Africa tolerated Garveyism because of its call for racial separatism. However, the UNIA was not without its detractors. The African Methodist Episcopal (AME) Church in both countries denounced Garveyism, viewing it more as a competitor than ally. On his 1921 tour of South Africa James Aggrey attacked the Garveyites for moving Africans away from multiracialism. In the United States W. E. B. Du Bois and many Afro-American intellectuals were sympathetic to Garvey's pan-Africanist sentiments but denounced his quest for voluntary racial segregation and for racial purity. As editor of the journal *Crisis* Du Bois condemned the Garveyites. But Du Bois and his own pan-Africanist organization failed to attract as wide a following among the South African masses. Indeed, South Africans played a comparatively small role in the four Pan-African congresses that were held in Europe and the United States in the 1920s.[159]

By the late 1920s Garveyism had acquired political overtones, and the Hertzog regime responded by banning the *New World* and harassing

UNIA members. Garvey was also under attack by the federal govern-ment in the United States, which expelled him from the country late in 1927. By then the movement in both countries was in full decline.

CONCLUSION

The period covered in this chapter was characterized by the United States' rapid and decisive responses first to Britain's exclusionary policies in the aftermath of the costly Boer War and then to the challenges and opportunities posed by the Hertzog administration's strategy of promot-ing national self-sufficiency through the creation of a dynamic domestic manufacturing sector. The United States emerged from World War I as a capital-rich creditor nation well prepared to export capital to South Africa and elsewhere. The postwar industrial boom forced American mining companies to look farther afield for essential ores, and for the first time private American portfolio capital was invested in indigenous and British-based South African enterprises, nearly all of it flowing into the extractive industries. South African entrepreneurs, notably Ernest Oppenheimer, needed capital to revive an aging gold industry and to open new areas for mineral exploitation. Unable to draw fully upon capital markets in war-torn Britain, they hesitatingly welcomed Ameri-can portfolio investments while fighting bitterly to prevent American mining MNCs from gaining majority control over the region's mineral resources.

Americans found the going a bit easier in other business ventures, particularly in manufacturing. The moment was propitious. Heretofore hesitant MNCs were willing to make substantial direct investments in the South African economy in order to preserve and expand their ex-tremely lucrative market share. The larger, highly capitalized MNCs matured rapidly after the war, decentralizing their corporate structures and becoming multidivisional in the process. They developed and mar-keted new product lines and diversified into consumer durables such as home appliances.

As in the past, the Americans proved to be consummate opportunists. Afrikaners had always bridled under British local and imperial economic domination, and Americans thus took advantage of Prime Minister Hertzog's desire to reduce that dependency by manufacturing locally and/or expanding their own marketing networks. This was nowhere more evident than in the motor vehicle, oil, and entertainment industries. The Afrikaners quickly forgot the United States' pro-British activities in the Boer War and embraced Americanism with its populistic rhetoric as an effective counter to the more rigid class-oriented local English-speaking populations. For the emerging Afrikaner businessman in search of self-confidence and identity the United States became a metaphor and symbol of economic modernization, success, and self-reliance.

Nevertheless, while the American business community was modern, or progressive, in its technology and management, it remained deeply conservative in its labor practices and apolitical in terms of its response to the domestic landscape. American businessmen looked askance at emerging urbanized and Western-educated Africans, viewing them as potentially leftist revolutionaries hostile to capitalism and capable of plunging the economy into chaos. Thus, Afrikaner leadership was embraced not only because it looked upon the United States with a mixture of fascination and respect but because it seemed to represent order and stability. Afrikaners symbolized the "rugged individualism" and republicanism that Americans mythologized as being a part of their own historical experience. Moreover, as the rate of urbanization accelerated from the late 1880s, the white-dominated entrepreneurial communities in both countries conducted business within the context of institutionalized segregation—a racial segregation that was crystallizing ideologically and structurally. It is therefore no surprise that so many members of the American business community passively accepted the apartheidization of the economy under the Afrikaner leaders Botha, Smuts, and ultimately Hertzog.

New players and new agenda appeared on the South African landscape after World War I. For the first time, in the 1920s, we see the entrance of private philanthropies as key advisors to missionary societies and colonial governments on such sensitive and controversial issues as the reform of "native" educational curricula and the government's role in African education. This touched off a long and acrimonious debate between and within racial communities in both the United States and South Africa.

If South Africans came to know more of the United States through the dissemination of mass culture within their own country, the Americans learned less about South Africans. Indeed, the news media disengaged from the region after the South African (Boer) War. The amnesia extended to the literati as well. Tragically, the period under study closed on the eve of a withdrawal by Afro-Americans. In both countries the Garvey movement came to be viewed by the white power structure as a political threat that required suppression. Similarly, the paternalistic AME Church ran afoul of its own South African congregations; and after the Bambata Rebellion of 1906 most separatist churches, especially the Ethiopian organizations, had to face increasing harassment from the South African authorities. The AME's Bethel Institute, which opened in 1902 with high hopes of evolving someday into a university for all South Africans, had by 1920 become a victim of American indifference and white South African scorn. The prosegregationist government-appointed South African Native Affairs Commission seemed almost embarrassed by the fact that in its heyday Bethel Institute attracted even a small number of English and Afrikaner students.

Late in 1929 the confidence of the business and financial communities in the United States was shaken to its core by the trauma of the Wall Street Crash. Americans entered the decade of the 1930s on a note of great uncertainty and trepidation. To their surprise, in a world of gathering storm clouds, the South African horizon turned out to be somewhat atypical. In chapter 5 I will first assess the impact of the Great Depression on American–South African relationships and then explore the reasons for the United States' wartime and postwar ascendancy.

NOTES

1. Shepard B. Clough, *A Century of American Life Insurance: A History of the Mutual Life Insurance Company of New York, 1843–1943*, p. 228.
2. W. J. De Kock, ed., *Dictionary of South African Biography*, 2:632. *Report upon the Returns for the Year 1919*, submitted by the Life Assurance Companies, Union Government, U.G. 20/21. (SAL).
3. C. Tsehloane Keto, "American Involvement in South Africa 1870–1915," p. 56. See also Robert Bruce Davies, *Peacefully Working to Conquer the World: Singer Sewing Machines in Foreign Markets, 1854–1920*, p. 137.
4. Alfred D. Chandler, "The Structure of American Industry in the 20th Century," *Business History Review* 43, 3 (Autumn 1969):272.
5. George Koether, *Ingersoll-Rand: The Building of Men, Machines, and a Company*, p. 73. See also "Investor," General Electric, p. 56; Davies, *Working*, p. 137.

6. Ingersoll-Rand, *Quarterly Report* (1st quarter) (Woodcliff Lake, N.J., 1985), p. 7. See also C. W. De Kiewiet, *A History of South Africa—Social and Economic*, p. 159.

7. H. A. Siepmann and J. A. Henry, *The First Hundred Years of the Standard Bank* (London, 1963), p. 329.

8. U.S. Department of State, *Monthly Consular and Trade Reports*, November 1909 (Washington, D.C., 1909), p. 11. See also Myra Goldstein, "The Genesis of Modern American Relations with South Africa, 1870–1914, Ph.D dissertation (State University of New York, Buffalo, 1972), *The Natal Directory, 1910* (Pietermaritzburg 1909).

9. Goldstein, "Genesis," p. 222. See also *Official Yearbook of the Union of South Africa, No. 27 1952–53* (Pretoria, 1953), p. 1933.

10. Thomas J. Noer, *Briton, Boer and Yankee: The United States and South Africa 1870–1914* (Kent, Ohio 1978), p. 100; Goldstein, "Genesis," p. 786; U.S. Department of Commerce, *Statistical Abstracts of the United States*, no. 35, 1913 p. 461.

11. Noer, *Briton, Boer*, p. 99. See also John G. B. Hutchins, "The American Shipping Industry since 1914," *Business History Review* 2 (1954): 110.

12. G. R. Berridge, *The Politics of the South Africa Run: European Shipping and Pretoria*, p. 7.

13. Hutchins, "Shipping Industry," p. 106. See also E. Glanville, comp., *The South African Almanack and Reference Book, 1911–1912.*

14. A. P. Walshe, "Southern Africa," in John D. Fage and Roland Oliver, eds., *Cambridge History of Africa* (London, 1986), 7:563.

15. C. G. W. Schumann, "Aspects of Economic Development in South Africa," in Marcell Kooy, ed., *Studies in Economics and Economic History*, p. 196. See also A. G. Kenwood and A. L. Lougheed, *The Growth of the International Economy, 1820–1980*, p. 219.

16. Ralph W. Hidy and Muriel E. Hidy, *History of the Standard Oil Company (New Jersey): Pioneering in Big Business 1882–1911*, p. 528.

17. Michael Tanzer, *The Race for Resources*, p. 167.

18. "Texaco" *Financial Mail*, September 6, 1986. p. 17.

19. Hidy and Hidy, *Standard Oil*, p. 219.

20. Raymond R. Sekaly, *Transnationalization of the Automotive Industry*, p. 28.

21. Alfred D. Chandler, *Giant Enterprise: Ford, General Motors, and the Automotive Industry*, p. 28.

22. Arthur Pound, *The Turning Wheel: The Story of General Motors through 25 Years, 1908–1933*, p. 174. See also Anonymous, *The Story of General Motors* (Detroit, 1957).

23. Robert Greenhalgh Albion, *Seaports South of the Sahara*, p. 33.

24. Eric Rosenthal, *The Rolling Years: Fifty Years of General Motors in South Africa*, p. 80.

25. L. Scott Bailey, *General Motors: The First Seventy-Five Years of Transportation Products*, p. 16.

26. Mira Wilkins and Frank E. Hill, *American Business Abroad: Ford on Six Continents*, p. 19.

27. Ibid., p. 18. See also Cleona Lewis, *America's Stake in International Investments*, p. 301.

28. Ibid., p. 304. See also C. H. Wendel, *One Hundred and Fifty Years of International Harvester*, p. 19; Fred V. Carstensen, *American Enterprise in Foreign Markets* (Chapel Hill, N.C. 1984), p. 133.

29. B. S. Cutler to W. C. Redfield, "Markets for Agricultural Machinery in South Africa," August 1, 1917, U.S. Bureau of Foreign Commerce, file 220/7/14 (Washington, D.C. 1918).

30. Michael French, "Structural Change and Competition in the U.S. Tire Industry, 1920–1937," *Business History Review* 60, 1 (Spring 1986), p. 66. See also Dick Clark, ed., *"U.S. Corporate Interests in South Africa" Report to the Committee on Foreign Relations*, U.S. Senate, 95th Cong., 2nd sess. (Washington, D.C. 1978).

31. B. R. Mitchell, Comp., *International Historical Statistics*, p. 420.

32. Emily S. Rosenberg, *Spreading the American Dream Abroad: American Economic and cultural Expansionism, 1890–1945*, p. 25. See also E. H. D. Arndt, *Banking and Currency Development in South Africa, 1652–1927* (Cape Town, 1928), p. 396.

33. Mitchell, *International Statistics*, p. 414.

34. U.S. Department of Commerce, I. W. Schlesinger, *"Investments: South Africa,"* file S/620, South Africa, 1920 (NAW).

35. Schumann, "Aspects of Economic Development," p. 168.

36. Cutler to Redfield, August 1, 1917, (DOC).

37. C. W. Harrison, *Harrison's Business and General Year Book of South Africa, 1927–1928*, p. 209.

38. Schlesinger, "Investments."

39. A. B. Lumby, in "The Development of Secondary Industry," Francis Coleman, ed., *Economic History of South Africa*, p. 201.

40. Cutler to Redfield, "Markets for Agricultural Machinery "August 1, 1917. U.S. Bureau of Foreign Commerce. *Report from The Consuls*. Washington, D.C. 1918. p. 19.

41. Carl P. Parrini, *Heir to Empire: U.S. Economic Diplomacy, 1916–1923*, p. 37.

42. Ibid., p. 22.

43. Rosenberg, *American Dream*, p. 57.

44. Ibid., p. 39.

45. Lewis, *America's Stake*, p. 195. See also S. H. Kim and S. W. Miller, *Competitive Structures of the International Banking Industry*, p. 66.

46. Alex Groner, *American Business and Industry* (New York, 1972), p. 97.

47. Parrini, *Heir to Empire*, p. 57. See Also William F. Notz and R. S. Harvey,

American Foreign Trade (New York, 1921), p. 443; C. K. Leith, J. W. Furness, and Cleona Lewis, *World Minerals and World Peace*, p. 147.

48. Mitchell, International Statistics, p. 473.

49. Leon M. S. Slawecki, *The Development of U.S. Foreign Policy Toward South Africa, 1948–1963*, p. 5. See also P. J. Stevenson to A. G. Goldsmith, letter no. 517, June 6, 1922, file 661/34/9 (DOC).

50. Harrison, *Year Book*, p. 143.

51. De Kiewiet, *South Africa*, p. 56.

52. C. G. W. Schumann, *Structural Changes and Business Cycles in South Africa, 1806–1936*, p. 67.

53. Harold van B. Cleveland and Thomas F. Huertas, *Citibank, 1812–1970*, p. 239.

54. Schumann, *Structural Changes*, p. 69.

55. P. J. Stevenson to Director, Department of Commerce Bureau of Foreign and Domestic Commerce, July 20, 1921 (DOC).

56. *Financial Mail*, November 1, 1985, p. 18. See also Price Waterhouse "Doing Business in South Africa," p. 43.

57. *Financial Mail*, November 29, 1985, p. 21. See also Brian Kantor, "The Evolution of Monetary Policy in South Africa," in Kooy, ed., *Studies in Economics*, p. 90; "The South African Reserve Bank: A Survey," *Financial Mail*, (November 7, 1986), pp. 9–50.

58. Parrini, *Heir to Empire*, p. 247; Rosenberg, *American Dream*, p. 25.

59. Ralph Gray and John M. Peterson, *Economic Development of the United States* (Homewood, Ill., 1974), p. 561.

60. P. J. Stevenson to Office of the Industries Division, Pretoria, November 29, 1922 (DOC).

61. U.S. Department of State. I. W. Schlesinger to Fred Fisher, American Consul (confidential), June 30, 1921, file 610/F/M (JPL).

62. "Warm Skies," *Rotarian* (April 1960): 42. Rosenberg, *American Dream*, p. 111.

63. P. J. Stevenson to Department of Commerce, July 7, 1922 (DOC).

64. Kantor, "Monetary Policy," p. 94.

65. Jill Nattrass, *The South African Economy*, p. 27. See also Walshe, "Southern Africa," pp. 576–77.

66. Martin Fransman, "Capital Accumulation in South Africa," in M. Fransman, ed., *Industry and Accumulation in Africa* (London, 1982), p. 246. See also *South African Industry and Trade, 1907–1957: Golden Jubilee Number*, p. 129.

67. S. H. Frankel, *Capital Investment in Africa: Its Course and Effects*, p. 211. See also Harrison, *Year Book*, p. 208.

68. Albion, *Seaports*, p. 32.

69. Wilkins and Hill, *American Business*, p. 193.

70. U.S. Department of State, Despatches from Consuls in Pretoria, 1913 Special Agents Series No. 218 (NAW).

71. H. M. Moolman, ed., *South African–American Survey,* p. 16.
72. *Official Yearbook of the Union and of Basutoland, Bechuanaland, and Swaziland,* p. 207.
73. Hutchins, "American Shipping," p. 114.
74. Albion, *Seaports,* p. 90. See also Edward Chester, *Clash of Titans: Africa and U.S. Foreign Policy,* pp. 97–119.
75. Albion, *Seaports,* p. 11.
76. Wilkins and Hill, *American Business,* p. 122.
77. Ibid., p. 274.
78. *Journal of Commerce* (New York) 220, 16,907 (May 31, 1949):39. See also T. S. Lovering, *Minerals in World Affairs.*
79. Albion, *Seaports* p. 36. See also Wayne G. Broehl, Jr., *John Deere's Company.*
80. *Financial Mail,* October 10, 1986, p. 44.
81. Hugh Murray, ed., *ESCOM: A Leadership Corporate Profile* (Cape Town, 1986), p. 9.
82. Kantor, "Monetary Policy," p. 97. See also Mary Locke Eysenbach, *American Manufactured Exports, 1879–1914.*
83. Groner, *American Business,* p. 246.
84. Ibid, p. 293.
85. Milton Friedman and Anne Jacobson Schwartz, *A Monetary History of the United States, 1867–1960* (Princeton, 1963), p. 396. See also J. Patrick Ryan, "Gold," in U.S. Department of the Interior, Bureau of Mines, *Mineral Facts and Problems,* p. 387.
86. Frankel, *Capital Investment,* p. 241. See also *State of the Union: Economic, Financial and Statistical Yearbook for the Union of South Africa,* p. 318.
87. Ralph H. Blodgett, *Our Expanding Economy* (New York, 1955), p. 847. See also Parrini, *Heir to Empire,* p. 37.
88. Ibid., p. 44.
89. David K. Eiteman and Authur I. Stonehill, *Multinational Business Finance,* p. 42. Kantor "Monetary Policy," p. 67; See also W. H. Clegg, "Currency," *Monthly Journal of the Johannesburg Chamber of Commerce* 25 (March 1925), p. 19.
90. E. W. Kemmerer and G. Vissering, *Report on the Resumption of Gold Payments by the Union of South Africa,* p. iii.
91. Schumann, *Structural Changes,* p. 114.
92. De Kock, ed., *Dictionary,* 1:211.
93. Harry Oppenheimer, "The Anglo-American Corporation's Role in South Africa's Gold Mining Industry" *Optima* 34, 2 (June 1986):81.
94. Anthony Hocking, *Oppenheimer and Son,* p. 77.
95. Ibid., p. 82.
96. Anglo-American Corporation of South Africa, *Third Annual Report of the Director for the Year Ending 31 December 1919* (Johannesburg, 1920) p. 4.

97. Duncan Innes, *Anglo-American and the Rise of Modern South Africa,* p. 92.
98. Leith, Furness, and Lewis, *World Minerals,* p. 176.
99. Chandler, "American Industry," p. 268.
100. Lane to Redfield, April 2, 1917, U.S. Bureau of Foreign Commerce, file 71652/32 RG 40 (NAW). See also R. Lael, "Platinum Policy During World War One," pp. 546–47; Donald A. Brobst and Walden P. Pratt, eds., *United States Mineral Resources.*
101. A. J. R. van Rhijn, "The Importance of the South African Mining Industry," *African Affairs* 58, 232 (July 1959): 229–37.
102. C. K. Leith, *World Minerals and World Politics* (New York, 1931), p. 97.
103. John H. Davis, *The Guggenheims: An American Epic,* p. 97.
104. Robert W. Dunn, *American Foreign Investments,* p. 170.
105. Alex Skelton "Africa," in Willian Y. Elliot, ed., *International Control in the Non-Ferrous Metals,* p. 377.
106. Ibid., p. 400. See also Andrew Roberts, "The Political History of 20th century Zambia," in T. O. Ranger, ed., *Aspects of Central African History* (London, 1968).
107. Skelton," Africa," p. 459.
108. Frankel, *Capital Investment,* p. 94.
109. Davis, *Guggenheims,* p. 114.
110. Ibid., p. 182.
111. Skelton, "Africa," p. 416. See also F. V. Meyer, *Britain's Colonies in World Trade* (New York, 1948), p. 204.
112. S. E. Katzenellenbogan, "The Building of the Benguela Railway, 1900–1931," Ph.D. dissertation (Oxford University, 1968) p. 290.
113. Leroy Vail, "The Political Economy of East-Central Africa," in David Birmingham and Phyllis M. Martin, eds., *History of Central Africa,* 2:203.
114. Stanlake Samkange, *Origins of Rhodesia* (New York, 1969) pp. 68–86.
115. L. H. Gann, *A History of Southern Rhodesia: Early Days to 1934* (New York, 1969), pp. 82–84.
116. Davis, *Guggenheims,* p. iii.
117. Kenneth Bradley, *Copper Venture: The Discovery and Development of Roan Antelope and Mufulira,* p. 79. See also Edwin P. Hoyt, Jr., *The Guggenheims and the American Dream* (New York, 1977), p. 140.
118. Hocking, *Oppenheimer,* p. 143. See also Patrick Manning, "Draft: Notes Toward a History of American Technical Assistance in Southern Africa from 1870–1950" (California Institute of Technology n.d.), p. 24.
119. P. E. N. Tindall, *History of Central Africa* (London, 1968), p. 272.
120. Innes, *Anglo-American,* p. 330. See also B. W. E. Alford and C. E. Harvey, "Copperbelt Merger: The Formation of the Rhokana Corporation, 1930–1932," pp. 336–37.
121. Richard L. Sklar, *Corporate Power in an African State,* p. 48. See also: Lewis, *America's Stake,* p. 244. Manning, "Draft," p. 27.

122. Sklar, *Corporate Power,* p. 48.
123. Mira Wilkins, *The Maturing of Multinational Enterprise: American Business Abroad, 1914–1970,* p. 110.
124. R. W. Holliday, "Chromium," in U.S. Department of the Interior, Bureau of Mines, *Mineral Facts and Poblems,* p. 211.
125. Frankel, *Capital Investment,* p. 266.
126. *State of the Union, 1957,* p. 311.
127. W. J. De Kock, ed., *South African Who's Who: Social, Business, and Farming, 1921–1922.*
128. U.S. Department of State, "South Africa," Publication no. 8021 (Washington, D.C. 1985).
129. See R. Hyam, *The Failure of South African Expansion, 1908–1948* (London, 1972).
130. Muriel Horrell, *Race Relations as Regulated by Law in South Africa, 1948–1979* (Johannesburg, 1982). See also Annual Report of the Native Affairs Commission, 1927, UG 26/1927 (Pretoria, 1928).
131. Kevin Danaher, *The Political Economy of U.S. Policy Towards South Africa,* p. 32.
132. Walshe, "Southern Africa," p. 584.
133. Daan Prinsloo, *U.S. Foreign Policy and the Republic of South Africa,* p. 46. See also U.S. Department of State, Papers Relating to the Foreign Relations of the United States, 1929 (Washington, 1944), 3:847.
134. Fred Field Goodsell, *You Shall Be My Witness,* p. 40.
135. William Beinart and Colin Bundy, *Hidden Struggles in Rural South Africa* (Johannesburg, 1987), p. 117. See also Keto, "American Involvement," p. 202.
136. Julia C. Wells, "Black American Influences in South African Political Thinking: Charlotte Manye Maxeke's Lost Vision," unpublished manuscript (n.d.). See also Thomas Karis and Gwendolen M. Carter, eds., *From Protest to Challenge: Documentary History of African Politics in South Africa, 1882–1964,* 4:81–82.
137. Arthur F. Christofersen, *Adventuring with God: The Story of the American Board Mission in South Africa.* See also Oscar Dhlomo "A Survey of Some Aspects of the Educational Activities of the American Board in Natal As Reflected in the History of Amanzimtoti, 1835–1956."
138. Anonymous, "The Advance of the Rhodesian Mission," file S/AD 804, 1953 (NAZ). See also Department of Agriculture, Annual Report, Southern Rhodesia, Year ending June 30, 1922, file S/AA 241, 1922 (NAZ); George P. Ferguson, *The Builders of Huguenot* (Cape Town, 1932), p. 64; Anonymous, "Frederick Brainerd Bridgman," p. 19.
139. Thomas Jesse Jones, *Educational Adaptations: Report of Ten Years' Work of the Phelps-Stokes Fund, 1910–1920,* p. 11.
140. Charles T. Loram, *Education of the South African Native* (Cape Town, 1917.).

174 *American Enterprise in South Africa*

141. D. Flood, "The Jeanes Movement," *NADA* 10, 3 (1971):15. See also Norman Atkinson, *Teaching Rhodesians: A History of Educational Policy in Rhodesia* (London, 1972).
142. Thomas Jesse Jones, *Education in Africa: A Study of West, South, and Equatorial Africa by the African Education Commission, Under the Auspices of the Phelps-Stokes Fund and Foreign Mission Societies of North America and Europe* (New York, 1922), p. 10.
143. Thomas Jesse Jones, *Education in East Africa: A Study of East, Central, and South Africa*, p. 72.
144. Kenneth James King, *Pan-Africanism and Education: A Study of Race Philanthropy and Education in the Southern States of America and East Africa*, p. 49; Sylvia Jacobs, *The African Nexus: Black American Perspectives on the Partitioning of Africa, 1880–1920*, p. 147.
145. Edwin W. Smith, *Aggrey of Africa: A Study in Black and White*, p. 143. See also L. H. Ofosu-Appiah, *The Life of Dr. J. E. K. Aggrey* (Accra, 1975).
146. Paul B. Rich, *White Power and the Liberal Conscience: Racial Segregation and South African Liberalism* (Johannesburg, 1984), p. 19.
147. King, *Pan-Africanism*, p. 29. For a more sympathetic analysis of the foundation, see L. J. Lewis, *Phelps-Stokes Reports on Education in Africa*.
148. A. Victor Murray, *The School in the Bush: A Critical Study of the Theory and Practice of Native Education in Africa*, p. 309.
149. Edward H. Berman, "Educational Colonialism in Africa," in Robert F. Arnove, ed., *Philanthropy and Cultural Imperialism*. See also Edward H. Berman "Education in Africa and America: A History of the Phelps-Stokes Fund, 1911–1945," Ph.D. dissertation (Columbia University, 1969); R. Hunt Davis, "Charles T. Loram and the American Model for African Education in South Africa," in Peter Kallaway, ed., *Apartheid and Education*, p. 111.
150. Milton J. Ferguson, *Libraries in the Union of South Africa, Rhodesia and Kenya Colony*. See also Merle Curti, *American Philanthropy Abroad*, pp. 321–22.
151. Rich, *White Power*, p. 18.
152. Raymond Leslie Buell, *The Native Problem in Africa* (New York, 1928). For Ross, see Peter Wickens, *Africa, 1880–1890* (New York, 1986), p. 150.
153. David Anthony, "Max Yergan and South Africa," manuscript (n.d.). See also Max Yergan, *Golden Poverty in South Africa* (New York, 1938).
154. Peter Duignan and L. H. Gann, *The United States and Africa*, p. 235.
155. Thelma Gutsche, *The Historical and Social Significance of the Motion Picture in South Africa, 1895–1940*, p. 326.
156. Kristin Thompson, *Exporting Entertainment: America in the World Film Market, 1907–34*, p. 46.
157. *The Kruger National Park: Hints and General Information* (Pretoria, 1933).

158. Krysko (Coca-Cola Corporation) to Hull, correspondance, April 4, 1986. See also Alden Hatch, *American Express: A Century of Service*, p. 145. See also *Anonymous, Promises to Pay: The Story of American Express Company* (New York, 1977), p. 243.
159. John H. Clarke, ed., *Marcus Garvey and the Vision of Africa* (New York, 1974), pp. 163–80. See also Robert A. Hill and Barbara Blair, eds., *Marcus Garvey: Life and Lessons* (Berkeley, 1987), pp. 311–19; Tony Martin, *The Pan-African Connection: From Slavery to Garvey*, passim.

FIVE

America's Ascendancy, 1930–1960

This chapter commences with an assessement of the critical role of gold and monetary policies in insulating South Africa from the ravages of the Great Depression and in shaping the country's relationship with the United States. It also examines the shift in the British Empire in the early 1930s towards more protectionist trade policies and the American responses to it. During World War II and its immediate aftermath United States–South African relations reached a great turning point. The chapter describes how the various strategies employed by the United States to restructure the postwar global economy created fundamentally new and unprecedently auspicious conditions for American trade and investment in South Africa and in the region as a whole. It surveys the restructuring of the South African economy in the decade after the Nationalists' rise to power in 1948 and the ways it stimulated the flow and determined the nature of American trade, technology, loans, and direct investments. The chapter also assesses the effects of the Cold War and Korean conflict on this rapidly evolving bilateral relationship and how the United States' almost obsessive fear of future strategic minerals deficits drew the country more deeply into the South African economy and compromised its ability to formulate policies consistent with concerns over that government's implementation of apartheid and more extensive repression of its black population. South Africa had never been an independent concern of U.S. corporate and foreign policy. Indeed, Americans did not look at South African issues on their own merits or demerits, but considered instead how the country fit into wider British and East-West relations. While the United States' economic and cultural engagement with the country intensified, the missionaries, who had been the traditional arm of American culture in South Africa for over a century, began an agonizing process of disengagement. But in the missionary twilight were glimmerings of a new corporate dawn.

IMPACT OF THE GREAT DEPRESSION

The early 1930s in South Africa and in the United States were marked by an accelerating trend away from economic liberalism and towards economic nationalism. The financial malaise and uncertainties of the early 1930s sparked the collapse of the multilateral trade and payments system that had emerged in the late nineteenth century. In the United States the economic depression that had begun in late 1929 deepened in the early months of 1930. In June Congress enacted the Smoot-Hawley bill in hopes of protecting domestic industry by imposing high duties on a broad range of imports. Smoot-Hawley, one of the highest tariffs in American history, was also the last one set unilaterally by Congress. But instead of rejuvenating industry, it contributed to a massive contraction in international trade and provoked retaliation from the United States' major trading partners, especially Canada and Great Britain.[1] At the Imperial Conference in Ottawa in July 1932 a series of trade agreements were negotiated among members of the British Commonwealth for reciprocal tariff preferences. The system of imperial preferences, now extended and strengthened, posed an enormous challenge to U.S. trade with sterling-zone countries, including the Union of South Africa.

South Africa had already moved into a protectionist mode. Since 1924 the Nationalist-Labor Pact government under Hertzog had pursued a determined policy of greater self-sufficiency through industrialization. The government itself represented an alliance between white English-speaking blue-collar labor and white Afrikaner-dominated rural capital. The prospect of economic depression only deepened the regime's resolve to protect itself from external forces.

The tidal waves of the Great Depression did not roll into South Africa until late 1930. But within a year the total value of exports fell by a quarter. Diamond sales almost collapsed, local agricultural prices weakened, and overall government revenues plunged precipitously. The regime quickly responded with a series of protective measures, beginning with the 1931 Export Subsidies Act, which remained in force until 1937.[2] Import duties were placed on a broad range of consumer goods and the government plowed more than £11 million into export subsidies. In 1931 South Africa also rushed through a Flour and Meat Importation Restriction Act, followed four years later by the Wheat Industry Control Act, laws that served to increase the country's food self-sufficiency by substantially reducing purchases of costly American wheat.

The economic depression in the northern hemisphere deepened in 1931. The collapse of the Austrian banking system that year sent spasms of fear and uncertainty into the world financial community and contributed to the decision of many trading nations to abandon the gold standard and to devalue their currency. Britain went off the gold standard in September 1931, thus dropping the link between its currency and gold. The pound sterling, now freely floating like a balloon out of control, fell like a boulder from $4.86 to $3.25.[3] This contributed to a precipitous worldwide drop in prices, particularly for commodities. It can be argued that it also was partially responsible for falling incomes and profits, which in turn led to recurring waves of cuts in production, employment, and prices.

Britain's abandonment of gold led to a unprecedented bullion outflow from the United States, which had been accumulating gold for more than forty years. In 1931 the nation's gold reserves stood at their highest level in history, amounting to 40 percent of the world's monetary gold stock.[4] Britain's dramatic shift in monetary policy presented challenges and great dangers to Americans as well as to South Africans. In South Africa investors withdrew their capital and sent it overseas in desperate expectation that if the government followed Britain's lead, their funds could be repatriated at considerable profit. For some, it must have seemed like a self-fulfilling prophecy. In December 1932 South Africa left the gold standard and devalued its currency in an effort to stem the alarming and unprecedented capital flight.[5] In this agonizing process gold coins were withdrawn permanently and bank notes were no longer convertible into bullion. The Reserve Bank greatly expanded its role in the economy by acquiring sweeping powers over currency and foreign exchange dealings. These unprecedented measures led to the stirrings of the country's economic recovery early in 1933. But even more important to South Africa's ability to pull itself out of depression quickly were the monetary policies of the Roosevelt administration.

The United States depression reached its nadir in March 1933. World trade seemed frozen in place, and the domestic and international banking systems hovered on the brink of collapse. The nation's bullion-based circulatory system lay in full hemorrhage. Within weeks newly elected President Roosevelt suspended gold payments in the mistaken belief that if gold prices rose, commodity prices would automatically follow.

Roosevelt's abandonment of gold marked an end of the gold standard in the United States. The general discontinuation of the gold standard by key trading nations had the immediate effect of lowering the volume of global lending and contributing to the emergence of regional currency blocs. The Americans had to face the uncomfortable fact that loans floated in London would be largely confined to British Commonwealth members who operated within the sterling zone.[6]

The deepening crisis in trade demanded a substantial modification in Roosevelt's monetary strategies. In 1934 the U.S. dollar was devalued by raising the official price of gold from $20.67 an ounce, where it had been for years, to $35.00. Gold trading was resumed, though by law only between central banks, not private citizens. From that time until the end of World War II exchange rates were determined by each currency's value in terms of gold. Only the U.S. dollar, however, was convertible into the yellow metal. With these reforms in place the government resumed the stockpiling of bullion, with gold reserves at Fort Knox, the main repository, rising in the process from $7.4 billion to $11.3 billion between 1934 and 1937. With more than half of the world's monetary reserves in its vaults, the United States was poised to penetrate overseas markets aggressively.[7]

Globally, gold prices soared in response to the abandonment of the gold standard and the attendant monetary reforms made by Great Britain, South Africa, and the United States. South Africa greatly expanded its gold output because production costs were considerably less than the new U.S. fixed price of $35 per ounce. Washington's demands for gold soared, and in 1939 South Africa made its first direct shipment of bullion to the United States.[8]

AN ENVIED RECOVERY

South Africa benefited enormously from American gold purchases and from the general rise in gold prices. Its protectionist trade policies and the return of normal rainfall by late 1933 had set the economy along the road to recovery. The strong price of gold insulated South Africa's economy from the full force of the world depression. The metal's dramatic ascent, rising in value by nearly 50 percent between 1932 and 1933, sparked off an enormous expansion of the extractive industries. The foreign exchange obtained from gold exports also played a major role in financing the extensive importation of capital goods needed for the burgeoning industrial sector. Moreover, it enhanced the government's ability to borrow in local and foreign financial markets and to finance the diversification of the economy into manufacturing and services.

Never before had South Africa employed with such determination and effect the instruments of quotas, tariffs, and direct subsidies to expand local industry. Its policies were clearly directed at import replacement and the use of local materials. From 1933 South Africa entered a period of rapid industrialization and rising consumer demand that continued almost without interruption to 1951. Between 1933 and 1939, when most of the industrialized world still staggered under the weight of economic depression, South Africa's GDP rose an astonishing 67 percent while the retail price index increased by a modest 7.2 percent.[9] Few countries in the world could have boasted of such glittering statistics. Not surprisingly, in 1936 the American magazine *Businessweek* portrayed South Africa as "one of the most spectacular markets in the world."[10]

South Africa's trade policies were designed to foster import replacement and to encourage the utilization of local materials. The regime relaxed its restrictions on the import of capital goods and looked to the United States as an important supplier. Crippled by depression, the United States was taking little more than 1 percent of South Africa's exports. The trade balance had almost always been in the United States favor, and now, just when the Americans desperately needed markets, South Africa was there, ready and willing to buy. Already, by the close of 1934, 17 percent of South Africa's imports were from the United

States. Britain worried over this trend and was even more alarmed by the prospect of losing South Africa as an inexpensive supplier of raw materials, Thus, in 1932, as a result of the Ottawa Conference, South African goods were allowed to enter Britain duty-free.[11] It is therefore little wonder that in the 1930s the United States rarely took more than 1 percent of South Africa's direct exports.

Economic and political nationalism raged in white South Africa in the 1930s. After the 1933 general elections, J. B. Hertzog and Jan Smuts formed a coalition government, with the former serving as prime minister and the latter as deputy prime minister and minister of justice. Britain's economically weakened condition encouraged Hertzog to press even more vigorously for greater self-determination for white South Africa. Early in 1934 Britain budged by passing the Status of the Union Act, which affirmed the position of the Union of South Africa as a "sovereign independent state" with the right to conduct its own foreign policy. South Africa thus achieved the status of a sovereign country, or Dominion, within the British Empire. Its only juridical tie with the mother country lay with the British monarch, who served as titular head of state. Henceforth, acts of the British Parliament in London were not valid in South Africa unless enacted by the South African Parliament as well.[12]

Hertzog, confident of South Africa's new-found independence from Great Britain, allowed his National party to fuse in September 1934 with Smuts's South African party into a new grouping, the United party. Through the so-called Fusion government that followed, the English-speaking white community, which historically controlled most major businesses and financial houses, entered into an era of cooperation with the entrepreneurial elements in the Afrikaner community. The more conservative Afrikaner MPs, who tended to reflect the views of the blue-collar workers and farmers, hived off under Dr. Daniel F. Malan and formed a Purified Nationalist party, consisting overwhelmingly of lower-middle-class Afrikaners.

The confident Afrikaners also pushed vigorously for greater control over their economic destiny. In the same year Volkskas was established as the first Afrikaner-controlled bank and was designed to provide capital to fledgling Afrikaner enterprises. During the second half of the 1930s domestic banks and finance houses, including Volkskas, increased their liquidity and injected locally formed capital into mining and manufacturing. The results were stunning: South African equity in mining shares grew from 14 percent in 1913 to nearly 40 percent by 1937.[13]

As the economy expanded, so did government revenue and public funds for the development of the country's infrastructure. In the process the government assumed a more interventionist role. Greater state aid was made available to white farming, manufacturing, and mining. New parastatals were created and older ones were strengthened. The almost decade-old Iron and Steel Corporation (ISCOR) finally came into production in 1933. The Electricity and Supply Commission (ESCOM), a state power utility established in 1923, was enlarged and soon supplied South Africa with nearly a third of its power.

THE GROWTH OF AMERICAN INVESTMENTS

South African demand for American consumer goods accelerated in the 1930s despite uncertainties in the world economy. Possibly through film, South Africans acquired a taste for American products, which undoubtedly contributed to the resurgence in U.S. trade and investment. Merchandise imports from the United States grew from $22 million in 1933 to $89 million in 1937 and soared to $187 million four years later.[14] By then, more than half of the country's non-British imports came directly from the United States and an even larger volume arrived indirectly from American-owned subsidiaries in the British Isles and Canada. American investors had also begun to discover the South African market, and by 1938 their long-term investments in the country had reached $72.9 million.[15]

As World War II unfolded, the book value of U.S. direct investments in southern Africa exceeded its level of 1929. This was quite extraordinary because overall American direct investments overseas actually declined in most regions of the world between the Great Depression and the outbreak of war. By 1943 American-owned assets in South Africa alone reached $86.6 million, including $50.7 million in direct investments.[16]

By effecting sweeping reforms in its trade policies in 1934, the United States was able to take advantage of South Africa's early economic recovery and its desire to diversify away from Great Britain. The economic depression of the early 1930s took an enormous toll on America's commerce with South Africa and the entire world, for that matter. In an effort to restart international trade, Roosevelt rushed the Reciprocal Trade Agreements Act through Congress in 1934. For the first time in history the executive branch was empowered to reduce U.S. tariff levels on a bilateral basis in exchange for a reduction of tariffs on goods exported by the United States. By giving the president the right to enter into bilateral trade negotiations, Congress relinquished its own authority to set individual tariff rates. The Reciprocal Trade Agreements Act, which was presented to Congress as an emergency measure to revive U.S. exports, provided the legislative basis for the U.S. trade policy for the next twenty-eight years.

The United States' expanding trade, especially in oils, metals, and heavy vehicular and mining equipment awakened the U.S. government to the need for enlarging and modernizing its long-neglected merchant marine. American shipping underwent a fundamental reorganization as a result of the Merchant Marine Act of 1936,[17] key legislation that launched a cargo ship construction program and led to the establishment of a highly organized, well-equipped cargo service along the major sea lanes of the world. Much of the impetus for this dramatic growth came from James Farrell, former president of the United States Steel Corporation, who in 1925 established the first regular steamer service to South Africa under an American flag. Farrell's American–South African Line, which had been in operation since 1925, provided the first refrigerated freight service between the United States and South Africa in 1936. The eastern seaboard was supplied with South African lobster, fruit, and wines. Farrell also began operating a twelve-passenger vessel between New York City and Cape Town.[18] Other American lines followed Farrell's lead in the field of freight. Lykes Brothers, the big Gulf operator, began services to South Africa in 1933, though not on a regular basis for another eight years. Two years later an independent operator, the Seas Shipping Company, entered the U.S–South African trade on a nonconference basis and ran its Robin Line with monthly sailings to Cape Town.

South African prosperity was reflected by a growing demand for personal-care products. In 1930, the Johnson and Johnson Company of New Jersey began marketing hospital supply and baby-care products while Colgate-Palmolive found eager consumers for its toiletries. Initially, their products were distributed to local retail stores through

"Greatest Car I've Ever Driven"

"Like An Airplane"

"Amazing Comfort and Balance"

"Remarkable Gasoline Mileage"

These are just a few of the many comments about the New Ford Eight. You'll be even more enthusiastic when you drive it.   Words can't begin to describe the thrill of its performance.

Have you heard about the speedometer? The top figure is now 90, instead of 80. You can go places—quickly—in the New Ford Eight.   It's comfortable, too!

THE NEW FORD EIGHT

There is also a new Ford Four with new speed, new comfort, new beauty, new smoothness and new economy. Have you driven it?

STEYNS GARAGE, LIMITED,

274 St. Andries Street, Pretoria.   'Phones 1940-41.

9. A South African advertisement for Ford automobiles, 1933. *Source: The Kruger National Park: Hints and General Information* (Pretoria: Government Printer, 1933), p. 2.

wholesalers. South Africa's new-found prosperity also stimulated demand for beverages, and here too American entrepreneurs quickly responded. In 1930 the Coca-Cola Company of Atlanta, Georgia, formed an export corporation and began to market aggressively overseas. Coke was soon introduced to South Africans, and its popularity led to the opening of a Coca-Cola office in Johannesburg in 1938.[19] Coca-Cola was possibly the first American company to establish joint ventures with local entrepreneurs as a vehicle for market penetration. Though the patented syrup and concentrates were shipped to South Africa from New York, local companies were given full responsibility for bottling and distribution.

South African demand for American products was perhaps best demonstrated by the success of the corporate-rating services. R. G. Dun and Company had been offering credit services to South African banking, commercial, and insurance interests since the turn of the century. However, their South African operations were greatly expanded and assumed a dominant position in the field after their acquisition of the venerable Bradstreet Company in 1933. In the years ahead Dun and Bradstreet played an important role in building domestic business confidence in American companies and their products.

Popular consumer interest in American products was further kindled by explosive growth in the distribution of American films. The 1930s witnessed the beginnings of American direct investment in South Africa's entertainment industry. We must recall that on the eve of World War I, I. W. Schlesinger, the American-born entrepreneur, had begun distributing American films to local vaudeville theaters. Then, after the Wall Street Crash of 1929, the major movie companies in the United States were reorganized and recapitalized under new leadership. They embarked on a vigorous program of overseas expansion, in many cases building their own theaters and taking over the distribution of their own films. Anticipating the challenge, South African companies that had been distributing American films were amalgamated in 1931 into two large enterprises: African Consolidated Theatres and African Consolidated Films. A year later Metro-Goldwyn-Mayer (MGM) entered the country and established its own distributing agency in Johannesburg. Formerly, most of its films were released through Union Theatres, an agency controlled by Schlesinger family interests. MGM then constructed a chain of large theaters, employing the designs of Thomas W. Lamb, a renowned theater architect in the United States who was responsible for many of New York's most opulent cinemas.[20]

Competition for this extremely lucrative business intensified after U.S.-based Twentieth Century Fox set up a South African-incorporated subsidiary in 1937. William Fox, one of the great pioneers of the American film industry, had lost control over the Fox Film Corporation shortly after the Crash, and in 1935 the firm merged with Twentieth Century Pictures to become Twentieth Century Fox. Between 1939 and 1940 the new enterprise constructed a number of theaters in South African cities for the exclusive showing of its films.

By the early 1930s Hollywood's films commanded larger audiences than their British counterparts, and by the end of the decade MGM and Twentieth Century Fox had achieved almost complete domination over the field of film distribution in South Africa.[21] Their influence and distribution had also begun to extend into the Rhodesias. So profitable was the business that by World War II American-produced films had become a major export to the region.

American record companies also enjoyed a full measure of success. Columbia Records opened a branch in Johannesburg in the early 1930s and in 1932, Gallo, a distributor for U.S. firms, set up the first recording studio in South Africa.[22] To an unprecedented extent and with breathtaking speed southern Africans of all races were exposed to American popular culture through film and records. With little effort the U.S. had secured an important place in South Africa's entertainment industry.

Even more lucrative gains were made in the transportation and petroleum sectors. By the mid-1930s, South Africa had become the seventh largest market for American auto parts and accessories and was the top purchaser of American passenger cars outside of North America. The number of licensed motor vehicles in South Africa rose from 86,000 in 1926 to an astounding 280,000 a decade later.[23] In 1937 Ford alone sold a record 9,829 vehicles in South Africa. By the eve of World War II 83 percent of the autos sold in South Africa were manufactured by American companies.[24]

The Firestone Tire Company of Akron, Ohio, with its vast rubber plantations in Liberia, West Africa, was well positioned to penetrate the African market. In 1936 it opened a tire and tube factory in Port Elizabeth and became the first American tire manufacturer in sub-Saharan Africa, second only to the British Dunlop Tyre Company.[25]

10. Harley-Davidson motorcycles on display, Durban, ca. 1929. (National Archives)

Expansion in automotive and tire production had an impact on the demand for petroleum. After dramatic growth in the 1920s and severe competition for global markets the American petroleum industry experienced a decade of corporate restructuring that ensured its continuing domination over the markets of southern Africa. Without this transformation the lead in oil distribution would undoubtedly have passed to the British. The explosion in the number of motor vehicles worldwide and rising demand, especially in South Africa, for fuel oil to furnish power for industrial plants and transport spurred competition among the oil producers. This occurred at a time of considerable turmoil in the world's petroleum industry. Global competition for oil in the years after World War I became so ruinous that the world's major petroleum companies adopted an oligopolistic strategy in order to preserve their hegemonic position. In the process resources and markets were shared or divided through the creation of joint ventures.

In 1931 the powerful Socony-Vacuum Company (later Mobil Oil) was created out of a Supreme Court-approved acquisition of the Vacuum Oil Company by Standard Oil of New York.[26] Vacuum already controlled an extensive marketing network in South Africa. The process of corporate consolidation was taken a step further in 1933, when Socony-Vacuum and Standard Oil of New Jersey formed a fifty-fifty joint venture, incorporated in the following year under the name Standard Vacuum Oil Company, or Stanvac. This was done to increase the efficiency of its overseas operations. Jersey and Socony turned over to Stanvac all of the producing, refining, transporting, and marketing interests south and east of Suez. Faced with this new and potentially dangerous competition, the Texas Oil Company (Texaco) formed a joint venture in 1936 with Standard Oil of California, called the California Texas Oil Company, or Caltex. By then, the Americans, mainly Stanvac and Caltex, were supplying South Africa with nearly 66 percent of its gasoline and more than 85 percent of its lubricating oils.[27]

The American oil companies had traditionally exported petroleum products from refineries in the United States and the Dutch West Indies. But as the Middle East operations of British Petroleum and Dutch Shell grew, American firms found the competition much tougher, and they too began to secure drilling concessions.[28] Standard Oil of California and Texaco formed a cooperative in Middle East oil production, and in 1936 they built a refinery in Bahrain. Within a year South Africa was being supplied mostly from the Middle East, first out of the Bahrain refinery and soon from Saudi Arabian installations as well. By then nearly all of southern Africa's gasoline supplies originated in the Middle East, especially the Persian Gulf. British Petroleum and Royal Dutch Shell, also in South Africa, though on a smaller scale, were unable or unwilling to meet the challenge. The American position was strengthened in 1940 when Caltex Africa was incorporated in South Africa in order to handle sales formerly controlled by Texaco.[29]

THE UNITED STATES' NEW MINERAL QUEST

South Africa had greatly expanded and diversified its own mineral output and by the 1930s had become a major source of strategic minerals. Surely gold was not all that glittered in the 1930s. From 1934 South Africa and Canada led the world in the production of platinum-group metals and greatly increased their share of manganese output. South African manganese production soared, and by 1938 Nazi Germany and the United States, both deficient in the strategic ore, had emerged as South Africa's top purchasers.[30] Vanadium production was also increased to meet exploding world demand. One of the largest mines was operated by the South-West Africa Company, which was half-owned by the New York-based Vanadium Corporation of America.[31]

The United States' rush for southern Africa's minerals must be viewed in the context of the country's evolution of thinking about minerals as a vital element in national defense. Interest in overseas mineral sourcing developed out of a growing awareness of the finiteness of domestic supplies. In the 1880s and 1890s U.S. dominance weakened in the production of certain minerals considered essential to industrial and military development. Other countries gradually surpassed America in output as well as in the efficiency and cost-effectiveness of extraction. In the early period this impending crisis was most visible in the domestic production of chrome, which started its descent in the 1880s, at a time when imports seemed to rise commensurately with increases in consumer demand. Previously, mineral shortages in the United States were of little public concern because the nation's natural resources were perceived to be virtually unlimited. Vast tracts of land, much of them owned or controlled by the federal government, still lay unexploited.

American appreciation of the importance of South African minerals did not develop until 1893, after the minicrash of the New York Stock market. Some contemporary observers argued that the fall was brought on in part by a decline in the supply of gold bullion. By 1895, when U.S. gold reserves were seriously depleted, it was not lost upon Wall Street

WET WOOD WILL BURN   *Certainly*

SO WILL "WET" PETROL   *But*

for a quick hot fire there is nothing like
dry wood. And for a quick response to the
spark there is nothing like "dry" petrol.
TEXACO forms a completely vaporised
mixture of air and petrol—a dry gas which
ignites instantly and burns completely.

TEXACO

PETROL AND MOTOR OILS

It's Better because it's Dry.

11. A South African advertisement for Texaco products, 1933. *Source: The Kruger National Park: Hints and General Information* (Pretoria: Government Printer, 1933), p. 6.

that South Africa was emerging as the world's largest producer of the precious metal. By the turn of the century mining engineers like John Hays Hammond and Gardner Williams focused in their writings and speeches on their experiences in South Africa on the importance of gold

12. A South African advertisement for Texaco products in the Afrikaans language, 1933. *Source: The Kruger National Park: Hints and General Information* (Pretoria: Government Printer, 1933), p. 6.

and industrial diamonds to the nation's own fiscal and economic vitality.

World War I generated fears of future extensive mineral deficiencies. The war dramatically increased public- and private-sector demands for a wide variety and an enormous quantity of minerals, demands that unex-

Ja, u is op die
regte pad-

●

na gelyke en ekonomiese
prestasie van u motor
solank as wat u
PEGASUS PETROL en
GARGOYLE MOBILOIL
gebruik.

PEGASUS & Mobiloil

Die VACUUM ongeëwenaarde kragspan.

VACUUM OIL COMPANY of SOUTH AFRICA, Ltd.

13. South African advertisement for Mobil products in the Afrikaans language, 1933. *Source: The Kruger National Park: Hints and General Information* (Pretoria: Government Printer, 1933), p. 2.

Yes! you're on the right road–

●

**to smooth and
economical performance
of your car as long
as you use
PEGASUS PETROL and
GARGOYLE MOBILOIL**

PEGASUS & Mobiloil

The VACUUM Unbeatable Power Team

VACUUM OIL COMPANY of SOUTH AFRICA, Ltd.

14. A South African advertisement for Mobil products, 1933. *Source: The Kruger National Park: Hints and General Information* (Pretoria: Government Printer, 1933), p. 6.

pectedly continued well into the postwar period. Stephen Krasner notes that the war also revealed for the first time the potential importance of foreign raw materials.[32] American entrepreneurs, whose foreign operations began in Latin America at the turn of the century, now looked farther afield, to southern Africa and beyond. The explosive demand for copper by the communications and transportation industries and earlier by the military during the war years was of special and deepening concern. By 1928 the United States, historically a net copper exporter, had begun a feverish search beyond its national frontiers for new sources.[33]

The idea of stockpiling strategic minerals emerged from the war and was made explicit in the National Defense Act of 1920, which charged the assistant secretary of war with procurement of all military supplies to ensure "adequate provision for the mobilization of material . . . essential to wartime needs."[34] Though never fully implemented, the act did provide the initiative for a conference of mining experts, held at Williamstown, Massachusetts, in 1923 on "Raw Materials and Foodstuffs in the Commercial Policies of Nations."[35]

Interest in the national-security dimension of strategic mineral sourcing was brought into sharper focus in 1925 with the appearance of *International Control of Minerals,* a publication of the influential American Institute of Mining and Metallurgical Engineers. In 1929 the country's mineral dependency became even more apparent through a Commerce Department publication, *Mineral Raw Materials: A Survey of Commerce and Sources in Major Industrial Countries,* produced by J. W. Furness and L. M. Jones, two of the nation's leading authorities.[36]

Four years later the so-called Mineral Inquiry, made up of some of the United States' most prominent mining experts, sponsored a well-attended conference in New York City on "Minerals in Their Political and International Relations."[37] It culminated a decade of cooperative research and spawned a mass of serious literature underwritten by such foundations as the Carnegie Endowment, the Council on Foreign Relations, the Foreign Policy Association, and the World Peace Foundation. Not surprisingly, southern Africa figured prominently in nearly all the works.

The onset of World War II greatly heightened American fears of mineral deficiencies. After intense discussion in Congress, a National Stockpiling Act was passed in 1939, enabling the federal government to acquire minerals needed for national defense.[38] This marked the commencement of a U.S. minerals policy. But curiously, instead of promoting self-sufficiency as called for in the bill, the United States would rely primarily on the stockpiling of imported ores. Many in Congress reasoned that their own resources were like savings in a bank, only to be drawn upon in dire emergencies and as a last resort.

AFRICAN EDUCATION: THE CONTROVERSY GROWS

As I noted in chapter 4, the Phelps-Stokes philosophy of education and community development was largely implemented in Africa through the Jeanes schools. It should also be recalled that the Phelps-Stokes Fund was responsible in the 1920s for introducing colonial Africa to the Jeanes method of education. Initially, Jan Smuts in South Africa favored the idea not for its educational component but because of its agrarian thrust and its apparent emphasis on holding Africans in the rural areas. He saw Jeanes schools as an instrument for slowing the process of African detribalization and urbanization. Smuts best summed up his feelings about African urbanization in a work published in 1930. He suggested that were it not for the "case of the urbanised or detribalised natives, the colour problem . . . would be shorn of most of its difficulties. . . . [The] situation in South Africa is therefore a lesson to all the younger British communities farther north to prevent as much as possible the detachment of the native from his tribal connexion and to enforce from the very start the system of segregation with its conservation of separate native institutions."[39] Smuts and many other white leaders in southern Africa viewed the Phelps-Stokes programs as a potentially effective instrument for keeping Africans in a traditionalist cocoon.

Tragically, the segregationist intentions expressed by Smuts and other local white leaders robbed the Jeanes experiments of their potential worth to African peasants. Indeed, the Jeanes philosophy was hijacked by the proponents of racial segregation, who wished to use it for their own political ends. Many Africans, who at first regarded the Jeanes schools as a means of increasing self-reliance and boosting food production, eventually came to regard them as a subtle new instrument of white repression.

Unrelenting criticism in the United States of the Phelps-Stokes Commission's proposals for African education further weakened the foundation's enthusiasm for its own programs. As a result, only a handful of underfunded Jeanes schools were ever established: none in South Africa and only a few in the Rhodesias, Nyasaland, and Portuguese Mozambique. The reports' prescient remarks concerning agriculture and community development were lost in acrimonious debate over the personalities, intentions, and strategies of their authors and implementors. The economic depression of the early 1930s placed severe constraints on educational and agricultural budgets and dampened the enthusiasm of local educators and government administrators.

In 1932, on the urging of Dr. C. T. Loram, who headed their Visitors' Grants Committee in South Africa, the Carnegie Corporation sent out Reverend Anson Phelps Stokes to tour "native" schools in South Africa, the Rhodesias, Tanganyika, and Kenya. Stokes, while favoring the Jeanes experiments, criticized the system of Native Reserves and strongly supported greater government assistance to African education. Continuing neglect of African educational needs, he warned, would create "a far greater danger than that of bringing about through repression a sullen and hostile native population."[40] Lamentably, Stokes' findings fell on deaf ears in South Africa and in the Rhodesias. Moreover, they did nothing to deflect criticism in the United States of the Fund's African programs.

The Jeanes program received a severe blow late in 1934, when Harold Jowitt, its major colonial supporter in Southern Rhodesia, bowed to criticism from the white Rhodesian settler community and resigned from his position as director of the Native Education Department. The department was then dismembered, and a major source of program funding was terminated.

The Jeanes experiments had become so controversial that in May 1935 an Interterritorial Jeanes Conference was convened in Salisbury, Southern Rhodesia, under the aegis of the Carnegie Corporation. Dr. Keppel, the foundation's president, came out from New York for the meeting, which was attended by well over one hundred black and white African educators and community leaders from South Africa and elsewhere on the continent. Out of this historic and unprecedented multiracial summit emerged a 428-page report that blasted the Jeanes schools and convinced the Carnegie Corporation to withdraw its support and to abandon plans for extending it into South Africa. Consequently, what started out as an ambitious effort to introduce agricultural and community development into the African curriculum came to an inglorious conclusion.[41]

The American disengagement may have assuaged the fears of the whites in southern Africa but it also intensified the frustrations of urban-oriented black American and African leaders who had vainly anticipated a shift in emphasis to urban concerns rather than a wholesale abandonment. The American foundations and missionary organizations, feeling the heat, simply withdrew, leaving the pieces to be managed by a suspicious and unenthuastic white colonial power structure. Thus, the 1935 conference in Salisbury marked a turning point. The supporters of African agricultural regeneration were defeated, and the Jeanes schools quietly faded into oblivion.

Throughout southern Africa American Board missionaries placed increasing emphasis on African education. In Natal the venerable Amanzimtoti Institute was renamed Adams College in 1935 and became an important venue for interracial conferences. Its distinguished faculty already included Albert Lutuli and Z. K. Matthews, two leaders in the African National Congress, while in the student body were the intellectuals Jordan Ngubane and Anton Lembede, both of whom played important roles in the founding of the ANC Youth League in 1944. Lembede became the leading theoretician of pan-Africanism and black consciousness in South Africa. Adams College, a nursery of modern African nationalism, boasted of a prep school, an industrial department, a teacher training department, an academically oriented high school, and a theological seminary.[42] Students were drawn from throughout southern Africa, including Southern Rhodesia, where the American Board completed a new hospital at Mount Selinda in 1935 and initiated an African nursing program. Mount Selinda also drew African students from South Africa as well as the Rhodesias.

THE CARNEGIE CORPORATION AND THE "POOR WHITE" PROBLEM

The late 1920s and early 1930s witnessed a deepening involvement of the Carnegie Corporation in urban social issues. Carnegie officials developed a keen interest in the social consequences of urbanization and industrialization and gave their financial support to a number of privately initiated projects in southern Africa. In the Union of South Africa, the corporation was particularly concerned with the issues of structural unemployment among white workers. Since the Boer War (1899–1902), white, predominately Afrikaner, marginal farm laborers had been migrating to urban areas in search of employment. Between 1921 and 1936 the number of whites in urban centers increased by half, while it more than doubled for Africans.

The PACT government feared the potential of unemployed black and white workers joining ranks and launching a class war against the regime. The Carnegie Corporation, strongly influenced at the time by Jan Smuts and by English-speaking liberals in the white business and professional communities, responded in 1929 by launching a major study of the country's "poor white" problem.[43] Nearly three years later its commission issued a five-volume report covering the health, educational, and psychosocial dimensions of poverty in the white community. The report concluded that poor white poverty in South Africa was essentially caused by low wages, not unemployment, and that the solutions had to be found in the urban-industrial sector rather than on the farm.[44] The study was greeted enthusiastically by the government, which used it to justify a substantial increase in public spending on white housing, health, and employment opportunities. The Carnegie commission went further than the report itself by supporting import-protection policies in the hopes that they would stimulate local industry and generate white employment.

The plight of Africans, on the other hand, was almost completely ignored in the Carnegie Report. In the 1930s government attempts to alleviate black urban poverty were half-hearted and largely ineffectual. Indeed, the government seemed preoccupied with stemming and attempting to reverse the urban drift through demographic control. Legislation in 1927 and 1937 empowered municipalities to require Africans to live in designated areas and force them to leave if they became unemployed. Nevertheless, in 1932 the racially segregated township of Orlando was opened fifteen kilometers from Johannesburg as the first of the new racially segregated periurban African townships.[45] Orlando and the others that followed were woefully inadequate in terms of amenities. Many government officials reasoned that providing a better life for Africans in the urban areas would only accelerate the population flow. Others argued that black urbanization must be discouraged because it intensified the competition among blacks and whites for urban jobs.

Carnegie attention to the issue of black poverty was thus deflected to the north. In 1933 it cosponsored with the Phelps-Stokes Fund a study of the impact of the copper industry of Katanga and the Copperbelt on African society and missionary enterprise. The project was initiated by J. H. Oldham, the secretary of the International Missionary Council, on behalf of the several large British missionary societies. Merle Davis, a prominent American sociologist, directed the research with the assistance of Charles Coulter, a professor of sociology at Ohio Wesleyan University and Dr. Ray Phillips, an American social worker and Congregational missionary. From this emerged Davis' anthology *Modern Industry and the African* (1933), one of the first professional analyses of the impact of migrancy, urbanization, and industrialization on Africans. Almost prophetically, it warned of the disruptive impact of rapid urbanization on African food self-sufficiency. It noted, for example, that in cassava planting, whereby a cycle of two or three years of crops were tended simultaneously, the absence of the cultivator for a single season resulted in the cutting off of the food supply for two years.[46] Davis, a proponent of the Jeanes school approach, concluded that industrialization must go hand in hand with agricultural development and that missionaries must grasp the interrelationship.

Unfortunately, colonial officials and missionaries largely ignored the findings, and the book was consigned to the dusty shelves of American libraries. Dr. Ray Phillips, however, returned to South Africa and became principal of the newly established Jan Hofmeyr School of Social Work in Johannesburg. In 1941 the institution began to train South Africa's first black social workers.[47]

Phillips also organized a number of multiracial Gamma Sigma Clubs in the black townships, which provided an urban venue for blacks and whites to debate social issues and a place where African musicians and artists could develop their talents. Phillips' brilliant socioanthropological work, *The Bantu in the City: A Study of Cultural Adjustment on the Witwatersrand*, (1938), was one of the first studies of its kind and did much to awaken Americans to the urban dimension of black life in South Africa.[48]

Arguably the most influential and monumental contemporary work on the continent and one supported by the Carnegie Corporation, was the *Survey of Africa*, the product of a multicolonial field project directed by W. M. H. Hailey, a leading British authority on colonial questions.[49]

At the suggestion of Jan Smuts the Carnegie Corporation awarded the Royal Institute of International Affairs funds to undertake the comprehensive four-year project. The outcome was the most exhaustive study ever made of colonial Africa. With a strong Eurocolonialist bias *The Survey of Africa* covered a breathtaking array of topics, including health, labor, education, law, agriculture, government, taxation, and transportation. The well-written and lucid work contained a wealth of useful data drawn from interviews and reports of leading white officials. Yet it was flawed by a paucity of African input. Nevertheless, Hailey's *Survey*, first published in 1938, and subsequently updated, remained the standard reference work on Africa for nearly three decades.

THE CHALLENGES AND OPPORTUNITIES OF WAR

As the clouds of war gathered over Europe in the late 1930s, Prime Minister Hertzog and most Afrikaners resisted the efforts by Smuts and the English-speaking white population to formally ally with Great Britain. In his "South Africa First" policy Hertzog argued for strict neutrality. After all, Boers had fought their own wars against what they perceived to be British imperialism. Afrikaners, who were becoming intensely nationalistic in the 1930s, did not want to fight "England's wars." In 1938, in a symbolic gesture of defiance against Great Britain, Hertzog required that "Die Stem van Suid-Afrika," the Afrikaner's national anthem, be played at all official occasions together with "God Save the King," the traditional anthem.

In the economic realm the Afrikaner prime minister seized upon opportunities to increase South Africa's trade with the United States and the Axis powers. The country's mineral exports to Germany and Japan grew enormously after the bilateral agreements of 1934.[50] Jan Smuts, the Anglophile Afrikaner deputy prime minister, became alarmed and stepped up pressure for closer diplomatic ties with Great Britain. Hertzog, on the other hand, was convinced that South Africa's entry into Britain's war would compromise its own sovereignty. But in September 1939 he lost in a parliamentary showdown on the issue of neutrality.[51] Smuts carried an amendment in favor of breaking relations with Germany. In protest Hertzog and his newly constituted National party withdrew from the government and entered into a political alliance with Dr. Daniel Malan and his Purified Nationalists. Smuts, under the United party banner, succeeded as prime minister and drew South Africa into the war.

During World War II, as during World War I, South Africa found itself largely cut off from its traditional sources of supply in Great Britain and had to rely more heavily on its own resources and on those of the United States. By 1941 imports from the United States surpassed those from Britain, 38 percent to 30 percent.[52] The book value of American private investment in South Africa also soared to $86.6 million by 1943 with nearly $51 million in direct investments, the bulk, of which was in petroleum ($36 million) and manufacturing ($11 million).[53] Significantly, only $4 million was in mining, a sector still firmly under British and English-speaking South African control.

South Africa's balance of payments remained favorable during the war years. Gold and foreign exchange reserves rose as domestic industries sold minerals to the United States under lend-lease agreements and exported minerals and military supplies to Great Britain. Gold again became a critical factor. The London market was now bypassed, and South African gold was shipped directly to the United States in order to pay South African as well as British lend-lease obligations to the Americans. Between 1941 and 1946 the United States extended $234 million in lend-lease exports.[54] After 1942, for the first time in history, South Africa's commercial banks resisted keeping their gold reserves in war-torn London, preferring instead the safety of their own cities. With plentiful supplies of gold the country was in an extremely favorable position to purchase American products.

During the war years the United States became a large trader on its own account. The country's great gains in the South African trade were partially the result of exports of heavy capital equipment, mainly to keep the mines operating. However, the South African government also became an important buyer of American-made aircraft. Previously, South African Airways, a parastatal corporation, had bought mostly German Junkers. Now, with Germany as an enemy and the British under seige, it looked to the Americans. Early in the 1940s the airline ordered a fleet of twenty-eight Lockheed Lodestar aircraft in its first significant purchase from an American manufacturer. Because of war needs, the planes were actually destined to South Africa's Department of Defence. Four years later the South African Airforce acquired five Douglas Dakota DC-3s, and in late 1945 South African Airways, back in full passenger service, bought three four-engine Douglas DC-4 Skymasters.[55] South Africa had discovered another American product, and in subsequent decades U.S.-manufactured aircraft commanded a major share of the market.

The demands of war compelled the United States to expand its mineral reserves, especially the ferro-alloys. A government mission was sent to South Africa in 1942 to press for an increase in the production of strategic minerals. South Africa complied, and the Americans were soon importing an enormous volume of platinum, used in the manufacture of sparkplugs and magnetos and as a catalyst in explosives. The United States also imported industrial diamonds for drill bits. And from the Rhodesias came copper for brass cartridges and shells. Vanadium was also imported, for the fabrication of aircraft fuselages. In addition, South Africa's seaports handled asbestos, tungsten, chrome, and mica from mines in the Katanga region of the Belgian Congo as well as from the Rhodesias. Much of this material was destined for America's eastern seaboard. By the war's end the United States had emerged as the largest purchaser of Rhodesian copper and a major buyer of most of South Africa's minerals.[56]

American shipping was greatly stimulated by the huge volume of ores imported through South Africa's harbors. By 1945 ten American shipping lines were providing regular service to South Africa from ports in Philadelphia, New York, New Orleans, Baltimore, Galveston, Houston, and San Francisco.[57]

MULTILATERALISM AS AN INSTRUMENT OF AMERICAN EXPANSIONISM

The war had offered the United States an unprecedented opportunity to bring the world capitalist economy under closer control and to establish institutions that could revive the war-torn European economies and ensure their economic stability. The process got under way in 1944 at the Bretton Woods Conference with the founding of the International Monetary Fund (IMF). The IMF, as it was envisaged by its founders, would provide a stable system of international payments for a world of fixed exchange rates. It would also assist member countries experiencing structural trade problems and defend their currencies against severe cyclical fluctuations. To overcome short-term trade-related balance-of-payments crises, individual IMF members could draw on an IMF pool of funds to supplement their own foreign reserves.[58]

At the inception of the IMF the forty-four charter member countries pledged to contribute capital on a regular basis. The accumulated funds were to be used to finance IMF lending operations. The United States' contribution was overwhelmingly the largest and ensured it of a preeminent position in the organization. Twenty-five percent of each country's quota had to be paid in gold or currency convertible into gold—currency that was effectively the U.S. dollar because it was the only currency still convertible directly into gold. In this way the American dollar was enshrined as the prime instrument for international trade and investment and the principal reserve asset for central banks. Thus, through the Bretton Woods Agreement the major currencies of the world were linked with gold through the U.S. dollar. Formerly, the gold standard was essentially a British sterling exchange standard because the pound sterling for decades had been the most widely used of the world's currencies for current and capital account transactions.[59]

The Americans thus created and dominated a new global monetary system. The IMF quickly set fixed prices for the major currencies and pegged them to the U.S. dollar, enabling the Americans to regulate exchange rates and draw member countries back into a common currency standard. The dollar was linked to gold at $35 per ounce for purposes of international currency settlements between central banks. Each currency was forbidden to fluctuate beyond a narrow parity spectrum. Through this arrangement the currencies of the world developed a heavy reliance on the United States dollar. By obliging IMF members to establish a par value for their currency, fixed either by the dollar or gold, the United States gained control over the monetary systems of the non-Communist world.[60] Thus, after 1947 the United States was able to manage the international monetary system, largely by providing liquidity and current adjustment.

The United States was also instrumental in establishing the International Bank for Reconstruction and Development, or World Bank. Like the IMF it was chartered as a multinational institution with capital provided by member nations. The United States was able to play a decisive role in this powerful institution as well by furnishing more than a third of the total contribution. The World Bank became another key vehicle in the United States' quest for postwar economic leadership.

Initially designed to help finance postwar economic reconstruction in Europe, the bank eventually broadened its operations to other regions of the world. By the mid-1950s it had become the largest multilateral provider of long-term developmental finance to the third world. The IMF and the World Bank were the first institutions in history to perform central bank functions for the international system. South Africa joined both the IMF and the World Bank within a year after the Bretton Woods Conference, and in doing so, it became more closely linked to the U.S. dollar and more susceptible to U.S. fiscal and monetary policies. South Africa also obtained a vital new source of inexpensive capital for infrastructural development. In 1951 the World Bank made its first significant loan to South Africa, consisting of a twenty-year $30 million credit at 4 percent to the Electricity Supply Commission for power development and a fifteen-year $20 million loan at 3.75 percent for expansion of transportation facilities.[61] With these funds the two parastatals purchased from American firms a number of locomotives, rolling stock, structural materials, and electrical equipment. In 1954 the World Bank extended an additional $60 million to the same sectors of the economy.[62]

With the non-Communist world's monetary system firmly under its control, the United States turned its attention to the expansion of world trade and investment. The first step was taken in 1945, when the Export-Import (Exim) Bank, founded in 1934, was restructured as an independent U.S. government agency with the purpose of facilitating trade by loans, loan guarantees, and insurance. Initially concerned with overseas importers interested in purchasing American manufactures, the Exim Bank soon expanded its operations to American exporters and to countries seeking funds for infrastructural development. South Africa found it an extremely useful instrument, and between 1946 and 1955 it borrowed more than $150 million for the modernization of its harbors and national road network.[63]

Indirectly related to the IMF and World Bank was the General Agreement on Tariffs and Trade (GATT), which came into operation in 1948. This multilateral organization aimed at moderating trade barriers between countries and ensuring equal access to each other's markets on a most-favored-nation basis. The GATT operated under the principles that trade must be conducted without discrimination and that protection of domestic industries must be undertaken through customs tariffs rather than by means of import quotas. Member nations, however, were allowed to impose temporary import restrictions against sudden increases in imports of specific products.

The GATT played a major role in the progressive liberalization of world trade in the postwar era. The United States assumed a dominant position in the organization and used it to open the world, including South Africa, to American technology, capital, and manufactured exports. To open the doors further still, the United States in 1948 passed the Economic Cooperation Act, which enabled it to sign a treaty with South Africa that protected American investors from double taxation.

U.S. trade and investment in South Africa was also spurred on by the Merchant Ship Sales Act of 1946, which enabled the government to sell to the private sector its huge, and now obsolete, naval fleets.[64] The Farrell Lines of New York and the Lykes Lines of New Orleans were among the first major American shipping companies to profit from the legislation. Both lines were able to expand their own fleets and to extend their services to a number of ports in southern Africa, including Durban, Port Elizabeth, and Lourenco-Marques in Mozambique.

South Africa, like the United States, emerged from World War II in a remarkably strong position economically and financially. Some sectors of the economy had made impressive strides under the stimulus of war. Gold and foreign exchange reserves had risen substantially, and money supply had expanded rapidly, while the country's debt had grown only moderately. Thus, the monetary situation was extremely liquid, and the banking system enjoyed ample reserves of foreign exchange. Investment funds and consumer demand, pent up during the war, were released with explosive force. The boom was accelerated by an exceptionally heavy flow of capital to the Union from overseas in 1947 and 1948 and by credit expansion within South Africa. War-induced backlogs in the supply of durable and nondurable consumer goods as well as heavy demands for capital equipment for the new projects already underway enabled South Africa's imports to more than double between 1945 and 1946. A year later they increased an additional 40 percent.[65]

By 1947 U.S. trade with the Union of South Africa had reached an all-time high. The value of American exports amounted to $414 million, or more than five times the figure for 1938. Imports of South African merchandise were $111 million, nearly seven and a half times the value on the eve of the war. Taking gold into consideration, direct imports from South Africa exceeded $268 million, still leaving the United States with a comfortable trade balance. The import values would have been even greater if South African gold and diamonds arriving via third countries, particularly Britain, were added to the calculations. American demands for South African diamonds rose spectacularly because of the recent adoption of cemented-carbide tools by the metal-cutting industries. But diamond sales were also given a huge boost after 1940, when Ayers Advertising of Philadelphia received the coveted De Beers account.[66] For the consuming masses of the United States South Africa came to represent the land of diamonds and gold. No one seemed to appreciate or understand the political and economic forces at work behind the scenes in South Africa. In the years to come those forces would be shaped not by the captains of industry but by the politicians, who were driven by the rapidly politicizing Afrikaner farmers, mineworkers, and civil servants.

CONFRONTING AFRIKANER NATIONALISM

Part of South Africa's postwar attraction to American enterprise was its low labor costs and compliant African workforce. The government had broken the back of African labor. Toward the end of the war and immediately afterward the government was confronted with waves of wildcat strikes by African workers who complained of meager food rations and whose jobs were threatened by the returning war veterans.[67] Labor demands during the war had resulted in a massive expansion of the working class and a resurgence of labor union activity. Africans flooded the urban-industrial areas to fill new positions as well as existing ones vacated by whites departing for military service. To weaken the Africans' bargaining power, the government in 1945 passed the Urban Areas Act, which prevented Africans from residing permanently in the areas of their employment.[68] This first comprehensive program of influx-control legislation was matched by brutal police suppression of the strikers and a purging of the union ranks of Communists and militant socialists. Such extreme tactics were partially motivated by the highly successful African mineworkers' strike of 1946, when nearly a hundred thousand workers shut down twenty-one mines and almost paralyzed the extractive industries.[69]

By 1947 the Smuts regime was well along the way to reversing a trend of rising African wages and growing unions that had been gaining momentum since the late 1930s. However, massive African urbanization and the threat of future competition for jobs only heightened feelings of insecurity among the rising middle class of predominantly white Afrikaners.

Smuts' United party was deeply divided over how to deal with black urbanization and the escalating labor demands of industry. The government's Fagan Report of 1948 rejected the premise that Africans were "temporary sojourners" in the urban areas.[70] The report was highly critical of the color bar, the pass laws, and the oscillating migratory nature of African labor. It maintained that the urban-industrial workers must be recognized as a permanent feature of South African society.

The United party supported the Fagan Report in principle, even though many whites, especially the workers, were not prepared for such a heavy dose of reality. Massive African urbanization and labor turmoil had heightened white insecurity. White workers were angered by an apparent erosion of segregationist labor policies. Their fear and anger were given visible expression in the general elections of 1948, when Jan Smuts and his predominantly English-speaking party suffered a stunning upset. The almost exclusively Afrikaans-speaking National party, under Daniel Malan, was swept into power on promises to shield the white workers from what they perceived to be the *swart gevaar* (black threat) and to protect them at the same time from manufactured imports that might stifle local industries and the workers employed by them. For the first time since the formation of the Union the party in power was exclusively Afrikaner. It was intensely nationalistic, with a bias against British capital and British business interests. And like its Krugerian and Hertzogian predecessors, this regime sought to diversify its markets and investors while fervently protecting its own industries. Not since the heyday of Afrikaner rule in the late nineteenth century was the United States confronted by such a potent combination of challenge and opportunity.

The months leading up to the elections and the immediate aftermath triggered a flight of British capital. Measures had already been taken by the government in March 1948 to restrict capital transfers. Later in the year the new Afrikaner regime reimposed restrictions on imports, largely in response to the country's huge trade deficit with the United States.[71] South Africa sharply curbed its American imports, including dollar payments for freight. In July 1949 the government prohibited the import of assembled cars. At the time only Ford and Vauxhall assembled automobiles in South Africa; others were imported as knocked-down models. The move was coupled with a devaluation of the currency, which reduced the serious balance-of-payments crisis by controlling nonsterling imports, while the enhanced prices of gold lifted the value of exports. The government also introduced a scheme of granting quotas of nonsterling exchange to importers, equal to fifty percent of the amount spent on nonsterling imports during 1947.[72] From South Africa's standpoint the moves were beneficial: The balance of payments moved sharply into surplus.

The Americans were deeply troubled by the new protectionist trend, and U.S. shipping lines responded by drastically reducing their schedules to adjust to the precipitous fall in trade. U.S. manufacturers were particularly disturbed for they had just for the first time in history superseded Britain as the major supplier to South Africa. Moreover, South Africa in 1948 had emerged as the eighth largest customer of the United States, taking $492 million of its exports.[73]

Further complicating matters, Americans had to deal with the South African government's formulation of a "prohibited list," which included a wide range of luxury consumer items. Fortunately, essential raw materials and capital equipment were exempted. Nevertheless, South Africa had begun to strictly ration its nonsterling foreign exchange and sharply cut its imports from the United States, including dollar payments for freight.

The postwar economic boom created an enormous demand for shipping. The Union-Castle Line, a major British liner company, had dominated the monopolistic South African Conference since the turn of the century. It held the lucrative mail contract from South Africa and in return received an annual subsidy and berthing priority in South African ports.[74] But Union-Castle lost more than a third of its fleet during the war and was unable to meet the new demands, especially along the routes to North America. Consequently, the South African government decided to form its own indigenous shipping concern. Thus, in 1947 the South African Marine Corporation (Safmarine) was established as a shipping parastatal and immediately began to receive heavy government subsidies. It is noteworthy that Safmarine was initially capitalized by Anglo-American Corporation and Anglo-Transvaal Consolidated, two

South Africa-based firms. Managerial expertise however, was furnished by an American shipping line, the States Marine Corporation. In 1947, with three "Victory" ships purchased from the U.S. Maritime Commission, Safmarine launched a regular service to North American ports.[75]

The results of South Africa's return to protectionism were quite dramatic. American shipping lines substantially reduced their operations. Moreover, the import restrictions forced some vehicle plants to assemble British and continental (French and German) makes in place of their American models. Not surprisingly, U.S. exports to South Africa fell from $492 million in 1948 to $266 million a year later. By 1950 they had sunk to $120 million. And between 1948 and 1950, America's share of total South African imports dropped in value from 35 percent to 16 percent.[76] Yet from an investment point of view the conditions for highly profitable enterprises were exceptionally favorable. Consumer demand was growing, and organized labor was weak. Since the 1920s the government had been developing a symbiotic relationship with the private sector designed to promote local private enterprise.

AMERICAN TECHNOLOGY AND SOUTH AFRICA'S MANUFACTURING REVOLUTION

South Africa's policy of import substitution played an important role in the dramatic postwar growth in manufacturing, especially in the production of intermediate and processed minerals. As a result the country enjoyed a decade of rapid industrialization between 1946 and 1956. The National government maintained a strong balance-of-payments position by boosting exports and domestic industrial production through its encouragement of trade and foreign investment. The government was anxious to induce American companies to locate manufacturing plants in South Africa and also to increase American loans to and investment in the extractive industries. At the end of the war a law was enacted requiring firms that were incorporated overseas to pay an annual license fee based on corporate capital. Significantly, firms could evade this by establishing a local subsidiary. American firms wishing to set up a branch or subsidiary received a variety of tax or regulatory concessions. Consequently, private American direct investment grew, from $51 million in

1943 to $140 million in 1950,[77] a 300 percent growth in direct investment alone, nearly half of it in the form of reinvested earnings. By 1950 the percentage of net earnings on U.S. investments in South Africa exceeded 27 percent.

Tariffs on U.S. consumer goods after 1949 became so high that American multinational firms either had to leave or to manufacture in South Africa to remain competitive. Many chose the latter, and when their position in South Africa was threatened, firms generating strong profits tended to establish a subsidiary in an effort to retain their markets. The major automobile manufacturers did this in response to the tariffs of the 1920s, and the petroleum and entertainment industries followed in the late 1930s. The trend greatly accelerated after World War II. Following the lead of Firestone, Goodyear Tire and Rubber Company of Akron, Ohio, which had been selling tires in South Africa since 1915, established a locally incorporated entity and in 1947 opened a factory at Uitenhage, a major manufacturing center on the eastern coast. Pepsi-Cola opened its first franchise in South Africa in 1948 and emulated Coca-Cola by distributing its syrup to independently owned and operated local bottling concerns that distributed it under license. Other major American firms that entered immediately after the war were Chesebrough-Ponds in 1946 with its patented Vaseline Petroleum Jelly, and Lilly Laboratories, which opened for business a year later.[78]

The South African government was determined to provide a stable political environment to attract overseas capital. Thus, the Durban race riots of January 1949 were brutally suppressed, leaving 142 dead and thousands injured.[79] The American business community seemed satisfied, and between 1948 and 1960 at least forty-two firms set up subsidiaries, representing a broad range of products, including paper, processed food, chemicals, and pharmaceuticals.[80]

South Africa gave special encouragement to companies that offered new technology, fresh capital, and products that generated employment and did not compete with goods produced locally. It discouraged firms that might compete with economic sectors already entrenched or under government ownership. This was most telling in the insurance business. For example, as early as 1943, an Insurance Act compelled the major American insurance companies, notably Cigna and the American International Group, to hold assets in South Africa equal to 53 percent of their net liabilities. Moreover, American insurers not registered prior to 1943 could not do so unless they had been established for at least twenty years.[81] Enormous pressure was put on the companies to deposit their investments and profits in government securities. Not surprisingly, South Africa became unattractive to American insurance firms. An analogous situation prevailed in the banking sector, where only British banks were allowed to establish branch operations.

By contrast, American firms offering new technology were strongly encouraged. The postwar technological superiority of American MNCs over domestic and British companies gave them a decisive competitive advantage in opening new markets or in penetrating and dominating old ones. The 1940s and 1950s witnessed a phenomenal growth in proprietary technology covered by key patents that were held in many cases by American firms. The pharmaceutical industry provides one of the best examples.

The advent of World War II sped the pace of pharmacological innovation in the United States. As early as 1943 fermentation technology enabled penicillin to assume commercial scale production and within a decade enormous strides had been made in antibiotic therapy. The extraordinary growth of industrial laboratories greatly accelerated after the war. The crash program in the commercial development of penicillin during the war had demonstrated the vast potential of pharmaceutical research and development. Pfizer, founded as a chemical company in the United States in 1849, achieved an early lead in the 1950s in the development of antibiotics. Terramycin was first marketed by Pfizer in March, 1950, and overnight the small firm was transformed into a full-scale pharmaceutical multinational.[82] The demand for antibiotics around the world provided Pfizer with enormous market opportunities. Through licensing agreements companies overseas were given the right to manufacture, distribute, and sell products manufactured by Pfizer and other American pharmaceutical companies. Pfizer's operations in South Africa began in 1953, and business was brisk from the start. A wide range of new pharmaceutical products were developed and patented by other American firms that also soon entered the South African market. Taking advantage of the withdrawal of German competition from South Africa during the war, American companies moved in aggressively and quickly stole market share from the large and well-established British and Swiss firms. The intensive investigation and regulation of the pharmaceutical industry by the U.S. government in the early 1950s provided an added incentive to expand operations overseas, beyond federal control. By 1955 thirteen American pharmaceutical companies were conducting business in South Africa, and all but three of them chose to manufacture locally.

The computer industry also serves as a fine illustration of market penetration and domination through technological superiority. International Business Machines (IBM) pioneered with the first large computer in 1953 (the "700" series) and began marketing operations in South Africa a year later. It gained an immediate dominance of the computer market and maintained it for more than three decades.[83]

Americans likewise pioneered in the field of airconditioning, an amenity that found eager buyers in warm climates. After the war the Carrier Corporation developed an inexpensive and efficient system that secured for the firm a profitable niche in the South African economy from the early 1950s.

American enterprises also made impressive strides in the processed and quick-frozen food industry. The Birdseye Company achieved early superiority in frozen fruit and vegetable technology, which was introduced to South Africans after the war. Profits were even more handsome in the area of processed breakfast foods. The Kellogg Company, established in Michigan in 1906, introduced a line of toasted breakfast cereals that, along with Quaker Oats,[84] became enormously popular in South Africa from the early 1950s.

Possibly the greatest American postwar investments in the nonmining sector of the South African economy were in transportation and petroleum. The automobile industry resumed its robust growth after the war, and licensed vehicles soared from an already impressive 390,000 in 1946 to 970,000 a decade later.[85] By 1956 twelve U.S. auto companies were selling vehicles in South Africa, eight of them operating their own assembly plants or having arrangements with local firms to assemble knocked-down kits. Nevertheless, Ford and General Motors maintained their overwhelming lead, especially after the series of amalgamations of the smaller U.S. auto companies in the mid-1950s. By 1960 Nash, Hudson, Studebaker, Packard, Kaiser-Fraser, and Willys-Overland had disappeared, along with their small South African distributing networks. Only the Chrysler Corporation, which had opened its first assembly plant near

Cape Town in 1958, remained to compete with the two American giants and their less extensive British and European counterparts.

In the mid-1950s the Nationalist government began to promote an aggressive local-content program in auto assembly, compelling the American companies to expand their domestic operations. Thus, as demand grew, so did government pressures for greater local content. Manufacturers responded through a process of vertical and horizontal integration, involving local acquisition of inputs from domestic-supplier industries.

The spectacular growth in vehicle output fueled demands for petroleum products. Socony-Vacuum responded in 1954 by building a multimillion dollar oil refinery, South Africa's first, near Durban.[86] A year later, the firm changed its name to Socony Mobil Oil Company and vastly extended its marketing network into the white rural communities. Also in 1954 Goodyear, Firestone, and General Tire (the latter had arrived in 1949) enlarged their plants at Port Elizabeth.[87]

DRAWING CLOSER:
THE COLD WAR AND STRATEGIC MINERALS

The postwar era witnessed moves toward closer cooperation between the governments of the United States and the Union of South Africa. The issue of strategic mineral sourcing became an important factor in determining U.S. policy towards the South Africans. The United States' monopoly over nuclear technology and weaponry was broken in July 1949, when the Soviet Union exploded an atomic bomb, an event that heightened American concern over its supply and sourcing of uranium, an essential ingredient in the manufacture of nuclear products. South Africa, with its reputed reserves of uranium, had to be factored into the calculations.

The United States' concern over uranium sourcing actually dates to the war era, when the country began to develop the atomic bomb. In the early 1940s the Combined Development Agency (CDA) was organized by the governments of Canada, Great Britain, and the United States to conduct a global search for uranium for manufacture in atomic bombs.[88] Uranium had been discovered in South Africa as far back as 1922, but little had been done to exploit the mineral. Then, in 1944 an American geologist discovered vast new reserves in South Africa. By 1945 South Africa joined the British and the Americans in a joint nuclear research program.[89] The exchange of American nuclear technology for South Africa's uranium ores initiated an era of close cooperation between the two countries. That cooperation began in 1949, when the United States helped South Africa set up an Atomic Energy Board.[90] Also in 1949 President Truman agreed to upgrading both countries' diplomatic missions to full embassies. In a State Department assessment that year, much attention was given to South Africa as a force for anti-Communism as well as a source for strategic minerals, including gold and uranium.[91]

U.S. policies toward South Africa after 1949 were guided by cold war concerns. After the outbreak of the Korean War in June 1950 American policymakers became fearful of the potential threat of the Soviet Union's depriving the West of vital industrial raw materials. As early as 1946 the U.S. had passed the Strategic Critical Materials Stockpiling Act to encourage greater domestic production. It became the key legislative instrument guiding U.S. stockpiling policy for decades afterward.[92]

But higher budgetary priorities in Washington in the immediate postwar period delayed the actual accumulation of stocks. Then came the Korean War and the passage of the Defense Production Act of 1950, authorizing the president to press for expansion of foreign as well as domestic production. In November 1950 South Africa agreed to sell uranium to the United States, and in less than a year, it also became one of several countries to sign a Mutual Defense Assistance Agreement.[93]

Bilateral military cooperation had, however, already begun. South Africa was one of the first countries to join the Americans in the Berlin airlift of 1949. A year later it became one of the first to contribute a military contingent to the Korean conflict.

Early in the 1950s it was discovered that many of South Africa's gold mines could produce uranium oxide as a byproduct. Thus, the United States pressed American investors to help South Africa to develop its gold and its uranium resources. Gold, of course, had also become vital to the United States in its new postwar role as the West's monetary leader. Henceforth, every effort was made to assist South Africa in the development of both resources.

The West Rand Consolidated Mines started uranium extraction in 1952, and by October of that year the first South African nuclear plant went into production.[94] Within four years South Africa built fourteen nuclear plants with financial and technical assistance from the United States. The Export-Import Bank advanced $130 million to South African mining companies participating in uranium programs—that is, to companies producing uranium from the waste of the gold mines. The Exim Bank added another $20 million of support in 1957–1958.[95] Altogether, the undertaking was enormously beneficial to the United States. Between 1953 and 1971 the Americans imported 43,260 tons of South Africa's uranium oxide, meeting nearly 20 percent of their requirements.[96] It is said that the United States' access to South Africa's mines in the 1950s was a major boost for the U.S. buildup of its nuclear arsenal during the Cold War era. By the end of that decade South Africa had become the Western world's third largest uranium producer.

The Korean War was what finally induced Congress to provide substantial support for mineral stockpiling. In 1951 President Harry Truman established the Materials Policy Commission to study the issue of strategic minerals. The commission was chaired by William S. Paley, president of Columbia Broadcasting System (CBS). The ensuing Paley Report of 1952, entitled "Resources for Freedom," was the most systematic and extensive survey of resources ever undertaken by the United States government.[97] The report was sharply critical of the United States' failure to produce enough of its own minerals and expressed deep concern over potential shortages and the exhaustion of supply. The commission, which included Arthur Bunker, president of Climax Molybdenum, a firm with mining interests in southern Africa, placed renewed emphasis on the desirability for stockpiling raw materials and urged the government to foster greater private-sector investment and technology in foreign mining operations.

The United States possessed the capital and the managerial talent to develop the new minerals resources. Many experts, especially in the State Department opposed any preference for domestic materials, arguing that it would be cheaper to cover part of U.S. needs for strategic minerals by importation and that the country's own resources would be depleted too rapidly if a program of self-sufficiency was pursued. On the other hand, Congressmen from the mineral-rich western states promoted stockpiling legislation as a means of maintaining high-cost, less-viable mines that had been operating with government subsidization since the war.[98]

In October 1953 President Eisenhower appointed a cabinet committee to continue the examination of the nation's minerals policy. On his urging the Senate launched a huge research effort to assess the condition and extent of the United States strategic mineral reserves. The results appeared late in 1953 in the twelve-volume series *Stockpiling and Accessibility of Strategic and Critical Minerals to the United States in Time of War.* It suggested, among many things, that "South Africa represents a great and booming frontier of the future as the demand for raw materials throughout the free world increases." The report listed twenty-seven strategic minerals "without which our industrial economy would collapse."[99] It pointed out that South Africa had become a prime source of key strategic minerals, especially platinum-group metals and uranium.

In 1953 Eisenhower proposed an "Atoms for Peace" policy that would enable the United States to share its nuclear technology through bilateral agreements with friendly countries, including South Africa. It offered the South Africans a research reactor and a grant of $350,000 for its installation. In March 1956 the Safari I reactor went critical and South Africa entered the nuclear age.[100] A year later the United States signed a nuclear cooperation agreement with South Africa to facilitate further the acquisition of nuclear technology and to increase cooperation over "peaceful" uses of atomic energy. This gave the South Africans the means to create their own atomic power stations and to purchase from the United States enriched uranium and plutonium.

Beginning in the late 1950s the United States practically ceased stockpiling materials and turned its attention from minerals to space. Indeed, the Cold War rivalry assumed a new dimension after 1957 when the Soviet Union launched *Sputnik,* the first space capsule to orbit the earth. The United States entered the age of space satellites a year later, and in the spirit of earlier mutual defense agreements it negotiated with South Africa and other countries for the construction of satellite tracking stations. As the space program extended into the 1960s, the United States became increasingly dependent on its network of stations in key global sites to monitor its own satellites as well as Russia's. Consequently, South Africa took on a new importance. Within a year of the United States' first satellite launch, the U.S. Navy was using South African ports for refreshment; and in October 1959 the Americans joined South Africa, Great Britain, Portugal, and France in joint naval exercises, in what was essentially an antisubmarine operation.[101]

Official interest in Africa, generally, grew with the accelerating pace of European decolonization. In 1958 the State Department created a separate Bureau of African Affairs. A year later a fixed point in U.S. policy towards Africa was set when the first assistant secretary of state for African affairs, Joseph Satterthwaite, stated his support "for African political aspirations when they are moderate, non-violent and constructive and take into account their obligations towards interdependence with the world community."[102] The Americans made it clear that they favored stability over revolutionary change. Leading up to the presidential campaign, Senator John F. Kennedy had begun to take a personal interest in African issues and attacked the Eisenhower administration for inconsistently supporting both colonialism and anticolonialisim. Kennedy was instrumental in persuading the Senate Foreign Relations Committee in 1959 to establish a subcommittee on Africa.

THE NEW AMERICAN INVESTMENTS: GOLD AND BASE METALS

Nevertheless, southern Africa was often viewed from a different point of view in part because of its enormous mineral resources. Gold, that most alluring of metals, continued to hold a special attraction to American investors. In 1946 the richest gold ore ever struck in South Africa was discovered in the Orange Free State, giving the gold industry a new lease on life and providing South Africa with more time and capital to diversify away from gold toward industrialization. But to expand its mineral output, the country desperately needed capital and technology, both of which the United States was prepared to furnish.

After the war the trend in the United States was towards greater emphasis on supply-oriented investment—that is, investment in minerals. Gold figured prominently. The U.S. share of the world's gold reserves had risen from 33 percent in 1934 to nearly 72 percent by 1948. The following year gold prices rose by 44 percent in the wake of Britain's devaluation of sterling.[103] As a result exploitation of the Orange Free State mines became extremely attractive to American companies. In 1949 Kennecott Copper loaned the Anglo-Transvaal Consolidated Investment Company money to finance gold extraction in the Orange Free State, and in October of the same year the New York investment house of Dillon, Read and Company negotiated a $10 million three-year revolving credit for the South African government from four American banks. Gold output soared, and in 1953 Kennecott sank another $8 million into South Africa's gold development.[104]

American investment in South Africa's gold industry grew substantially through the efforts of Charles W. Engelhard, a New Jersey entrepreneur. In 1957 a consortium of New Jersey investors led by Engelhard acquired a block of stock in the Central Mining Company, or Corner House. At the time Corner House was the second largest holding company in the South African mining industry, with considerable shareholdings in Australian and Canadian extractive industries.[105] In a masterful stroke Engelhard became the most powerful single American investor in southern Africa. The acquisition gave him virtual control over Rand Mines Group, Ltd., which was one of the oldest and largest mining companies in South Africa, accounting for more than half the country's gold output.

Engelhard, anxious to spark greater American interest in gold investments, formed the "American–South African Investment Trust" in order to give Americans an opportunity to invest in South African gold bullion as well as in gold-mining operations. South Africa's gold production accelerated, and by the end of 1959 its new gold fields were accounting for over 85 percent of total output, while the country itself was producing 63 percent of the world's total.[106]

American investment in base metals also grew after the war in response to the acceleration of industrialization. In 1947 Newmont Mining and the American Metal Corporation had accepted a South African government invitation to purchase the Tsumeb Mining Company of South West Africa, formerly under German control. U.S. investors also looked northward beyond the Limpopo River, to the British Rhodesias. By the end of the 1950s $50 million in private American capital had been poured into the area, almost all of it for the development of copper, chrome, manganese, and lithium mines.[107]

The economic boom of the 1950s and the Korean War raised demand for base metals in the United States. Whereas before World War II the United States was a net exporter of most minerals, during World War II large quantities were imported, and the postwar economic boom sustained the demand. Almost from the outset of the war the United States imported increasing quantities of metallurgical ores from southern Africa. By then the country had become South Africa's biggest customer for manganese, mainly for use in the production of dry-cell batteries, and its sole buyer of corundum, an important industrial abrasive.[108]

After the war, U.S. demands for chrome exploded. By 1951, after duties were lifted, all American chromite was imported, mostly from Southern Rhodesia and South Africa. Chromite became a key refractory and chief alloying constituent of stainless steel. In 1956 alone the United States imported 476,000 tons of South African chrome, making it that country's largest customer for the ore.[109] Cobalt demands also skyrocketed with the Korean War. In Northern Rhodesia, cobalt, which was used in the manufacture of high-strength alloys as well as for magnets in loudspeakers, was being produced as a byproduct of copper processing by the Rhokana Corporation. Copper also came into great demand, mainly for the United States' electrical and telecommunications equipment. Between 1954 and 1958 an annual average of 49,000 short tons of copper was exported to the United States from the Rhodesias and 19,000 from South Africa.[110] By the 1950s South Africa also became a world leader in platinum and the largest U.S. source for the metal.

A DEEPENING ENGAGEMENT:
THE INVASION OF AMERICAN CAPITAL

It must be reemphasized that American trade and investment greatly expanded in the decade of the 1950s, especially after January 1951, when South Africa eased its import restrictions. Riding on handsome foreign exchange earnings from its export of minerals, South Africa entered into a new period of rapid economic expansion. Once the economy took off, it tended to be sustained by a high rate of reinvestment of profits and heavy infusions of fresh capital from Great Britain and the United States as well as from its own highly sophisticated financial institutions. Private capital inflows from the United States accelerated as American banks gave revolving credit for South African public and private agencies. The Industrial Development Corporation (IDC), which had been created by the government in 1940, now demanded capital to promote the nation's industrial development. The IDC assisted private enterprises and also encouraged the creation of state enterprises, including the mammoth South African Coal, Oil, and Gas Corporation (SA-

SOL). The first SASOL plant, which opened in 1955 for the purpose of extracting oil from coal, had an enormous effect on the expansion of the country's infant chemical industries.

The Netherlands Bank of South Africa, whose parent firm was in Amsterdam, began in the early 1950s to use the Irving Trust Company of New York as its correspondent bank. A turning point in South Africa's financial relations with the United States came in December 1952, when the Afrikaner government floated its first public loan on the American market ($20 million); and it was fully subscribed within two hours.[111]

The U.S. government, through its own postwar foreign aid programs, also made enormous contributions to this massive infusion of capital. Between 1945 and 1955 the U.S. extended $152 million to South Africa and $61 million to the British Rhodesias. In addition the World Bank in 1951 alone loaned South Africa $30 million for the expansion of the Electricity Supply Commission (ESCOM), its parastatal utility corporation, and $20 million for transportation. Between 1951 and 1957, the World Bank loaned South Africa altogether $160 million.[112]

American trade and investment in South Africa was moving into high gear when, in 1953, the U.S. Commerce Department began regular reporting on the country for the American business community. South Africa had become a keystone of the Cold War strategy, with the government and the private sector working hand in hand. Direct American investment in South Africa soared from $140 million in 1950 to $300 million in 1957. By 1959 it had reached $323 million, involving at least 160 American firms.[113] All but three of the fifteen largest corporations on *Fortune*'s index had investment portfolios that included holdings in South Africa. More trade was now being carried in American flagships than ever before, and a far higher percentage of them now traveled directly to South African ports, bypassing European intermediaries. South Africa greatly relaxed its import restrictions in 1957, and by the end of the following year the United States had become South Africa's second most important trading partner.

But the Union discovered that the ensuing expansion of imports had resulted by March 1958 in serious balance-of-payments deficits on both current and capital accounts. The government, however, encountered little difficulty in obtaining from the International Monetary Fund a gold-tranche drawing and a standby arrangement in order to maintain its weakening reserve situation and to obviate a reimposition of import restrictions.

The United States' economic ties with South Africa had become substantial enough to attract the attention of the larger banks, and a series of bank mergers in 1955—including National City Bank's merger with First National Bank to become the First National City Bank of New York and Chase National Bank's merger with the Bank of Manhattan Company to become Chase Manhattan[114]—enhanced the capability of several American banks to venture into Africa. In 1957 a revision of the Edge Act by the U.S. government gave banks wider authority to buy and sell foreign exchange and to operate overseas. A year later the First National City Bank returned to South Africa after a hiatus of thirty-six years. Also in 1958 the Netherlands Bank of South Africa (today Nedbank), opened a representative office in New York. Within three years Nedbank would become the largest South African-controlled banking group. In February 1959 Chase Manhattan Bank followed First National to Johannesburg. South Africa did not permit foreign banks to open branches, so it was necessary to establish a subsidiary. Both American banks were able to extend credit facilities and other services to American multinational corporations and their South African subsidiaries. It was only months before the two banks opened additional facilities in Cape Town. The ability of the two American banks to furnish loans in South African currency was of great service to the American MNCs that had formerly encountered problems in obtaining credit from South African banks, which tended to favor local firms.

MAKING THE CONNECTION EASIER: TRANSPORTATION, COMMUNICATIONS, AND TOURISM

The climate for American enterprise in South Africa greatly improved with advances in air transportation and communications. Pan American World Airways of New York inaugurated passenger air service between South Africa and the United States in 1947. Pan Am, chartered in the United States in 1927, got an early start as an international air carrier by servicing exclusive airmail contracts in runs to Latin America. In 1941 it moved into Africa when it assumed responsibility for Britain's trans-African air routes. A year after the war's end Pan Am was awarded the Africa and South Atlantic routes that its founder and owner, Juan Trippe, had pioneered in 1941. By 1949 the airline was offering two scheduled flights a week between New York City and Johannesburg. The fare was an exorbitant $917 one-way and the flight, following a route via the Azores, Lisbon, Dakar, and the capitals of equatorial Africa, consumed thirty-nine and a half hours. Nevertheless, it did represent an enormous reduction in traveling time for busy American executives.[115]

Communications were also greatly facilitated in 1949, when the Radio Corporation of America (RCA) established a direct link between the two countries with radio-telegraph and telephone service via American Telephone and Telegraph. RCA, founded three decades earlier, was the product of a joint effort by General Electric, Western Electric, American Marconi, and AT&T and was established to handle all foreign expansion of American radio communications. As early as 1930 South Africa was indirectly linked to the United States by RCA's London-based radiotelephones. The British had achieved an early domination of long-distance telephone service with its dominions through its monopolistic Empire Chain of stations, which connected the entire British Empire.[116]

Improved transport and communications helped to lubricate tourism between the two countries. In 1949 the South African Tourist Corporation (SATOUR) opened an office in New York City to promote South African tourism, while in October of the previous year the London branch of the American Express Company opened its first office, in Johannesburg. American Express did well in South Africa, and in 1950 it opened a branch in Cape Town.[117] It was not long before the firm was also conducting a booming business in the sale of travelers' checks and in handling land tours for American visitors. It also booked tours to the United States. American Express attributed much of its success to its popular weekly South African radio broadcast, "Abroad with American Express," which was first aired late in 1951.

It was also in that year that Farrell Lines, in cooperation with American Express, began to advertise fifty-five day all-expense "cruise tours" on its sister ships, the *African Endeavor* and the *American Enterprise*. Over the years, since the 1920s, the Farrell family had probably been more responsible than any single American entrepreneur for the promotion of passenger and freight traffic to southern Africa.

The flow of Americans to South Africa had grown substantially, from

The most wonderful travel adventure of all...

South Africa

...**plus
a superb voyage on a
modern transatlantic liner—
an unforgettable vacation in itself!**

South Africa's spectacular scenery, delightful climate, beaches and lakes will captivate you. Modern cities, Zulu villages. Big game or camera safaris arranged in advance. Also special 55-day, all-expense "Cruise-Tours."

SAILING REGULARLY—the sister-ships *African Endeavor* and *African Enterprise* assure a glorious ocean crossing . . . finest accommodations, service, cuisine. New York to Capetown, $650 up.

For full information, see your Travel Agent or write Dept. A.

FARRELL LINES

26 BEAVER STREET, NEW YORK 4, N. Y.

15. An advertisement for Farrell Line cruises to South Africa, 1951. (Courtesy, Farrell Lines)

402 visitors in 1930 to 819 in 1948 and 1,498 in 1953. By 1956 it had climbed to an annual 3,404 visitors.[118] Nevertheless, sea passenger traffic steadily lost ground as air travel time was reduced. Finally, in 1959 Farrell Lines, after losing money on the Cape Town run, withdrew its passenger service altogether.

Business and tourism were greatly stimulated by improvements in domestic and international air transportation. South African Airways launched an expansion program in the mid-1950s. In 1956 it took delivery of three Douglas DC-7-Bs, which at the time were the fastest piston-driven commerical aircraft in the world. South African Airways was the first airline outside the United States to use the aircraft. But advances in aircraft technology soon rendered even the DC-7-B obsolete. The first commercial jet made its Atlantic crossing in 1958, and within two years South African Airways and Pan Am entered the jet age with their acquisition of Boeing 707s.[119] Thus, 1960 marked a turning point. The jet age vastly shortened travelling time while expanding the entrepreneurs' vision and opportunities. Suddenly, South Africa seemed not too distant to the adventuresome American businessperson and tourist.

ENGAGING THE MASSES: FILM AND THEATER

Advances in telecommunications and transportation brought only a small number of South Africans into contact with Americans and their culture. It was the expansion of the U.S. entertainment industry that exposed the broad masses—blacks as well as whites—to the full spectrum of American life. And after World War II American culture spread more deeply and extensively in South Africa, primarily through the film industry. In the 1930s movies, especially with the widespread introduction of sound motion pictures, became the chief arm of American culture there.

After the war American films were marketed more aggressively as a result of the establishment of the Motion Picture Export Association of America (MPEAA). This was a trade association representing the major film producers and distributors. Some scholars have referred to it as the foreign policy wing of the American film industry.[120] In any case, MPEAA gave strong encouragement to the dissemination of American films throughout southern Africa. A number of American film companies entered the region for the first time in the 1950s, including United Artists

Take the fast way to Africa's fast-growing markets. Fly with us "International Style".

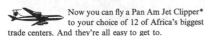 Now you can fly a Pan Am Jet Clipper* to your choice of 12 of Africa's biggest trade centers. And they're all easy to get to.

Pan Am is the only airline that flies straight through from New York to Rabat/Casablanca, Dakar, Conakry, Monrovia, Accra, Lagos, Abidjan, Cotonou, Douala, Leopoldville and Johannesburg.

You can see one city or see a handful. Prefer the latter? Our Extra Cities Plan makes it easy. Buy a round trip to Johannesburg, for instance, and you can visit other cities on the way there and on the way home.

And the fares? Here are a few round-trip 14-21 day Jet Economy samples: Rabat/Casablanca, $373. Dakar $557. Lagos, $689. Johannesburg, $946.

*Pan American Trade-Mark Reg. U.S. Pat. Off.

You'll fly a Pan Am Jet Clipper manned by a Pan Am crew. This is the same kind of jet that flies princes to Paris, millionaires to Montevideo and Jet-Setters to Japan. Take your choice of first-class *President Special* or *Rainbow* Economy service. Either way, you'll enjoy meals inspired by *Maxim's of Paris*. Whichever you choose, you'll be welcomed aboard by Pan Am's friendly cabin personnel.

And, best of all, you'll have the good feeling that comes from flying the very best there is.

For reservations, see your Pan Am Travel Agent or call Pan Am.

Reminder for businessmen: every Africa-bound Jet Clipper can carry up to 16,000 lbs. of cargo.

World's most experienced airline

FIRST ON THE ATLANTIC   FIRST ON THE PACIFIC   FIRST IN LATIN AMERICA   FIRST 'ROUND THE WORLD

16. A 1965 advertisement for Pan American World Airways. (Courtesy, Pan American World Airways)

Corporation, Loews International, and Warner Brothers. The competition intensified, and in 1956 Twentieth Century Fox, which had been in the country for some time, acquired the vast Schlesinger entertainment interests and merged them under the banner of the Johannesburg-based Twentieth Century Fox Organisation of Southern Africa. It was a major move because the Schlesinger family's African Theatres was the largest chain of cinemas in the region.[121]

Very little of South Africa could be found in the American cultural landscape. South African cinematographers had begun to develop their own motion picture industry but it was on an extremely small scale, and none of their films was commercially run in the United States. Instead, American eyes were opened by the stirring novel *Cry, The Beloved Country* by Alan Paton, a white liberal deeply concerned over racial discrimination in his own country. Shortly after its publication, American playwrights Kurt Weill and Maxwell Anderson transformed it into a popular musical, *Lost in the Stars*. Opening on Broadway in October 1949 and running for an astounding 289 performances,[122] this play provided the American masses with their first exposure to racial issues in South Africa. It would not be their last.

AFRICAN EDUCATION: MISSIONARY DISENGAGEMENT AND FOUNDATION REENGAGEMENT

The 1950s witnessed the effective retreat and withdrawal of American missionaries from the field of African education in South Africa. In 1949 the Bantu Education Commission, appointed by the Nationalist government, recommended greater central government control over African education.[123] It was a highly unrepresentative body, lacking participation from either Africans or missionary educators, even though the two groups had pioneered in the field of African education. The commissioners called for a separate educational system for Africans, including a different syllabus that would anchor students in their own traditional culture.

Their recommendations led to the notorious Bantu Education Act of 1953, which gave the white-staffed Department of Native Affairs control over all African schools, including those owned and operated by the American Board. The act transferred African education from the missionaries and provincial authorities to what shortly became the central government's Department of Bantu Education. It was further decreed that state subsidies to missionary-operated teacher training schools would be terminated and that those earmarked for mission-run primary and secondary schools would be phased out. Thus, the American Board's Inanda Seminary for Women in Natal became a government school. The Board's trustees in Boston protested in vain; in 1958 they terminated their financial support altogether. Adams College shared a similar fate, the government refusing to allow it to continue as a private independent school and forcing it to close down completely in 1956, after demanding that all teacher training be undertaken by the state.[124]

By the mid-1950s the American Board headquarters in Boston was suffering from financial and administrative problems, and its facilities throughout southern Africa had begun to deteriorate. The Board's trustees lacked the means and the will to fight the South African regime on the issue of apartheid. And with the loss of state subsidies from the South Africans the Board was unable to keep its educational institutions operating.

Nevertheless, by that time a more activist anti-apartheid concern was initiated, not by business leaders but by a new generation of American church leaders. At home a growing number of religious leaders were becoming political activists. Some were involved in the civil rights movement and were active in such multiracial organizations as the Congress of Racial Equality (CORE). They became sensitized to the issues of racial segregation and discrimination and began to view them in a wider global perspective. American civil rights leaders were deeply troubled by the new apartheid legislation of the Nationalist regime, especially the 1950 Group Areas Act, which intensified racial segregation on a geographical-residential basis. However, it was the 1952 Defiance Campaign against racial discrimination that brought the issue of apartheid vividly to the Americans and that sparked a new American concern over racial injustice in South Africa. The Defiance Campaign was a nationwide civil disobedience campaign in which more than 8,500 Africans and their supporters went to jail. The African National Congress, a key player in the campaign, had begun to shift to a more neo-Gandhian form of civil disobedience through passive resistance. The demonstrations broadened the ANC membership and transformed the organization into a mass movement.[125]

The Defiance Campaign received considerable media attention in the United States and drew keen interest from civil rights leaders. Inspired by the campaign, a multiracial group of attorneys, clergy and pacifists under the leadership of Reverend George M. Houser in 1953 organized in New York the American Committee on Africa (ACOA) with the prime objective of supporting the struggle for African liberation by educating and mobilizing the American public. Its major publication, *Africa Today*, was established by George Shepherd, later a University of Denver professor. From its inception the American Committee eschewed government support and relied heavily on donations from liberal inter-denominational church organizations.[126]

American academic interest in South Africa remained at a low level in the immediate postwar years. Between 1947 and 1951 the centrist Carnegie Corporation of New York had tried to generate more interest by sponsoring reconnaissance trips to East and South Africa. Between 1950 and 1952 it gave seed money to Northwestern University for African studies. Then, in 1951, the American Universities Field Staff (AUFS) was organized in New York as a nonprofit academic "foreign service" to generate more academic interest in contemporary world affairs. The AUFS sent Edwin Munger, a young scholar from California Tech, into the field to gather first-hand information and to report regularly from southern Africa. Munger's rambling observations were circulated periodically in loose form on campuses affiliated with the organization.[127] Another American scholar of South Africa was Gwendolen Carter, whose book *The Politics of Inequality: South Africa since 1949*, published in 1958, was the first comprehensive analysis of South African politics by an American political scientist.

Many people in the public and private sectors were concerned that prominent Africans on official visits to the United States be accorded a non-discriminatory reception and one befitting their role. Thus, in 1953, a group of black and white American educators, businessmen, and entertainers launched the African-American Institute (AAI) in Washington, D.C. Through donations from major banks and corporations doing business in Africa as well as funds from the government, the AAI emerged as a non-membership, non-partisan and non-profit organization.

The African-American Institute was also designed to assist African students in the United States with scholarships and to establish links between American business and political leaders and the emerging new generation of black African nationalist leaders. *Africa Report*, a monthly magazine, was launched by the AAI in 1956 to offer analysis of current political and economic developments throughout the continent.[128]

Working closely with the government, the Ford Foundation in 1953 established funds for the Foreign Areas Training Program and provided seed money for the creation of African studies centers on major American campuses, including Boston University (1953), Johns Hopkins (1957), and the University of California, Los Angeles (1957). At the time only Northwestern University had offered a program of African studies. Federal funding was substantially increased after 1957 through Title IV of the National Defense Act, which encouraged the study of non-Western languages and cultures.[129] In many ways the Ford decision marked the beginning of a new period of foundation rededication to Africa. The major concern this time was with educating Americans about the continent and preparing them for leadership roles in government and education. Very little attention, however, was given to training citizens for roles in international business.

Also in 1957 the African Studies Association (ASA) was founded at Columbia University by a group of academics under the leadership of Cornelius de Kiewiet, a South African emigré and president of Rochester University and the Association of American Universities, and Alan Pifer, head of the Carnegie Corporation. A year later, the Carnegie Corporation granted Columbia University funds to sponsor an American Assembly conference on "The United States and Africa." Leading experts from government, business, banking, and education attended.[130] Black American intellectuals, feeling excluded from these developments, organized the American Society of African Culture (AMSAC) in New York as their own forum. In some respects, AMSAC was a successor to the multiracial, though black-led, Council on African Affairs, which had been founded in the early 1940s by Paul Robeson and Max Yergan who, in the early years, were outspoken Russophiles. The Council, however, was more militantly anti-apartheid and fell victim in the early 1950s to the anti-Communist hysteria of the Cold War. Yergan, despite his long years in South Africa as an executive with the YMCA, subsequently resurfaced as a political conservative. Both organizations failed to receive support from the major foundations and eventually passed into oblivion.

THE MASS MEDIA DISCOVERS SOUTH AFRICA

American interest in Africa was rekindled by the achievement of Ghanaian independence in March 1957 and by the rapid growth of African nationalism in South Africa. The African National Congress drew closer to the black working class after the establishment in 1955 of the multiracial South African Congress of Trade Unions, a sister organization that affiliated itself with the Soviet-dominated World Federation of Trade Unions. A group of white South Africans and Americans, concerned with these trends, obtained funds from the Carnegie Corporation in 1958 to organize the United States–South Africa Leadership Exchange Program. USSALEP opened offices in Washington and Johannesburg and developed a Visitors' Exchange Program that bore strong resemblance to the one operated by the Carnegie Corporation in the 1920s and 1930s.

The human suffering, social upheaval, and violence generated by the government's implementation of apartheid began to draw the attention of civil rights leaders in the United States. In 1950 the Population Registration Act and Group Areas Act, respectively, classified the entire population by race and called for the division of the nation into separate areas for different races and black ethnic groups. Three years later the Reservation of Separate Amenities Act provided fines and possible imprisonment for attempts to integrate public facilities, and the Native Labour Act redefined the term *employee* to exclude Africans.[131]

These and other apartheid laws attracted the interest of the American media at a time when the United States was itself deeply concerned over racial discrimination and civil rights. John Gunther's *Inside Africa,* the first popular, serious survey of contemporary Africa ever published in the United States, appeared in 1955 and rapidly became a best-seller. In the same year John Hughes, a journalist with the Boston-based *Christian Science Monitor,* opened the first American news bureau in South Africa. *The New York Times* followed only months later. Both papers began to cover such events as forced removals of the black population under the Group Areas Act and the effects of the Industrial Conciliation Act, which provided for job reservation along racial lines. Considerable media attention was also given in 1956 to the removal of the constitutional clause that for a century had given Coloreds the right to vote. American interest in the process of newsgathering in Africa was articulated in 1956, when Ruth Sloan Associates in New York commissioned Helen Kitchen to edit *The Press in Africa*.

Soon after the triumphant Montgomery, Alabama, Bus Boycott in 1956, associates of civil rights leader Reverend Martin Luther King, Jr., journeyed to the teeming black ghettos of Alexandra in South Africa to help its residents organize a similar boycott. Bus boycotts were not new to South Africans, who had organized the first such boycott in modern history in the 1940s. However, King's followers had perfected the strategy of civil disobedience. The subsequent Alexandra Bus Boycott of 1957 lasted three months and proved to be the most dramatic passive resistance effort in South Africa's history. But while the Montgomery Bus Boycott had ended in victory when the U.S. Supreme Court declared segregation of buses unconstitutional, its Alexandra counterpart led to only greater entrenchment of segregationist policies.

CONCLUSION

The United States' position in South Africa was greatly expanded, deepened, and ultimately consolidated in the three decades following the Wall Street Crash of 1929. More than that, the Union became an American base for penetrating the markets and resources of British and Belgian possessions extending as far north as Kenya Colony. After 1953 South-Central Africa became an especially lucrative region, with the formation of the British-controlled Central African Federation, consisting of the two Rhodesias and Nyasaland. This was followed by a decade of massive infusions of British, South African, and American capital for private investment and public infrastructural development.

By the close of the 1950s American multinational corporations had deeply ensconced themselves in nearly every sector of South Africa's economy. Thus, what looked like ominous storm clouds and bolts of lightning on the economic horizon of late 1929 turned out to be the flashes of a bright new dawn, heralding a more aggressive and dynamic phase in the United States' engagement with South Africa. But this intensive involvement must be contrasted against the retreat of the old mainline missionary organizations and to a lesser extent the private foundations. In the 1930s the former had begun to address themselves to the urgent social and racial issues of the day, establishing community centers in black townships, studying white poverty and African migrancy, funding organizations dedicated to interracial dialogue, opening new hospitals and clinics, creating experimental farms and rural schools, and educating an African leadership that was becoming increasingly outspoken against white supremacy. But in the 1950s Americans retreated from their small, though ambitious, undertakings in the face of growing government intervention in African education and community development. American missionaries, whose historic involvement was mainly with English-speaking liberals, enjoyed little influence in Afrikaner government circles. In addition, they had to contend with diminishing support from home.

The United States' dramatic economic ascendancy in South Africa was achieved through a fascinatingly complex interplay of factors, which included adroit gold and dollar diplomacies, the creation and manipulation of postwar multilateral donor institutions and trade agreements, and the use of trade-related federal agencies like the Export-Import Bank. Great Britain's departure from the gold standard in 1931, an important turning point, ushered in a chaotic era of competitive devaluations, monetary disorder, and a British-imposed imperial preference tariff system designed in part to limit the United States' presence in traditional British overseas markets. But South Africa and the United States ultimately turned these exclusionary policies to their advantage, and by 1946 the Americans had imposed a new order, dominated by a gold-backed dollar.

The federal government became the engine of American expansion, subsidizing the merchant marine and Pan American Airways and encouraging loans to South Africa's public and private sectors for infrastructural expansion. Direct and portfolio investments in the postwar era soared, impelled by a burgeoning highly protected manufacturing sector and by seemingly insatiable demands for minerals from American industries. World War II and the Korean conflict, combined with the paranoia of the Cold War, heightened the United States' concern over mineral sourcing and more sharply focused the debate over South Africa's strategic importance in a world seemingly threatened by communism. The white power structure fed the fires of that evolving controversy by posing as a Western outpost of capitalist order and stability in an increasingly turbulent non-Western world. In the 1940s and 1950s the

United States' perception of southern Africa as a great mine of vital strategic minerals, a model of capitalist economic development and unlimited entrepreneurial opportunity, and a land of staggering physical beauty had the tragic effect of greatly obfuscating the harsh realities of an evolving racial domination. American investments, basking in spectacularly high rates of return, were undeterred by such upheavals as the Defiance Campaign. It would take the shock of a well-publicized massacre in a teeming black ghetto to open the eyes of Americans to the other side of the beguiling South African coin.

NOTES

1. U.S. Department of Commerce, *American Direct Investments in Foreign Countries,* Bulletin no. 731; U.S. Department of State, *The Trade Debate;* Stephanie A. Lenway, *The Politics of International Trade* (Boston, 1985), pp. 16–19.
2. C. W. De Kiewiet, *A History of South Africa: Social and Economic,* p. 44.
3. A. P. Walshe, "Southern Africa," A. D. Roberts, ed., *The Cambridge History of Africa* (London, 1986), p. 548; David K. Eiteman and Arthur I. Stonehill, *Multinational Business Finance,* pp. 42–43.
4. Alan Jeeves and David Yudelman, "The Closing of a Labor Frontier: Black Migrants to the South African Gold Mines, 1920–1985," paper presented at Wesleyan University, April 1986. See also Jonathan Hughes, *American Economic History* (Glenview, Ill., 1985), p. 233.
5. Brian Kantor, "Monetary Policy," in Marcelle Kooy, ed., *Studies in Economics and Economic History,* p. 67. See also S. Lumby, "Tariffs and Gold in South Africa, 1886–1939," p. 139; "The Country's Coachman," *Financial Mail* (Johannesburg) November 1, 1985, p. 49; David Yudelman, *The Emergence of Modern South Africa,* ch. 4 and passim.
6. G. W. G. Browne, "Fifty Years of Public Finance," *South African Journal of Economics* 51, 1 (March 1983). 136.
7. Merle Lipton, *Capitalism and Apartheid, 1910–1984,* pp. 110–11. Francis Wilson, "Southern Africa," in Roland Oliver, ed., *Cambridge History of Africa,* 7:260.
8. A. C. M. Webb, "Mining in South Africa," in Francis Coleman, ed., *Economic History of South Africa,* p. 191; Eiteman and Stonehill, *Multinational Business,* p. 42; A. B. Lumby, "Development of Secondary Industry," in Coleman, ed., *Economic History,* p. 137; Leo Katzen, *Gold and the South African Economy,* pp. 77–84.
9. C. G. W. Schumann, "Aspects of Economic Development in South Africa," in Kooy, ed., *Studies in Economics,* p. 10.

10. "South African Markets," *Businessweek,* December 12, 1936, p. 17. See also S. H. Frankel, *Capital Investment in Africa: Its Course and Effects,* p. 211; U.S. Department of Commerce, *American Direct Investments in Foreign Countries in 1936,* p. 16; Cleona Lewis, *America's Stake in International Investments,* pp. 44–49.

11. U.S. Bureau of Foreign Commerce, *Investment in the Union of South Africa: Conditions and Outlook.* (Washington, D.C., 1953), p. 23; *Economist,* February 13, 1988, pp. 70–73; *Financial Mail* (Johannesburg) November 7, 1986, p. 34.

12. Daan Prinsloo, *United States Foregin Policy and the Republic of South Africa,* p. 48; Eric A. Walker, *A History of Southern Africa* (London, 1957), p. 636.

13. C. G. W. Schumann, *Structural Changes and Business Cycles in South Africa, 1806–1936,* pp. 99–211. See also, S. H. Frankel, *Investment and Return to Equity Capital in the South African Gold Mining Industry,* p. 114.

14. B. R. Mitchell, comp., *International Historical Statistics,* p. 414. See also U.S. Department fo Commerce, *Annual Economic Review,* Special Report no. 28 (Washington D.C., 1935).

15. U.S. Department of Commerce. *Union of South Africa. Business Trade Information Service* (World Trade Series) no. 40, June 1951 (Washington, D.C.: US Dept. of Commerce, 1951) p. 19. See also U.S. Treasury Department, *Census of American-Owned Assets in Foreign Countries,* p. 411.

16. *State of the Union of South Africa and Statistical Year Book (1958),* (Cape Town, 1959), p. 133. See also Cleona Lewis, *The United States and Foreign Investment Problems,* p. 323.

17. Robert Greenhalgh Albion, *Seaports South of the Sahara,* p. 127. See also G. R. Berridge, *Politics of the South Africa Run: European Shipping and Pretoria,* p. 60 fn.

18. Investment in the Union, Appendix B, pp. 131–36. See also U.S. Department of Commerce, *Commerce Reports,* no. 28 (South Africa) July 13, 1935 (Washington, D.C., 1936), p. 22.

19. *South African Production* (Johannesburg, 1967), p. 271. See also Katherin Marton, *Multinationals, Technology, and Industrialization: Implications and Impact in Third World Countries,* p. 105, Edmund T. Pratt, *Pfizer: Bringing Science to Life,* p. 6.

20. Eric Rosenthal, *Stars and Stripes in Africa,* (Johannesburg, 1968), p. 27. See also Kristin Thompson, *Exporting Entertainment: America in the Film Market, 1907–34,* p. 171.

21. Anthony Slide, *The American Film Industry: A Historical Dictionary* (New York, 1986), pp. 209–10. See also Thelma Gutsche, *The History and Social Significance of the Motion Picture in South Africa, 1895–1940,* p. 256; *Our First Half Century, 1910–1960* (Johannesburg, 1960), p. 324.

22. H. M. Moolman, ed., *South African–American Survey,* p. 19.

23. Mira Wilkins, *The Maturing of Multinational Enterprise: American Business Abroad, 1914–1970*, p. 385.
24. Raymond Sekaly, *Transnationalization of the Automotive Industry*, p. 29.
25. Michael French, "Structural Change and Competition in the U.S. Tire Industry, 1920–1937," *Business History Review* 60 (Spring 1986): 28–29. See also *South African Industry and Trade, 1907–1957: Golden Jubilee Number* p. 271.
26. John M. Stopford and John H. Dunning, *The World Directory of Multinational Enterprises, 1982–83*, p. 1063. See also Henrietta Larson, Evelyn Knowlton, Charles Popple, *History of Standard Oil Company (New Jersey): New Horizons, 1927–1950*, p. 260.
27. Wilkins, *Maturing*, p. 344.
28. U.S. Department of State, *Efforts to Meet Complaints from South Africa that American Import Regulations Unduly Restrict South African Exports to USA*, in Foreign Relations of the United States, Diplomatic Papers, vol. 1, 1936 (Washington, D.C., 1936).
29. Stephen J. Randall, *United States Foreign Oil Policy: 1919–1948* (Montreal, 1985), p. 58.
30. Stopford and Dunning, *Multinational Enterprises*, p. 1066.
31. Robert W. Dunn. *American Foreign Investments* p. 66. See also Anonymous, *Journal of Commerce*, May 31, 1949, p. 5.
32. Stephen D. Krasner, *Defending the National Interests: Raw Materials Investments and U.S. Foreign Policy*, p. 48. See also C. K. Leith, J. W. Furness, and Cleona Lewis, *World Minerals and World Peace*.
33. Alex Skelton, "World Copper Mining," in William Y. Elliott, ed., *International Control in the Non-Ferrous Metals*, p. 337.
34. Brookes Emeny, *The Strategy of Raw Materials*, p. 99.
35. T. S. Lovering, *Minerals in World Affairs*, p. 216.
36. J. W. Furness and L. M. Jones, *Mineral Raw Materials. A Survey of Commerce and Sources in Major Industrial Countries*, pp. 5–6.
37. Leith, Furness, and Lewis, *World Minerals and World Peace*, p. 72. See also Emery N. Castle and Kent A. Price, eds., *United States Interests and Global Natural Resources*, p. 70.
38. Raymond Dumett, "Africa's Strategic Minerals During the Second World War," p. 383. See also Alan Bateman, "Wartime Dependence on Foreign Minerals"; Raymond Mikesell, *Stockpiling Strategic Minerals* (Washington, D.C. 1986), p. 9.
39. Kenneth Ingham, *Jan Christian Smuts. The Conscience of a South African* (London, 1986), p. 314.
40. Anson Phelps Stokes, *Report on Education, Native Welfare and Race Relations in East and Southern Africa* (New York, 1934).
41. "Report of the Interterritorial Jeanes Conference," Salisbury, May 1935 (Lovedale, South Africa, 1935), pp. 395–428.
42. Thomas Karis and Gwendolen M. Carter, eds., *From Protest to Challenge:*

Documentary History of African Politics in South Africa, 1882–1964, 4:55.

43. Merle Curti, *American Philanthropy Abroad*, p. 321. See also Richard D. Heyman, "The Role of the Carnegie Corporation of New York in African Education, 1925–1960," Ph.D. dissertation (Columbia University, 1970), pp. 88–94. For a critical examination of the role of the Phelps-Stokes Fund in Africa, see Edward H. Berman, "Education in Africa and America: A History of the Phelps-Stokes Fund, 1911–1945," D.Ed. dissertation (Columbia University, 1969).

44. J. F. W. Grosskopf, et al., *The Poor White Problem in South Africa: Report of the Carnegie Commission*.

45. Edgar H. Brookes, ed., *Apartheid: A Documentary Study* (London, 1968), pp. 33–34.

46. J. Merle Davis, *Modern Industry and the African*, p. 282.

47. Ray E. Phillips, *The Bantu in the City*, p. 38. See also Richard Elphick, "Missionary Christianity and Interwar Liberalism," in Jeffrey Butler, Richard Elphick, and David Welsh, eds., *Democratic Liberalism in South Africa: Its History and Prospects*, (Middletown, Mass., 1988), p. 69.

48. Phillips, *Bantu*, p. 111. See also Paul Rich, *White Power and the Liberal Conscience* (Johannesburg, 1984), pp. 24–25.

49. Lord Hailey, *An African Survey* (Oxford, 1937).

50. U.S. Department of Interior, Bureau of Mines, Bulletin No. 19. *The Minerals Yearbook for 1943* (Washington D.C., 1943).

51. Lipton, *Apartheid*, p. 272. See also Newell M. Stultz *Afrikaner Politics in South Africa, 1934–1948*, p. 55.

52. Mitchell, Comp. *International Statistics,* p. 426. See also E. W. Pehrson, "War and Strategic Minerals," *South African Mining and Engineering Journal* October 8, 1942.

53. *State of the Union (1957)*, p. 251. See also *Businessweek*, February 27, 1960. p. 86; "New U.S. Stake in South Africa," *Businessweek*, November 29, 1947, p. 16; Ian Mackler, *Pattern for Profit in Southern Africa*, p. 41. See also U.S. Department of Commerce, *Statistical Abstracts of the United States* no. 65, 1943.

54. "Lend-Lease Assistance," *Businessweek*, November 29, 1947, pp. 44–48. See also Andrew Kamarck, "The African Economy and International Trade," in Walter Goldschmidt, ed., *The United States and Africa*, American Assembly series (Arden, 1958).

55. Mackler, *Pattern for Profit*, p. 70. South African Airways, *Annual Report, 1956–1957* (Pretoria, 1958), p. 7. *South African Digest*, November 29, 1985, p. 1096. See also *South African Digest*, February 10, 1984, p. 15.

56. U.S. Department of Commerce, *Exporters' Digest and International Trade Review*, p. 22. See also Dumett, "Minerals," p. 80.

57. A. M. Fransman, "Capital Accumulation in South Africa," in A. M. Fransman, ed., *Industry and Accumulation in Africa* (London, Heinemann,

1982), p. 5. See also John G. B. Hutchins, "The American Shipping Industry Since 1914," 2 pp. 211–12,
58. Harry Venedikian and Gerald A. Warfield, *Export-Import Financing* (New York, 1985), pp. 82–83. See also *The Economist* Februaray 6, 1988, p. 70; *Economist* February 13, 1988, p. 40.
59. J. Keith Horsefield, ed., *The International Monetary Fund, 1945–1965* (Washington, D.C., 1969), 2:413–14. See also Stefanie A. Lenway, *The Politics of U.S. International Trade* (Boston, 1985), p. 6.
60. U.S. Department of Commerce, *The Foreign Investments of the United States*, Supplement, *Survey of Current Business* (Washington, D.C., 1953), p. 60. See also "Horns of a Dilemma," *New York Times*, October 13, 1987, p. D-5.
61. World Bank, *Sixth Annual Report, 1950–51* (Washington, D.C., 1952) p. 19. See also *ESCOM Sixty-First Annual Report Ending 31 December 1983* (Sandton, S. A., 1984).
62. World Bank, *Ninth Annual Report, 1953–54* (Washington, D.C., 1954) p. 22.
63. Department of Commerce, *Investment in the Union of South Africa: A Survey* (Washington; D.C. 1954), p. 60.
64. Albion, *Seaports*, p. 18.
65. U.S. Department of Commerce, Union of South Africa *Business Information Service* (World Trade Series), no. 40 (Washington, D.C. June 1951) p. 1. See also George Marais, "Foreign Trade of the Union of South Africa," Ph.D. dissertation, (University of Wisconsin, 1956).
66. U.S. Department of Commerce, *Investment in the Union of South Africa: Conditions and Outlook* (Washington, D.C., 1953), p. 22. See also *Businessweek*, May 27, 1950, p. 44.
67. Lipton, *Apartheid*, pp. 239–40. Tom Lodge, *Black Politics in South Africa Since 1945* (New York, 1983), ch. 1 and passim.
68. Alex Hepple, *South Africa: A Political and Economic History* (New York, 1968), p. 186. See also South Africa. Social and Economic Planning Council, Report no. 9 UG 32/1946 (Pretoria, 1946).
69. Lodge, *Black Politics*, pp. 19–20.
70. Union of South Africa, Department of Native Affairs, *Report of the Native Laws Commission, 1946–1948* (Fagan Commission) (Pretoria, 1948) pp. 17–24.
71. D. Hobart Houghton, *The South African Economy*, p. 140. See also A. B. Lumby, "The Development of Secondary Industry," in Coleman, ed., *Economic History*, p. 220.
72. U.S. Department of Commerce, *Business Information Service*, p. 4. see also *Economist*, August 6, 1949, p. 318; D. J. Botha, "On Tariff Policy: The Formative Years," *South African Journal of Economics* 41, 4 (December 1973): 117–18.
73. H. Zarenda, "Tariff Policy: Export Promotion versus Import Replace-

ment," *South African Journal of Economics* 43, 1 (March 1975): 23.

74. David Hughes, *In South African Waters: Passenger Lines Since 1930*, p. 46.

75. Albion, *Seaports*, p. 255. Berridge, *South Africa Run*, p. 19.

76. Business Trade Information Service (1951), p. 4. See also Kamarck, "African Economy," in G. Goldschmidt, ed., *United States and Africa*, p. 131.

77. *Investment in the Union of South Africa* (1953), p. 136. See also *Businessweek*, February 11, 1950, p. 106.

78. *South African Production*, p. 39.

79. Hermann Giliomee, "Apartheid, Verligtheid, and Liberalism," in Butler, Elphick, and Welsh, eds., *Democratic Liberalism in South Africa*, pp. 372–73.

80. *Investment in the Union of South Africa*, p. 2. See also Robert L. Sammone to Director of Foreign Reporting Services, "American Capital Investment in South Africa."

81. David Hauck, *U.S. Companies and Support for the South African Government: The Legal Requirements* (Washington, D.C., 1985), p. 7.

82. Barrie G. James, *The Future of the Multinational Pharmaceutical Industry to 1990*, p. 2. See also Stopford and Dunning, *Multinational Enterprise*, p. 223; *South African Production*, p. 11; Pratt, *Pfizer*, p. 16.

83. C. Joseph Pusateri, *A History of American Business*, (Arlington Hts, Ill., 1984) p. 280. See also Richard Leonard, *Computers in South Africa: A Survey of U.S. Companies*, p. 7.

84. Arthur Marguette, *Brands, Trademarks and Goodwill: The Story of the Quaker Oats Company* (New York, 1967); Stopford and Dunning, *Multinational Enterprise*, 2:211; E. W. Williams, *Frozen Foods: Biography of an Industry* (Boston, 1963), p. 14.

85. Bureau of Statistics, *Union Statistics for Fifty Years*, p. 14.

86. Donald McHenry, *United States Firms in South Africa*, p. 34. See also *State of the Union* (1957), p. 77; Mobil Oil Corporation, *Mobil in South Africa*.

87. Maurice O'Reilly, *The Goodyear Story*, p. 116. See also "Prospecsts in the Tire Industry," *Journal of Commerce* (New York, vol. 220, no. 16,907 (May 31, 1949), p. 44.

88. Prinsloo, *U.S. Foreign Policy*, p. 59. See also Oye Ogunbadejo, *The International Politics of Africa's Strategic Minerals*, p. 89.

89. *State of the Union* (1957), p. 183.

90. Anonymons, *Treaties and Alliances of the World* (New York, 1974), p. 175. See also *Facts on File*, December 17–23, 1950 New York, 1951), p. 1022. E. W. Anderson and G. H. Blake, *The Republic of South Africa as a Supplier of Strategic Minerals*.

91. Madeleine Kalb, *The Cold War in Africa: From Eisenhower to Kennedy*

(New York, 1982), p. 272. See also Thomas J. Noer, *Black Liberation: The United States and White Rule in Africa, 1948–1968*, ch. 1 and passim.
92. David A. V. Fischer, "Slowing the Spread of Nuclear Weapons" *Optima* 33, 3 (1985); 100. See also Mikesell, *Stockpiling Strategic Materials,* p. 11.
93. *Treaties and Alliances,* p. 174. See also Alfred E. Eckes, Jr., *The United States and the Global Struggle for Minerals* (Austin, 1981), p. 151.
94. *State of the Union (1957),* p. 185.
95. Van Rhijn, "The Importance of the South African Mining Industry," *African Affairs* 58, 232 (July 1959): 234. See also Harry Magdoff, "American Empire and the U.S. Economy," in Robert I. Rhodes, ed., *Imperialism and Underdevelopment* (New York, 1970), p. 81.
96. Castle and Price, *U.S. Interests,* pp. 70–72.
97. U.S. President's Materials Policy Commission (Paley Commission), *Resources for Freedom Report,* June 1952 (Washington, D.C., 1952).
98. W. C. J. van Rensburg, *Strategic Minerals: Major Mineral-Consuming Regions of the World,* 2:174.
99. U.S. Congress, Senate, Committee on Interior and Insular Affairs, *Stockpile and Accessibility of Strategic and Critical Materials to the United States in Time of War,* Hearings before the Special Subcommittee on Minerals, 83rd Cong., 1953, part 1 (Washington, D.C., 1953), pp. 37–39.
100. Ogunbadejo, *Strategic Minerals,* pp. 100–108.
101. Sanford D. Greenberg, "U.S. Policy Toward the Republic of South Africa, 1945–1964," pp. 55–57.
102. Crawford Young, "U.S. Policy Toward Africa," African Studies Association, Silver Anniversary Address (Boston, December 1983). See also Noer, *Black Liberation,* p. 94. Leon M. S. Slawecki, "The Development of U.S. Foreign Policy toward South Africa, 1948–1963," (YUL).
103. Ibid., p. 19.
104. Siegfried Stein, *The United States in International Banking* (New York, 1951), p. 415. See also Stewart Smith, *U.S. Neocolonialism in Africa.*
105. A. P. Cartwright, *Golden Age: The Story of the Industrialization of South Africa and the Role Played by the Corner House Group of Companies, 1910–1967,* p. 323 (RH).
106. J. Patrick Ryan, "Gold U.S. Department of the Interior, Bureau of Mines," in *Mineral Facts and Problems,* p. 309.
107. A.J. Wills, *The History of Central Africa* (New York, 1964), p. 338.
108. Donald A. Brobst and Walden P. Pratt, *United States Mineral Resources;* Dan O'Meara, *Volkskapitalisme: Class, Capital and Ideology in the Development of Afrikaner Nationalism, 1934–1948,* p. 249.
109. U.S. Department of the Interior, Bureau of Mines, *Mineral Facts,* p. 211.
110. Ibid., p. 288.
111. *State of the Union (1958),* p. 296. See also SASOL Ltd., *Annual Report, 1982* (Johannesburg, 1982), p. 8.

112. *Africa Report*, July (Washington, D.C., 1958), p. 9. World Bank, *Annual Report, 1961–1962* (Washington, D.C., 1963), pp. 18–19.

113. *State of the Union (1958)*, p. 291; U.S. Department of Commerce, *Statistical Abstracts on the United States*, no. 80, 1959.

114. Harold van B. Cleveland and Thomas F. Huertas, *Citibank, 1812–1970* p. 434. fn. See also S. H. Kim and S. W. Miller, *Competitive Structure of the International Banking Industry*, p. 55.

115. Deborah W. Ray, "Pan-American Airways and the Trans-African Air Base Program of World War II," Ph.D dissertation (New York University, 1973), pp. 62–64.

116. Stopford, and Dunning *Multinational Enterprise*, 2:425.

117. *Promises to Pay: The Story of the American Express Company* (New York, Amexco, 1977), p. 14.

118. "SATOUR," in *State of the Union (1958)*, p. 425. See also David Hughes, *In South African Waters: Passenger Lines Since 1930*, p. 46.

119. *South African Digest*, March 11, 1971, p. 11.

120. Rosaleen Smyth, "Factors Inhibiting the Development of Feature Film Production in English-Speaking Africa."

121. Slide, *Film Industry*, p. 210.

122. "Lost in the Stars Dazzled America," *Variety* October 16, 1952, p. 17.

123. *Apartheid: Its Effects on Education, Science, Culture, and Information* (Paris, 1968), pp. 30–95. See also Agnes Wood, *Shine Where You Are: A History of Inanda Seminary, 1869–1969*, p. 26.

124. Ibid., p. 126. See also Muriel Horrell, *Legislation and Race Relations* (Johannesburg, 1971), p. 64; Meg Voorhes, *American Universities and Black South African Education* (Washington, D.C., 1986).

125. Lodge, *Black Politics*, p. 158. See also Edward Roux, *Time Longer Than Rope: The Black Man's Struggle for Freedom in South Africa* (Madison, Wi, 1978), pp. 386ff.

126. George M. Houser, *No One Can Stop the Rain*, p. 63. USSALEP was founded in 1958. Richard E. Bissell, *South Africa and the United States: The Erosion of an Influence Relationship*, p. 132.

127. Edwin Munger, *American Universities Field Staff: Central and Southern Africa* (Washington, D.C., 1957), vol. 5.

128. Helen Kitchen, *U.S. Interests in Africa*, p. 8. See also Sanford J. Ungar, "South Africa in the American Media," in A. O. Hero and John Barratt, eds., *The American People and South Africa*, p. 25.

129. Edward H. Berman, *The Influence of the Carnegie, Ford, and Rockefeller Foundations on American Foreign Policy: The Ideology of Philanthropy*, pp. 40–44 and passim. See also Ford Foundation, *Annual Report, 1957* (New York; 1958).

130. Kamarck, "African Economy," p. 77. Roger Omond, *The Apartheid Handbook: A Guide to South Africa's Racial Policies* (New York, 1986),

pp. 36–40. See also Sheila T. Van der Horst, ed., *A Review of Race Discrimination in South Africa* (Cape Town, 1981), passim.

131. T. R. H. Davenport, *South Africa; A Modern History,* pp. 304–305. Roux, *Time Longer than Rope,* p. 385. William Minter, *King Solomon's Mines Revisited: Western Interests and the Burdened History of Southern Africa* (New York, 1986), p. 97.

SIX

From Sharpeville to Soweto, 1960–1975

Taken as a whole, the period 1960–1975 saw surging trade volume, impressive economic growth, and handsome profits for U.S. multinational corporations in South Africa. It was also an extremely propitious time for individual and portfolio investors. But during this period the economy was convulsed by domestic racial and labor turmoil and traumatized by external challenges the nature of which it had never before confronted. This chapter examines the measures taken by the South Africans and their American friends to stanch the capital hemorrhage, restore investor confidence, and dramatically restart an economy seemingly on the verge of collapse in 1960. It was a rescue operation that was repeated on several occasions in different forms. Many of these measures, however, were of such a Draconian nature that, while they achieved peace and restored a facade of domestic tranquility, they punctured the popular American illusion of a free-enterprise democratic South Africa. They helped give birth to a new generation of U.S. -based anti-apartheid organizations that stepped up the pressure for trade sanctions and questioned the very presence of American enterprise there, a presence that grew enormously in this period, fueled by a consumer and state-driven economic boom that generated fabulous profits for United States traders, manufacturers, and investors. This chapter examines the role of American enterprises—commercial, industrial, investment, and philanthropic —and their responses to these crises and opportunities. It identifies South Africa's growing dependence on the reinvested earnings of multinational corporations and foreign capital to sustain the boom. It was a prosperity that overlooked certain structural and institutional weaknesses in the economy and that masked the inability of semiskilled employment to keep pace with population growth. The erosion of civil rights in South Africa and the interracial stress generated by the imbalances in the economy's advance only highlighted the inconsistencies of a U.S. foreign policy that swung like a pendulum between pious declarations and a hard-headed pursuit of narrow and short-term national and corporate interests.

THE CRISIS OF CONFIDENCE

The year 1960 represented a truly historic turning point for the South African economy with the massacre on March 21 of sixty-nine Africans by the South African Police in the segregated Transvaal township of Sharpeville. The tragic incident had grown out of African anger and frustration over the hated pass system. The African National Congress (ANC) and the Pan-Africanist Congress (PAC), which had broken away from the ANC only a year earlier, had separately decided on a series of mass protest campaigns and pass-burning exercises. Sharpeville's was meant to be the first of many scheduled throughout the nation.

African nationalism was spreading like a brushfire throughout sub-Saharan Africa. In 1960 seventeen new African nations achieved independence from the various colonial powers and were admitted to the United Nations. This rapid process of independence touched off a revolution of rising expectations throughout southern Africa. In February 1960 in Cape Town Prime Minister Harold Macmillan warned Parliament of the "winds of change" sweeping across Africa and urged whites to initiate reforms.[1] Blacks took heart, while whites prepared to dig in.

American public consciousness of Africa had begun to awaken, and in March the U.S. Senate Foreign Relations Committee held unprecedented day-long open hearings to seek ways to forge an African policy. With great prescience, George Houser of the American Committee on Africa (ACOA) urged the senators not to view Africa in a narrow East-West context or out of fear of Soviet expansionism.[2] But many viewed Houser as a naive radical, and in the final analysis American policy remained a hostage of Cold War concerns. Even John F. Kennedy, who as a junior senator in 1956 had voiced opposition to the East-West analysis, had by the early 1960s reversed himself in the wake of Soviet intervention in

Cuba and in the former Belgian Congo. Richard Mahoney contends that "for the sake of Soviet containment . . . Kennedy retreated from an African policy based on African interests."[3]

The Sharpeville massacre and the tragic events immediately following in the African township of Langa near Cape Town, where hundreds were injured and approximately eighteen thousand were detained, were the first racial incidents in South Africa to shake the world, especially the international business community. In the 1950s the American business community had failed to perceive the gathering momentum of black protest sweeping through the urban industrial areas. Now it stood almost in disbelief as the Sharpeville and Langa incidents led to massive work stoppages and to an unprecedented declaration of a state of emergency throughout much of the nation. American entrepreneurs and investors suddenly lost confidence in the government's ability to control the turmoil. Some feared these events heralded a period of escalating racial turmoil and that white South Africa would soon fall before the wave of African nationalism sweeping over the continent. As blacks in South Africa moved toward confrontation with whites, civil disobedience and protest hardened into resistance laced with revolutionary rhetoric. The American media, new to the South African scene, confidently predicted that South Africa was nearing the end of its tether. Would the falling dominoes soon reach southward across the Zambezi and Limpopo rivers?

Given the context, it is not surprising that the Sharpeville and Langa tragedies triggered a massive flight of capital. Actually, the net outflow had begun three years earlier, though at a rate that caused little notice or concern. But things were dramatically different now. From March 1960 to June 1961 more than R248 million left the country. Gold and foreign exchange reserves fell by nearly a half, from R315 million to R142 million, clearly more than the current account could cover.[4] A substantial portion of the capital outflow consisted of the withdrawal of foreign portfolio and direct investments and of contractual repayments on loans. South Africa had to confront a balance-of-payments crisis greater in severity than any experienced since the dismal days of 1932, when the fabric of the nation seemed to be unravelling.

For a brief moment in 1960 it appeared that the entire capitalist economy would collapse and with it the sinews of white supremacy. To save itself, the government had to act quickly, imaginatively, and forcefully. Drastic and historically unprecedented measures were in order. Firstly, in early April the ANC and PAC were banned, and over the next three months thousands of so-called terrorists were imprisoned or detained. Turmoil subsided in the industrial heartland, and the government turned to fiscal issues. The Sharpeville aftermath had led to a substantial drain on reserves, which caused a sharp decline in liquidity of the commercial and other banking institutions. The incident was also damaging to trade and to the country's ability to attract foreign capital and technology on favorable terms. Restrictions were thus imposed on commercial bank loans for hire-purchase. Foreign exchange controls were intensified and severe limits placed on capital outflows. The government blocked the repatriation of profits earned by foreign investors. Indeed, Americans wishing to sell stocks on the Johannesburg Stock Exchange could not repatriate their profits but had to reinvest them in securities quoted on the exchange.[5]

RESTORING BUSINESS CONFIDENCE

To the astonishment of many, the draconian measures led rapidly to an accumulation of capital within the country and to a dramatic strengthening of the foreign exchange position. A favorable balance of the current account was quickly achieved. Thus, the government's fast and effective action had restored a large measure of foreign investor confidence.

But South Africa desperately needed to obtain international loans to reverse the capital outflow and attract new foreign investment. In those objectives it received vital assistance from key American bankers and investors, notably Charles W. Engelhard, who was the largest single American investor in the economy and who had much to lose by a financial collapse. Engelhard's extensive mineral-processing businesses in the United States depended heavily on imports of ores from southern Africa. Moreover, as head of the Precious Metals Corporation he operated an extremely profitable enterprise that allegedly evaded South African prohibitions on private bullion exports by fabricating jewelry from gold bars and then reprocessing it into bullion after its export overseas.[6] Engelhard enjoyed powerful connections, not only on Wall Street but in the very corridors of power in Washington. He was a personal friend of Lyndon B. Johnson and a major contributor to the Democratic party.

By the time of Sharpeville the total value of U.S. direct investments in South Africa stood at $350 million, almost double the figure of two decades earlier.[7] Engelhard and his group of mainly New Jersey investors had contributed much to that impressive growth. They had a considerable stake in the country's gold industry and were anxious to counteract the capital flight—indeed, to reverse the flow before the extractive industries collapsed altogether. Under Engelhard's forceful leadership a group of American financiers obtained a vital $150 million loan for the South African government. In late December 1960, through his urgings, another lifeline of support came from the American-dominated International Monetary Fund (IMF) in the form of permission for South Africa to draw $18.8 million.[8] In the same month the World Bank came forward with a $25 million loan to the South African government.[9] Though the country's balance of payments on current accounts had returned to surplus, the massive outflow of capital had led to a large decline in reserves. The IMF and World Bank injections helped to replenish them and to give the regime a desperately needed "good housekeeping seal of approval." Ultimately, the IMF allowed South Africa to draw down some 75 percent of its $150 million credit with the institution.

As 1961 unfolded, the economy showed signs of rapid recovery. Political disaster was soon overtaken by financial windfall. Relative calm returned to the black townships, and in September Anglo-American's Rand Selection Corporation, South Africa's largest investment company, was able to borrow $30 million from a group of American institutional investors, with Engelhard again playing an instrumental role in the arrangements. This was the first major loan obtained by a South African institution since Sharpeville and the largest loan ever arranged by a South African firm from overseas private investors. Within a week First National City Bank of New York, which had recently opened offices in South Africa, topped it up by offering the government's Industrial Development Corporation an unsecured revolving credit facility with a cap of $5 million. In December twelve of the largest U.S. banks, including Chase and First National, renewed for two years a $40 million revolving credit for South Africa, which had been in effect since 1950. This impressive lending consortium was formed and administered by Dillon, Read and Company of New York.[10] Some of the participating banks, including First National Boston Corporation, already had affiliates in South Africa. In the same month the World Bank extended a $14 million loan to the state-owned Electricity Supply Commission (ESCOM) for electric power development and an additional $11 million to South African Railways, another government entity. A number of American banks participated in the latter loan, including Bank of America, Morgan Guaranty, the Riggs National Bank of Washington, D.C., and Fidelity-Philadelphia Trust Company. The railway loan was designed to furnish capital for a massive expansion and modernization program.[11] Over the years the World Bank had already made a series of loans to the South African Railways and Harbors Administration totaling $137 million. South Africa gained richly from the World Bank, considering that its voting power stood at slightly less than 1 percent, as opposed to 31 percent for the United States.[12] These and other loan facilities went a long way toward enabling Prime Minister Verwoerd and his Nationalist regime to recharge the economy by increasing public expenditures, especially through an expansion of industries in the state-controlled sector.

It is reasonable to conclude that Engelhard, the IMF, World Bank, and key American private banking institutions and institutional investors played an important role in restoring business confidence in South Africa and in saving the economy from possible collapse. Some would argue further that the injection of predominantly American capital was instrumental in triggering an economic boom. Surely, in the decade from 1961 South Africa enjoyed one of the highest real growth rates in the world, with annual rates of between 5 and 7 percent. During the period the country's GNP, alone, rose by more than 76 percent.

THE SIXTIES: BOOM YEARS

Clearly, the expansion of the capitalist world economy in the 1960s lifted demand for South African exports, especially minerals, and provided a powerful stimulus for autonomous growth. But much of that growth, at least between 1961 and 1968, derived from lowered corporation tax rates and a more aggressive pursuit of import replacement. Indeed, import substitution, or displacement, through protective tariffs was key to the government's efforts to develop new industries and to ensure greater national security. In other words, growth was fostered by the high protection offered to domestic manufacturing through preferences for raw materials and the exclusion of many foreign goods. Much of the fuel for this astounding recovery came from foreign exchange earnings from gold and other minerals as well as from fresh overseas capital in the form of loans and investments. Without the considerable inflows of capital in the months after Sharpeville such a growth rate would have been extremely difficult to achieve.

Viewing events from a broader perspective, the 1960s was a decade of enormous worldwide growth for American multinational corporations. Large American firms were becoming multi-industrial, through a process of diversification by way of acquisitions or mergers. Many corporations, traditionally known for a specific product, began producing a range of often regulated goods. For example, Sara Lee, a Chicago-based subsidiary of Consolidated Foods, built a factory in South Africa to manufacture analgesics, antacids, and shoe-care products. Other American MNCs began to manufacture in one country and export their product in a semifinished state to a branch in another country for completion, sale, or reexport to a third country. The growth of intrafirm trade gave rise to new opportunities for shifting capital and components between different countries. In the 1960s General Motors of South Africa imported components from Germany and Japan for the manufacture of its Opel cars and Isuzu trucks. Similar arrangements were initiated by Ford and Chrysler, who, respectively, purchased a 25 percent share of Mazda and 30 percent of Mitsubishi, both Japanese firms.[13] South Africa readily accepted the new order of things and allowed American corporations to devise ingenious diversification strategies that resulted in both forward and backward integration of operations. Though most firms went forward into the marketing and distribution of their finished products, nearly every form of diversification was resorted to, horizontal as well as vertical. Nevertheless, for labor-intensive industries, particularly vehicles, South Africa continued to maintain strict local-content regulations to ensure that production was much more than simply an assembly operation in which components were imported from the U.S. or Canada in a semimanufactured condition.

In the 1960s U.S. corporations captured new markets in South Africa not only as a result of their extraordinary advances in scale and capitalization but also because rapid technological strides had been made since the beginning of the Second World War as a result of enormous expenditures on research and development. Especially rapid progress was made in the areas of office equipment, electronics, and pharmaceuticals. I have already noted that in the postwar era the United States gained a high reputation for superior technology, management, and marketing. In the 1960s this was nowhere more visible than in the computer business. We have seen that IBM pioneered in South Africa in the early 1950s and had carved out an enormously profitable niche for itself in an entirely new field. Competition arrived a decade later, when Burroughs (now Unisys) began selling mainframe computers and peripherals and Control Data Corporation of Minneapolis came in with a unique line of "supercomputers." NCR (National Cash Register), already a household name in South Africa for its venerable cash registers, also introduced a line of computers, while in 1968 Hewlett-Packard completed the American circle. American computer firms jealously guarded their technology and did not establish plants in the country, choosing instead to maintain huge sales and service networks.

Americans also took an early lead in instant cameras and photocopiers. In 1948 Dr. Edwin Land came out with an innovative Polaroid camera that developed and printed pictures in the camera in sixty seconds. Polaroid cameras gained wide popularity, and in 1962, Land marketed an adaptation that gave natural color prints. A year later Kodak introduced the pocket Instamatic, with inexpensive quick-loading film cartridges. The Xerox Corporation, a pioneer in photocopying equipment, entered South Africa in 1964 through its British subsidiary, Rank Xerox, which was 51 percent owned by its New York parent. Within three years "xerox" became a verb equivalent to "copy" in South Africa.

Between 1961 and 1965 capital flows from the United States in the form of direct and portfolio investments increased steadily. Exact dollar figures are extremely difficult to obtain because no international consensus exists on what constitutes foreign direct investment—that is, the percentage of equity stake that distinguishes "portfolio" from "direct" investment. Moreover, the stock of investment is recorded at book value, which is usually less than its market value. Nevertheless, in the early 1960s substantial portfolio investments were being made in both the mining and manufacturing sectors. By mid-decade Engelhard's consortium, the South African Investment Company, held at least $60 million in assets, most of its portfolio apparently in gold-mining stocks.[14] Engelhard's efforts to rescue South Africa from the post-Sharpeville trough won him many accolades, including a directorship on the powerful and prestigious South African Chamber of Mines. Probably no American entrepreneur since John Hays Hammond in the late nineteenth century had wielded as much power and influence over the South African extractive industries.

The country's investment climate in the 1960s was exceptionally good. The government was extremely receptive to American capitalists, and enormous profits could be reaped as consumer spending skyrocketed. By 1966 the return on U.S. investments in the country averaged 20.6 percent, which at the time was the highest obtained in the world. Japan, at 12 percent, was a distant second, and Canada, with the most American investments, could boast a return of only 7.4 percent.[15] In 1962 alone American firms in South Africa garnered well over $72 million in profits. And between 1961 and 1965 repatriated profits and dividends on direct investments exceeded U.S. net capital inflows. By 1965 the total value of U.S. investments had soared to over a half-billion dollars, of which at least $529 million was in the form of direct investment. As 1966 drew to a stunning close, American investment had reached a new high of $597 million, accounting for more than 14 percent of total foreign direct investment in South Africa.[16]

Nonetheless, it was not widely recognized at the time that much of the growth in American investments in South Africa resulted not from fresh capital from home but from reinvestment of exceedingly high local earnings. Indeed, a large proportion of American investments in South Africa in the early 1960s was financed by retained earnings. Less than a third came from fresh capital inflows. This was not a new development. In the previous decade local capital formation in the country provided close to nine-tenths of total fixed investment. Since the late 1960s, for example, foreign mining and petroleum companies were required to ensure that a major portion of earnings remained in South Africa to finance expansion of the extractive and refining industries. What was so threatening immediately after Sharpeville was that much of the bottled-up portfolio investment evaporated. The loss needed to be restored quickly, for only through such a restoration could investor confidence return.

BUYING INTO SOUTH AFRICA: AMERICAN INVESTMENTS

Many American businesses that generated substantial local profits in the 1960s used them to buy minority and majority interests in domestic firms. Kimberley-Clark, the paper products manufacturer, acquired 38 percent interest in Carlton Paper, Owens-Illinois bought 20 percent of Consolidated Glass, and ITT acquired 30 percent of African Telephone Cables, as well as Rhodesia's major radio manufacturer. St. Regis Paper Company obtained 25 percent equity in the Rhodesian Pulp and Paper Company, while the Phelps Dodge Corporation bought a 49 percent interest in Black Mountain Mineral Development Company, which operated lead-silver and copper mines in the Cape province. Newmont and American Metal Climax (Amax) each acquired a minority interest in the Tsumeb Corporation in Namibia, but taken together, they gained a 65 percent ownership, which assured their control over the territory's largest nondiamond mining operation. By the end of the decade Tsumeb accounted for 80 percent of Namibia's output of base metals, and the operation represented 90 percent of American investment in the territory. Newmont, in control of management at Tsumeb, then secured a 57 percent stake in Namibia's O'Okiep Copper, Amax took a 46 percent interest in Roan Selection Trust, a giant in the extractive industries of southern Africa, and Amax and Newmont together bought into Palabora Mining, a huge copper operation in the northern Transvaal.

The pace of buy-ins quickened in the mid-1960s. In 1965 Chase Manhattan Bank merged with Standard Bank and gained a 14 percent interest. Coca-Cola secured a 51 percent stake in the huge Amalgamated Beverage Canners. ITT picked up a car brake company, and Allegheny International bought into the enormous Lion Match Company. Caltex poured its tremendous local profits into the construction of a refinery, its first in South Africa. The $45 million Durban facility became operational in 1963, saving South Africa more than $10 million in foreign exchange in the first year, alone.[17]

A few American firms consolidated their positions by buying up smaller local competitors. John Deere, for example, bought 75 percent of the stock of a South African implement-manufacturing establishment that was growing rapidly but needed more working capital.[18] Deere and others also had substantial amounts of capital outlay to expand their own distribution and service networks. American chemical, fertilizer, and farm equipment manufacturers took full advantage of the transition in the white agricultural community to larger, more mechanized, and more capital-intensive farming. Unfortunately, these trends only further eroded the competitive position of African farmers, who lacked the capital to purchase the new inputs. Agricultural output in the Republic soared, but the gap in income and productivity between whites and blacks widened still further.

In the manufacturing sector American investment in the 1960s in South Africa took the form mostly of direct investment, with a predilection for wholly owned subsidiaries. This was in contrast to independent black-ruled Africa, where Americans preferred joint ventures with local principals. Often, American MNCs entered South Africa by way of licensing agreements with local firms to distribute or manufacture their products. However, in most cases, they retained their ownership of proprietary technology, patents, and brand names.

Market-oriented investments expanded in the 1960s with the explosive growth in consumer demand. Many American firms increased their branch operations or, as we have seen, acquired equity in local firms. Others entered the economy to supply existing firms. Dresser Industries, for example, came to South Africa in the 1960s to supply equipment to the well-established American petroleum companies and then stayed on and reaped considerable profits.

American businesses responded enthusiastically to South Africa's strategy of state-supported industrial expansion. Since the mid-1950s there had been a relative decline in U.S. investment in mining and an increase in manufacturing, a trend that greatly accelerated in the post-Sharpeville era. By 1965 the manufacturing sector was attracting the largest share of American direct investment (45 percent), with petroleum garnering 23 percent and mining only 12 percent. Manufacturing output in South Africa increased by 70 percent between 1960 and 1965. In the decade after Sharpeville the value of output in manufacturing grew at an average annual rate of 18 percent, compared with 8 percent for mining and 6 percent for agriculture.[19] The country was quickly becoming self-sufficient in the production of a broad range of consumer goods, reflecting in considerable measure the contributions of American-owned capital and technology.

The United States' presence in the manufacturing field had grown in the first half of the 1960s at an unprecedented pace. By 1965 there were 237 subsidiaries and branches in South Africa, a majority of them in the manufacturing sector.[20] Management, on the other hand, remained predominantly in the hands of local white citizens. Of the managing directors of the twenty top American MNCs, more than 43 percent were English-speaking white South Africans.

American MNCs benefited from outstanding local institutions of higher learning that adapted their curricula to meet the demands of technological and managerial change. But as we shall soon discover, the rapidly expanding universities were all but off-limits to nonwhites. Since the Separation of Universities Act (1959) Africans were effectively barred from attending white universities. Nonwhites could obtain a higher education at the multiracial University of South Africa, but it was a correspondence institution of uneven quality.

The post-Sharpeville boom intensified the pressures from urban employers for the utilization of Africans in greater numbers and at higher skills. American joined local employers in clamoring for labor incentives and an easing of the color bar in skilled employment. The government, strongly under the influence of organized white labor, remained stubbornly determined to keep Africans out of skilled jobs. In 1970 this was made crystal clear with the passage of the Bantu Labour Amendment Act, which actually extended job reservation restrictions.[21] Nevertheless, by 1974 the demand for skilled labor in the construction industry had become so great that many employers simply ignored job reservation regulations.

American entrepreneurs were not without growing competition from other countries. In the 1940s and 1950s American manufacturers were either introducing new product lines or taking market share from the British. In those halcyon days South Africa was regarded as one of the most promising new frontiers for the expansion of American capitalism. A dominant position in several key sectors was easily achieved: notably in elevators, computers, pharmaceuticals, breakfast cereals, oil refining and distribution, motor vehicles, movies, detergents, office equipment, and cosmetics. Yet from the mid-1960s the Americans had to confront increasing competition from other industrialized states, especially West Germany and Japan. Initially, the competition was most intense in the automotive industry. In 1956 Volkswagen of West Germany purchased a controlling interest in a local assembly plant; and the Japanese began assembling cars, the Datsuns, three years later. The competition intensified after 1961, when Toyota of Japan entered the market. Within three years, Toyota rose to fourth place in the commercial vehicle market, primarily through a distribution network pioneered by Albert Wessels, an Afrikaner businessman.[22]

In the boom years of the 1960s consumer demand was high and there seemed to have been plenty of room for all competitors, especially in the transportation sector. The number of licensed vehicles exploded from 970,000 in 1956 to 1.8 million a decade later, then shot up to a breathtaking 3.5 million at the close of 1975.[23] Ford and GM remained the giants in the field and piled up impressive profits. However, as early as the mid-1960s they had begun to lose market share to the Japanese. The American manufacturers were caught off guard by the sudden surge in world demand for smaller, fuel-efficient cars, brought on after 1973 by the Arab oil boycott following the Yom Kippur War in the Middle East. The Japanese responded quickly to the change in consumer preference and within a few years had secured a commanding position in the small-car market.

In contrast to these developments, South African laws made it extremely difficult for its own companies to make capital investments overseas. Through unusual circumstances, however, the huge Anglo-American Corporation became a rare exception. When the government of Zambia decided to participate in the extractive industries of its own country, it paid for its 51 percent stake in Anglo-American's subsidiary in American dollars. Anglo used the money to establish the Bermuda-based Minerals and Resources Corporation (Minorco). The subsequent death of Charles Engelhard in 1971 provided Anglo-American with a unique opportunity to expand into the United States. From Engelhard's heirs Anglo-American acquired 30 percent of the common stock and 20 percent of the preferred stock of Engelhard Minerals and Chemicals in the United States. Largely through its offshore Minorco corporation, Anglo-American had by the early 1980s become one of the largest foreign investors in the United States. From its Bermuda base Anglo-American managed to get hundreds of millions of dollars into foreign subsidiaries before South African laws slowed overseas investments. From Bermuda, Anglo began buying Consolidated Gold Fields, headquartered in London, which in turn bought into New York-based Newmont Mining through a tangled web of companies. It also acquired extensive blocks of urban real estate along the eastern seaboard.[24] Other South African investors had to content themselves with capital investments in local American subsidiaries. For example, in the 1970s South African stockholders in Avis Car Rentals secured a controlling interest in the American firm even though the corporate name and logo were retained.[25] Slowly, and almost unnoticed, South African investors had begun to acquire a capital stake in the growing American presence in the Republic, thus forming an extremely complex and interlocking web.

BUSINESS IN THE SHADOW OF APARTHEID

We have seen that by 1964 the South African government had restored investor confidence by reestablishing a degree of tranquility and security in the wake of the Sharpeville trauma. It had been achieved in part through brilliant and remarkably effective economic policies. But it was also accomplished through a series of brutally repressive laws and tactics that were aimed at destroying the African opposition and implementing the official policy of apartheid. In the aftermath of Sharpeville the ANC and PAC, frustrated by the failure of passive resistance, decided to shift tactics and to create their own clandestine sabotage units. But from the start they were infiltrated by government multiracial intelligence units. A mass of coercive legislation was passed, eliminating the right of habeus corpus and empowering the government to arrest and detain individuals for extensive periods. ANC leader Nelson Mandela was arrested in August 1962 and eventually sentenced to life imprisonment. And between 1962 and 1965 several thousand of his comrades were also imprisoned as a result of a series of treason and security-related trials. PAC leaders, including Robert Sobukwe, were also imprisoned—in the case of Sobukwe, without formal charges or a trial.[26]

The government was thus able to neutralize and decapitate the revolutionary underground and to cut it off from its externally based cells. The Criminal Procedure Act of 1965 allowed for arrest and detention of up to six months. And the Terrorism Acts of 1967 closed off almost all remaining channels for the physical expression of anti-apartheid sentiment. The government also moved against organized black labor. By 1964 the leadership of the South African Congress of Trade Unions, which since its founding in 1955 had been closely allied to the ANC, had been driven into exile.[27] Surveillance of opposition groups was intensified after 1969 with the formation of the Bureau of State Security (BOSS).

The strong feelings of insecurity generated by the Sharpeville incident encouraged the government to implement its apartheid policies more aggressively. In late 1962 the Group Areas Act (1950) began to be executed more forcefully and broadly with the proclamation of residential "areas" reserved for specific African ethnic groups. Pretoria also enforced more vigorously the section of the act that restricted African business enterprise to the black townships and the rural reserves. Within a year whole populations of workers and budding entrepreneurs were uprooted and moved to new, racially segregated locations. A year later influx control was broadened when the pass system was extended to African women.

Even before Sharpeville the government had begun to enact laws and to establish public corporations aimed at implementing geopolitical apartheid. The Promotion of Bantu Self-Government Act (1959) was designed to consolidate the scattered native reserves into self-governing Bantu states, or Bantustans, while the Bantu Investment Corporation (1959) served as a financing mechanism for economic development in the segregated areas. Actual development of the Bantustans began in 1960 with the unveiling of the first Plan for the Transkei and the creation of the Xhosa Development Corporation. In subsequent years foreign and domestic corporations were urged to relocate to the borders of these segregated zones. American firms that were already well established in the industrial heartland successfully resisted the decentralization plan, arguing not on moral grounds but that distant border industries, removed from skilled labor and from adequate infrastructure, would be more costly to operate and more difficult to staff with managers. The Chrysler Corporation became one of the few to bow to these pressures when, in 1967, it opened a new plant in the Transvaal, just beyond the border of the Bophuthatswana Bantustan.[28]

Sharpeville and the repressive measures that followed drew unprecedented international censure. As criticism mounted, the Afrikaner-dominated government became more defensive and nationalistic. In May 1961 it declared itself an independent republic and six months later it withdrew from the British Commonwealth in the face of warnings that it would be expelled. The currency, based since the early nineteenth century on British sterling and long a symbol of British financial domination, was decimalized and the rand was adopted as the new monetary unit in place of the pound.

In leaving the Commonwealth, South Africa lost a number of British preferential trade quotas. But the Americans were only too willing to compensate, at first by establishing an official and extremely generous quota for South African sugar. In the decade ahead the American business community richly capitalized on the loosening of Britain's hold on the South African economy and on growing anti-British feelings among important Afrikaner figures in the ministries of trade, industry, and finance.

Nevertheless, the events surrounding Sharpeville altered the terms and tenor of American attitudes toward South Africa. Certainly after Sharpeville the anti-apartheid rhetoric in the United States and in Great Britain became more strident. American MNCs, however, reacted defensively, arguing that they were apolitical and that it was inappropriate for them to take positions on the policies of host governments. More will be said of this later. Officially, U.S. policy reflected a contradiction between rhetoric and practice. U.S. relations with South Africa became ambiguous and confused. The National Security Action Memorandum 33 was revised in 1962 to suggest noncooperation in areas relative to South Africa's apartheid policies but to support continuing cooperation in other fields.[29] The Western industrialized countries earnestly hoped for a peaceful solution to South Africa's racial problems and gave greater prominence to African moderates. In December 1961 Chief Albert Lutuli, ANC president, received a Nobel Peace Prize for his efforts to effect change through nonviolent tactics. The United States would more openly support peaceful change but refused to go so far as to support Lutuli's call for sanctions. Thus, the Americans voted "no" in November 1962 on a United Nations General Assembly vote that member nations should break diplomatic relations with South Africa, expel it from the international organization, and boycott all South African exports.[30] President Kennedy wanted to deal cautiously with the country, perhaps because the United States was preparing to undergo a rapid expansion of its space program and would need a network of stations in key sites around the world to monitor Soviet satellites as well as its own. In September 1960, only months after Sharpeville, the United States and South Africa reached an agreement on three National Aeronautics and Space Administration (NASA) satellite tracking stations, and within months the Americans set up a radio space research station near Cape Town. Then, in 1962 an agreement was concluded with South Africa for the establishment of Defense Department space-tracking facilities independent of the NASA installations. As a quid pro quo, Kennedy agreed in June 1962 to sell military equipment to the South Africans to "contain Communist aggression".[31]

United States policy towards South Africa changed course dramatically in late 1963, after the conclusion of a Nuclear Test Ban Treaty with the Soviet Union. East-West tensions subsided, and in his first official attack on apartheid Kennedy unilaterally banned the export of combat equipment to South Africa. In August 1963 U.N. Ambassador Adlai Stevenson voted in favor of a U.N. Security Council call for an embargo on the sale and shipment to South Africa of arms, ammunition, and military vehicles as well as machinery for the manufacture of such.[32] But from the start both bans were riddled with loopholes, and U.S. government agencies failed to adopt procedures to implement the bans. Consequently equipment exports continued covertly, occasionally with the knowledge and tacit approval of key Commerce Department personnel. Some American arms manufacturers simply exported through Canada or other third parties. Moreover, the embargos did not specify so-called dual-purpose equipment, used for both military and civilian purposes. Computers and small aircraft fell into this category. In 1964 the Johnson administration half-heartedly attempted to close the loopholes by banning the sale of all military equipment to the South African police, military, and paramilitary units engaged in training as well as in combat.[33] Unfortunately, this did not prevent some American firms from making arrangements with foreign manufacturers to produce weapons under special license. The latter were then free to export the items directly to South Africa. Nor did the Johnson administration put pressure on Israel, its client, to refrain from filling the vacuum left by the decline in the American arms trade to the apartheid regime. Indeed, after 1963 Israel became South Africa's prime external source of arms and military technology. The relationship, encouraged by American Zionist organizations, led to an Israeli–South African military-commercial pact just a decade later. Israel played a vital role in providing expertise for the creation in South Africa of a state armaments industry, called

ARMSCOR, in 1964. Another important U.S. loophole in the arms ban was plugged in 1968, when Johnson barred the use of American components in the foreign manufacture of weapons destined for South Africa.[34] But this did not stop the dramatic growth in arms exports and military technology from Israel.

Like its predecessors, the Johnson administration was not willing to go beyond limited military sanctions. The White House called for a termination of naval cooperation in 1964 and a ban on naval visits to South Africa three years later. Nonetheless, it ignored appeals in 1964 by Reverend Martin Luther King, Jr., and the American Negro Leadership Conference on Africa to ban future American private investments. Johnson was also deaf to their demands for U.S. support of a U.N. oil embargo. Instead, in 1965 the Johnson administration enunciated a vague economic policy towards South Africa, affirming that the United States would "neither encourage nor discourage private investment in the Republic."[35] Yet, in the future it continued to do both. In April 1966 the administration called upon the Export-Import Bank to stop extending direct loans to South Africa's public- and private-sector buyers of American goods. However, it did not discourage the bank from continuing to provide a wide range of services, including loan guarantees for payment of South African goods as well as insurance for American bank loans and for privately financed exports to the United States.

American attitudes and actions toward South Africa were strongly influenced by concern over strategic minerals. In the 1960s the U.S. was becoming increasingly dependent on external sources of supply for critical ores. South Africa, Southern Rhodesia, and the Philippines had become the country's principal suppliers of chromium, partially as a result of the loss of supply from Cuba after the Castro revolution in 1962 and the cessation of its extraction in the United States. Moreover, in the 1960s demand for cobalt escalated with the development of jet engines for commercial use. Though cobalt was generally purchased elsewhere in southern Africa, particularly in Southern Rhodesia, much of it was exported to the West through South African seaports. Manganese also became important, especially after 1963, when American production fell to almost nil.

Nonetheless, only small amounts of minerals were purchased for the nation's stockpile during the Kennedy and Johnson administrations. Market prices for base metals were so high that both administrations sold off portions of the national stockpile to alleviate inflation and to help the budget, especially after the costs of war in Vietnam began to skyrocket.[36]

The United States' collaboration with South Africa on strategic minerals revolved primarily around uranium and atomic energy. Between 1961 and 1965 the Milwaukee-based Allis Chalmers Corporation, under the "Atoms-for Peace" program, helped South Africa with the construction of Safari I, the country's first nuclear reactor. Under the program South African technicians received training at the U.S. Nuclear Corporation's fuel-fabricating facility in Tennessee.[37] Before long South Africa was able to undertake its own program of nuclear development. In 1969 the federal government began enriching commercial uranium fuel and became the only non-Communist supplier for nuclear utilities. South Africa looked to the United States, and in the 1970s it depended heavily on the Americans for enriching its own uranium.

The Johnson administration's reluctance to discourage trade with South Africa may have stemmed in part from America's evolving balance-of-payments problems in world trade generally. The United States had begun to come to grips with the dilemma in 1962 with the Trade Expansion Act, which was the first major initiative in trade liberalization since the Reciprocal Trade Agreements Act of 1934. The new law empowered the president to use an across-the-board method of tariff negotiations and opened the way for substantial tariff reductions. In the trade with South Africa the effect was immediate and dramatic. From 1962 to 1965, the balance shifted from a negative $35.6 million to a healthy surplus of $207.3 million,[38] the latter figure reflecting the sale of five Boeing 727s to the government-owned South African Airways. Nevertheless, from the perspective of the United States' total world trade, exports to South Africa amounted to a mere 1 percent of all American exports by value—a proportion that had remained remarkably constant throughout history.

In broad global terms the United States continued to experience deepening balance-of-payment problems. In February 1965 President Johnson urged American firms to export and borrow more in overseas financial markets rather than to export precious American capital. In the case of South Africa Americans were succeeding. By the end of 1969 17 percent of South Africa's imports were from the United States, and 8.4 percent of its exports went there.[39] Over the decade of the 1960s U.S.

export trade to South Africa grew by a hefty 103 percent while its imports expanded by only 44 percent. Few members of Congress in Washington were prepared to bend to pressures to shut off one of the major "bright spots" in an otherwise dismal record of American trade.

GOLD REDUX

For South Africa gold remained the keystone of its economy and an important card to play in international monetary diplomacy. Postwar production increased steadily, mainly as a result of the discoveries of huge deposits in the Orange Free State. As a share of total world output (excluding the Soviet Union) it rose from 49 percent in 1953 to 63 percent in 1960 and 75 percent in 1965.[40]

We must remember that during the era of the gold standard, gold was the international means of payment, and each currency was assessed according to its gold value. One could exchange dollars for pounds sterling in exact proportion to their gold value. Adjustments in exchange rates occurred rarely. Thus, gold bullion was the major instrument for settling international transactions. However, in the late 1960s and early 70s international trade and financial transactions reached a point where the direct link of currencies to a gold standard with fixed parities exploded.

For years the United States had viewed gold as a key instrument for reducing its deficits. It should be reemphasized that the Bretton Woods agreements had linked the non-Communist world's major currencies with gold through the dollar. The U.S. dollar thereby became the key currency for international trade. Its value was tied to gold and the value of the other currencies was tied to the dollar. Countries were expected to maintain the value of their own currencies by using dollars to buy and sell them. In other words, the United States assumed the role of paying gold to buy dollars from governments that had amassed them. In effect, the Bretton Woods system had aimed at limiting the competition among countries for gold by promoting the outflow of dollar balances as an alternative.[41] The system worked to the United States' advantage until the late 1950s, when deficits began to accumulate. Usually, they had to be settled in gold rather than in dollars, thus reflecting the asset preferences of the Bretton Woods countries. Nevertheless, by the early

1960s the Treasury Department had become alarmed over the growing quantity of U.S. deficits that were being transferred in the form of gold rather than dollars. The country's gold stock had fallen from over $22 billion in 1950 to $15.5 billion in 1964 and then to a paltry $10 billion by March 1968.[42]

From 1961 to 1968 the United States had attempted to stabilize and reduce world gold prices by means of an international gold pool. The effort proved fruitless, and there was a new run on the precious ore. Thus, in March 1968, in an effort to demonetize gold, the world's leading central banks established on American initiative a two-tier system, separating official transactions at the fixed price of $35 a fine ounce from free-market transactions in privately owned and newly mined gold. In other words, central banks had to trade at the official price, but a market was now established for other investors where the price fluctuated freely. At a stroke gold was liberated from the straitjacket of the fixed price imposed for the previous thirty-four years.

Thus, the Bretton Woods system, which had delivered stable exchange rates through a gold-linked dollar, was fundamentally altered. Initially, South Africa perceived this as a threat and responded by adopting its own two-tier gold market. Then it drastically reduced its gold exports and refused to sell on the free market, anticipating that this would force up gold prices. As a consequence, South Africa's gold and foreign exchange reserves skyrocketed, though world gold prices did not budge, mainly because the United States refused to purchase the newly mined gold. The effort was abandoned after a year of desultory results. When South Africa reappeared on the market, free prices fell back from $45 per ounce to the old $35 per ounce floor.[43] But by then, the South African economy was booming, and the country's gold and foreign exchange reserves reached a historic high in April 1969 of $1.7 billion, up from $907 million only two months earlier and from $800 million in 1963.[44] Finally, in December 1969 South Africa reached an agreement with the IMF for a more structured system of gold marketing, whereby South Africa was permitted to sell gold to the IMF, but not to other central banks, and only after the price had fallen below $35 per ounce.[45] Nevertheless, the free market for nonmonetary gold remained in place and South Africa now sought to take advantage of this new opportunity to influence the market for gold, especially in the areas of carat jewelry and electronics. The government was particularly anxious to promote gold sales abroad in the free market. In 1970 it decided to mass-market its gold Krugerrand coin, which had been introduced only three years earlier, by emphasizing its advantages as an investment. Then, in 1971 six members of the Chamber of Mines established the International Gold Corporation, or Intergold, to promote the metal in the world's key jewelry and industrial markets. Previously, no one had given much thought to marketing gold in the same manner as other metals. World demand for gold was increasing dramatically, and this was clearly reflected in South African output, which increased handsomely from $500 million in 1959 to $2.6 billion in 1974. A series of crucial shifts in gold policy by the American government in the early 1970s profoundly impacted on world gold prices and hence on South Africa's economic fortunes, as I shall further discuss later.[46]

MONETARY MANIPULATIONS

As the 1970s opened, the United States was still encountering balance-of-payments problems of its own. Over the years enormous quantities of U.S. dollars had been accumulating overseas; and in 1971 a U.S. world trade deficit was recorded for the first time in recent history. While Western Europe and Japan competed more effectively against the United States in world markets, American direct investments in many countries grew larger than the value of trade. South Africa continued to be an exception. American investment there grew vigorously, and the balance of trade jumped from $275 million in 1970 to $336 million only a year later.[47] However, even in South Africa, the Americans had begun to lose their market share to other countries. As early as 1968 Japan had surged ahead to become, albeit briefly, South Africa's second biggest trading partner, after Great Britain.

It must be remembered that since the Bretton Woods Conference of 1944 the role of the United States in the world's monetary order was to pay gold for dollars from foreign governments that amassed American currency as a result of their efforts to support its price. The system, however, was severely undermined when soaring debts and inflation in the United States encouraged speculators to unload their dollars. This placed enormous pressures on U.S. gold reserves, and in early 1971, the U.S. gold stock fell below the psychological floor of $10 billion.[48]

Faced with this depletion and the gnawing balance-of-payments problems worldwide, President Nixon announced in August 1971 that the United States would scrap the Bretton Woods Agreement altogether. Official purchases or sales of gold by the United States Treasury were suspended. U.S. dollars would no longer be used as the basis for the gold-exchange standard. In other words the dollar could no longer be converted into gold. Thus, the U.S. had suspended gold payments and detached the metal from its dollar par value because more dollars were being held abroad than the total gold reserves in the United States.[49] Bretton Woods had outlived its utility to the United States and was consigned by Nixon to the dustbin of history.

The dollar was then devalued by being allowed to float. A key objective in the entire exercise was to force the other major governments to depreciate the dollar on their foreign exchange markets. The international monetary system by this time was evolving towards a system of floating exchange rates. Within a few years exchange-rate parities were no longer fixed by governments but fluctuated according to supply and demand. It should also be noted that in 1970 Special Drawing Rights (SDRs) were created by the International Monetary fund (IMF) to supplement gold and the U.S. dollar as international reserves.[50]

South Africa responded to Nixon's initiative by modifying its own exchange-rate policy, tying its currency, the rand, to the U.S. dollar and allowing it to float together against other international currencies. And to deal with its own chronic balance-of-payments situation, it devalued the rand and tightened import controls.[51] But this devaluation counteroffensive, as a way of slowing the continuing flood of American imports, was foredoomed.

The Americans hoped that government-initiated export stimulation would improve their balance-of-payments problems. In 1971 Congress passed the Export Expansion Finance Act, which increased the overall amount of export loans, insurance, and guarantees that could be extended by the Export-Import Bank. The bank was now better able to provide financing on competitive terms and to help exporters with the necessary financial support. Hence, trade expansion in the 1970s was facilitated by U.S. credit agencies. Exim Bank Chairman William Casey strongly favored greater trade with South Africa, a country that appeared to hold enormous market potential.[52]

Between 1972 and 1976 the Exim Bank alone vastly increased its exposure in South Africa by authorizing $205 million for insurance and loan guarantees to a number of MNCs, including General Electric's sale of diesel locomotives to the South African Railways Corporation.[53] In addition, between 1972 and 1976 the Commodity Credit Corporation financed $46 million worth of commodities for export to the Republic. The results were astounding. Trade volume soared more than 20 percent in 1973 alone. In 1975 U.S. exports to South Africa climbed to $1.3 billion from only $401 million in 1966, but imports rose to $850 million from $249 million.[54] The United States had become South Africa's third largest source for imports, accounting for nearly 17 percent of its foreign purchases.

The South African government, deeply concerned over the country's growing trade imbalances, had already established an investigatory commission. The resultant Reynders Report (1972) blamed the balance-of-payments problems on the poor performance of the overly protected manufacturing sector in foreign markets. It noted that since the end of World War II the country had suffered from almost continuous deficits on the current account of the balance of payments and that this situation had become a serious constraint on economic growth. High protectionist policies had raised the cost structure of the South African economy because expensive local inputs had to be utilized in preference to less-expensive imports. Manufactured exports were only about 10 percent of gross value of manufacturing output and only a quarter of total exports in 1970. The commission therefore urged greater exports of manufactured goods and government-initiated efforts to improve efficiency in the manufacturing sector to overcome the chronic balance-of-payments deficits. It concluded with a warning that South Africa urgently needed to become more competitive in world markets. The Reynders Report was of considerable significance in that it set the stage for a switch in government policy to aggressive export promotion.[55]

GROWTH STIMULATION AND
THE APARTHEID STATE

South Africa's imports continued to grow at a faster pace than its exports. Since the end of World War II the country had suffered an almost continuous deficit on its current account balance of payments.

Only briefly, in 1968, was it on the positive side. The problem became especially acute with the rise in public expenditures after Sharpeville. From 1962 South Africa pursued a determined policy of growth stimulation through the instrument of government and its state corporations. The state accelerated its policy of making huge investments in the public sector, which was most visible in its spending on mammoth public sector projects, including the development of Richards Bay on the Natal coast as an export point for coal, the establishment of the state arms industry, the vast expansion of the state Iron and Steel Corporation (ISCOR), the modernization of the chemicals industry, and the rehabilitation and expansion of the transportation infrastructure. Heavy expenditures were also made on energy production, particularly the state Electricity Supply Commission (ESCOM), while the state Industrial Development Corporation (IDC) greatly increased its financing of ventures in the mining sector. Altogether, the government's share of gross fixed investments rose from slightly less than a third in 1950 to just under half twenty years later.

South Africa had also begun to increase its expenditures on African education, and the results were rather startling. The number of black students in secondary education alone rose between 1960 and 1975 from 47,600 to 318,000 and in primary education from 1.4 million to 3.4 million.[56] Much of this growth occurred in the 1973–1975 period, when support for African education shifted from the less-equitable direct taxation on Africans to general reserve funds from the government treasury.

South Africa's rapid expansion on the educational, industrial, and infrastructural fronts necessitated heavy importation of capital goods as well as capital. Moreover, consumer demand for imported items had been running strong since 1962, when the bank rate was substantially reduced. Traditional fiscal and monetary policies could no longer be used to cope with the situation. By 1969 a crossroads had been reached: South Africa had to increase its foreign borrowing or risk stalling economic growth. The time seemed ripe for increased borrowing. Over the previous decade the country enjoyed one of the highest growth rates in the world, and the South Africans felt confident that major increases in their debts could easily be serviced out of future growth.

This seemed to be a most propitious moment for pursuing a policy of expansive foreign borrowing. The 1960s had witnessed a phenomenal growth in multinational banking, especially in the United States. Over the decade an increasing proportion of American banking profits were derived from foreign lending activities. The growth in foreign branches of American banking began in 1958 and accelerated in the 1960s and 1970s. American banks established new overseas branches to participate in European money and capital markets and to make Eurodollar loans because U.S. laws restricted the outflow of capital abroad. This, of course, occurred at a time when government demands in South Africa for capital were escalating, with money needed for the burgeoning security aparatus, the state enterprises, and "black development" within the apartheid context. The vast liquidity at the start of the 1970s enabled American bankers to become more aggressive and reckless in seeking new borrowers.

In 1970 an international consortium was set up under the leadership of the European-American Banking Corporation. Over the next three years it made six loans to South Africa's public sector, totalling $210 million.[57] The bulk of the loans were funneled through the Finance Ministry and to such parastatals as ESCOM and ISCOR. In the years ahead a significant portion of South Africa's Eurocurrency loans were from U.S.-based banks or their foreign subsidiaries.

American investments in South Africa had grown impressively in the early 1970s. In the decade's first year alone they expanded by 11 percent. A year later, the United States was providing 20 percent of all foreign direct investment in the country, up from 14 percent in 1966. Much of that growth was concentrated in a few companies that were mainly involved in petroleum, vehicle assembly, and pharmaceuticals.

In corporate America an argument was building for a stronger U.S. private presence in South Africa. David Rockefeller, whose Chase Manhattan Bank was conducting a brisk business in South Africa, suggested that U.S. corporations in the country had a vital role to play in improving communications through trade. Rockefeller's view seemed to represent a wide consensus in the American business community that U.S. banks and MNCs could serve as effective instruments of multiracial dialogue. American entrepreneurs argued that the long-term effect of sustained economic growth would be to undermine apartheid by bringing people together into a pool of common economic interests. A survey conducted at the Massachusetts Institute of Technology in 1974, involving 252 U.S. corporations, revealed strong opposition to any withdrawal of American investments. I shall address this issue further on.

By 1973 U.S. direct investment in South Africa reached $1.2 billion. It soared to $1.5 billion a year later, up from only $600 million a decade earlier.[58] American direct investments were even greater because figures did not take into account American investments in South Africa via third countries. Indeed, many American companies continued to enter the South African market through an existing subsidiary, often based in Great Britain.

American direct investments included all flows—equity as well as reinvested earnings—between the foreign investor and the investment enterprise in the host country. They were widely dispersed but significant in three sectors: autos, petroleum, and computers. The firms in control of those sectors increased their assets by nearly half in the early 1970s. Some American companies enjoyed the commanding heights in their field. Gilbarco, for example, controlled 43 percent of South Africa's fuel-pump market and 66 percent of its gasoline-pump servicing market.

The economic prosperity of the 1960s and early 1970s transformed manufacturing into South Africa's leading growth sector, accounting for 24 percent of the GDP in 1970. For American entrepreneurs the early 1970s was a time of plant expansion. Pharmaceutical companies, notably Eli Lilly, opened new factories and greatly increased their output. Goodyear Tire also significantly expanded production facilities, and General Motors opened a new diesel-electric locomotive plant with 30 percent local-content capacity. Many other MNCs launched ambitious expansion projects; the largest may have been Caltex, which in 1967 invested $24 million in South Africa's second oil refinery.[59] Such was the extent of American business confidence in South Africa's economic future.

A TURNING POINT:
THE PETROLEUM CRISIS

The boom years, fed by soaring world prices for minerals, contributed to great expectations for sustained economic growth. Between 1972 and 1973 a tremendous hoarding of minerals in the West pushed mineral prices to record levels. This encouraged producers in southern Africa to increase their output. In an eighteen-month period, between 1972 and

1974, raw materials prices in world markets rose more sharply than during any previous such period in the past two centuries.

In South Africa the euphoria over booming prices for minerals was tempered in October 1973, when world oil prices began to rise precipitously. This was followed by the oil embargo and the quadrupling of prices by early 1974.[60] A wave of uncertainty swept over the country as consumer purchasing power waned, corporate profits plunged, and equity investments almost came to a grinding halt. Ending a twenty-five year era of high economic growth, the oil crisis represented a turning point. By mid-1974 a recession loomed menacingly in the face of a general collapse of demand for most minerals.

As they had done in the past, the South Africans looked to gold to save them from what seemed like an impending catastrophe. Gold earnings had always been the principal stimulant and financial base for the government's own investment activities. And it must be remembered that South African gold output climbed from $365 million in 1955 to over $2.6 billion in 1975. The free-market gold price had begun its rapid ascent in 1972 after breaking through the $58 per ounce ceiling. It accelerated a year later, driven by the U.S. abandonment of the gold standard and the loss of confidence in the dollar in the face of threats of a total Arab oil embargo.

Significantly, from the recession of 1974 private American banks, with Citibank leading, began to fund ever larger proportions of South Africa's burgeoning debt. Because of the recession in the United States, corporate demand for loans had shriveled, and banks were thus anxious to increase their lending to governments and parastatals. Moreover, U.S. repeal of foreign capital and credit controls in 1974 allowed American banks to increase their share of international credit. The U.S. government, strapped for funds to expand foreign aid programs, put greater pressure on the private sector to increase its flows of loan money overseas. Already since the early 1970s scores of American banks had established correspondent relationships with South African counterparts, partially in order to handle the accounts of the growing number of American MNCs as well as to facilitate trade financing. Through these correspondent relationships American banks approved a growing volume of letters of credit and interbank loans. In 1974 Citicorp managed a $100 million loan to ISCOR and another $50 million a year later, while it also lent $30 million to ESCOM for construction of nuclear reactors and $10 million to a parastatal, the Industrial Development Corporation.[61] The capital continued to flow in as the U.S. government repealed its own foreign capital and credit restrictions. By the end of 1975, 20 percent of South Africa's foreign debt liabilities were owed to the United States, up from 14 percent a decade earlier. Thus, from about 1974 international credit provided much of the financing of South Africa's public projects. With American financial assistance, the South African government was able to vastly expand its participation in the country's economy and to develop a state capitalism almost unrivalled in extent by any major Western country.

South Africa's economic uncertainties persisted through the first half of 1975 as gold and foreign exchange revenues began their descent. South Africa's terms of trade weakened in response to the general recession in the West and the fall of commodity prices. In the process inflation soared from 9.6 percent in 1973 to nearly 12 percent. South Africa had begun to incur a huge deficit on its current account. In September 1975 the government responded this time by devaluing the rand by more than 18 percent against the dollar.[62]

Fortunately for South Africa, gold was poised for another rally. On December 31, 1974, the United States, which had abandoned the gold standard two years earlier, made it legal again for private citizens to purchase gold and to trade in bullion. South African gold Krugerrands were now able to enter the U.S. market. The demand for the coins was strong from the start, thanks to an aggressive marketing program launched by Doyle Dane and Bernbach, the American advertising agency handling the Krugerrand account for South Africa. In 1975 alone Americans purchased nearly 15 percent of the coin's output.[63] The American appetite for gold became so great that in 1977 the Johannesburg-based Intergold opened a regional head office in New York. Never before in history had the South Africans marketed a metal in the United States so aggressively and with such stunning success.

The world petroleum crisis of 1973–1974 posed an enormous threat and challenge to South Africa, which had no crude petroleum resources of its own. The country, already moving toward greater energy self-sufficiency, now had to double its efforts. An important leg of the quest for such self-sufficiency was the construction of nuclear power generating facilities. In 1974 the United States agreed to buy raw uranium from South Africa for enrichment at the government's atomic energy facility in Oak Ridge, Tennessee. From there, it was shipped to France for fabrication into fuel rods and resold to South Africa for the projected Koeberg power plant outside Cape Town. The purchase of South African uranium was not unprecedented. Over the years the United States had bought 45,000 tons of uranium oxide from South Africa for its own use.[64] Indeed, by 1974 over 20 percent of U.S. domestic requirements were met by South Africa.

South Africa also stepped up its program to extract oil from its extensive natural resources of coal. As far back as 1935 the Anglo-Transvaal Consolidated Investment Company acquired a license for the Fischer-Tropsch process for synthesizing oil from coal. But further development was halted by World War II. After the war the government acquired an American adaptation of the process that allowed for vastly greater output. It should be recalled that in the 1950s a huge parastatal, the South African Coal, Oil, and Gas Corporation, or SASOL, was created to ensure greater fuel independence. The project, which came on stream in 1955, marked the world's first commercial use of the coal liquifaction process and represented an enormous technological breakthrough for South Africa. SASOL I was small and contributed only a minute proportion of the country's liquid fuel needs. Then came the petroleum crisis of 1973–1974 and rising international pressure for oil sanctions against the apartheid regime. The need for a vast expansion, mainly to protect against the threat of an international petroleum boycott, was immediately recognized. Again, South Africa turned to the Americans for capital and engineering expertise. In March 1975 J. Robert Fluor's Fluor Corporation of California secured a multimillion dollar turnkey contract from SASOL to provide the engineering and to oversee construction of the SASOL II facility.[65] The second SASOL project had wider economic ramifications, vastly increasing gasoline output and providing an enormous range of byproducts, including nitrogenous fertilizers for agriculture, plastics, detergents, and synthetic rubber. Thus, SASOL II offered a greater degree of energy security and served as an important generator of new petrochemical industries.

Americans also played a critical role in boosting South Africa's capacity for refining imported oil. In 1975 Caltex, which was half-owned by Standard Oil of California and half by Texaco, began to expand its Milnerton refinery near Cape Town, at a cost of $134 million.[66] Even before its completion, nearly 40 percent of South Africa's oil-refining capacity lay in the hands of Caltex and Mobil. But the two American oil giants did not welcome South Africa's synfuel program, and only half-hearted efforts were made to promote SASOL's products. Consequently, the Afrikaners created their own corporation, Trek, which actively marketed synfuels at its own filling stations.

NIXON AND THE RAPPROCHEMENT

The Nixon admininstration's policies toward South Africa were very much the work of Secretary of State Henry Kissinger. They reflected efforts to extricate the United States from Vietnam without forfeiting power in Southeast Asia or Africa to the Chinese or Russians. Thus, the policy détente with South Africa grew out of the wreckage of Vietnam. South Africa was viewed as a stable ally, and Nixon committed himself to a policy of diplomatic rapprochement with the South Africans. Kissinger believed in the concept of "linkage," whereby the problems of southern Africa had to be placed and resolved within the wider context of Eastern issues.

Concern was also reemerging over the question of strategic minerals. The National Materials Policy Act of 1970 mandated the creation of the National Commission on Materials Policy, the first major group to study natural resources since the Paley Commission nearly twenty years earlier. To South Africa's disappointment the subsequent report placed only minor emphasis on the United States' strategic mineral deficiencies.[67] But then again its findings were made before the OPEC-induced petroleum crisis.

In January 1970 Kissinger gave Nixon his set of five options on South African policy, with his own recommendations. The document, known as the National Security Study Memorandum (NSSM) 39, rested on the premise that the whites of southern Africa were there to stay and that change could only come about through a constructive engagement with them. Kissinger's report added that "there is no hope for the blacks to gain the political rights they seek through violence, which will only lead to chaos and increased opportunities for the Communists."[68] Détente, Kissinger argued, would produce political reform. NSSM Option Two, favored by Kissinger and ultimately adopted, called for closer association with South Africa. Kissinger's approach was little more than an echo of the remarks made by Satterthwaite of the State Department almost a decade earlier.

In the minds of many Washington policymakers loomed the perennial question of minerals. By this time U.S. domestic consumption of minerals was consistently higher than production. The Nixon administration was fearful that any escalation of turmoil in southern Africa would weaken the investment climate, especially for the mining companies. Australia, Canada, and South Africa were viewed as the only three key mineral countries with a measure of political stability. Kissinger, anxious to ease the region into reform without compromising political stability, recommended a gradual and selective relaxation of economic restrictions against South Africa and Rhodesia, hoping in return to win the cooperation of the white leadership. The American business community, anxious to avoid a political revolution at all costs, enthusiastically and unaminously endorsed the Kissinger thesis.

To expedite the process, John Hurd, an American entrepreneur, was appointed ambassador to South Africa. On Kissinger's advice the Nixon administration adopted a permissive interpretation of the 1963 arms embargo and allowed the resumption of exports of so-called dual-purpose military aircraft.[69] Almost immediately, the South African government began purchasing Lockheed aircraft for cargo and other purposes. Nixon also loosened sanctions against Rhodesia, whose white population had unilaterally declared independence from Britain in November 1965.

In light of these events the Byrd amendment easily sailed through Congress in November 1971. It forbade the U.S. president to prevent the importation of strategic materials from any non-Communist country as long as the same material was being purchased from a Communist country.[70] This provision enabled the American MNCs to import chrome and ferrochrome from Rhodesia in contravention of United Nations sanctions. Those who supported the sanction-busting amendment argued that 98 percent of the world's chromite ore was located in South Africa and Rhodesia. Without access, the United States could become almost totally reliant on the Soviet Union. Consequently, the chrome ban was lifted, much to the relief of whites in Rhodesia and South Africa as well as American mineral importers and processors. The era of economic sanctions against Rhodesia was significant in that it encouraged American mining companies to become more deeply involved in the extraction of ores from South Africa as an alternative to Rhodesià. It also forced American mining companies to explore sources outside the region and to develop synthetics and other substitutes.

IN THE WAKE OF THE DURBAN STRIKES

In 1973–1974, the South African labor scene was rocked by a series of crippling industrial strikes initiated by African workers in and around Durban. They were provoked by the enormous gap between black and white wages and by the generally low wages and benefits paid by employers.[71] The U.S. government was stunned by the rapid escalation of black labor militancy and for the first time began to put quiet pressure on American MNCs to improve their wages, benefits, and working conditions. The State Department published guidelines for American companies, pointing out that they were behind the West Germans on average wages. It was no secret that wage differentials between black and white workers in South Africa were enormous. In 1971 it was estimated that on average white wages were 643 percent higher than their African counterparts.[72] Most American MNCs resisted these pressures and did little to improve working conditions. However, there were a few important exceptions, and they will be discussed later.

The United States was forced into a reformulation of its policies on southern Africa in response to the rapid and totally unforeseen decolonization of Portuguese Africa. The military coup in Lisbon in April 1974 and the rapid decolonization and independence of Mozambique and Angola only a year later destroyed the relevancy and assumptions of Kissinger's NSSM 39 insofar as the events challenged the premise that whites were an immovable force. The Nixon administration's gross miscalculation of trends in southern Africa left the United States unprepared to deal with the aftermath of the Portuguese coup. Within South Africa the business community nervously looked northward to their Lusophonic neighbors and realized that the white Portuguese *cordon sanitaire* had suddenly evaporated into a seemingly Marxist landscape.

After some initial hesitancy and intense debate the Americans recognized the government of Samora Machel in Mozambique in September 1975 but balked at the Neto government in Angola, especially after it had called upon Castro's Cuba to save it from an invasion by South

Africa. Kissinger directed the Central Intelligence Agency to finance a campaign against the Marxist regime. But in December 1975 the Senate passed the Clark amendment, banning aid to any party in the unfolding Angolan civil war.[73] South Africa's invasion of Angola, condoned by key players in the Nixon administration, was thus repudiated by Congress.

Mozambique closed its border with Rhodesia in March 1976, cutting off an important lifeline to the outside world. By 1977 the guerrilla war in the white redoubt had begun to turn in favor of the African liberation movements, who were now being supplied from friendly neighboring front-line states. Time seemed to be running out, and the United States put pressure on South Africa to work toward a negotiated settlement between the Rhodesian whites under Ian Smith and black moderates in hopes of foreclosing a Marxist takeover.[74]

The United States now began to distance itself from the South Africans. In 1974 Nigeria had surpassed South Africa as the United States' major trade partner in Africa, mainly because of the dramatic increase in oil imports. Meanwhile, the Nigerians assumed a leading role among African nations in the anti-apartheid struggle at the United Nations. It was suddenly important for the Americans to cultivate good relations with a nation upon whom they depended so heavily for petroleum. A year later the United States stopped exporting enriched uranium to South Africa, ostensibly because of its refusal to sign the Nuclear Non-Proliferation Treaty of 1968. The decision had negligible impact on the American economy, which by then had an overabundance of uranium, thanks to the opening up of vast Canadian resources. Hence, South African supplies and cooperation were no longer considered essential. In the same year, after intense congressional debate, the United States closed down its NASA tracking facility after declining to renew the contract. It can therefore be argued that the Nixon version of détente and engagement ended late in 1975 and was not revived for nearly seven years, until the accession of Ronald Reagan. Thus, the first foray into constructive engagement ended on a note of frustration and lack of accomplishment. The South African power structure was not about to be dictated to by the Americans, who, in their minds, had let them down over the issue of Angola.

PRESSURES ON APARTHEID:
HOLDING THE ENTREPRENEURS ACCOUNTABLE

The 1960s witnessed the twilight of mainline American missionaries in southern Africa and the opening of a new era in church-supported activism. In 1964 the American Board of Commissioners for Foreign Missions in Boston was dissolved after 128 years of activity.[75] For South Africa it marked the end of the American missionary era. The demise of missionary organizations may be attributed in part to the government's assumption of almost complete control over African education.

But church organizations in the United States had also become increasingly hostile to apartheid and were calling for disengagement at all levels. A new generation of leadership was emerging in the old mainline churches in America, in the form of a pastorate that favored socialistic democracy and support for groups struggling for social justice and civil rights. In the United States many of their concerns and accomplishments were bound up in the Civil Rights Act of 1964, which banned discrimination in the use of public facilities and employment wherever the federal government had jurisdiction. It was a leadership that saw capitalism and its emphasis on individual advancement as antithetical to racial equality. Freedom, it was argued, cannot be gained through private enterprise or in the free marketplace; it could only be achieved by means of political mobilization of the exploited masses. Missionary stations of old were stereotyped as instruments of the status quo and upholders of traditions that were no longer appropriate or relevant to the world. Thus, the 1960s witnessed the decline of missionary proselytization and the rise of liberation theology. The American missionary as private entrepreneur and advocate of the capitalist ethic had become a relic of the past. For pastors in the civil rights movement even the activities of progressive missionaries such as Reverend Ray Phillips and Drs. McCord and Bridgman, who had been in the vanguard of social and educational reform in the past, were unacceptable because of their very engagement, however indirect, with the racist state. In many ways church leaders in the 1960s and 1970s had moved beyond their congregations on social issues. Some church members, especially in the South, recoiled from the new activism by hiving off into more conservative charismatic and pentecostal organizations. These fundamentalist movements tended to remain apolitical and noncommittal on issues such as apartheid, and their evangelical missionary endeavors continued.

The emergence of independent black-ruled Africa and tragic events such as those in Sharpeville and Langa attracted wide media attention. Not since the Second Boer War had sub-Saharan Africa figured so prominently in American newspapers. In 1961 *Newsweek*'s first bureau in Africa was opened in Nairobi, Kenya, and the *Washington Post* began regular coverage of sub-Saharan Africa with a Lagos-based British stringer who became full-time a year later. Most American journalists responsible for South Africa were still based in London, though special reports were filed from Nairobi and Lagos. By 1963 fifty-nine correspondents, mostly stringers, reported to the American media from Africa, though most of them were British citizens. The political tempo accelerated and by mid-1965 the *New York Times,* the *Los Angeles Times,* and the *Christian Science Monitor* had full-time resident correspondents in Africa. The latter's was based in Salisbury, while the *Los Angeles Times*'s correspondent resided in Leopoldville. Closest to the South African scene was United Press International, which by 1966 had a staff bureau in Johannesburg.

Anti-apartheid activism moved into higher gear in the early 1960s, in the aftermath of Sharpeville and Langa. Campaigns calling for economic sanctions were launched in the major American cities. In March 1964 the International Conference on Economic Sanctions Against South Africa was held in London and attended by representatives of anti-apartheid groups in forty nations.[76] Not surprisingly, religious denominations and ecumenical organizations were in the forefront of the early debates on apartheid in South Africa.

In 1965, several small conferences on apartheid were sponsored by the International Division of the National Council of Churches in New York. In the same year the first large expression of student activism was forthcoming in a demonstration at Chase Manhattan Bank's Wall Street headquarters. Local college students, led by the Students for a Democratic Society (SDS) and the National Student Christian Federation, protested against the renewal of bank loans to the South African government. Also in 1965, the influential Carnegie Endowment for International Peace published "Apartheid and the United Nations' Collective Measures,"[77] a report that objectively weighed the arguments for and against economic sanctions. Meanwhile, a growing minority in the aca-

17. An anti-apartheid student demonstration, ca. 1985. (Photo credit, African News/Erin Sweeney)

demic community had begun to argue that only through U.S. disengagement from South Africa could Americans hope to cultivate a fund of trust and goodwill in black Africa. Further, it was maintained that the economic growth of the 1960s, far from undermining apartheid, actually consolidated it and helped it to mature into a more subtle and sophisticated socioeconomic system.

Support for refugees of apartheid also began to arise. In 1966 the American Committee on Africa (ACOA) set up the Africa Fund to provide humanitarian assistance to South African political refugees.[78] A year later the American legal profession became involved in the issue of apartheid when the Lawyers Committee for Civil Rights Under Law launched the Southern Africa Project to build bridges between the domestic civil rights movement and the global struggle for human rights.[79] The committee also worked to increase awareness in the American legal profession of South Africa's evasion of rule of law.

The corporate stock divestment drive, which eventually became one of the most potent anti-apartheid weapons, began in 1968 with Princeton University student demands that their trustees divest the institution's portfolio of stocks in companies conducting business in South Africa. In the same year anti-apartheid demonstrators made similar demands on the campuses of the University of Wisconsin, Cornell, and elsewhere. Also in 1968 the Ford and Rockefeller foundations cosponsored *Southern Africa and the United States,* a short book designed to bring the issues of apartheid and economic sanctions into sharper focus.[80] Within months sixteen representatives had organized themselves into the Congressional Black Caucus to mobilize support for a broad range of civil rights laws, including legislation against the white regimes of South Africa and Rhodesia.

In the case of Rhodesia it was becoming apparent that sanctions were not entirely effective. Indeed, export volumes from the country actually rose between 1966 and 1970 from $238 million to $346 million.[81] Such statistics seemed to strengthen the case against sanctions for South Africa. Even most sanctions supporters had not yet recognized that for Rhodesia the terms of trade had begun to deteriorate and that limited sanctions had deprived its industries of the technology needed to maintain competitiveness in world markets. As early as 1967 Ford had quietly shut down its Rhodesian assembly plant after losing most of its export markets.

The anti-apartheid movement was somewhat overshadowed in the late 1960s by Vietnam and the civil war in Nigeria. Militants found themselves deeply divided over the issue of Biafran independence. However, a crucial turning point for the movement came in 1970, when the Securities and Exchange Commission ruled that shareholders could submit public-interest shareholder resolutions on specific social responsibility issues.[82] Within a year the first church-supported resolution was brought forward by the national organization of the Episcopal Church. It called upon General Motors, one of the largest employers of Africans, to cease its manufacturing operations in South Africa. The mammoth corporation launched a successful campaign against the resolution, which received only 1 percent of the stockholders' votes. Nevertheless, 1971 marked the commencement of the strategy of using institutional investors as a tool for pressuring American corporations into improving the conditions of employment of their African workers.

CORPORATE REACTIONS:
PUTTING ON A GOOD FACE

How did the private, corporate sector respond to the mounting pressures in favor of economic sanctions and boycotts against South Africa? Historically, American MNCs had been insensitive to the issues of racial discrimination. Corporate annual reports rarely mentioned the ideology, theory, or business dimensions of apartheid. Executives were loath to make public statements regarding political currents in the countries where they conducted business, and South Africa was certainly no exception. MNCs reiterated their argument that they should not cast judgments over the internal affairs of host countries. Moreover, from the 1960s the trend was towards greater local control over subsidiaries. Managing directors, often South African-born, tended to soft-pedal racial issues and shield headquarters from the harsh realities of apartheid. Business policy generally allowed the local managing directors to identify and resolve their problems in accordance with the interests of the host country as long as growth and profits could be realized for the subsidiary.

The Boston-based Polaroid Corporation was the first American firm to respond to anti-apartheid pressure when in 1970 its black American employees pressured it into establishing a program in South Africa to improve labor conditions. Polaroid's black workers in Massachusetts were protesting the production and processing of Polaroid film for use by the South African government in its passbook system.[83] It must be remembered that the passbooks were an integral part of the country's influx-control system and thus an important pillar of apartheid. By January 1971 Polaroid was contributing five hundred scholarships for South African students. The Polaroid experiment forced business into a defensive posture and revealed its vulnerability to anti-apartheid pressures. Moreover, both the Department of Commerce and the Department of State lauded the Polaroid programs as instruments for apartheid reform, and they urged other American MNCs to take similar steps. General Motors followed Polaroid's initiatives a year later with a program to improve the wages and benefits of its own black employes, and by the end of 1973 more than a dozen American MNCs had put into place programs similar to Polaroid's. A new emphasis was placed on upgrading the skills of black workers. In 1973 the Carnegie Corporation funded several career and leadership development programs, including a startup grant to the United States–South African Leadership Exchange Program's Careers Development Project.[84] Nevertheless, nearly all American corporations and foundations had spurned calls from anti-apartheid organizations to withdraw from the country altogether or to establish a code of business conduct.

The first corporate moves towards disinvestment were made in 1973, when Weyerhaeuser, the huge timber and paper company, pulled out and MGM discontinued its film distribution after more than four decades in South Africa.[85] But this did not establish a trend. Moreover, some argued that the MGM decision was part of a corporate restructuring that involved the sell-off of most of its theaters outside of the United States. In the years ahead most American MNCs followed John Deere's lead in making public statements to their stockholders and to the press of their intention to remain in South Africa as a "force for change."[86]

In the early 1970s demands for corporate accountability on a broad range of domestic and international issues had begun to gather momentum. In 1971 in New York the Interfaith Center on Corporate Responsibility (ICCR) was formed by a group of Protestant and Catholic organizations and sponsored by the prestigious National Council of Churches. The ICCR ultimately served as a coordinating body for nineteen Protestant agencies and 210 Catholic orders.[87] Its aim was to influence corporate behavior on a broad range of moral and ethical issues, including South Africa. It published briefs—in reality exposés—and began to look for institutional investors, such as foundations and religious organizations, to support shareholder resolutions at annual meetings of corporate stockholders. In the same year the Pacific Northwest Research Center was formed in Oregon to investigate and assess corporate performance in a wide variety of political and economic problems, including apartheid. In 1972 the Investor Responsibility Research Center (IRRC) was founded in Washington, D.C., as an independent, nonprofit corporation to conduct research and publish impartial reports on contemporary social and public policy issues and the impact of those policies on major corporations and institutional investors.[88] Ultimately, its support came from more than three hundred investing institutions. In the same year the American Committee on Africa's office in Washington was transformed into the independent and jointly sponsored Washington Office on Africa. With its activities funded from a wide spectrum of denominations, including the Methodists, Presbyterians, United Church of Christ, and the Episcopalians, the aim of the office was to lobby for passage of legislation to cut off all U.S. support for South Africa. By 1972 ACOA had established both the Southern Africa Committee and a magazine *Southern Africa* to garner membership and to keep Americans abreast of civil and human rights violations in the white regimes. Nevertheless, in the early years the ACOA remained on the margins of legislative and corporate power in the United States, membership and support coming primarily from the religious, labor, and academic communities.

These movements took heart in the progress of liberation in Rhodesia. In 1972–1973 the guerrilla struggle was transformed into a civil war as the liberation movements began to infiltrate the country. Sanctions at last seemed to be working. Despite the outward appearance of domestic prosperity, the country's current account had remained in deficit since its unilaterial declaration of independence in 1965, and by the early 1970s the Smith regime had to drastically reduce its imports to save on foreign exchange.

Nonetheless, national opinion polls indicated that most Americans knew little and cared even less about events in southern Africa.[89] Obviously, advocates of economic sanctions and disengagement would have to educate American voters and investors before corporate and legislative resolutions and votes could be carried. An important step in that direction was taken in 1973, when the Africa News Service was started in North Carolina by a group of moderate Duke University graduates. Their biweekly publication, *Africa News,* did much to inform its readers of current trends on the continent. Later they carried news on Africa over radio stations throughout the country, particularly in the black communities. British organizations were also having an influence. In Cambridge, Massachusetts, South African exile Reverend Kenneth Carstens established a chapter of the British-based International Defence and Aid Fund for Southern Africa to help defend political detainees in South Africa and Namibia. IDAF's newsletter kept Americans abreast of human rights violations and did much to introduce prominent American experts in international law to the legal ramifications of apartheid.[90]

By the early 1970s pressure was also building to discourage American participation in South African athletic events. In 1972 the American boxer Muhammad Ali, bowing to pressure from South African exile

Dennis Brutus and the United Nations Special Committee on Apartheid, refused an offer to fight in the Republic.[91] Nevertheless, a year later Arthur Ashe played several matches there. Clearly, there was still a lack of consensus, even among black Americans, over how best to fight apartheid. The approaches ran the gamut, from total boycott to total engagement.

Surprisingly little attention was given in the academic community to the development of curriculum and serious research on South Africa. Universities and foundations tended to fund research in black African nations that had already achieved their independence. Moreover, only a few dozen specialists on South Africa taught in the United States; most of them were British or South African-born and trained in the disciplines of history and political science. One of the few American scholars to directly address the issue of the United States' corporate role in South Africa was the black intellectual Donald McHenry, who in 1975 published a short study entitled *U.S. Firms in South Africa.*[92]

Nevertheless, in the 1960s African studies on American campuses grew at an astonishingly fast pace. It can be argued that by 1970 the United States had pulled ahead of Great Britain as the leader in African studies outside the African continent. An African Studies Center was organized at Michigan State University in 1960 and at the University of Wisconsin in Madison a year later. Federal government involvement in the development of African studies began to expand rapidly in the early 1960s through the vehicle of the Office of Education. Early emphasis was placed on language and cultural studies in countries under African majority rule. In 1965 the University of Wisconsin was among the first to be designated as a Language and Area Center by the Office of Education.[93]

The whole tradition of area studies on American campuses was influenced initially by the requirements, interests, and goals of Congress and the federal government. In the early 1960s some of the major African studies programs were initiated and directed by former and current members of the American intelligence community, particularly the CIA and received the bulk of their financial support from the federal government. By contrast, the U.S. business community expressed comparatively little interest in advancing research on South Africa, or even African studies for that matter.

Some faculty eventually left the centers and went into government service. Surprisingly few Africa specialists pursued careers in the private sector. Indeed, nearly all of the African studies centers were biased against business and finance; and courses in African economics and agronomy were practically nonexistent. Additionally, most of the major African studies programs, as well as the national African Studies Association, were dominated by politically moderate white academics. The issue of racial bias came to a head in 1969 at the annual convention of the African Studies Association, held in Montreal. John Henrik Clarke, a black American Africanist from New York, led many Afro-Americans out of the African Studies Association and established the African Heritage Studies Association, based in New York City.[94] But even that group tended to focus on the cultural history and Afro-American connections of societies north of the Zambezi. Throughout the 1960s few American scholars specialized in southern African studies and still fewer offered courses on the region.

Political repression in South Africa drove many students into exile in North America. By 1965 over 435 South Africans were studying in American colleges and universities, but only a handful of them were enrolled in studies concerning their own country.[95] By contrast, South African universities were not generally popular with American youth because of their racial segregation, and they failed to draw more than a hundred Americans in any academic year.

More attractive to Americans were the country's well-organized game parks, spectacular natural vistas, and world-class hotels and resorts. Few other subtropical countries were as well prepared for international tourism, and not surprisingly the 1960s witnessed modest though substantial growth in Yankee tourism. American hotel and motel chains entered South Africa, beginning with Holiday Inns in the late 1960s. Pan American Airways also capitalized on the surge in tourism by building Intercontinental hotels throughout Africa wherever its planes flew. In 1969 Western International Hotels merged with United Airlines and opened facilities in southern Africa. In the same year Avis, the American car rental company, became a subsidiary of ITT and opened offices in Johannesburg. Avis initially entered into a fifty-fifty partnership with a local firm, but by 1975 the local Avis had risen to number one in South Africa's car rental business and was essentially a South African-owned business.

Tourism and business in general were given an enormous boost by advances in the speed and comfort of air transportation. Jet aircraft vastly shortened traveling time between the United States and South Africa. Initially, Pan Am jet Clipper service between New York and Cape Town consumed an average of twenty-two hours, as opposed to thirteen days by Farrell Lines. It did not take a Cassandra to see that the era of regular transoceanic passenger service was rapidly sailing into the twilight zone. The shipping lines tried to survive by offering luxury cruises with a South African stopover on extensive itineraries. In 1960 Moore-McCormack Lines of New York entered the business with its Sea Safari cruises to Africa, although the route proved to be unprofitable and was soon abandoned.[96] Meanwhile, inflation-adjusted airfares fell drastically, and passenger volume soared. In 1964 Pan Am carried 1,937 passengers into Johannesburg and 2,041 out. Pan Am, the only carrier to fly between the two countries, had reduced its roundtrip fare by half, to $946 and cut its traveling time to nineteen and a half hours.[97] Passenger demand grew steadily, and profits mounted. Competition began in February 1969, when South African Airways, a government airline, launched its own Johannesburg–New York service.[98] Passenger volume grew steadily and then accelerated spectacularly after 1973, when both carriers began to purchase the huge, long-distance Boeing SP747s. The two airlines also obtained Civil Aeronautics Board (CAB) approval to fly via Cape Verde islands, thus by-passing Lisbon and shaving another three hours off traveling time.

Spectacular advances in telecommunications also brought the United States closer to South Africa. It should be recalled that telephone service between the two countries began in the mid-1930s via England by a single-circuit submarine cable to London and then onward to New York via radio-telephone. Gradually, the number of circuits grew. However, a technological breakthrough was achieved in 1975, when direct-dialing facilities became operational. In a stroke South Africa was integrated into the global satellite system, which was operated by the International Telecommunications Satellite Organization, or INTELSAT. More calls could be placed simultaneously and at less cost.[99]

Cultural exchange, long in a state of hibernation, also experienced a moderate revival between 1965 and 1975. Beginning in the early 1960s South African culture trickled into the United States, mainly through the medium of drama. Alan Paton's *Sponono*, with several Africans in the cast and with music by Gideon Nxumalo, was performed at the Cort

Theater on Broadway and at the World's Fair in New York in 1964. Theater critics slammed it as an Uncle Tom play laden with condescending black stereotypes, and both productions failed to draw large or enthusiastic audiences.[100]

In the aftermath of Sharpeville many black musicians and composers, frustrated by racial discrimination in South Africa, exiled themselves to the United States. Artists like Miriam Makeba, Dollar Brand, and Hugh Masekela became well known to American audiences. Black South African actors began to make their mark before American audiences in 1974, when John Kani and Winston Ntshona won Tony awards for their Broadway performances in *Sizwe Bansi is Dead*, a drama by Athol Fugard, an Afrikaner playwright.

Black South Africans had begun to reawaken to the civil rights movement in the United States after the assassination of Reverend Martin Luther King, Jr. The upsurge in political and cultural consciousness grew out of the ferment in the high schools of the urban black townships. In 1968 the student Steve Biko and others broke from the white-dominated National Union of South African Students and formed their all-black South African Students Organization, which became the prime mover in the unfolding Black Consciousness Movement in South Africa.[101] In its 1971 manifesto black consciousness was described as a state of mind. The movement, as well as the student unrest that emerged in 1972, seemed to draw much of its early inspiration from the works of such militant black Americans as Stokeley Carmichael, former chairman of the Student Nonviolent Coordinating Committee (SNCC), and Charles Hamilton, as well as from the speeches and writings of Malcolm X and LeRoi Jones of the Republic of New Africa movement. Robert Fatton has suggested that "what the American Black Power ideology provided was a theoretical source for the renewal of black South African thinking."[102] Gail Gerhart in her research noted the "terminological revolution" in the use of the word *black*. In the early 1970s South African militants began to adopt such popular American slogans as Black Power and Black Is Beautiful and to reject as antirevolutionary the appellations *colored, negro, native, bantu,* and *nonwhite.*"[103]

Initially, the Black Consciousness Movement was tolerated by the Nationalist regime under Prime Minister John Vorster, which saw it as a new nonviolent and theoretical framework for racial separatism. But after the pro-Frelimo rallies in September 1974 which supported the liberation of Mozambique, it was clear that the cultural movement had developed strong political and panethnic overtones. Consequently, these and similar demonstrations on school campuses throughout the country were followed by large-scale detentions of black consciousness leaders. Nevertheless, the tempo of student resistance heightened in 1975, when Portugal gave independence to neighboring Mozambique and Angola. This abrupt decolonization after years of guerrilla struggle gave black South African students a new and more profound sense of urgency and expectancy.

CONCLUSION

One of the most striking aspects of the United States' relationship with South Africa in the period 1960 to 1975 was the great public awakening to the system of apartheid and its assaults on human and civil rights. Sharpeville, the explosive growth of African nationalism, and the unfolding civil rights movement in the United States had begun to sensitize young people to the issue of black empowerment. In the United States citizen activism had led to the passage of the landmark Civil Rights Act of 1964. But among some activists the spirit of expectancy soon eroded into a sense of frustration and a mood of militancy. The separatist Black Power movement, which gained momentum in 1966, was followed by urban racial disorders a summer later.

Private foundations and educational institutions, which had hitherto been at the trailing edge of the civil rights movement, cautiously began to address the issue of "equal opportunity," which they considered the ultimate civil right. The Rockefeller Foundation became one of the first to develop a strategy to identify and develop moderate leadership in the United States' black ghettos. Then in 1968 under the direction of Alan Pifer the Carnegie Corporation began supporting the training of black lawyers to become active in the civil rights movement. Funds were also extended to the New York Legal Aid Society for community law offices in Harlem. However, the foundations' overarching objective was to solve the plight of blacks through the provision of greater educational access and the expansion of the frontiers of universal opportunity within the context of the free enterprise system. It must be remembered that American philanthropic interest in blacks derived from a long tradition of concern over the need to provide leaders with skills and techniques for economic self-sufficiency, not from an ideological commitment to the principle of political empowerment.

Out of these growing domestic civil rights concerns, as well as the evolving worry over the environmental consequences of industrial pollution, grew strident demands for corporate responsibility and accountability. What is important for this study is that in the 1960s and early 1970s these concerns and strategies were extended to the civil and human rights crises in southern Africa in the form of anti-apartheid activism. At the forefront of the new movement were white and black political exiles from South Africa and American civil rights workers. In the United States the enforcement machinery of the federal government had seemingly begun to facilitate black advancement. With similar pressures, could not the South African government be forced to move in a similar direction? Americans looked at South Africa through the lens of the American civil rights experience and the easy rush to independence in the European colonies of East and West Africa. In the immediate aftermath of Sharpeville some Americans felt that African majority rule was at hand. But they miscalculated the resiliency of the South African economy, adjuvated by massive capital infusions, and the determination of the government to suppress, neutralize, marginalize, and co-opt its real and potential opponents.

During this period gold continued to be a crucial factor in the survival of the South African economy. A definitive history of gold in the world economy has yet to be written; when it is, South Africa will figure prominently. The white power structure survived the shocks of Sharpeville through a complex combination of gold exports and the infusions of foreign capital, a substantial proportion of it under American control. Years of protectionist policies in South Africa may have contributed to domestic economic growth, but they also created a hothouse effect preventing the country's manufactures from competing effectively in world markets. Consequently, government efforts to diversify away from the yellow metal were not fully successful, and South Africa continued to be a hostage to the vagaries of world gold prices and foreign monetary policies. On the other hand, the United States responded to South Africa's protectionism by increasing the flow of investments, either directly or through joint ventures.

U.S. presence in the South African economy grew rapidly in the years after Sharpeville, undeterred by the increasingly strident voices of the anti-apartheid movement at home and the growth of black intellectual and labor militancy in South Africa. South Africa's post-Sharpeville policies of growth stimulation and the search for autarky required foreign capital and technology that the United States was prepared to furnish. The role of the United States in restoring international investor confidence in the immediate post-Sharpeville days was extremely important in this calculus. However, it may be argued that what counted most was not the enormous capital infusions via consortia of individual and institutional investors, bankers, and multilateral donors but the very act of taking the investment risks in a climate of extreme uncertainty. The Sharpeville massacre and the government repression that followed unmasked the realities of South Africa's racial and political problems and sounded the first knell to the dissolving epoch of illusion. On the other hand, the spectacular post-Sharpeville recovery led many unwary American entrepreneurs to believe in an illusion of new South African prosperity, which by 1984 had proved to be a thin veneer, polished by the glitter of gold, diamonds, and rich black coal, the lifeblood of the country's exports. In the final analysis, the behavior of U.S. private and public sectors in the 1960s and 1970s must be viewed within two contexts: that of lingering Cold War fears over losing access to the strategic minerals of southern Africa and that of the incomparably high rates of return on capital investments.

The year 1975 marked the end of the Sharpeville era and the beginning of American ponderings over the very future of white rule, not only in southern Africa but in South Africa itself. Events forced Americans in both the private and public sectors to reassess their raison d'être in the white redoubts. The war in southeast Asia and the civil rights struggle in the United States wound down, and the spotlight again shifted to southern Africa. But henceforth a far more complicated and less predictable amalgam of attitudes and strategies began to merge in the United States as well as in South Africa.

NOTES

1. J. C. Van Zyl and H. J. Reynders, "Foreign Trade Policy in South Africa," in J. A. Lombard, ed., *Economic Policy in South Africa* (Cape Town,

1973), p. 344. See also D. Hobart Houghton, *The South African Economy*, p. 66; Merle Lipton, *Capitalism and Apartheid, 1910–1984*, p. 143; J. Keith Horsefield, ed., *The International Monetary Fund 1945–1965*, vol. 2, *Analysis* (Washington, D.C., 1969), p. 414.

2. George M. Houser, "What the U.S. Can Do About Apartheid," *Africa Today* 8 (March 1966): 4–6ff. See also Thomas J. Noer, *Black Liberation: The U.S. and White Rule in Africa, 1948–1968*, p. 211.

3. Richard D. Mahoney, *JFK: Ordeal in Africa* (New York, 1983), pp. 188–90. See also Victor Razis, *The American Connection: The Influence of United States Business on South Africa*, p. 44.

4. J. C. du Plessis, "Foreign Investment in South Africa," in I. A. Litvak and C. J. Maule, eds., *Foreign Investment: The Experience of Host Countries*, p. 192. See also Leo Katzen, "The Economy," *Africa South of the Sahara Annual, 1978–1979* (London, 1979), p. 888.

5. Houghton, *South African Economy*, p. 187; Lipton, *Capitalism and Apartheid*, p. 144.

6. Minter, *King Solomon's Mines Revisited, Western Interests and the Burdened History of Southern Africa*, pp. 73–77. See also "The Engelhard Touch," *Forbes* (August 1969), p. 23.

7. Theodore Nelson, "Republic of South Africa." See also "South Africa," *Businessweek*, October 7, 1961, p. 61; Daan Prinsloo, *U.S. Foreign Policy and the Republic of South Africa*, p. 51.

8. Horsefield, *The International Monetary Fund*, 2:414.

9. World Bank, *Seventeenth Annual Report, 1961–1962* (Washington, D.C., 1962), p. 94. *Facts on File* 21 (New York, 1962): 499.

10. Ann and Neva Seidman, *South Africa and United States Multinational Corporations*, p. 116. See also H. Wachtel, *The New Gnomes: Multinational Banking in the Third World* (Washington, D.C., 1977), p.8.

11. *ESCOM: A Leadership Corporate Profile*, October 1986 (Cape Town, 1986), passim.

12. World Bank, *Seventeenth Annual Report*, appendix, p. vii.

13. *The Washington Post*, December 2, 1984, p. 1; *Financial Mail*, (Johannesburg), October 3, 1986, p. 40: *African Business* (London), July 1987, p. 7.

14. Duncan Innes, *Anglo-American and the Rise of Modern South Africa, 1980/81: Official Yearbook*. (Johannesburg, 1981), p. 490.

15. Seidman and Seidman, *South Africa*, p. 235; *South Africa*, p. 80. See also Colin Legum, ed., *Africa: Contemporary Record, Annual Survey and Documents 1973/74*, p. 342.

16. McHenry, *U.S. Firms*, p. 14. See also J. N. Friedlin and L. A. Lupo "U.S. Direct Investment Abroad," U.S. Bureau of Foreign and Domestic Commerce, 54, 8 Part 2, August 1974 (Washington, D.C., 1974), p. 18.

17. American Committee on Africa, *Challenge of New Investments in South Africa* (New York, 1976). See also Thomas Gladwin and Ingo Walter, *Multinationals Under Fire*, p. 201.

18. Wayne G. Broehl, Jr., *John Deere's Company,* p. 707. See also *South Africa/Namibia Update* 6, 4 (September 1981):3.
19. *South Africa: Guide to Foreign Investors* (Johannesburg, 1977), p. 27. See also *Standard Encyclopedia of Southern Africa* (Johannesburg, 1970), 1:617.
20. Dick Clark, et al., *U.S. Corporate Interests in South Africa, Report to the Committee on Foreign Relations.* See also *Africa* 62 (October 1976):26.
21. John Dugard and W. H. B. Dean, "The Just Legal Order," in van der Horst, ed., *Race Discrimination,* pp. 20–21.
22. "The Man, the Castle," *Financial Mail* Supplement, September 5, 1986, p. 9.
23. Eric Rosenthal, *The Rolling Years: Fifty Years of General Motors in South Africa,* p. 72.
24. Innes, *Anglo-American,* pp. 235–36. See also Harry Oppenheimer, "The Anglo-American Corporation's Role in South Africa's Gold Mining Industry," *Optima* 34, 2 (June 1986):19.
25. "No Brakes on Growth," *Financial Mail,* Special Corporate Supplement, April 18, 1986, p. 9.
26. Stephen M. Davis, *Apartheid's Rebels* (New Haven, 1987), pp. 49–50.
27. Tom Lodge, *Black Politics in South Africa since 1945,* p. 20.
28. Muriel Horrell, ed., *Survey of Race Relations in South Africa 1975* (Johannesburg, 1976), pp. 183–88. See also Seidman and Seidman, *South Africa,* p. 98; Lipton, *Apartheid,* pp. 30–31.
29. Anthony Lake, "Caution and Concern: The Making of American Policy Toward South Africa, 1946–1971," Ph.D dissertation (University of Wisconsin, 1974), passim.
30. Henry F. Jackson, *From the Congo to Soweto: US Foreign Policy Toward Africa Since 1960,* p. 146.
31. Thomas Karis, "U.S. Policy Toward South Africa," in G. M. Carter and Patrick O'Meara, eds., *Southern Africa: The Continuing Crisis,* p. 327.
32. William Foltz, "U.S. Policy Toward Southern Africa," in René Lemarchand, ed., *American Policy in Southern Africa: The States and Stance,* p. 263.
33. *Africa News,* April 26, 1982, p. 7; Prinsloo, *U.S. Foreign Policy,* p. 61; Sanford D. Greenberg, "U.S. Policy Toward the Republic of South Africa, 1945–1964," Ph.D. dissertation (Harvard University, 1965), pp. 199–200.
34. U.S. Congress, House Committee on Foreign Affairs, *Hearings on U.S.–South African Relations,* 89th Cong., 2nd sess. 1966. See also Richard E. Bissell, South Africa and the United States: *The Erosion of an Influence Relationship,* p. 24.
35. Chester, *Clash of Titans: Africa and U.S. Foreign Policy,* p. 217.
36. John Walton Cotman, "South African Strategic Minerals and U.S. Foreign

Policy, 1961–1968," p. 277. See also Raymond Mikesell, *Stockpiling Strategic Minerals* (Washington, D.C., 1986), p. 18.

37. Robert Denerstein, "Update," *Africa Report* 20, 3 (May–June 1975): 33.

38. S. A. Department of Commerce, *South Africa's Trade with the United States,* p. 12. See also U.N. Department of Political and Security Council Affairs, Unit on Apartheid, *Foreign Investments in South Africa* (New York, 1968).

39. U.S. Department of State, *South Africa. Background Notes, March 1971* (Washington, D.C., 1971). See also *Standard Encyclopedia of Southern Africa,* 1:22.

40. S. A. Department of Commerce, *South Africa's Trade,* p. 3.

41. Francis Cassell, *Gold of Credit?: Economics and Politics of International Money* (New York, 1965), p. 40.

42. David T. Devlin, "The Balance of Payments," in Ingo Walter, ed., *Handbook of International Business* (New York, 1982), pp. 61–66.

43. *Africa Digest* 17, 4 (August 1970). pp. 2–3. See also Benjamin Cohen, *Organizing the World's Money: The Political Economy of International Monetary Relations* (New York, 1977), p. 51.

44. Volkskas. *Economic Spotlight.* March 1985 (Johannesburg; 1985), p. 1.

45. Horsefield, *International Monetary Fund,* 2:413.

46. Legum, ed., *Africa Contemporary Record: 1973/74,* p. 177.

47. Colin Legum, *A Republic in Trouble: South Africa, 1972–73* (London, 1973), pp. 34–35. See also H. Zarenda, "Tariff Policy: Export Promotion versus Import Replacement," *South African Journal of Economics* 43,1 (March 1975), p. 74.

48. Devlin, "Balance of Payments," p. 63. See also Cohen, *Organizing,* p. 179.

49. U.S. House of Representatives, *U.S. Business Investment in Southern Africa,* part 2, Hearings before the Committee on Foreign Affairs, 92nd Cong., 1st sess. (Washington, D.C., 1972). See also Joyce Kolko, *Restructuring the World Economy* (New York, 1988), p. 334; David Eiteman and Arthur I Stonehill, *Multinational Business Finance,* pp. 26, 47; Harry M. Venedikian and Gerald A. Warfield, *Export-Import Financing* (New York, 1985), pp. 164–65.

50. Eiteman and Stonehill, *Business Finance,* pp. 48–49; John S. Odell, *United States International Monetary Policy* (Princeton, 1982), p. 194.

51. *South Africa, 1980/81 Official Yearbook,* p. 487. See also African-American Chamber of Commerce, "News," March (New York, 1972).

52. U.S. House of Representatives, *U.S. Business Involvement in Southern Africa,* part 3, Hearings before the Committee on Foreign Affairs, 93rd Cong., 1st sess. (Washington, D.C., 1973).

53. Richard Synge, ed., *South Africa: A Guide* (London, 1977), p. 19.

54. Barbara Rogers, *White Wealth and Black Poverty: American Investments in Southern Africa,* p. 196.

55. Jill Nattrass, *The South African Economy,* p. 271. See also Lipton, *Capitalism and Apartheid,* pp. 240–41.

56. *South African Digest,* October 29, 1976, p. 4.

57. Donald McHenry, *U.S. Firms,* p. 32.

58. J. N. Friedlin and L. A. Lupo, "U.S. Direct Investments Abroad, 1973," U.S. Bureau of Foreign and Domestic Commerce, *Survey of Current Business,* 54, 8 part 2 (Washington, D.C., August 1974), p. 18. See also Legum, *Africa Contemporary Record,* 1973, p. 272.

59. Stopford and Dunning, *Multinational Enterprise,* 1:444.

60. Joan E. Spero, *The Politics of International Economic Relations* (New York, 1985), p. 336.

61. Interfaith Center on Corporate Responsibility, *South Africa Brief,* May (New York, 1980), p. 3-A

62. *South African Digest,* June 30, 1978, p. 19.

63. D. Brooks, "The Krugerrand Connection," American Committee on Africa Special Report (New York, 1985), p. 3.

64. Ronald Walters, "Uranium Politics and U.S. Foreign Policy," *Journal of Southern African Affairs,* 4, 3 (July 1979):281–301. See also Cotman, "South African Strategic Minerals and U.S. Foreign Policy," p. 277.

65. Heidi Tietjen, "Fluor" in Africa Fund, *Southern African Perspectives,* August (New York, 1979), pp. 1–6. See also *Financial Mail,* March 29, 1985, p. 56.

66. South African Embassy, *The United States and South Africa.* Occasional paper no. 14 (Washington, D.C., 1979).

67. Mikesell, *Minerals,* p. 20.

68. *The Kissinger Study of Southern Africa: National Security Study Memorandum 39,* passim.

69. Michael T. Klau and Eric Prokosch, "Getting Arms to South Africa," *Nation,* July 8–15, 1978, pp. 50–51.

70. Robert Pastor, *Congress and the Politics of U.S. Foreign Economic Policy, 1929–1976,* pp. 97–98.

71. C. Joakimidis and A. Sitas, "A Study of Strikes in the 1970s," *Work in Progress* (Johannesburg) November 6, 1987, pp. 105–12. See also Lodge, *Black Politics,* pp. 59–60; *Africa Confidential* 14, 20 (November 1969)13:6.

72. Paul Irish, "U.S. Corporations in South Africa," paper presented to International Seminar on the Role of Transnational Corporations in South Africa (London, 1979).

73. Dick Clark, "American Policy Towards Southern Africa," *Issue: A Quarterly Journal of Africanist Opinion* 7, 1 (Spring 1977):21–22.

74. Franklin A. Thomas, et al., *South Africa: Time Running Out,* passim.

75. Fred Field Goodsell, *Among the Bantu in Africa: Story of the American Board of Commissioners for Foreign Missions South of the Equator, 1835–1960.*

76. *Africa Digest* December 19, 1964, p. 12.

77. E. Jefferson Murphy, *Creative Philanthropy: Carnegie Corporation and Africa, 1953–1973.*
78. The Africa Fund, *Annual Report, 1986* (New York, 1986), p. 1.
79. Avery Russell, "Pursuing Justice in an Unjust Society," *Carnegie Quarterly* 29, 1 (Winter 1981):1–7.
80. Ford Foundation. *Annual Report, 1968* (New York, 1969), p. 4.
81. Alan Best and Harm de Blij, *African Survey* (New York, 1977), p. 294.
82. Philip L. Christenson, "U.S.–South African Economic Relations," in Barratt and hero, eds., *American People*, p. 48.
83. By 1971 Polaroid was contributing over five hundred scholarships in South Africa for blacks. Christopher Coker, "Collective Bargaining As an International Sanction: The Role of U.S. Corporations in South Africa," *Journal of Modern African Studies* 19, 4 (1981):653–54. See also Legum, ed., *Africa Contemporary Record, 1970–1971*, p. A54.
84. Carnegic Corporation *Annual Report, 1973* (New York, 1974). See also Karis "Black Politics in South Africa," *Foreign Affairs* 30 (Winter 1983):392–406.
85. Anthony Slide, *The American Film Industry: A Historical Dictionary* (Westport, CT, 1986), pp. 358–59.
86. Broehl, *John Deere*, p. 234.
87. Interfaith Center for Corporate Responsibility, *The Corporate Examiner* 9, 12 (December 1980):4–6.
88. Roger Walke and Richard Knight, *Unified List of U.S. Companies with Investments or Loans in South Africa and Namibia.*
89. See Helen Kitchen, ed., *Africa: From Mystery to Maze.*
90. International Defense and Aid Fund for Southern Africa, *News Notes,* June (Boston, 1982), p. 2. See also Paul Holenbeck, "Out of Africa," *Duke* 73, 3 (March 1987):37–39.
91. Jeffrey Sammons, *Beyond the Ring: The Role of Boxing in American Society* (Chicago, 1988), pp. 230–31.
92. McHenry, *U.S. Firms*, p. 50.
93. Philip D. Curtin, "African History," *African Studies Association Newsletter* 12 (1974): p. 11.
94. "The 1969 Annual Meeting," *African Studies Newsletter* 2, 6–7 (November–December 1969):1–38.
95. Meg Voorhes, "American Universities and Black South African Education," *IRRC Special Report,* February 25, 1985 (New York, 1985). U.S. House of Representatives, Committee on Foreign Affairs, "African Students and Study Programs in the United States," Report of the Sub committee on Africa, 89th Cong., 1st sess. (Washington, D.C., 1965), pp. 14–17.
96. G. R. Berridge, *The Politics of the South Africa Run: European Shipping and Pretoria*, p. 219. See also Pan-American/Farrell Lines, *African Marketing Guide, 1968*, p. 5.
97. *Africa Report* (February 1965), p. 36. See also South African Airways.

Annual Report, 1956/57 (Johannesburg, 1957), p. 5; *South African Digest,* (December 9, 1964), p. 3.

98. *South African Digest,* February 22, 1969, p. 1
99. *South Africa 1983: Official Yearbook of the Republic of South Africa* (Pretoria, 1983), pp. 435–36.
100. Colby Kullman and William C. Young, *Theatre Companies of the World* (New York, 1986), p. 92.
101. Mokgethi Motlhabi, *The Theory and Practice of Black Resistance to Apartheid* (Johannesburg, 1984), p. 24 and passim. See also S. M. Motsuenyane, "Black Consciousness and the Economic Position of the Black Man in South Africa," in T. Thoahlane, ed., *Black Renaissance, Papers from the Black Renaissance Convention* (Johannesburg, 1975).
102. Robert Fatton, Jr., *Black Consciousness in South Africa,* pp. 67–68. See also "SASO Policy Manifesto," *SASO Newsletter* 1, 3 (August 1971):11; John Kane-Berman, *Soweto: Black Revolt, White Reaction* (Johannesburg, 1978), pp. 1–25.
103. Gail Gerhart, *Black Power in South Africa* (Berkeley, Univ. 1978), p. ii.

SEVEN

The Post-Sowetan Years, 1976–1987

The years 1976 and 1984 were important milestones in the long history of United States–South African economic relations. Rivulets of protest suddenly merged into a torrent of outrage that forced a fundamental reassessment of the United States' stance and stakes. Other trends unfolded independently of South Africa yet had a profound impact on the conduct of international business. From 1976 a consensus had begun to emerge that the world economic crisis was not cyclical but structural. In the decade ahead the international business community, in its quest for viability, resorted to new corporate strategies at home and abroad. These included intrafirm trade, acquisitions and mergers, takeovers, leveraged buyouts, and divestitures by conglomerates of previously held companies. A sea change occurred in the ways multinational banks handled foreign exchange and debt. And from the late 1970s the United States began to launch a new era in monetary history.

This chapter, however, focuses on the cataclysmic events and policies in South Africa that reawakened Americans to the unfolding crisis of apartheid and contributed to important shifts in public opinion and in the strategies of governments, anti-apartheid organizations, foundations, and multinational banks and corporations. It surveys the growth and maturation of the anti-apartheid movement, analyzes the responses of investors and entrepreneurs, and weighs the impact of disinvestment, divestment, and sanctions on South Africa's beleaguered economy. The chapter also attempts to explain why some American enterprises readily capitulated to the anti-apartheid avalanche and withdrew completely while others devised stratagems for maintaining some form of corporate presence.

A new era in black protest was launched on June 16, 1976, in Johannesburg's sprawling township of Soweto. What started out as a student demonstration over the imposition of Afrikaans as the medium of instruction ended in the death of over six hundred youths at the hands of the South African police. A wave of rioting, looting, arson, and general violence spread across the country. Not since Sharpeville sixteen years earlier had the black population seemed so bold and the white population so uncertain and insecure.

The booming South African economy of the 1960s and early 1970s had resulted in a nearly fourfold increase in the black student population and an explosion in the number of secondary school graduates. At no time since the frenetic economic activity of the World War II years did the economy appear so robust and so able to fund a wide variety of projects. Yet this touched off a revolution of rising expectations that was not matched by a commensurate expansion in educational facilities, urban housing, and job opportunities. Recently kindled African hopes turned to despair and frustration in 1975 as the period of growth in African wages came to an abrupt end.

THE UNEXPECTED RECESSION

The South African economy entered the year of the Soweto rebellion in a weakened condition. A recession had begun abruptly in 1974, and from late 1975 gold prices had begun to turn down after a steady rise from $40 per ounce in 1971 to $159 per ounce on the eve of the recession.[1] In the early 1970s South Africa had succeeded in raising the price of gold from its fixed convertibility to the dollar by restricting supply. But then the United States began to depress prices by selling off a proportion of its reserves on the private market. Commodity prices were also softening in world markets, which further aggravated the deterioration in South Africa's terms of trade. To the distress of government planners the rate of growth in real GDP slowed from 2.1 percent in 1975 to 1.4 percent a year later.[2] And as early as February 1976 the prices of essential foods and public transportation began to soar, a trend that was felt most severely in the urban black ghettos.

This unexpected recession stimulated a dramatic increase in foreign borrowings and lured scores of American banks into correspondent relationships with their South African counterparts. Indeed, since the onset of recession in 1974 South Africa had become increasingly dependent on international capital and credit. In February 1976 ESCOM, the utility parastatal, secured a $200 million five-year loan from a consortium of twenty-eight U.S. banks. A month later, Citibank put together a twelve-bank consortium loan of $150 million for a project to exploit titanium, a rare ore used in manufacturing jet engines.[3]

It must be recalled that even before the economic downturn South Africa had embarked on a program of massive infrastructural development, partly to expedite the expansion of exports of nonprecious metals, especially coal and iron, but also to implement its apartheid programs of separate economic and political development. U.S. banks enthusiastically participated in multibank consortia to finance the government's ambitious projects. On the eve of the Soweto rebellion government ministries and parastatals were dramatically increasing their borrowings in both American and European financial markets. By April of 1976 U.S. bank loans were at a record $350 million and would have been considerably higher if their European branches were factored into the calculations.[4] Most of South Africa's Eurocurrency loans were actually from American-based banks or their foreign subsidiaries. By the year's end the country's overseas bank debt equalled $7.6 billion, of which at least $2.2 billion was owed to banks in the United States.[5] Without precedent and to the knowledge of very few, no less than a third of all bank claims on the Republic were owed to U.S. banks and their foreign branches. Quietly, though assuredly, South African dependence on U.S. financial institutions was growing.

On the other hand, by 1976 the country had become an important supplier to the United States of key strategic minerals, especially platinum group metals. American demands for platinum soared in response to the Clean Air Act of 1974, which created a new demand for platinum catalysts in vehicular converters for the reduction of exhaust emissions. It was also employed in refining processes to produce unleaded fuel and as a catalyst in chemical processing. Late in the decade South Africa was supplying more than half of U.S. platinum imports and 80 percent of its foreign purchases of vanadium, used in strengthening steel.

U.S. equities had also become quite substantial, accounting for 16 percent of total foreign investments in South Africa. By 1976 the book value of American corporate investment had reached $1.6 billion or 37 percent of total American investments in Africa.[6] At the same time individual portfolio investors owned more than a quarter of the country's gold shares.

AN AMERICAN REASSESSMENT

On the eve of the Soweto rebellion the United States had begun a reassessment of long-term prospects for South Africa and neighboring Rhodesia. Uppermost in the minds of Washington policymakers was the vital need to maintain substantial private investments in southern Africa and to preserve access to the minerals without Soviet competition. A region of compliant states was therefore seen to be critically important. In April 1976 in Lusaka, Zambia, Secretary of State Henry Kissinger admitted that time was running out for whites in southern Africa. The *cordon sanitaire* of conservative Portuguese colonies had snapped with the abrupt decolonization of Angola and Mozambique. In a sharp reversal of policy, Kissinger set fourth a ten-point program aimed at facilitating southern African negotiations with moderate blacks. He also called for the establishment of majority rule in Rhodesia before the grant of formal independence. He assured South Africans that the United States would ease restrictions on American trade and investment in their country if they would establish a timetable for Namibian independence and put pressure on the Rhodesians to share power with their African majority. In other words, Kissinger implied that the white leadership in southern Africa must develop a cooptionist strategy in order to derail or forestall black radicalism. He warned Prime Minister Vorster that South Africa might be the next candidate for international sanctions if it failed to sever its ties with the illegal Smith regime in Rhodesia.[7]

The rising turmoil in southern Africa had already begun to attract wider American media attention, and anti-apartheid South African novelists such as Nadine Gordimer, Alan Paton, Elsa Joubert, J. M. Coetzee, and André Brink found prestigious publishing houses in the United States eager to promote their works. Their popular and heart-wrenching stories quickly sensitized the American intelligentsia to the human costs of apartheid. The time of media reengagement was at hand; and in May 1976, after a hiatus of ten years, the *New York Times* reopened its Johannesburg office, anticipating that the turmoil in South Africa would soon escalate. The *Times* had closed shop in 1966, shortly after the expulsion of its correspondent, Joseph Lelyveld, who had filed stories critical of government policies. Now, in 1976, the more prescient observers had begun to sense that the structural decline of South Africa's growth rate had commenced and that black unemployment had become a chronic rather than a cyclical problem. The time bomb seemed to have been set. When it would go off was anyone's guess. But the American media wanted to be there when it did. Thus, the Soweto rebellion and the subsequent turmoil received extensive media coverage. Overnight, Soweto became known to millions of Americans, who reacted with outrage and shock to the brutal means employed by the government to suppress the turmoil. No other event in South African history received so much coverage and, through the newspaper and magazine media, so vividly.

It was not long before the widespread turmoil in the wake of the Soweto rebellion touched off a reaction in the international financial community remarkably similar to that in the aftermath of Sharpeville. It triggered another massive hemorrhage of capital that placed enormous stress on the current and capital accounts. As the risk climate deteriorated, bankers became more apprehensive and the tendency for lending changed rather abruptly from long-term public bonds to shorter-term credits. This shift reflected banking concern over the country's growing political and economic uncertainties. In 1976 alone there was a 35 percent reduction in long-term capital inflows.[8]

In the decade after Soweto a growing outflow of capital forced the country to undertake greater short-term borrowing in order to keep the foreign exchange reserves at an acceptable level. Moreover, lending institutions, still nervous over the Soweto conflagration, were reluctant to lend long term, as I shall discuss further below. Economists would argue that the net outflow of funds on combined current and capital accounts was a reflection of poor export performance and of the unattractiveness of South Africa's economy to long-term foreign investors.[9] It required no special expertise to see that in every year but one, between 1976 and 1986, South Africa would record an accumulated current account deficit.

The Soweto incident, which took most South African organizations, including the African liberation movements, by surprise, led almost immediately to a sharp fall-off in private capital investment, which forced the government to impose an import surcharge in order to protect the balance of payments. In the longer term the rate of new equity investment fell and a growing proportion of new capital derived not from fresh infusions overseas but from reinvested, bottled-up earnings on U.S. and other foreign subsidiaries. Nonetheless, in the months after Soweto the government turned, as it had after Sharpeville, to American-controlled lending institutions. Engelhard had died a few years earlier and left no one to fill his shoes as a lifesaver for white South African capitalism. Nevertheless, the government found emergency support from the multinationals, the IMF alone providing $365 million in credits.[10]

Soweto reignited the public debate in the United States over the role and performance of American firms in South Africa. Fuel for the controversy came from the sudden expansion of the American media's presence in South Africa. The major dailies vastly expanded their coverage, and through the Associated Press and United Press International offices in Johannesburg, the flow of information increased considerably.

Congressmen had to respond to such a high visibility issue, and in September 1976 the House of Representatives' Africa subcommittee opened hearings on the question of U.S. lending to South Africa and the services rendered by the Export-Import Bank. The Congressional Black Caucus produced the "Afro-American Manifesto on Southern Africa," which attacked the Ford administration for its anti-Mozambique policy and called for the liberation of all southern Africa from white rule.

The American Committee on Africa, sensing growing domestic concern over apartheid, went beyond the call for comprehensive economic sanctions by formulating a strategy that focused on three key objectives: to seek shareholder divestment of stocks in firms doing any kind of business in South Africa, to force a disinvestment by companies with South African subsidiaries, and to outlaw the sale of gold Krugerrands. High-visibility American MNCs employing large numbers of blacks either in the United States or in South Africa would be targeted for special pressure. The grand plan was to force American enterprises to cease trading and to withdraw from South Africa altogether.

The Soweto rebellion led to a recrudescence of severe government repression and to a mass northward exodus of black youths to neighboring countries. Many found their way into military training camps of the African National Congress (ANC) in Zambia, Mozambique, and Tanzania, while others wound up in schools in East Germany.[11] Americans were concerned over the Soweto refugees, fearing they would become partisans of Marxist revolutionary movements. To counter the threat, the State Department crafted a policy with private foundations to co-opt this new generation of black militants by educating them in American institutions. Late in 1976 the African-American Institute (AAI) initiated, with State Department funding, the Southern African Training Program to provide postsecondary development-related training for student refugees.[12] And in September of 1977 the Agency for International Development (AID) helped the financially strapped Phelps-Stokes Fund to launch its own Southern African Refugee Scholarship Program, aimed at providing Namibian and South African students in political exile an opportunity to continue their education in an American setting.[13] But in the early years, relative calm returned to South Africa and the government and foundations gave little more than lip service to the program. Over the decade, only 263 South Africans and 118 Namibians received AAI support. Nevertheless, the AAI commissioned its Africa Policy Information Center to focus more sharply on the volatile southern African region, recognizing full well that it was a smoldering volcano. In May 1977 the Institute launched a monthly *South Africa/Namibia Update,* which objectively surveyed key current political and economic events. The newsletter's major purpose was to provide information to American businessmen, academics, and policymakers.

THE CARTER IMPERATIVE

In January 1977 Jimmy Carter took office as president, and relations with Southern Africa took a new tack in the face of changing political winds. From the start the Carter administration announced it would seek a fundamental shift in American policy towards South Africa, vowing to speak out against human and civil rights violations. On the other hand, Carter, like his predecessors, though more deliberately, attempted to use American MNCs as an instrument to force political change in the apartheid state. The White House reasoned that by putting on a human face, American corporations would set a high example that might be emulated by others.[14]

For the first time in history, American businesses in South Africa began to coalesce in response to the threat of black militancy as well as to the challenge of Carter's humanistic approach. The first American Chamber of Commerce on the African continent in half a century was established in Johannesburg in early 1977 by more than 130 multinational corporations.[15] Meanwhile in Philadelphia a set of six principles to guide American business performance in South Africa had been promulgated by a black Baptist minister, Reverend Leon Sullivan, who also gained a seat on General Motors' board of directors.

The Sullivan Code of Corporate Conduct, as it was called, was designed to encourage American corporations to promote racial equality in their employment practices. Over the years revisions and additions, or "amplifications," were made to the code, but its objective remained constant: to engage and reform, not withdraw. Sullivan's premise bore remarkable similarity to Carter's: namely, that American enterprise could be a force for structural reform in South Africa.

In the annals of American business history the document is quite remarkable. It called for desegregation of the workplace, equal employment practices for all races, and equal pay for equal work. It also demanded training programs for nonwhites as well as massive corporate spending on housing, education, and other social services. Through the accounting firm of Arthur D. Little each company was evaluated and rated annually.[16] The scorecard became a public record, available to stockholders as well as to the media.

From the start the Sullivan Code was greeted with mixed reviews. Many companies grudgingly subscribed to the code as a justification for continued operations in South Africa. A number of the larger, labor-intensive, and high-visibility MNCs with substantial fixed assets in South Africa signed it willingly. Others resented any intrusions into their corporate behavior and policies or argued that they could not afford to make the requisite reforms. Still others dissented. The anti-apartheid groups attacked the code vigorously, as did the NAACP and the AFL-

18. A U.S. labor organization demonstrates against South Africa, ca. 1985. (Photo credit, Africa News/Erin Sweeney)

CIO. These groups ultimately called for total corporate withdrawal, arguing that apartheid could not be reformed but had to be destroyed, along with the government that upheld it. American MNCs felt otherwise and began to lay the groundwork for the establishment of affirmative action programs.

President Carter, himself a former businessman, continued to maintain that U.S. trade and investment in South Africa, if guided by such high principles as the Sullivan Code, were beneficial and that a buoyant economy would keep all boats afloat. The administration therefore supported the code, but as Christopher Coker says, they refused to make it mandatory.[17] Andrew Young, the United States ambassador to the United Nations and a prominent black American, shared President Carter's conviction that enlightened capitalism could affect change. Hence, the new administration condemned apartheid in high moral tones, while encouraging big business to help bring about change in South Africa's domestic policies. The State Department and the American private sector were urged to work together to promote human rights in pursuit of majority rule. Nevertheless, while Washington spoke out against human and civil rights violations against Africans, similar infractions against the civil liberties of white South African apartheid opponents and the fact that white opponents of apartheid were also lingering in South African jails, went largely unnoticed.

Thus, the White House engaged in a more strident anti-apartheid rhetoric and in greater official distancing of the United States from Pretoria. It was the first time that an American president officially and openly attacked apartheid. But Carter's policies, like those of his predecessors, fluctuated between idealistic declarations and a dogged pursuit of national interest.[18] The White House was convinced of the strategic importance of the Cape route in the shipment of oil from the Middle East to the industrialized countries of the West. It also appreciated the enormous southern African reserves of minerals that were believed to be critical to U.S. defense industries. Yet the president was also realistic enough to grasp that time was running out on the white regime in Rhodesia and that a deal would have to be cut with the African majority. What kind of a deal and with whom were questions left unanswered. Ultimately, the United States' equivocation became Britain's opportunity. The path to a peaceful transfer of power was blazed by the British. The embargo of Rhodesian chrome was reimposed when in March

1977 Congress, on Carter's urging, repealed the controversial Byrd amendment. This time around no cries of displeasure were heard from Union Carbide and the other American mining companies because a new process had been discovered to smelt lower-grade and less expensive chrome ores, available outside the white redoubt.[19] By then Union Carbide was producing 20 percent of South Africa's chrome and could expand its operations there to compensate for losses from Rhodesia. For the Rhodesian diehards the United States' return to a sanctions policy meant serious losses in foreign exchange earnings. Revocation of the sanctions loophole was a contributing factor in the inability of the Smith regime to finance its civil war against the African forces of national liberation.[20] To the acute observer it seemed possible that the Rhodesian experience could be replayed in South Africa at some future date. The Rhodesian experience demonstrated that while in the short term sanctions can stimulate domestic economies and promote autarky, in the long run they contribute to economic disequilibrium and a lack of competitiveness in world markets.

South Africa's national elections in mid-1977 gave the ruling National party its largest parliamentary majority since coming to power in 1948. Pieter W. Botha became prime minister in 1978, after serving for twelve years as defense minister. In the latter capacity he had been the prime architect of the strategy of cross-border attacks into Angola. Now in power, Botha gave a greater role to the military, not only in matters of national defense and internal security but in administrative decision-making. Military spending had already begun its spectacular and seemingly uncontrollable ascent. In the decade from 1971 defense expenditures exploded by 860 percent, reflecting an escalation of the war in Namibia and Angola and heightened fears among whites in the wake of Portuguese decolonization and the Soweto rebellion.[21]

Botha immediately addressed himself to the problem of restoring a sense of security in the white community by intensifying the crackdown on black militants. The process was well underway even before he assumed office. Steve Biko, the eloquent and charismatic Black Consciousness leader was arrested and murdered by the police in September 1977. In the following month the new Internal Security Act banned all Black Consciousness organizations, including the Black Peoples Convention and the South African Students Organization (SASO). Their leaders were placed in detention or forced to flee into exile.[22] The campaign of raids, arrests, detentions, and bannings all but crushed black conscious-ness as a force of opposition. Biko's death by police torture and the public inquest into the circumstances behind it produced considerable evidence of police brutality. The entire Biko affair was transformed by the media into a cause célèbre, thanks in part to the keen investigative reporting of Donald Woods, a white South Africa newspaper editor. In his own country Biko, who was hitherto almost unknown to whites, became a martyr in the cause of black liberation. The American public's fresh awareness of the brutality of apartheid was clearly revealed in a Harris poll in December 1977, which found a majority of respondents opposing further business investment in South Africa.[23]

Holding to his policy of human rights, President Carter responded to the tragic events surrounding the Biko affair by banning "gray-area" sales to South Africa of any nonmilitary products that might have stra-tegic application during a period of national emergency. He also sup-ported the United Nations mandatory arms embargo, which prohibited exports of products with military applications.[24] The Interfaith Center on Corporate Responsibility (ICCR) reacted to the Biko incident by intensifying its strategy of shareholder resolutions. In June, even before Biko's death, the American Committee on Africa (ACOA) launched the Committee to Oppose Bank Loans to South Africa with wide church support. A major target was Citibank, which since 1972 had been the top U.S. lender to South Africa.

Anti-apartheid groups, including Protestant and Catholic organiza-tions, began to file shareholder resolutions in numerous banks. By then, U.S. banks held nearly 21 percent of all foreign loans to South Africa. Indeed, no fewer than forty-one American banks had extended credits to the Republic, with Citibank, Chase, Bank of America, Chemical, Manu-facturers Hanover, and Morgan Guaranty in the lead.[25]

It must be remembered that in the 1960s and 1970s American banks had undergone a process of globalization. Citicorp and Chase Manhat-tan, in particular, borrowed money from other banks and the money markets in order to lend it at higher rates to businesses and countries overseas. However, this innovative money-renting business began to decline in the late 1970s. Chase and Citicorp were never able to build a strong local deposit base. Neither had enough branches to conduct a viable banking business, and both failed to break through the oligopoly of the big local and British banks, especially Standard Chartered. In about 1976 Citibank terminated its retail banking business in the country and henceforth concentrated on serving its corporate clients.[26] Citibank was the only American bank that operated as a full-service entity rather than as a representative office.

Bowing to pressure from the anti-apartheid groups, Chase Manhattan terminated its lending to the South African government and its agencies. In March 1978 the Bank of Boston and Citibank followed Chase's lead, although Citibank continued to make trade-related loans. Still, by the year's end, most American banks had ceased to grant medium-term loans to any entity dealing directly with South Africa's government. Short-term loans, on the other hand, continued to grow in both value and volume.

American banks did not stop all loans to the public sector. In 1980 Citibank resumed loaning to government agencies, but it had modified its policies in response to anti-apartheid pressures by refusing to fund projects that had the potential for advancing the cause of apartheid. Consequently, its syndicated loans to the South African government that year were earmarked for public housing projects for black workers. In the same year three other U.S. banks lent the private Urban Foundation $33 million for similar low-income housing projects.[27] Founded in 1977 on the initiative of Harry Oppenheimer, chairman of Anglo-American, the Urban Foundation aimed at raising money from the private sector to initiate self-help projects in the African townships.

Activists were less successful in convincing the Carter administration to stop Exim Bank loan guarantees. Carter was generally opposed to disinvestment and comprehensive economic sanctions and clung to the premise of his Republican predecessors that engagement and involvement in South Africa would give the United States greater leverage to force change.[28] Congress, however, proved more malleable, and in October 1978, over White House opposition, it voted for a policy modification. Indeed, the Evans amendment (to the Exim Bank Act of 1945) forbade the use of Exim Bank facilities for any export that would contribute to the maintenance of apartheid or any export to the government of South Africa unless the president notified Congress that significant South African progress was being made in eliminating apartheid. In other words, no Exim facilities could be granted in sales to nongovernment entities unless they adhered to Sullivan Code principles.[29] So in short the Evans amendment restricted government-subsidized loans to

South Africa. The amendment was actually a compromise proposed by a conservative congressman to stave off tougher restrictions. Yet, in the wake of this legislation, the Exim Bank reduced its exposure from $265 million in 1976 to $132 million in 1980.[30]

THE NEW WAVE

In the months leading up to the congressional vote the American Committee on Africa helped to launch a new wave of divestment campaigns, beginning at the University of Massachusetts and Hampshire College in late 1977. A year later Oregon's became the first public university system to sell holdings in corporations doing business in South Africa. And at the national convention of the African Studies Association in November 1977 a group of academics organized themselves into the autonomous Association of Concerned Africa Scholars to promote studies on alternative government policies toward southern Africa and to lobby Congress for tougher sanctions.[31] In the same month the Boston-based Polaroid Corporation and Wang Laboratories announced they would leave South Africa. Polaroid pulled out completely, in protest over its distributors' dealings with the South African government. It was a truly historic move, for no other American business had publicly said it was leaving South Africa for moral reasons. Wang, on the other hand, may have been the first American MNC to experiment with a modified form of withdrawal—one that came to serve as a model for the disengagement process of the mid-1980s. Although Wang sold its South African subsidiary to a local firm, it retained a distribution agreement that enabled the selling of its computers to continue.[32] In 1979, for the first time in the history of American business in South Africa, there was a net divestiture. It amounted to only $164 million, but it was an ominous warning, little noticed at the time, of future trends.

The black American community was also reawakening after a long slumber to the plight of Africans under apartheid. Since the late 1960s militants in the United States had been preoccupied with their own black consciousness, or Black Power phenomenon. Within a decade the more violent elements had been suppressed by the federal government or had adopted less militant strategies. Now, a new generation of more middle-class black Americans was emerging and was prepared to work within the system to achieve change. Anti-apartheid protesters were quietly shaving their beards and removing their sandals. They were leaving the streets and moving into the boardrooms—to the very centers of American corporate power. Thus, the anti-apartheid movement was maturing and in the process becoming wiser and more sophisticated.

In 1977 TransAfrica, having grown out of a meeting of the Black Leadership Conference on Southern Africa that had met only months before,[33] was formally established in Washington, D.C., as a legislative lobby in favor of a broad range of issues affecting blacks in the United States, the Caribbean, and Africa. It became the first black American policy lobby. Perhaps no other black American did more to bring the issues of apartheid into sharper focus for Americans than the Reverend Jesse Jackson. In August 1979 the flamboyant and eloquent pastor undertook a well-publicized two-week visit to South Africa. Not long after returning, his PUSH organization helped to organize the American Coordinating Committee for Equality in Sport and Society to fight South African sports in the United States.[34] Jackson also called for civil disobedience in South Africa and for withdrawal of U.S. investments as a means of coercing the Botha regime into changing its policies. TransAfrica picked up the thread of Jackson's approach and in early 1980 came out with a statement of policy calling for a wide array of actions against South Africa, including a ban on new investment, a comprehensive trade embargo, a mandatory phased corporate withdrawal, and a termination of air travel between the two countries.[35] Jackson and Carter shared the popular American conviction that the United States had the power to force the Botha government's hand. They differed primarily in their approach.

The tragic events surrounding Soweto also induced the major American philanthropies into a fundamental reassessment of their philanthropic activities. Deep concern was now voiced over the erosion of the rule of law and the devastating invasions of civil liberties. The foundations remained committed to funding organizations that encouraged interracial communication, as evidenced by support given by Phelps-Stokes, Ford, and Carnegie for the Centre for Intergroup Studies, which had been established by an Afrikaner liberal scholar in 1968 as an autonomous research institute on the campus of the University of Cape Town[36] and which sponsored training programs in conflict resolution. Nevertheless, from 1979 Carnegie and the Ford Foundation began to shift the thrust of their concerns to the support of organizations fighting apartheid, particularly to those offering legal counsel to victims of apartheid laws. A number of legal centers were funded, notably the Centre for Applied Legal Studies, which was a University of Witwatersrand-based independent organization seeking to promote legal reform in the area of African civil rights. The center also produced information on the legal rights of black workers and trade unionists and defended Africans in apartheid-related court cases.[37] Through the Washington-based Lawyers' Committee on Civil Rights Under Law, Ford also made grants to assist lawyers' defense work in political trials. Later, the Lawyers' Committee sponsored studies on the feasibility of economic sanctions. In the early 1980s Rockefeller Brothers Fund first became involved in South Africa, when it joined Ford and Carnegie in support of the Legal Resources Centre in Johannesburg, a public interest law firm that advised and defended black workers and trade unionists accused of violating apartheid laws.[38]

A HESITANT RECOVERY

The South African economy had weakened considerably in the months following Soweto, especially its external payments position. The government took forceful measures to deal with the crisis in August 1976, when it introduced an import deposit scheme to reduce its overseas purchases. This was replaced in May 1977 by a surcharge on a broader range of imports. Domestically, the real GNP growth rate for 1977 dropped to zero as gold prices remained in the doldrums and hovered at $130 per ounce.[39]

The "Soweto recession" ended in December 1977, almost as abruptly as it had begun, and the country experienced a mild recovery until September 1981. The sudden turnaround may have been triggered by a dramatic improvement in gold prices. In 1978 gold soared to $193 per ounce, and the economic growth rate registered 3.2 percent for the year, far beyond anyone's expectations.[40] In 1978, as a hedge against raging inflation at home, American citizens doubled their purchases of gold by buying Krugerrands and making portfolio investments in the extractive industries. American shareholdings in the mining houses were estimated at $2.3 billion, or approximately a quarter of total mining shares. American direct investment had climbed to $2 billion, and approximately 5 percent of all capital stock in South Africa's manufacturing industry was in American hands. Altogether, by the end of 1978 foreign investments equalled nearly 20 percent of the total value of all private investment in the Republic.[41]

Nevertheless, American firms with fixed assets in South Africa had begun to feel uneasy about the long-term prospects in the wake of Soweto. Late in the 1970s some of them had begun to reduce their exposure. In November 1977 Polaroid became the first company with a subsidiary to disengage completely. In March of the following year, General Electric sold off its consumer goods business. Then, in September of 1979 General Tire relinquished its 27 percent stake in its South African subsidiary. At the time, tire companies in the United States had begun to suffer from bulging inventories and were losing money at a dangerous rate. General's first reaction was to scale back its overseas operations.

American MNCs were also becoming concerned over the escalation in labor turmoil and the pressures from African employees for higher wages. In 1979 the government, responding to the recommendations of its Wiehahn Commission, legalized black labor organizations and made them register in an effort to bring them under closer supervision.[42] The Wiehahn reform was followed by rapid growth among African unions. In April the nonracial Federation of South African Trade Unions (FOSATU) was formed and within months drew tens of thousands of workers under its umbrella. In 1979 Ford Motor Company became the first U.S. MNC in South Africa to recognize a black union. Kellogg followed only months later. The Wiehahn reform triggered rising expectations among African workers. It also increased labors' concern with political issues and its willingness to confront management. This became visibly apparent in November 1979, when a wave of strikes spread to Ford, General Motors, and Goodyear Tire. Never before had American multinationals in South Africa come under such a withering and sustained attack by organized African labor and at a time when they had begun to make substantial reforms at the workplace. It soon became frustratingly evident that the companies most vulnerable to attack were those that were seemingly moving into a reformist mode. None of the firms had developed a strategy to deal with what appeared to be a catch-22 phenomenon.

Pretoria was determined to push on with its grand apartheid policies while ensuring security at home and along its frontiers. The government pursued more vigorously its policy of granting independence to the homelands in an effort to appear to be amenable to African nationalism as well as to reverse the African drift towards the established urban centers. In 1976 the Transkei was granted nominal independence, followed a year later by Bophuthatswana. Then came Venda in 1979 and the Ciskei two years afterward. The Botha government needed enormous amounts of capital to expand the military and to develop industries and infrastructure along the borders of the homelands. Money was also required to assist the homelands in their own development. The United States, bowing to pressures from the Organization of African Unity, refused to recognize the independence of the homelands and urged American MNCs not to invest in them.

In January 1979 the financial wizards of Pretoria instituted an ingenious monetary reform to stimulate direct foreign investment and to slow the outflow of capital. This was undertaken through the establishment of the "financial rand," which could be used by companies setting up their own subsidiaries in the country. The rand was transformed into a more flexible currency after being freed from the U.S. dollar and placed under a managed float.

From an investment standpoint the reform bore fruit. Capital flowed in from Europe, Asia, and the United States in almost record volume. The balance of payments situation also dramatically improved. In 1979 gold exports rose in value by 60 percent, and the value of merchandise exports also accelerated by a third over a twelve-month period. The year registered a record surplus on the current account of $43.7 billion, more than double that of the preceding year.[43]

The economic recovery accelerated in 1980. The GDP growth rate jumped from 5.5 percent in 1979 to a breathtaking 8 percent in 1980, possibly the highest growth rate of any country on earth.[44] Uncertainty in the world over oil, especially after the fall of the shah of Iran in early 1979, and global inflation made gold more attractive to investors everywhere. Its price reached a historic high of $850 per ounce in January 1980 before levelling off to a still strong $525 per ounce in March.[45] Merchandise exports (excluding gold) rose by another 20 percent while the value of gold output increased by an unprecedented 80 percent. South Africa's reserve position improved dramatically, enough for the post-Soweto import surcharge to be removed. The effects of the gold boom were spectacular, and the huge windfall profits of the gold-mining industry provided the state with a desperately needed infusion of revenue.

But there was another side of that glittering gold coin. The shah of Iran had supplied South Africa with most of its oil and at favorable prices. With the shah gone, much of the country's oil had to be purchased on the spot markets, at exorbitantly high prices. Suddenly, South Africa's fears of an international oil boycott were revived. Consequently, the government decided to launch a huge expansion of its SASOL II coal conversion plant, at a cost of $6.9 billion.[46] It also vastly increased its expenditures on nuclear power development. In both endeavors American entrepreneurs played a critical role.

Despite those concerns, an air of confidence, however false and fleeting, returned to South Africa, and suddenly corporate talk about disinvestment was placed on the back burner. American trade and investment boomed. Between 1980 and 1981 the book value of American companies operating in South Africa rose from $2.4 billion to $2.6 billion, an all-time high. U.S. direct investment was providing more than 17 percent of total foreign investment in the country.[47] Nevertheless, from 1979 the U.S. share in new investment fell as other nations, particularly West Germany and Switzerland, advanced their economic stake. The Japanese presence also grew dramatically, though not in the form of direct investments since Japanese law allowed only the expansion of trade.

South Africa's exports to the United States rose steadily, from $1.3 billion in 1977 to $2.3 billion in 1978. U.S. exports to South Africa jumped 30 percent in 1979 alone, to $1.4 billion.[48] In 1980 the United States became South Africa's largest trading partner for the first time in history and soon furnished more than 15 percent of the country's total imports and took nearly 18 percent of its merchandise exports. More than six thousand American companies were doing business in South Africa, most of them through sales agents and distributors.

In 1979–1980 increasing amounts of capital were spent on modernization and expansion of the extractive industries, especially gold, uranium, and coal. Large volumes of U.S. mining equipment were exported, particularly by Ingersoll-Rand, Dresser Industries, and Joy Manufacturing. This activity came at a time of deepening American concern over strategic mineral sourcing. It must be recalled that since 1947 the United States had maintained a strategic stockpile of minerals deemed vital to support defense, industrial, and civilian requirements. But over the years the stockpile had been neglected and much of it had been sold off or reduced. In 1976, after a hiatus of nearly two decades, President Gerald Ford began to rebuild inventories. Carter continued the practice. A report in 1978 concluded that the United States was strategically more vulnerable to a long-term chromium embargo than to an embargo of any other natural resource, including petroleum.[49] New concerns over mineral dependence led to the Strategic and Critical Materials Stockpiling Act of 1979, which required the United States to establish an expanded national stockpile capable of sustaining the country for up to three years in the event of a national emergency.

In 1980 South Africa took advantage of this anxiety by allowing mineral rights to be purchased through the financial rand. In the same year Congressman Ray Santini (D-Nevada) returned from a fact-finding tour of the Republic and issued a report that emphasized the importance of southern Africa's minerals for the West. The Santini report warned that U.S. dependence on foreign sources was in excess of 50 percent for twenty-four of thirty-two minerals considered essential for national survival. The report noted that South Africa was already supplying 38 percent of U.S. imports of chromite, half of its platinum and palladium, more than 80 percent of its vanadium, three quarters of its ferro-chrome, 45 percent of its ferromanganese, 67 percent of its gold imports, and well over half of its industrial diamonds.[50] Santini, from a state that depended heavily on local mineral output for its own employment and revenue, was arguing not for increased imports from southern Africa but for greater support for domestic mineral extraction to reduce American dependence on foreign sources. However, from Washington's view his report clearly demonstrated the critical importance of South Africa to the United States' industrial strength and national defense. Consequently, in 1980 Congress passed the National Materials and Minerals Policy, Research, and Development Act, which called for the formulation of a national minerals policy. The United States was thus poised for a mineral reengagement with the apartheid republic.

REAGAN AND THE ERA OF REENGAGEMENT

Ronald Reagan came to power in January 1981, determined to improve relations between South Africa and the United States. In a March CBS television interview, he asked rhetorically if America could "abandon a country that has stood by us in every war we have ever fought, a country that is strategically essential to the free world in its production of minerals that we all must have?"[51] The same month witnessed the first large-scale South African invasion of Angola since the 1978 offensive. Then in May President Reagan announced that he would pursue a new policy of "constructive engagement" with South Africa crafted by his new assistant secretary of state for African affairs, Chester Crocker. Constructive engagement was based on the old premise that the United States had the power to influence the course of events in southern Africa. Crocker anticipated that quiet diplomacy, coupled with economic assistance, would help to bring about peaceful change. His policy was intended to reduce Afrikanerdom's siege mentality, raise its sense of security, and thus facilitate internal reform.[52] But there was a fixed point in American policy, one that had remained constant for more than a quarter century: If there would be any change in South Africa, it must be achieved through nonviolent and nonrevolutionary means.

In the pursuit of this new form of constructive engagement the White House toned down public criticism of apartheid while quietly increasing private dialogue with the Botha administration—to encourage peaceful change through "communication and confidence-building." The first visible expression of the Reagan policy was made in the same month when the United States ambassador to the United Nations cast a veto in the Security Council to defeat four resolutions that called for oil and arms embargoes against the apartheid regime. This was the first open break between the new administration and black Africa on a major African issue. However, not more than two months before the launch of constructive engagement, covert meetings had occurred for the first time since 1963 between senior American and South African military personnel. In June the news leaked out and the Organisation of African Unity unanimously adopted a resolution condemning the United States for its "collusion" with South Africa.

A shift in the mood of Congress appeared to be taking place when in

September the Senate voted to repeal the Clark amendment and thus to allow a resumption of support to the Union for the Total Independence of Angola (UNITA) rebels attempting to overthrow the Marxist regime in Angola. The Reagan administration then went on to suggest, much to Pretoria's delight, that a South African withdrawal from Namibia be linked to a withdrawal of some 35,000 Cuban troops from Angola. The administration had certainly built up Afrikaner confidence, to the extent that in November 1981 an emboldened South Africa staged its deepest invasion into Angola.

Then, on March 1, 1982, in a sharp reversal of Carter's policy, the Reagan administration announced the relaxation of trade restrictions imposed in 1977 in the wake of Biko's death. Most significant was the easing of export controls over sales of nonmilitary goods to the South African military and police. From 1983 through 1985, the U.S. State Department licensed the export to South Africa of more than $18 million worth of goods included on its official munitions list of weapons and weapons-related technology. American stockholders in the defense industries remained unpersuaded by arguments against arms sales. Indeed, a proposal in 1983 not to sell Xerox equipment to the South African Defence Force won votes representing less than seven per cent of the company's stock. By this time, South Africa had expanded its military trade with other countries, particularly Israel, one of the United States' most important clients and itself a major recipient of U.S. military weapons and technology. It should be recalled that the U.S. arms embargo of the 1960s helped to propel South Africa into a closer relationship with suppliers from the Middle East and shaped its decision to develop its own arms industry.

This trade relaxation was part of a major administration thrust to increase trade internationally. One of the keystones, the Export Trading Companies Act, sailed through Congress in 1982 under the expectation that it would increase the ailing export trade by inducing small- and medium-size enterprises to export more. It was the first legislation in over a decade to aid American exporters in penetrating and expanding their markets in Africa.

The Commerce Department opened a trade promotion office in Johannesburg; within a year it had greatly increased the the volume of export licenses to the South African trade. Dual-purpose equipment, such as computers and aircraft, was again permitted for export. Not surprisingly, this resulted in a huge jump in exports of computers and data encryption devices used in automatic teller machines.

COPING WITH A MINI-RECESSION

The South African economy had already begun to show ominous signs of losing steam again. Late in 1981 gold prices retreated, and the country began to feel the impact of world recession. The annual GDP growth rate fell by half, to 4 percent, reflecting a decline in foreign demand.[53] Disturbingly, the volume of imports was rising uncontrollably, a partial reflection of America's aggressive export stimulation programs. The balance of trade swung from a $7 billion surplus in 1980 to a deficit of almost half a billion in 1981, while the current account fell into a deficit of almost $4.5 billion.[54]

Hard times seemed to be returning, and some American MNCs started to take another long hard look at the relative advantages of operating in South Africa. Again, some firms decided to jettison portions of their operations. The American Express Company sold most of its equity to Anglo-American's Freight Services and ailing Firestone unloaded its majority holdings in several of its local subsidiaries as part of a global sell-out of its less profitable plants. Between 1980 and the close of 1984 forty-one American companies sold a portion of their equity in their South African operations or withdrew completely.

Investor confidence was shaken with the publication of the Rockefeller Foundation–funded study *South Africa: Time Running Out* in June 1981. The conservative and prestigious Rockefeller Foundation was a relative newcomer to South Africa, having entered the arena four years earlier with funds to launch the massive study. In its subsequent findings the Rockefeller commission ruled out a strategy of comprehensive trade sanctions, but recommended a moratorium on business expansion and new investment. The commission echoed fears of the former Carter administration that sanctions could fortify right-wing elements and also invite trade retaliation. On the positive side the study pointed to the emergence of new black leaders in South Africa and to the urgent need for Americans to open an era of engagement with them, calling upon foundations, government, and the private sector to support black leadership development.[55]

As the South African economy weakened, its need grew for more foreign capital to sustain its ambitious development projects. In February 1982 the Reagan administration urged a $1.1 billion IMF loan. It was the biggest international loan in South Africa's history and the largest one ever awarded from the IMF's Compensatory Financing Facility. The request, and approval, touched off an outcry in the anti-apartheid movement, and in late 1983 public pressure forced the United States to place strict guidelines on future South African draws. Indeed, Congress passed a Replenishment Act in 1983, which directed the U.S. representative to the IMF to vote against all future loans to the regime.

The year 1981 had been a fairly good one for South Africa until the final quarter. And even in 1982 American private direct investment climbed to $2.8 billion, its highest peak ever. By the end of 1983 the United States was responsible for just under 20 percent of total foreign direct investment in South Africa, trailing both West Germany and Great Britain.[56] The rates of return in mining and manufacturing, at an astonishing 25 percent and 18 percent, respectively could not be matched anywhere in the world. Yet much of the increase in American investment continued to be attributed to higher levels of retained earnings by well-established subsidiaries. Some cash-rich American firms, particularly John Deere, had made earlier commitments to open new manufacturing facilities. But in almost all cases they were financed out of locally accumulated capital. Admittedly, a few new enterprises appeared on the scene, notably American fast-food chains. Pizza Hut, Kentucky Fried Chicken, and the Carvel Corporation of New York, an ice cream retailer, opened franchises in 1982. Kentucky Fried Chicken was an instant success, and within a few years it could boast of over 180 outlets, mostly African-controlled franchises, selling chicken under their trade name. In most cases franchisers financed their fast-food enterprises with local capital.

The strong American presence in South Africa was revealed in the expanding volume of air traffic. South African Airways acquired several Boeing 747 SPs in 1976, and flying time between Johannesburg and New York was reduced to less than fourteen hours. In 1982 the carrier began weekly flights to Houston, Texas.[57] But the planes were not loaded with exports from South African farms, mines, and factories. Instead, they carried skilled professionals, mainly English-speaking whites, in search of a new home for themselves and their capital. The white brain drain to America had indeed begun in earnest.

Surely, all was not well with the South African economy. The poor performance of the current account between 1981 and 1984 resulted in a sharp increase in foreign debt, both in absolute and relative terms to the GDP. With mining output stagnating again and manufacturing growth slowing, South Africa became increasingly concerned with its accumulating current account deficit, which had mushroomed since 1976. The rise in short-term liabilities was especially acute. Foreign debt rose from $17 billion to $23 billion in the 1981–1984 period.[58] And as the rand depreciated from 1981, imports of machinery and other essential items rose sharply. The balance of payments pendulated from a surplus of nearly $3 billion to a deficit of $3.7 billion. By late August 1982 the country's foreign exchange reserves were barely enough to cover a single week's imports. With imports growing strongly, the demand for trade financing surged and South Africa turned to more offshore financing. Many banks were willing to oblige. However, South Africa had to make painful adjustments in its budget. Real capital spending between 1979 and 1984 fell by more than 12 percent, while in the same period current expenditures rose, largely because of soaring military expenditures and ballooning debt service.[59] A decline in personal net savings in the same time frame only increased the country's reliance on foreign capital.

Steps had to be taken to control inflation and to end the deterioration in South Africa's export situation, which probably reflected slackening demand in the recession-ravaged West. South Africa took the gamble of lifting controls on a wide range of products to force local industry to become more competitive. In February 1983 the financial rand was abolished, and the country returned to a unitary exchange rate system. The rand could now change to an undervalued position, thus making South African exports more competitive in world markets. On the other hand, the reform also lifted exchange controls over nonresidents and triggered an even greater capital outflow as Americans and others divested by selling their gold shares and equity in their subsidiaries to South African residents. The latter found themselves in a favorable position to buy the investments off-loaded by the foreigners because exchange controls prevented them from legally investing their capital overseas.

To protect foreign exchange reserves, the Reserve Bank urged local private banks to increase their overseas borrowings. In 1983 Nedbank opened a full branch in New York City, and later that year its branch arranged a $200 million loan facility for the South African Treasury.[60] In the same year, for the first time in recent history, the government began to finance a portion of its recurrent expenditures by borrowing. With less private investment as a source of finance, the regime took advantage of the cheap money that American banks at the time were so eager to lend. Faced with a crippling drought, the country was forced to spend precious foreign exchange on purchases of corn from the United States and Zimbabwe.

TAKING ADVANTAGE OF A BRIEF RESPITE

South Africa won a brief respite in a boomlet that ran from mid-1983 to mid-1984, as the United States and other Western countries were pulling out of their recessions and world trade rebounded moderately. South African export volume exploded with volcanic force. Krugerrand sales in 1984 skyrocketed and became South Africa's largest single export to the United States, accounting for about a quarter of the total value of its trade with the Americans. Gold in general comprised nearly half of the country's export earnings, and in terms of capital inflows, a healthy proportion came from Americans investing in gold and precious-metals funds. Nonetheless, this sudden flush masked the uncomfortable reality that since 1979 the percentage of gold shares owned by Americans had actually fallen.

Trade may have turned up, but the investment picture became gloomier. Overall, gross domestic fixed investment fell by 8 percent in 1983, reaching its lowest point in four years.[61] Virtually no new American enterprises were established in South Africa during the period. Indeed, some MNCs took advantage of the currency reform and miniboom to resume selling off their equity participation in local firms. Chrysler sold its 25 percent stake in Sigma Motor Corporation to Anglo-American, which already held three quarters of its shares. Others, notably Motorola, which had been battered in the United States by Japanese competition, sold off some of their weaker divisions. Withdrawals during 1983 included the largest disinvestments ever occurring in South Africa. Associated British Foods sold its 52 percent of the local Premier Food Group for nearly $130 million, and the Hong Kong trading house Jardine Matheson disposed of its majority interest in a South African transport and hotel conglomerate for about $188 million. Portfolio investments also declined as foreign investors unloaded large parcels of gold and other mining stocks.

South Africa's monetary reform of February 1983, which opened the door for disinvestment, added new fuel to anti-apartheid lobbies in the United States. Already in 1980 there were forty-five shareholder resolutions proposed to thirty-seven corporations. Many resolutions to banks and companies urged an end to the marketing of Krugerrands. Protesters escalated their demands for disinvestment, or the sale by American companies of subsidiaries doing business in South Africa, and called upon colleges and other nonprofit institutions and foundations to divest themselves of stock in companies doing business in South Africa. At the same time, pressure increased on states to pass laws to curtail investments, and to withdraw public funds from companies whose investments in South Africa appeared to help apartheid. Big breakthroughs had already been achieved in 1982 when the Michigan legislature instructed its university system to purge its investment portfolios of companies operating in the Republic. In that year, Massachusetts, Michigan, Connecticut, and the city of Philadelphia all passed legislation barring public pension fund investment in firms doing business in South Africa.

American foundations meanwhile had begun to increase their support for scholarships. In 1981 the Phelps-Stokes Fund beefed up its newly organized Southern African Refugee Scholarship Program as well as its Southern African Manpower Development Assistance Project, the latter being a training and technical support program administered in cooperation with the U.S. Agency for International Development. The Phelps-Stokes effort complemented the 'Southern African Training Program', which was set up by the African-American Institute in 1976 to provide postsecondary development-related training for refugees.

The Carnegie Corporation also took a renewed interest in South Africa, and in April 1982 it initiated the massive "Second Inquiry Into Poverty and Development in South Africa". Unlike its report on poor whites, undertaken more than half a century earlier, this project focused on the blacks. For direction of the vast undertaking, Carnegie turned to Francis Wilson, a prominent white South African sociologist based at the University of Cape Town. The research phase culminated exactly two years later in a huge conference at the University of Cape Town, where more than three hundred papers were presented, surveying the causes, nature, and content of black poverty in South Africa. The Cape Town Carnegie Conference was unprecedented in its scope and in the breadth of its contributors, consisting of South Africans of different racial, ethnic, and ideological backgrounds as well as Americans. A smaller, follow-up conference summarizing the meeting's findings was held in New York months later.

Carnegie was not alone in launching bold new initiatives. Between 1980 and 1986 the number of American foundations making grants in South Africa began to grow rapidly. By far the most significant new player was the W. K. Kellogg Foundation, one of America's largest philanthropies, which made its first South African grant in 1986. Within two years it had made commitments of approximately $12 million in the southern African region, mainly in the form of scholarships to train black youths to take future leadership positions in a post-apartheid South Africa.[62]

A RETURN TO TURMOIL

In August 1984 the South African government, deeply concerned over the mounting current account deficits as well as the escalating rates of interest and inflation, abruptly returned to tighter fiscal and monetary policies. The rand was again devalued, and restrictions were placed on imports, which led to a rapid improvement in the current account. But the depreciated rand only drove up the cost of essential imports and pushed up the rand value of overseas loans and credits. It also raised the interest payments in rands on overseas debt. It may be argued that through its August 1984 measures the government was attempting to force down inflation by deliberately imposing a recession on the domestic economy. To compound the misery the government also announced a substantial increase in the general sales tax. Thus, from August 1984 consumer demand plunged, and the economy was jolted into a new period of stagflation. Industrial output fell, building activity slowed, and unemployment soared. South Africa's black population was exploding at 2.6 percent a year, and African unemployment was surpassing 25 percent. African labor unions had become larger, better organized, and more sophisticated. The National Union of Mineworkers, founded only two years earlier, already boasted of a membership exceeding two hundred thousand.[63] A record number of strikes rocked the country in 1984 as South Africa experienced its worst industrial turmoil in decades.

Not suprisingly, a new spasm of violence began in several black townships in September 1984. Tension had been building for weeks with school stayaways and election boycotts against the impending new parliamentary structure. The September outbreak coincided with the inauguration of the new constitution. The immediate cause of the riots, which left twenty-nine dead and more than three hundred injured, was a rise in rents and electric rates in public housing.[64] But blacks were also angry over the new constitution, which created a segregated tricameral parliament of whites, Indians, and Coloreds and totally excluded Africans. Moreover, they resented the new municipal councils, which were packed by officials whom they regarded as incompetents and government collaborators.

New groups had begun to form a year earlier to fight the constitutional proposals, which the white electorate subsequently approved in a November 1983 referendum. Then, in late September 1983, they coalesced into a new organization, the United Democratic Front (UDF), and launched a campaign to keep voters away from the polls for the election of Coloreds and Indians. The UDF was an umbrella organization representing a broad geographical, ethnic, and demographic base and bringing together radicals as well as moderates, whites as well as blacks. Nevertheless, its cutting edge was the black youth movements, which accounted for almost half of the UDF's affiliated membership at the time of its national launch.

As 1983 unfolded, the cruel fact of persistent high youth unemployment in the urban areas became more glaringly apparent. Large numbers of the highly politicized veterans of the Soweto rebellion of 1976 remained in the festering black townships, grouped loosely around the Congress of South African Students, the nation's largest and best-organized youth movement. Early in November 1984 black trade unions joined the UDF in a mass strike. The magnitude of the demonstrations was a clear indication that South Africa had entered a new era of protest, with students and workers united under a single UDF banner. The overall effect of the mass strikes of late 1984 and 1985 was to move the African National Congress (ANC) back into the mainstream of politics via the UDF and to trigger an intensification of the worldwide debate on sanctions and disinvestment.

This most massive display of African protest in South African history and the most protracted unrest since the Second Boer War hit the industrial heartland with explosive force. The incidence of sabotage and politically motivated violence dramatically escalated. The upheaval was characterized by unparalleled unity in the resistance movement. In 1984 South Africa found it had experienced a record number of strikes, longer, deeper, more massive, and better organized than ever before. In the face of what seemed like a national uprising the government panicked and for the first time ever decided to deploy the army to control the black townships. By December 1984 thousands of civil rights activists and trade unionists found themselves banned or in preventive detention.

The specter of mass violence made Americans extremely apprehensive, affecting banks and investors as well as individuals and institutions. A substantial erosion of foreign and domestic confidence within the business community began to occur. As early as September 1984 American banks began cutting back on loans, reducing their exposure in South Africa by selling their loans to institutions that were not fully aware of the situation in South Africa—in other words to smaller U.S. banks and Japanese institutions. The practice was not altogether unprecedented. Since the early 1980s banks in the United States had developed a market among themselves in trading and selling loans. Indeed, loan participations were bought and sold much like bonds or foreign exchange. Generally, there was a contraction in new American overseas lending in 1983 for the first time in two decades, and it continued well into 1985. Between September 1984 and March 1985 overall lending by U.S. banks to South Africa dropped a disturbing 16 percent to $4.2 billion.[65]

In 1985 there was continuing weakness in the economy and endemic political turmoil. Fixed capital formation continued to decline, and the rand depreciated by 38 percent against the dollar. As the rand fell, imports from the United States and elsewhere became more dear. The 325 or so American subsidiaries found they had to pay more for imports of essential components. Thus, the cost of materials rose at the same time that black labor militancy, consumer boycotts, and escalating wage and benefits demands began to cut deeply into corporate profits. Labor-management tensions began to build anew, especially conflicts between the auto makers and the National Automobile and Allied Workers Union (NAAWU). Some companies were forced into liquidation; others agreed to merge with more viable enterprises. The auto industry was especially hard hit. Output had fallen steadily since 1984, and in February 1985, Ford, South Africa's second largest American carmaker, reduced its stake to 42 percent by selling over half of its interest to the locally owned South Africa Motor Corporation (SAMCOR). SAMCOR was put together out of the motor interests of the South African subsidiary of Ford of Canada and Anglo-American's AMCAR. In the merger Ford relinquished its management responsibilities. The strong U.S. dollar gave Japan an artificial cost advantage, and Japanese entrepreneurs began to eat into the American share of the market. Caterpillar, for example, had to face increasing competition from Komatsu, which produced similar machinery at lower cost to the consumer.[66]

As acquisitions and merger-mania spread across South Africa, the economic health of the nation fell into the hands of progressively fewer state and privately owned corporations. South Africa was becoming riddled with cartels and monopolies. Already by 1983, 80 percent of the value of shares listed on the Johannesburg Stock Exchange (JSE) were held by only seven companies, three of them insurance groups. This trend was greatly accelerated from 1985 by the mergers and takeovers that resulted from the new wave of disinvestment. With so much pent-up capital in the country, South African entrepreneurs were only too happy to buy up foreign subsidiaries. Typically, U.S. MNCs sold their subsidiaries to their local management or to a holding company usually established by a consortium of South African banks or to such cash-rich corporate conglomerates as the life insurance companies. In other cases the American firms sold their subsidiary to a South African trust of its own design, often comprising its rank-and-file employees and/or its management. The MNC thus sold the trust, often financed the sales, and held the debt. Over time the trust was expected to pay back the loan. Usually, in the process of transfer the MNC ensured that its products would continue to be sold by the former subsidiary. Some firms retained buy-back options that allowed them to return at a future date.

The Botha regime found it extremely difficult to contain the mounting turmoil that had become so endemic. Many in government blamed the problems on hyperinflation. Thus, early in 1985 Botha tried unsuccessfully to reduce inflation by raising interest rates to record levels. This effort failed, however, because of government overspending and the precipitous freefall of the rand. The economy continued its decline, and social turmoil rose as the twenty-fifth anniversary of the Sharpeville massacre approached. Civil government had practically collapsed in the black urban areas. In the eastern Cape shops were shuttered by widespread consumer boycotts. On March 21 in Langa, a black township in the Eastern Cape, the South African Police massacred twenty Africans en route to a funeral. The Langa incident provided a new focus for American outrage and hastened the gathering momentum for economic sanctions. In frustration over the inability to contain the turbulence and to show toughness to an increasingly polarized and restive white electorate, Botha declared on July 21, 1985, another national state of emergency in most of the Republic's industrial areas. Sweeping police and military powers were imposed in the black suburbs of Johannesburg and near the industrial centers of the eastern Cape province. The American business community was shocked and viewed Botha's draconian measures as the actions of a weak, uncertain, and desperate man. Many Americans had anticipated that Botha would respond to the crisis with a statement of broad reform. Instead, they were jolted by the beleaguered president's tough reaffirmation of law and order through an intensification of repression. Botha's Durban speech was a great turning point in that it deprived the American business community of its argument that the private sector had the leverage to force the regime into a reformist posture. Thus, in a very real sense Botha had unwittingly pulled the rug out from under the American business community and left it dangerously vulnerable to frontal attack from the anti-apartheid forces that were rapidly regaining momentum back home in the United States.

THE LIQUIDITY CRISIS: PULLING THE PLUG

Botha's emergency decree seemed to kill any chance of political negotiations. And it entailed the most far-reaching restrictions in South African history. In the first eleven days of the emergency gold stocks plunged by 20 percent in value. There was rapid selling on the JSE, and capital outflows accelerated. Krugerrand sales in the United States had already begun to plummet in April to 54,000 ounces, down from 255,000 only a year earlier.[67] The business community viewed the Botha regime as not moving to end white supremacy but rather as initiating reforms to preserve it. Then, at the August National Party Congress in Durban, the president failed to announce a widely expected new reform program. Americans were stunned and impatiently asked: What had become of Washington's much-touted leverage? Constructive Engagement, it seemed, had failed to push the regime into a reformist mode.

The crisis of July 1985 greatly aggravated the debt situation, which had become critical by June, when the debt-service ratio hit 62 percent.[68] New long-term capital had virtually ceased to flow into the country, and the total amount of short-term foreign debt was in excess of foreign reserves. Public corporations found they were no longer able to borrow abroad to fund their ongoing capital expansion projects. South African businessmen had to face the distressing fact that between 1980 and 1985 the country's foreign debt had mushroomed a staggering 293 percent in rand terms. Moreover, the capital flow of American MNCs in investments and loans to subsidiaries fell from a $71 million positive flow to South Africa in 1982 to a net outflow of $17 million in 1985. Already in March 1985 a U.S. bank startled American creditors with a report that South Africa's external finances were in chaos.[69]

The crisis came to a head in late August 1985, when key foreign banks, on the initiative of New York's Chase Manhattan Bank, refused to roll over their credit lines to South African banks. That forced the finance minister to close both the foreign-exchange market and the Johannesburg Stock Exchange on September 1 and to place a four-month freeze on repayment of $14 billion in foreign loans. The government also reintroduced the financial rand and reimposed exchange controls over nonresidents. The measures were ostensibly taken to protect the rand exchange rate against further outflows of funds from the capital account of the balance of payments. The finance minister was deeply uncomfortable over the prospect that $14 billion of the $24 billion of the country's foreign debt would fall due within the year. This liquidity crisis was thus triggered by the foreign banks' withdrawal of short-term credit lines more than by the disinvestment by nonresidents.

The reinstatement of the financial rand was also intended to discourage disinvestment. Under the two-tier currency system MNCs could only exchange their proceeds from the sale of their subsidiaries in financial rands, which were worth less than the commercial rand. It was expected that the financial rand would trade at a discount to the commercial rand and thus slow the rate of disinvestment. This, of course, did not happen. The rate of disinvestment accelerated. Moreover, the two-tier system constituted a disincentive to new direct investment as well as discouraging equity and indirect investment. It did, however, penalize disinvestment because sellers had to take their proceeds in the cheaper financial rand. Many avoided this problem by structuring deals around repayment of internal corporate debt rather than outright cash payment. Some also disinvested by remitting overseas the maximum dividend possible to their American shareholders. Others illegally transferred funds by over-invoicing imports and underinvoicing exports.[70]

BREATHING NEW LIFE INTO THE ANTI-APARTHEID MOVEMENT

The events of late 1984 through August 1985 represented a turning point in the anti-apartheid movement. The turmoil in South Africa received extensive and unprecedented coverage in the American media at a time when other regions of the world were relatively quiet. That coverage gave enormous new fuel to the anti-apartheid organizations and greatly strengthened their lobbying efforts at all levels of government—county, state, and federal. Since the early 1980s, strategy had shifted to proxy campaigns by a coalition of church organizations. In March 1982, for the first time, two public pension funds in California (California Teachers' Retirement System and California Public Employees' Retirement System) joined the coalition in sponsoring a shareholders' resolution, in this case against Xerox's operations in South Africa. The campaign to ban the sale of gold Krugerrands, launched in late 1979 after Jesse Jackson's South African trip, also gained fresh momentum. A complex offensive against the apartheid regime was beginning to emerge, characterized by campaigns to force banks and corporations to cease doing business in South Africa and to persuade institutional investors, especially municipal pension funds, to divest their portfolios of stocks of companies with operations or significant trade in the republic. There were also campaigns to ban the sale of Krugerrands, to institute comprehensive economic sanctions, and to boycott cultural and athletic events that involved South Africa.

In August 1984 the New York City Council voted to divest the city's largest employee pension fund of holdings in companies doing business in South Africa and agreed on a five-year divestment plan for its employee retirement system. Then in February 1985 it passed an ordinance banning the deposit of city funds in banks promoting Krugerrand sales and penalizing firms that refused to sign the Sullivan Code.

The stunning victories in New York and California breathed new life into the surging anti-apartheid movement. The pressure now began to build on banks, legislatures, and educational institutions. In March 1985 the First Chicago Corporation announced it would make no new loans to the South Africa government. A string of other prominent banks, including Morgan Guaranty Trust, followed in April. The Bank of Boston went farthest by announcing it would end all loans to South Africa, to the private as well as to the public sector. Anticipating greater pressure, many of the largest U.S. banks began to develop policies banning new loans.

By October 1985 eleven states and thirty-five cities across the country had taken some kind of economic action against South Africa. Twenty-four major colleges and universities had announced their intention to divest themselves of stocks in companies doing business in South Africa. Nonprofit institutions had begun to adopt South Africa–free investment policies. In addition several investment counseling firms had established a stock index of U.S. companies that did not do business in South Africa. The Investor Responsibility Research Center published a report in 1985 analyzing the impact of South Africa–related divestment on portfolio performance. Some companies with high visibility consumer products decided to withdraw from South Africa for fear that their products would be boycotted in the United States by local governments and state purchasing agencies.[71]

American labor, slow at first to respond to events, saw an opportunity to exert some influence beginning in 1979, when black unions were again legalized in South Africa after a hiatus of many years. American labor's programs in South Africa were launched in the early 1980s by the AFL-CIO's African-American Labor Center in New York. The center had already received federal support for a variety of activities in Africa and for years its policies had closely reflected the broad aims of the United States. In 1980 the AFL-CIO sponsored a seminar at Cornell University in an effort to establish personal ties with the new labor leaders and to become better acquainted with their needs and objectives. American union funds for South African labor organizations now began to grow quickly, from $27,000 in 1981 to $875,000 three years later.

Organized labor's interest in South African issues greatly intensified after the formation of the Congress of South African Trade Unions (COSATU) in December 1985. Rising like a phoenix from the apartheid landscape, COSATU began as a federation of thirty-six unions with more than six hundred thousand members.[72] The rate and numerical proportions of consolidation of organized labor was historically unprecedented in southern Africa. Not since the days of Clements Kadalie and his Industrial and Commercial Workers' Union in the 1920s had the pace of unionization been so rapid. And while labor unions in the rest of Africa were weakening in the face of internal dissension and government repression, South Africa's were growing at breathtaking speed. By the end of 1986, 18 percent of black industrial labor in South Africa was unionized, more than triple the figure obtained on the eve of Sharpeville. The African labor factor in the South African equation had become too important for Americans to ignore.

Prosperity had given muscle to black industrial workers. Though whites still controlled 82 percent of skilled jobs, the need for highly trained labor was growing faster than the growth of the white labor pool. With higher wages for blacks came greater consumer spending. Whereas in 1960 black consumer spending accounted for 26 percent of the total, by 1982 it had reached 48 percent. Thus, the black population had gained greater leverage, and the threat of strikes and consumer boycotts was real.[73] As the number of strikes and work actions exploded in the early 1980s, black workers revealed a new spirit of unity and confidence. Some workers had even begun to support cohorts in other sections of a given industry. For American firms, all this had ominous implications.

The anti-apartheid campaign greatly profited from the media exposure given to Bishop Desmond Tutu, who received a Nobel Peace Prize late in 1984 and then journeyed to the United States to condemn President Reagan's policy of Constructive Engagement as "immoral and un-Christian." No other visiting South African, white or black, had ever received such intensive media coverage or drawn such enormous crowds. Tutu's tumultuous reception was followed by Senator Edward Kennedy's well-publicized visit to South Africa early in 1985. These emotionally charged events led to the establishment of the Free South Africa Movement, a TransAfrica-initiated coalition of labor unions, religious organizations, campus groups, and mainline anti-apartheid lobbies opposed to constructive engagement. Disillusionment was growing over the Reagan administration's lack of progress in reaching a settlement in Namibia and in the Botha regime's refusal to repeal apartheid laws. In March 1985 the movement gained national recognition with the arrest outside the South African Embassy in Washington, D.C., of Reverend Jesse Jackson and prominent labor leaders. By July twenty-two members of Congress had been arrested while they were picketing the South African Embassy, and more than four thousand other citizens shared a similar fate when demonstrating in cities across the nation. As a growing number of members of Congress got arrested at the doorstep of the South African Embassy, images of black unrest and white repression radiated from the televisions, radios, and newspapers. Never before in history had South Africa been so completely in the public eye.

Pressure now began to build from representatives in the Congressional Black Caucus for a comprehensive anti-apartheid bill. After nearly a quarter century of demonstrations the anti-apartheid movement had made racial discrimination in South Africa a major domestic American issue. Many conservative members of congress countered that the sanctions and disinvestment campaigns had been transformed into a domestic civil rights issue, exploited by Democrats eager to mobilize black constituents. The Democratic leadership sidestepped the charges. With a barrage of statistical data the prosanctions lobbyists launched a new offensive against the conservatives' argument that South Africa was strategically important to the West for its minerals as well as for its Cape route. They countered that the real choke point for Western oil supplies was at their source in the Persian Gulf's Strait of Hormuz. They also argued that the strategic minerals found in such abundance in South Africa could be sourced elsewhere and that substitutes were available for some of them.

The events from March onward put increasing pressure on the Reagan administration to reassess its policy of Constructive Engagement. President Reagan had already begun his efforts to preempt the anti-South African organizations by attempting to put a human face on Constructive Engagement. In 1984 the South African Human Rights Program was established and administered from Johannesburg through the U.S. Agency for International Development (USAID) and began to extend grants to local community projects. Then in March 1985 the United States voted affirmatively on a U.N. Security Council resolution condemning apartheid. The resolution passed unanimously. In July Reagan signed an Export Administration Act, which reimposed the export controls on South Africa that had been adopted by the Carter administration years earlier and resumed the total embargo of exports to South Africa's military and police and prohibited sales of computers to its government.[74]

By August a constellation of anti-apartheid bills were before both houses of Congress and state legislatures. But legislators were running ahead of their constituents, for a Gallup poll taken in September 1985 revealed that only 13 percent of respondents favored a trade embargo or sanctions and a mere 3 percent supported divestment. A nationwide *Businessweek*/Harris poll in February 1985 indicated that only 18 percent wanted U.S. corporations out of South Africa.[75] Most respondents held to the traditional view that trade and investment would erode apartheid and accelerate the trend toward reform.

Nevertheless, to head off pending congressional sanctions, Reagan imposed limited sanctions of his own. On September 9, 1985, he signed an executive order that banned the import of Krugerrands and prohibited the export of computers, nuclear technology, and weapons or ammunition to the South African government or its agencies. It also prohibited government export assistance to any American firm employing at least twenty-five persons in South Africa and not adhering to the fair labor principles embodied in the Sullivan Code. Reagan's order further banned loans by any financial institution to entities owned or controlled by the South African government. On the positive side the executive order called for greater public support for black scholarships in South Africa and for human rights organizations.[76] Reagan's order hit most directly American firms that were major government suppliers and military contractors.

The debate heated up over whether the American public and private sectors possessed sufficient leverage to end apartheid. It was observed that few citizens held seats on the boards of key South African mining and manufacturing firms. Moreover, managing directors of American subsidiaries tended to be local South Africans, mostly English-speakers who were not members of the ruling National party and whose influence in the corridors of power was extremely limited. American citizens owned about 15 percent of all mining shares, and about 70 percent were in the gold-producing sector, which was the largest employer of black labor. However, most of these mining shares were held by individuals, not by public or private institutions. On the other hand, the United States held just under 20 percent of total foreign direct investments and was strong in key growth sectors, particularly oil (44 percent), autos (33 percent), and computers (70 percent). Surely, argued many, American corporations in those sectors had the power to affect substantial change in the South African economy.

THE COUNTER-OFFENSIVE

In any case, American MNCs seemed unprepared to deal with the growing anti-apartheid pressures on Congress. In late 1984 an anti-apartheid bill passed the House of Representatives and was only narrowly defeated in the Republican-controlled Senate. Until the events of 1985 American corporate CEOs usually deferred to their men in the field in charge of their local subsidiaries for assessments of domestic political issues. This now began to change quite dramatically as officers from headquarters made their own reconnaissance missions to South Africa. From March 1985, with American banks announcing the cessation of new loans, executives in home offices became more outspoken against apartheid and developed a more activist approach. And as the disinvestment campaign gathered momentum in the United States, a sense of urgency seized the business community in South Africa and speeded its efforts to blunt the campaign. In the first six months of 1985 the number of Sullivan Code signatories went from 129 to 153 and then reached 178 by November.[77] The signatory corporations accounted for nearly three quarters of all workers in American firms.

Under intensifying pressure from anti-apartheid lobbies in the United States and from African trade unions as well as enlightened self-interest, American companies began to take a wider view of their responsibilities towards their black South African employees, their families, and their communities. Some, like John Deere, had begun to make improvements as early as 1973. By 1980 most American MNCs including many of those that had not signed the Sullivan Code, had achieved complete desegregation of their facilities. In the first half of the 1980s enormous and historically unprecedented sums were expended on educational projects. More than a hundred American MNCs contributed to the construction of the Project for the Advancement of Commercial Education, or

PACE Commercial High School, a coeducational school for six hundred African students in the very heart of the teeming African ghetto of Soweto. The $4.5 million facility, with state-of-the-art equipment, opened its doors in July 1981 as a visible testimony of the private sector's new commitment to black educational development. Additionally, in the early 1980s Crocker National Bank and Citibank participated in a $25 million loan to help finance the construction of MEDUNSA (Medical University of southern Africa), South Africa's first medical school for Africans.[78]

Individual American MNCs also undertook their own projects. John Deere pioneered again when it launched a white-employees' reorientation program to improve race relations. And in 1981 the John Deere Foundation spent $420,000 to build a technical high school near its plant at Nigel.[79] IBM, meanwhile, introduced a computer-based system to teach children literacy. In July 1985 the computer giant announced new grants totalling $15 million over five years to enhance literacy skills and to foster black enterprise and legal reform. Indeed, it committed itself to supplying 250 South African schools with "Writing-to-Read" laboratories at a cost of $10 million for 37,000 black elementary school students.[80] Goodyear Tire spent $6 million on black education and housing. Mobil Oil committed itself to $20 million over five years after it had launched a Teacher Opportunity Program. Johnson and Johnson and Unisys (formerly Burroughs) promised to devote millions to programs to upgrade science teaching. In 1985 Coca-Cola made an initial commitment of $10 million to support a variety of educational and housing programs. Unisys could boast of an educational project in forty-four schools with six thousand black students. And Honeywell, General Motors, Ford, and Firestone Tire established a sprawling technical college near their plants in Port Elizabeth. By the end of 1987 thirty-six American companies in South Africa could collectively claim to have initiated 1,394 projects, many of them involving black education and the promotion of African entrepreneurship.

Quietly and with little media notice, the Americans were beginning to shift their attention to the promotion of black private enterprise in the South African townships in hopes of creating a new black bourgeoisie favorably inclined towards capitalism. Several American MNCs cooperated with the locally based Small Business Development Corporation in training Africans to become entrepreneurs and to establish their own businesses. By the beginning of 1986 Sullivan signatory companies alone had spent more than $250 million in 'social responsibility' programs and had committed many millions more.[81] Schools and clinics had been opened, and there was an enormous expansion in affordable housing and recreational facilities. In this new thrust the private sector received strong support from the Reagan administration. In fiscal year 1987 the U.S. government, through AID, authorized a seven-year Black Private Enterprise Development Project at $19.5 million. Concurrently, a scheme was initiated in South Africa by the American-based International Executive Service Corps (IESC). Retired executives from all fields of business and industry began to volunteer their time and expertise to help black South African entrepreneurs to improve their management skills.[82] By the end of 1987 IESC had launched more than fifty projects.

American banks, MNCs, and government agencies quickly discovered, however, that such achievements were unable to deflect attacks on them by anti-apartheid groups. They were not winning points with anyone, and the ambitious programs were costing them dearly at a time when

19. Promoting African private enterprise in South Africa. Mr. Houghton, a representative of the nonprofit International Executive Service Corps (IESC), listening to a client, Francis Magam, owner of Woolcraft, a clothing manufacturer in Johannesburg, 1987. (Courtesy, IESC)

local profit margins were falling. Throughout 1985 The South African economy had shown signs of continuing weakness. By the end of the year inflation reached 18.4 percent, a sixty-year high, and real GDP for the year was a negative 1.2 percent.[83] Nevertheless, throughout the year the export picture remained surprisingly strong. South Africa drastically reduced its imports to conserve on foreign exchange while boosting exports. For example, exports to the U.S. in 1985 reached $2.17 billion, while imports fell to $1.26 billion. In the overall picture total exports for the year amounted to an astonishing $16.5 billion, while imports levelled out at $11.5 billion.[84] Thus, despite the severe fiscal crisis, the trade surplus in dollar terms was more than double the surplus of the previous year. The gold price had fallen to $315 per ounce, but South Africa compensated by increasing its output to the point where gold represented nearly two-thirds of total export revenue. South Africa was able to market its metals quite well, in light of the fact that in 1985 the value of the rand declined by 26 percent against the U.S. dollar, after falling nearly 39 percent the year before.[85] Indeed, the continuing decline in the rand in 1985–1986 boosted the competitiveness of South Africa's mineral exports. South Africa, a petroleum importer, was also able to take advantage of the collapse in world oil prices.

The worsening political and economic situation encouraged a flow of political manifestoes from most South African business associations. In March 1985, shortly before sanctions bills were introduced before both houses of Congress, the American Chamber of Commerce in South Africa for the first time applied pressure on the Botha regime by imploring it to abolish influx control, extend voting rights to blacks, and open a dialogue with all races and political movements.[86] And just after Reagan signed his executive order, eighty chief executive officers of the largest American firms operating in South Africa issued public appeals in South African newspapers for reform. In the United States they formed the U.S. Corporate Council on South Africa. Altogether, the 104 council members, led by the CEOs of Burroughs and General Motors, vowed they would lobby for political reform in South Africa. Their concern stemmed from the rising tide of companies announcing their intention to disinvest or to reduce their stake in local subsidiaries to minority holdings.

The disinvestment trend gained momentum throughout 1985. The year opened with Pepsico announcing it would sell both its bottling plants. In March, after nearly forty years of service to South Africa, ailing Pan Am discontinued its flights. More announcements were forthcoming. The process accelerated after Reagan's executive order in September. Singer sold its marketing and distribution operations; Motorola disposed of its subsidiary; Apple Computer announced a full shutdown; General Foods sold its 20 percent stake in Cerebos. New York-based Phibro-Salomon, a major commodities trading firm, began to sell off some of its $400 million assets in South Africa, Batten, Barton, Durstine, and Osborn (BBDO) International sold 75 percent ownership in its South African agency to local directors. Some companies pulled out as a result of wider corporate liquidation plans. For example, International Harvester sold its truck operations and agricultural division to J. I. Case, which had recently become a Tenneco subsidiary. By the close of 1985 at least thirty-nine major American firms had left South Africa, up from only seven the year before.

Much of the disinvestment may have been part of a wider move. American MNCs in other regions of the world were reducing their direct investments and cutting their foreign assets. The weak dollar had made overseas investment more expensive, and American tax reform had rendered domestic operations, in the United States itself, comparatively more profitable and less risky. Consequently, a growing number of MNCs shifted emphasis away from overseas investment and export. A change of attitude of companies toward world markets was occurring. And as the value of the U.S. dollar rose by more than 40 percent between 1980 and 1985, the U.S. trade balance in the world steadily deteriorated from a surplus of $25 billion to a deficit of nearly $80 billion.[87]

The early 1980s were marked by rampant corporate restructuring in the United States, a process that may have made corporate decisions to disinvest far easier. Dozens of MNCs had begun to cut their ties to their less profitable overseas subsidiaries in South Africa and elsewhere. Many had started to accumulate debt and were therefore ripe for a hostile or friendly takeover. Some sold portions of their assets to pay down debt for their acquirers or to prevent a hostile domestic takeover, as with Union Carbide's efforts to stop a GAF threat. In fact, a company could improve its public image by withdrawing from South Africa for apparently moral reasons when in reality other considerations also influenced the decision.

Despite the rising pressures for economic sanctions, the United States actually stepped up its mineral purchases. In 1985 at least eighteen utility companies were buying uranium from South Africa, and the country was supplying the Americans with a growing proportion of its imports of platinum. The United States was now importing all of its manganese from abroad and 92 percent of its platinum group metals (nearly half from South Africa). The Americans were also importing 95 percent of their cobalt needs, mainly from Zaire and Zambia via South African seaports. In May 1985 representatives of the Department of Defense and the Department of Commerce visited South Africa to assess the condition of the country's extractive industries. In a report published in July the mission concluded that free-market access to South Africa's strategic minerals was vital for U.S. defense and industrial preparedness in the event of a national security crisis.[88] The study's findings renewed the old debate over the importance of dependency on South Africa for national security. Some groups favored greater political support for the Botha regime as a counter to the perceived "Communist onslaught," while others pressed for a renewed effort to find alternative sources and synthetics.

CONSTRUCTIVE ENGAGEMENT UNRAVELS

Throughout 1986 pressures for stronger measures against South Africa continued to build in both houses of Congress and in state legislatures. In March 1986 the AFL-CIO sponsored a "Day of Solidarity With Victims of Apartheid" rally in Washington, D.C. The Washington-based Investor Responsibility Research Center (IRRC) published the most comprehensive study ever carried out of American business involvement in South Africa, a 240-page directory of U.S. and Canadian investment in South Africa, that revealed that disinvestment and divestment were well underway.[89]

A number of large institutional investors had at last been won over to the anti-apartheid cause and had become extremely effective in forcing American firms and banks to cut their South African links. A huge breakthrough came in July 1986, when the Teachers Insurance and Annuity Association and College Retirement Equities Fund, or TIAA-CREF, the mammoth teachers' pension fund, asked all U.S. corporations in its multibillion dollar portfolio to withdraw from South Africa. CREF also began to sponsor shareholder resolutions at thirty companies, asking them to pull out. The divestment campaign received an even bigger shot in the arm when California's legislature voted to withdraw $11 billion in state pension funds from corporations investing in South Africa. This was the greatest divestment commitment in American history by a single entity. The State of New Jersey had already sold $1.5 billion of pension fund investments and in October 1986 said it would sell $4.3 billion more. Meanwhile, American MNCs continued their departure plans. Publishing houses such as the venerable John Wiley and Son announced their intention to leave. AT&T said it would no longer use South African metals in its telephone equipment, and the ailing Bank of America stated it would halt all lending to the country. A great psychological blow came in April 1986, when the venerable General Electric sold its industrial machinery division to a South African company. General Electric had been one of the first American MNCs to establish a subsidiary in the country, back in the late nineteenth century, and it commanded an enormous presence. The GE decision contributed greatly to the atmosphere of confusion and uncertainty. At the end of 1986 U.S. direct investments in South Africa stood at $1.1 billion, a drop from $1.2 billion in 1985 and a continuation of the downward trend that began in 1982.[90]

A similar frenetic ambience prevailed on Capitol Hill. Differences of opinion over sanctions raged within both political parties. Conservatives were deeply split, some fearing that a weak anti-apartheid stance might place them on the wrong side of the moral fence. Most Democrats believed that a strong vote on sanctions would stem the apparent erosion of party support from the American black community. The White House asserted that constructive engagement was beginning to work and that the Botha regime had begun to institute reforms, pointing to the scrapping of job reservation, the restoration of citizenship to blacks permanently resident in the townships, the repeal of the Prohibition of Mixed Marriages Act, and the amendment to the Group Areas Act to open business districts to entrepreneurs of all races.

Congress was not impressed. In September 1986 it passed the Comprehensive Anti-Apartheid Act and forwarded it to President Reagan, who vetoed it. Within weeks a flurry of major companies, including Coca-Cola, announced they would pull out as extreme uncertainty over the economy continued to persist. Between 1980 and 1986 private consumption growth dropped from 6.3 percent to 1.7 percent, and gross fixed investment in manufacturing capacity crashed from 100 percent in 1980 to 42 percent six years later.[91] The era of huge profits seemed to be ending.

In October Congress overrode the veto by overwhelming margins in both houses. Thus, the Comprehensive Anti-Apartheid Act, with its eighteen different types of sanctions, became the law of the land. It reinstituted the ban on computer sales to the South African government or agencies and forbade new loans or investments unless they were destined for black-owned businesses. Loans to the South African government were prohibited, and U.S. banks were not permitted to accept South African government deposits. Profits of American MNCs in South Africa could only be used to maintain existing operations, not for expansion. In the area of trade the act terminated the sugar quota, giving it to the Philippines, banned imports of South African iron, steel, coal, uranium, textiles, petroleum, and agricultural products, and stipulated that no goods manufactured by South African parastatals could be imported either. The act also breached an international agreement by revoking South African Airways' landing rights in American terminals.

But an important loophole was placed in the legislation.[92] The president could permit the importation of products considered vital to U.S. interests. And, indeed, in February 1987 the White House exempted ten minerals it considered "strategic" from the sanctions list after the State Department informed Congress that the economy depended on them for its national security. Nevertheless, in November 1986 the government named 166 South African firms that would be prohibited from exporting to the United States. In a "positive" vein the Anti-Apartheid Act authorized Congress to expend $40 million over two years for education and training of South African blacks in fields including entrepreneurship and labor and social work. In December 1987 Congress added another, extremely potent economic sanction, changing the tax treatment of U.S. investment by prohibiting American taxpayers from claiming tax credits for taxes paid to the government of South Africa.[93]

The American business community was stunned by the Congressional assertiveness. Some viewed with alarm this new government intrusion into the private sector. Under the Comprehensive Anti-Apartheid Act corporations with more than twenty-five employees in South Africa were required to comply with the Sullivan principles or submit to an annual evaluation by the Department of State. Rarely in peacetime had government interfered so openly and explicitly in the private sector. Corporate concerns deepened after the congressional elections in late 1986 removed the Republicans from their majority position in the Senate. In December the American Management Association held a day-long seminar in New York for senior-level corporate executives to discuss the implications of this historically unprecedented legislation and to speculate on the anti-apartheid inclinations of the new, more liberal Congress.

These new political developments at home did much to speed the exodus of American firms from South Africa. Warner Communications announced it would sell its record operations, which, in a joint venture with Paramount Pictures and Universal, held approximately a third of the South African record market. CBS followed Warner's lead, along with Bell and Howell. Honeywell, the Minnesota-based maker of computers and electronic control systems, said it would sell to a local engineering and construction firm, and Dun and Bradstreet prepared to sell its financial services subsidiary. Revlon, the New York cosmetics manufacturer, under pressure from a massive black American boycott of its products, agreed to sell its South African subsidiary, which made black hair-care products. By the end of 1986 at least fifty American firms had announced plans to withdraw. But as disinvestment accelerated, the number of Sullivan signatories dropped, from 179 in 1986 to ninety-two at the end of 1987. Having left South Africa, few American firms were willing to continue to fulfill their earlier pledges to their former black employees who either lost their jobs or were left to the mercies of their new South African employers.

Official ties between the United States and South Africa steadily deteriorated during the disinvestment process. In March 1986 a ranking South African military aide was expelled in protest over South African raids on ANC bases in the front-line states. In the same month, the U.S. Embassy in Pretoria sent for the first time an official representative to the funeral of a black political activist—but only after every other Western embassy announced its intention of attending. In June 1986 the reinstitution of the state of emergency seemed to kill any chance of political negotiations and suggested that Botha was abandoning his reform initiative. Then in October, in a gesture of displeasure over Botha's policies, an American career diplomat, Edward Perkins, was confirmed by Congress as the United States' first black ambassador to South Africa.

Sentiment against the Botha regime was growing even within the president's circle of advisers at the White House. In February 1987 the secretary of state's twelve-member Advisory Committee on South Africa, consisting of leaders from business and labor, recommended that only stronger economic and political sanctions would force South Africa to negotiate with the black majority and abolish apartheid. The committee also cautioned against endorsement of any reforms that failed to address the concerns of blacks.[94] Yet in the same month the United States and Great Britain vetoed a U.N. Security Council resolution calling for broad mandatory economic sanctions. The American representative at the United Nations boldly asserted that his country "totally rejected the notion that we should eliminate apartheid by provoking the collapse of the South African economy and a subsequent violent revolution."[95] At the same time the White House continued to press for greater assistance to the Southern African Development Coordination Conference (SADCC) as well as to Mozambique, a nominally Marxist country that had made gestures of détente to Washington. Both SADCC and Mozambique were desperately seeking to reduce their dependence on South Africa for trade and communications.

A HESITANT DEPARTURE

Between 1984 and the close of 1987, at least 162 U.S.-owned companies withdrew, leaving behind an almost equal number. On the other hand, approximately 350 U.S. firms with minority equity investments also departed. In the first six months of 1987 alone more than twenty-five firms signalled their impending departure, including Merck, a pharmaceutical firm that had been there since 1917, and Firestone, which agreed to sell its remaining quarter interest to Federale Volksbeleggings, a local Afrikaner-dominated industrial holding company. Proctor and Gamble and Union Carbide quietly began to sell their assets, and in June alone Citicorp, ITT, Xerox, McGraw-Hill, and Ford Motor Company announced plans for departure. Ford, the last U.S. motor company to have interests in South Africa, divested itself of its 42 percent equity in a subsidiary, the South African Motor Company (SAMCOR). A portion of the proceeds were then plowed back into SAMCOR for new equipment. But in return the local company had to agree to transfer nearly a quarter of its stock to an employee-owned trust fund. Citicorp's local subsidiary, Citibank, was sold to First National Bank (formerly Barclays). Some companies, like the subsidiary of CPC International, were sold to a consortia of South African and European investors. Others, notably American Brands, the U.S. packaging giant, had few fixed assets and prepared for a more rapid disengagement.

However, as the year 1987 unfolded, it was becoming doubtful if sanctions, divestment, and even disinvestment were having the desired effect. Some departing firms began to renege on or terminate their commitments to social responsibility projects. In November 1986 PACE Commercial High School closed its doors, in part because of a drop in American corporate support. Often white South African buyers of American subsidiaries lacked the capital resources or the will to continue such expensive programs. Moreover, they were no longer exposed to shareholder pressures from America or held to the criteria of the Sullivan Code. In June 1987, Reverend Sullivan, in the face of pressures from the black American community and anti-apartheid groups, disassociated himself from the code of conduct he had created just a decade earlier. Despite strong evidence to the contrary, Sullivan contended that the code had failed and that only a mass corporate exodus and broad economic sanctions would achieve fundamental change. He therefore urged all American companies to leave South Africa and to take steps to prevent their products from being sold there. Sullivan signatories in 1985 employed 71 percent of all those who worked for American MNCs in South Africa and employed more than 39,000 blacks, including Coloreds.[96]

The accelerated withdrawal of American firms led to a dramatic decline in private corporate contributions to community development programs in the African townships. The U.S. government tried to make up for the shortfall, but African organizations spurned its overtures, fearing that official assistance from a government source would weaken their credibility and their autonomy. Indeed, the American Embassy, flooded with largess amounting to nearly $22 million from official sources in Washington, became hard pressed to find recipients among authentic black community groups. At the same time South African black organizations began to launch fundraising efforts aimed at private philanthropies in the United States. However, private foundation support for South Africans remained narrowly based. A 1987 survey by the Institute of International Education in New York found only twenty-five organizations with established records of support for South African-related programs.

By early 1987 it had become painfully apparent to anti-apartheid groups that the withdrawal of American MNCs from South Africa did not necessarily mean the end of their presence there. Only twenty-one of the companies that had announced their intention to leave had actually done so completely. Some simply shifted their investments into non-equity links and managed to keep their products and services available. Indeed, most of the MNCs that disinvested retained substantial business connections through distribution, licensing, or technology agreements. And not a few still received trademark or patent royalties. Their management also remained intact for the most part. In short, though no longer under the influence of anti-apartheid pressures emanating from the United States, American MNCs sought to retain access to South African markets without subjecting themselves to anti-apartheid pressures at home.

Thus, for many firms a sell-off or disinvestment of a subsidiary did not lead to a full close-down. Many continued to supply the South African market with their goods through import houses or to maintain exclusive, long-term distribution contracts that allowed the successor South African firms to assemble and sell their products. Sanctions-busting techniques ranged from mislabelling exports to the United States and shipping through intermediate countries to completing the assemblage of a product overseas. A few companies moved portions of their operations to neighboring countries. Colgate-Palmolive, for example, opened a packaging plant in Botswana, and Coca-Cola shifted its concentrate-manufacturing facility from Durban to the Kingdom of Swaziland.

Kodak was one of the few companies that said it would disinvest completely. Nevertheless, although Kodak attempted to withdraw its products completely, the company found doing so impossible because its products could be purchased by local companies from third parties. Most of the companies that disinvested completely were small distribution or marketing operations that could continue with little disruption under a distribution agreement. Thus, in some cases companies simply reduced their exposure by converting their subsidiaries into licensing arrangements, in some instances going so far as to rename their products to avoid political repercussions. Thus, when it pulled out, GE left behind forty-two distribution agents covering a wide range of electrical, electronic, and industrial products. General Motors sold its assembly plant but continued to make its product line available to the companies buying them out. IBM's products and services continued to be available in South Africa through a local supplier. AT&T still offered its international long-distance telephone service. Some companies, like Exxon Corporation, were unable to find local buyers for their affiliates and therefore established special trusts (one is nonprofit) and sold shares in them in order to avoid closing their operations down completely. Trust arrangements became the preferred method for companies intending to reestablish a direct investment position in the future.

At first, the South African economy seemed almost mysteriously unaffected by the gathering storm clouds of sanctions and disinvestment. The value of American investments, direct and indirect, had actually increased nearly 10 percent in the 1984–1986 period, from $2.04 billion to $2.23 billion, at a time when South Africa was at the height of its domestic turmoil. But this was largely the result of the accumulation of reinvested earnings that could not be legally repatriated.

Beginning in June 1986 the economy seemed almost to defy external attacks and showed signs of rebounding from the trauma of the mid-1980s. Gold regained its luster as early as July 1986, and prices rose from $345 an ounce in the first half of the year to $425 an ounce by October and upward to $477 ten months later.[97] International gold demand soared at a most critical and propitious moment for South Africa. The good year in gold sales in 1986 was due in large measure to the dramatic increase in Japan's import of gold to mint its coins commemorating the sixtieth year of Emperor Hirohito's accession to the throne. Gold prices also surged as international tensions in the Persian Gulf raised fears of high oil prices and greater inflation. As in the past, gold again proved to be a haven for investors and speculators in times of uncertainty. By the close of 1987, U.S. citizens still held 14 percent of all South African mining shares. About 70 percent or $3.2 billion was in gold-mining companies. Nevertheless, the value of the shares had fallen by nearly a third since 1982. Diamond prices rebounded too, partially a result of the depreciation of the U.S. dollar against major currencies, and platinum sales also skyrocketed to record levels.

In 1985–1986 the declining rand stimulated demand for South African exports and helped to curb imports, leaving the country with a record trade surplus of $7 billion in 1986. Indeed, exports rose 27 percent in value between the months of February 1986 and 1987, despite a steady appreciation of the rand against the dollar.[98] By early 1987 net capital inflows occurred again, to the delight of the South African financial wizards. South Africa had dramatically returned to a sizeable surplus on its current account, and gold and foreign exchange reserves began to climb back again.

The government responded to impending sanctions with an aggressive new import replacement strategy and an intensified export promotion program. The South African business community had begun to turn its attention to breaking sanctions by diversifying away from American markets. Indeed, the private sector engaged in a desperate search to compensate for evaporating markets in the United States. Quite spectacularly, trade began to shift towards the Pacific Rim, in the direction of Taiwan, Hong Kong, South Korea, Singapore, and Japan. Trade with Japan, alone, expanded by 25 percent in 1986.

The euphoria of 1986 turned to confusion and uncertainty in 1987. True, outwardly the economy seemed to continue to make a modest recovery. The gross domestic product increased by 2.6 percent; but this was mainly in response to shifts in inventory and to a surge in private and government consumption in the face of cheaper oil imports and strong gold prices.[99] Wage increases triggered the consumer boom that generated a new wave of imports. As a result, the trade surplus began to narrow. Moreover, the surplus on the current account had to finance the enormous drain on the capital account in the balance of payments. Thus, in many respects the growth of 1986 and early 1987 was a thin veneer, derived largely from an increase in consumption expenditure. Ominously, the rate of fixed investment continued its precipitous descent thus reflecting the lack of investor confidence in the economy. By the middle of the third quarter of 1987 the economy appeared to be on the blink. Overall balance of payments on both current and capital accounts had slipped back into a deficit position, which was reflected in the continuing drain on gold and foreign exchange reserves. Even more ominous for the future, black unemployment had climbed to 40 percent, up from less than 25 percent three decades earlier. The population exceeded 35 million and was increasing at about 2.5 percent annually.[100]

In late 1987 the impact of the Anti-Apartheid Act began to ripple through the South African economy. After sanctions direct investments fell by nearly 5 percent to $2.12 billion. Bilateral trade was even more dramatically affected by the American legislation. By the close of 1987 imports from South Africa were about 40 percent less in terms of value than the previous year, or $1 billion compared to $1.8 billion.[101] This reflected substantial reductions in purchases of diamonds and gold as well as of embargoed items. Indeed, diamond exports to the United States plunged alarmingly. Between 1983 and 1985 exports to the United States averaged 5.6 million carats a year, while in 1987 they fell to a mere 139,000 carats. With moderate success South Africa got around this by selling to its American customers indirectly, through middlemen in Israel, Great Britain, and Ireland. But altogether trade between the United States and South Africa declined substantially. By the end of 1987 the United States was taking only 13 percent of South Africa's exports and supplying the country with only 11 percent of its imports. Japan had emerged as the apartheid regime's top trading partner, and the United States had slipped to fourth place.

Sanctions and disinvestment may have begun to harm the South African economy, but there was little evidence that they had forced the whites into a more reformist stance. Indeed, white South African politics appeared to move further rightward in the national elections of May 1987, which gave the pro-apartheid Conservative party 26 percent of all white votes cast and easily eclipsed the liberal Progressive Federal party as the official parliamentary opposition. In a dramatic shift nearly 40 percent of the white English speakers voted for the ruling National party, which had hitherto been overwhelmingly dominated by Afrikaners.[102] In the budget announced that year police expenditures were scheduled for a 50 percent increase and defense spending was to go up by a third.[103] South Africa gave the appearance of moving not in the direction of fundamental democratic reform but toward totalitarianism. Under Botha, government power was passing from parliament and the National party to the security establishment, namely the State Security Council (SSC) a committee of the state president's cabinet. The SSC's control was extended over all branches of the government and even over the heights of private enterprise.

In sharp contrast to the period following Sharpeville and Soweto the government this time had failed to restore the confidence of the American business community. The May elections were interpreted as a prelude to an escalation in regional and internal conflict and another blow to chances for political reform. The economy had improved, but investor confidence had not. Fixed investment, bank borrowing, and consumer-durables spending remained weak. Central government spending had grown by 23 percent in the year ending March 1987, while revenue expanded by only 16 percent.[104] The government continued to encounter difficulty in tapping foreign loan markets and therefore stimulated the economy by cutting taxes and increasing public expenditures, especially on security and black education. Nevertheless, in March 1987 South Africa and its creditors reached an agreement on repayment of $1.4 billion of the $13 billion frozen foreign debt, blocked in the fiscal crisis of September 1985. But it was not enough to restore the shaken confidence of the international financial community. U.S. bank lending to South Africa declined from a peak of $4.7 billion in 1984 to under $3 billion by March 1987.[105]

The Botha regime intensified its repression in a seemingly futile attempt to control the rising incidence of wildcat strikes and urban terrorism. Moreover, South Africa staged military raids into Zambia in April 1987 and into Mozambique in May, thus raising the level of regional tension. In the face of a growing number of work stoppages, the government also began a crackdown on the leadership within the United Democratic Front (UDF) and in the powerful Congress of South African Trade Unions (COSATU). COSATU had become South Africa's largest trade union federation under the powerful leadership of Cyril Ramaphosa and was a formidable black labor force with its twenty-five affiliated unions. It had drawn itself closer to the aims of the African National Congress (ANC) and had aligned itself with the UDF, an umbrella for nearly seven hundred organizations and disparate associations with little in common but their opposition to the government's "reform" program.[106] The mass imprisonment and detention of UDF leaders undermined the already precarious political discipline within the movement. Matters were made worse for the opposition in June 1987 with the renewal of the national state of emergency.

In the post-Sowetan era the American news media became the prime conveyor of information on current South African events. No longer did the U.S. news-gathering corporations rely on correspondents of British nationality. Through a mixture of truth and distortion, journalistic enterprise injected the deep-seated problems of racial injustice in South Africa into the living rooms of millions of mostly ignorant Americans. The subtle complexities and historical dynamics of apartheid were telescoped, processed, and simplified into staccato montages for general viewers and readers. And into the classrooms of U.S. public schools flowed extremely graphic anti-apartheid documentaries produced by a number of private companies, notably the California-based Southern Africa Media Center. Recognizing the enormous consciousness-raising quality of this investigative reporting, the Botha regime introduced a series of press restrictions that culminated in January 1987 with the expulsion of the *New York Times'* bureau chief in Johannesburg. It was not long before the volume of news from South Africa began to decline, and by the year's end the anti-apartheid momentum had slowed. Paradoxically, as Americans developed a greater awareness of the evils of apartheid, they became more confused by the complexity of the issues and more deeply divided over how they could be resolved. The initial manifestations of black against white conflict could be comprehended. But the power struggles within the various racial and ethnic communities were uncomfortably confusing to many.

Censorship of another kind had been emerging in the United States, in the form of calls for a total cultural boycott. In 1983 the United Nations Center Against Apartheid began issuing a register of performers to be boycotted because of their professional appearances in South Africa. Growing numbers of prominent white and black American stars were performing not only in the Republic but in the so-called independent homeland states. By 1987 the bitter controversy over the definition and parameters of "cultural boycott" led to the formation of Artists United Against Apartheid. The nonprofit organization of fifty-four leading performers was spearheaded by Sidney Poitier and Harry Belafonte. Out of their efforts came a popular anti-apartheid album entitled *Sun City*. This period of heightened awareness also saw the emergence of another influential organization, Filmmakers United Against Apartheid, cochaired by Jonathan Demme and Martin Scorsese.

Efforts to discourage cultural figures from performing in South Africa were matched by an equally determined effort to promote the works of South African apartheid opponents in the United States. In 1985 the nonprofit African Arts Fund was launched to assist refugee artists in completing their professional education in the United States.[107] The boycott issue became more intense in 1987, after Paul Simon, the American singer and composer, and his multiracial Graceland group toured southern Africa and drew enormous multiracial crowds. The tour was condemned by the ANC, but received mild support from a number of local UDF leaders, including Reverend Allan Boesak. The controversy had sharpened into the questions: do such tours serve to condone or legitimate apartheid or do they raise American consciousness of apartheid's evils?

CONCLUSION

For American enterprise the wildly gyrational eleven years following Soweto represented the best of times and the very worst of times. They witnessed the most intensive and frenetic engagement in nearly three centuries as well as the most compelling and frenzied disengagement. It was an epoch of turbulent confusion, of rapid advance and retreat, of mixed corporate and government signals overlaid by a bewildering conjunction of highly progressive corporate labor reforms and almost Machiavellian strategies of sanctions evasion. In this period American entrepreneurs began to speculate that time may indeed be running out on white minority rule and that their corporate policies and practices would have to undergo fundamental change. In May 1977 Vice President Mondale became the first person in high office to publicly call for majority rule in South Africa. His clarion message struck a note of realism that in the decade ahead came to have increasing urgency.

This was a time when the American private sector came under increasingly intensive public scrutiny. The major multinational corporations, supported by successive American presidents, clung to the premise that by example they could serve as an effective instrument of change. And in a remarkably short time dozens of major multinational corporations gathered their accumulated profits to embark on a seemingly desperate mini-Marshall Plan for black South Africa, building state-of-the-art schools, devising innovative curricula, offering housing for employees and scholarships for their children. It was an initiative that often exceeded anything offered to Afro-American employees in the United States or to employees in other countries. Smaller, less-capitalized MNCs felt that such reforms were too costly, and they either did nothing and took the anti-apartheid heat or withdrew.

It must be emphasized that after Soweto, the anti-apartheid movement in the United States had matured and had developed a more sharply focused and cohesive campaign. In the early 1980s it began to incorporate moderates as well as militants, business executives and attorneys as well as academics. The activists moved off the streets and into the board rooms of foundations, colleges, and major pension funds. They became allied with organizations involved in related issues and won over such prominent leaders as Jesse Jackson, Harry Belafonte, Congressmen Charles Rangel, Stephen Solarz, and Howard Wolpe, and Senator Edward Kennedy.

One can conclude here that a turning point came in late 1984 and early 1985 with the confluence of several important events: the consolidation of African resistance into the United Democratic Front and the Congress of South African Trade Unions; massive urban disturbances and consumer boycotts on a historically unprecedented scale, and the intensive American media coverage of these events and the activities of the eloquent Bishop Desmond Tutu. Indeed, the anti-apartheid cause gained international momentum with the award of the Nobel Peace Prize to Tutu in recognition of his efforts to end apartheid peacefully. Advocates of constructive engagement were almost completely overwhelmed by the Botha regime's refusal to open a dialogue with the new African players and by the stalling of reform in the face of a growing white conservative backlash. These events occurred at a moment when the South African economy was sliding into another economic recession and the rates of return on American investments were reaching historic lows. The year 1985 was beginning to look like a replay of the aftermaths of Sharpeville and Soweto. A state of emergency had returned to the country, and the forces of repression were unleashed again. This time, in the face of enormous media and anti-apartheid pressures at home, Americans were less prepared to help South Africa regain the confidence of the international financial community. The crisis came to a head in August 1985, when the big American banks closed their lending windows. The die had now been cast and a new era of American disengagement had begun, broader and more profound than ever before and involving an awesome range of disinvestment and divestment strategies. It can be argued that the momentum of disinvestment accelerated out of control when it became clear to a number of large and highly visible multinational corporations that the profits of doing business in South Africa had the potential of being outweighed by the cost of municipal and state pension fund divestment and by the boycott of public-sector purchasing agencies. The disinvestment trickle became a flood after the passage through Congress of the Comprehensive Anti-Apartheid Act. But, as we have seen, many American corporate entities, including private philanthropies, remained behind for reasons as diverse as their individual activities and objectives.

As the sun set on the final days of 1987, it was unclear to even the most astute observers just what the future would hold for American–South African relations. For nearly three centuries Americans have more often than not misjudged the enormously complicated dynamics of South African society. I must conclude that the private and the public sectors in the United States have yet to develop a consistent, coherent, or realistic set of strategies that can ensure a relationship that is mutually beneficial and satisfying and that can help to move South Africa toward a system of representative democracy.

NOTES

1. South African Information Ministry, "The Magic of Gold," *Backgrounder* (Washington, D.C., 1981), p. 2. See also Vella Pillay, "The Role of Gold in the Economy of Apartheid South Africa," United Nations Centre Against Apartheid, Department of Political and Security Council Affairs. *Notes and Documents,* March 1981 (New York, 1981), pp. 7–9; David Yudelman, *The Emergence of Modern South Africa,* p. 267.

2. Thomas Bray, "South Africa: Growth and Political Reform," *Wall Street Journal,* September 9, 1982, p. 1. See also *Doing Business in South Africa,* August 1977 (New York, 1977), p. 43.

3. Colin Legum, ed., *Africa Contemporary Record* (1977), p. A24. See also Nancy McKeon, "Update," *Africa Report* 20,3 (May–June 1976) p. 34.

4. U.S. House of Representatives, *U.S. Interests in Africa,* Hearings before the subcommittee on Africa, 96th Cong., 1st sess., 1979 (Washington, D.C., 1980), pp. 401–31.

5. Leo Katzen, "The South African Economy," in *Africa South of the Sahara, 1986,* p. 867. See also W. H. Thomas, "Structure of the South African Economy," in W. H. Thomas, ed., *The Condition of the Black Worker* (Uppsala, 1975), pp. 15–55.

6. Jonathan Leape, Bo Baskin, and S. Underhill eds., *Business in the Shadow of Apartheid: A Survey of U.S. Companies,* passim.
7. Dick Clark, "U.S. Corporate Interests in South Africa," Report to the Committee on Foreign Relations, U.S. Senate (Washington, D.C., 1978).
8. Paul D. Irish, "U.S. Corporations in South Africa," International Seminar on the Role of Transnational Corporations in South Africa (London), November 4, 1979) p. 10.
9. Barclays, *Business Brief* (Johannesburg, January 1986), p. 1. See also "South Africa", in Legum, ed., *Africa South of the Sahara, 1977–78* p. 827; G. W. G. Browne, "Fifty Years of Public Finance," *The South African Journal of Economics* 51, 1 (March 1983), p. 137.
10. Katzen, "The South African Economy," p. 896. Republic of South Africa, Department of Statistics, *South African Statistics, 1978* (Pretoria, 1978), pp. 77–78.
11. Ann Micou, ed., *U.S. College and University Initiatives to Expand Educational Opportunities for Black South Africans* (New York, 1988), passim.
12. African-American Institute, *Annual Report, 1984* (New York, 1985), p. 7.
13. Phelps-Stokes Fund, "Seventy-Five Years of Education for Human Development," *Annual Report, 1981/82,* Diamond Anniversary Issue 3, 2 (Spring 1986):3–7.
14. Christopher Coker, *The United States and South Africa, 1968–1985: Constructive Engagement and Its Critics,* pp. 72–74. See also Kevin Danaher, *The Political Economy of U.S. Policy Towards South Africa,* p. 40.
15. Ian Mackler, *Pattern for Profit in South Africa,* p. 37. See U.S. Department of State, *The Trade Debate,* Joseph Margolis, "Update," *Africa Report* 23,1 (January–February 1978), p. 30.
16. The Sullivan Statement of Principles, 4th Amplification, November 8, 1984 (Philadelphia, 1984), Appendix M. See also Karen Rothmyer, "Sullivan Principles," *Southern African Perspectives* (New York, August, 1979), pp. 1–4; Reverend Leon Sullivan "Agents for Change: The Mobilization of Multinational Companies in South Africa," *Law and Policy in International Business* 15, 2 (1983):427–44.
17. Coker, *United States and South Africa,* p. 93. See also *Africa News,* February 14, 1983, p. 3.
18. James A. Nathan and James K. Oliver, *Foreign Policy Making and the American Political System* (Boston, 1983), p. 219. See also *Africa Confidential* 19, 25 (December 15, 1978):3.
19. Thomas N. Gladwin and Ingo Walter, eds., *Multinationals Under Fire,* pp. 176–77. See also Richard W. Hull, "Rhodesia in Crisis," *Current History* 76, 445 (March 1979):105.
20. *The Christian Science Monitor,* October 20, 1986, p. 15. See also Richard Synge, ed., *Africa Guide, 1977* (Essex, 1976), pp. 51–53; William Minter and Elizabeth Schmidt, "When Sanctions Worked," *African Affairs* 87, 347 (April 1988):207–39.

21. Barclays, *Business Brief* (Johannesburg, October 1985), p. 1. See also *Financial Mail*, March 22, 1985, p. 65.
22. Donald Woods, *Biko* (New York; 1979), pp. 52–54. See also Muriel Horrell, ed., *Survey of Race Relations in South Africa, 1977* (Johannesburg, 1978), p. 62.
23. A. O. Hero, "The American Public in South Africa," in John Barratt and A. O. Hero, eds., *The American People and South Africa*, p. 8.
24. U.S. Senate, *U.S. Policy toward South Africa*, Hearings before the Committee on Foreign Affairs, Subcommittee on Africa, 96th Cong., 2nd sess., March 1980 (Washington, D.C., 1980).
25. Desaix Myers, "U.S. Domestic Controversy on American Business in South Africa," in Barratt and Hero, eds. *American People*, p. 69.
26. John David Wilson, *The Chase: Chase Manhattan Bank 1945–1985* (Boston, 1986), p. 82 fn. See also Gladwin and Walter, *Multinationals*, p. 101.
27. Joseph Margolis, "Update," *Africa Report* p. 35.
28. Robert M. Price, "U.S. Policy Toward Southern Africa," in G. M. Carter and Patrick O'Meara, eds., *International Politics in Southern Africa*, pp. 45–56.
29. Business International, *A Fresh Look at South Africa*, Business International Research Report (New York; 1982), p. 13.
30. Hal B. Lary, *Problems of the United States as World Trader and Banker*, passim; "South Africa," *Economist Intelligence Unit*, 4th quarter (London, 1976).
31. Richard E. Bissell, *South Africa and the United States: The Erosion of an Influence Relationship*, p. 121; Gladwin and Walter, *Multinationals*, p. 169.
32. George M. Houser, *The Story of the American Committee on Africa* (New York, n.d.), p. 7.
33. Desaix Myers, *U.S. Business in South Africa*, p. 298.
34. *Africa Report* 31, 3 (May–June 1986), pp. 33–36.
35. *Washington Report on Africa* 5, 26 (1987):1. See also *Economist*, March 16, 1985, p. 35.
36. Carnegie Corporation of New York. *Annual Report, 1987* (New York, 1988), pp. 58–59. See also Julie Gottlieb, "U.S. Professional Association Initiatives Related to Black South Africans," Paper delivered at the Institute of International Education (New York, October 1987); Landrum R. Bolling, *Private Foreign Aid: U.S. Philanthropy for Relief and Development*.
37. S. A. McLean and R. Kluger, "U.S. Foundation Giving to Enhance Educational Opportunities for Black South Africans," (New York, 1987), p. 11.
38. Ibid., p. 38.
39. Christopher Wilson, "South Africa's Debt Overhang" *Optima* 35, 2 (1987):21.

40. Barclays, *Business Brief* (Johannesburg, March 1985), p. 2. See also A. M. Fransman, "Capital Accumulation," in Martin Fransman, ed., *Industry and Accumulation in Africa* (London, 1982), p. 49.

41. *Africa News,* February 9, 1979, p. 3; Gary Nelson, "Marketing Kruger-rands," *Corporate Examiner* 9, 12 (December 1980):1.

42. Denis MacShane, Martin Plant, David Ward, *Power: Black Workers, Their Unions, and the Struggle for Freedom in South Africa* (Nottingham, 1984). See also Sheila T. van der Horst, *Race Discrimination in South Africa,* (Capetown, 1981), p. 34, Standard Bank, *Guide to Business in South Africa* (Johannesburg, July 1984), p. 1; Merle Lipton, *Capitalism and Apartheid, 1910–1984,* pp. 118–19.

43. Jill Nattrass, *The South African Economy,* p. 267. See also Central Statistical Services, *Statistics in Brief, 1979* (Pretoria, 1979), p. 2.

44. Nedbank Group, *Executive Guide to the Economy* (Johannesburg, June 1985), p. 1.

45. *International Trade, 1982/83* (Geneva, 1983), p. 206.

46. Rhys Jenkins, *Transnational Corporations and Uneven Development,* p. 5. See also *South African Digest,* August 11, 1980, p. 6.

47. *London Sunday Times,* May 9, 1982, p. 40; Business International, *A Fresh Look,* p. 4.

48. Standard Bank, *Standard Bank Review* (Johannesburg, March 1985), p. 2. See also "Sheltering Down Under," *Financial Mail,* June 27, 1986, p. 88; Nedbank, *Guide to the Economy* (May 1986), p. 1.

49. W. C. J. van Rensburg, *Strategic Minerals: Major Mineral-Consuming Regions of the World* 2:171.

50. U.S. Committee on Foreign Relations, Subcommittee on African Affairs "Imports of Minerals from South Africa," September 1980 (Washington, D.C., 1980), p. xii. See also U.S. Department of the Interior, Bureau of Mines, *Mineral Commodity Summaries.*

51. "A Conversation with the President," *CBS News Special Report with Walter Cronkite,* March 3, 1981, transcript, p. 8. See also R. Stephen Brent, "The Reagan Policy Toward South Africa."

52. Donald Rothchild and John Ravenhill, "Subordinating African Issues to Global Logic," in Kenneth Oye, Robert Lieber, and Donald Rothchild eds., *Eagle Resurgent: The Reagan Era in American Foreign Policy,* (p. 72; "Constructive Engagement," *Africa Confidential* 27, 15 July 16, 1986), p. 1.

53. Sandy Boyer, "Divesting from South Africa," Paper presented to the American Committee on Africa (New York, 1983). See also Investor Responsibility Research Center, *Reporter* (September 1985), p. 5; *International Trade, 1981/82* (Geneva, 1982), p. 164.

54. *International Trade, 1981/82* p. 166. See also *London Sunday Times* (London) October 7, 1984.

55. Franklin Thomas, et al., *South Africa: Time Running Out,* passim.

56. "South Africa," *Economist Intelligence Unit,* 4th quarter (London, 1983). See also "South Africa, 1983," in Frost and Sullivan, *Country Reports* (Syracuse, N.Y. 1983).

57. *South African Digest,* October 29, 1976, p. 14. The Boeing 747S was introduced in 1976 and cut flying time between New York and Johannesburg to fourteen hours. See also *South African Digest,* February 10, 1984, pp. 12–14.

58. *The Cape Argus,* March 27, 1985, p. 21. *Business Day* (Johannesburg), April 10, 1985, p. 1.

59. Nedbank Group, *Executive Guide to the Economy* (October 1985), pp. 1–3.

60. Nedbank. *Economic Roundup* (September 1985), p. 1.

61. *Keesing's Contemporary Archives* (Bristol, England) 30 (January 1984):3266. Katzen, "The Economy," p. 793.

62. M. R. Sinclair and J. L. Place, *Progress: Reports on Health and Development in Southern Africa* (Washington, D.C, 1988), p. 14. See also U.S. Department of State, *Background Notes: South Africa* (Washington, D.C., May 1985), pp. 7–8.

63. *South Africa/Namibia Update* 8, 1 (November 1984):1. Horrell, ed., *Survey of Race Relations, 1984* (Johannesburg, 1985), p. 252.

64. "South Africa, 1984," in Frost and Sullivan, *Country Reports* (1984). p. D-2. *South Africa/Namibia Update* 8, 11 (November 1984):2.

65. Investor Responsibility Research Center, *Review Service,* (New York, September 1985), p. 1. IRRC, *Reporter* (New York, September 1985), p. 3.

66. "Exodus of U.S. Firms," *Africa Economic Digest* 31 May 31, 1986, p. 18; *New York Times,* December 2, 1985, p. D2.

67. Nedbank Group, *Executive Guide to the Economy* (November 1985), p. 1.

68. Barclays, *Business Briefs* (January 1986), p. 3; *Africa Economic Digest,* November 30, 1985, p. 44.

69. David Niddrie, "The Economy," *Work in Progress* 56/57 (1988):p. 52; Standard Bank, *Standard Bank Review* (February 1985), p. 1. See also *African Business,* January 27, 1986; *New York Times,* December 31, 1986, p. D3.

70. *Forbes,* March 9, 1987, pp. 101–104; *Financial Mail,* June 20, 1986, p. 50. *New York Times,* August, 17, 1986, p. D2; *New York Times,* October 6, 1986, p. D-5. See also Audna England, ed., "South Africa: Myths and Realities of Divestiture," Paper delivered at the Council on Religion and International Affairs (New York, 1985).

71. Investor Responsibility Research Center, "Tightening Credit," South Africa Review Service, *Reporter* 3, 3 (September 1985):37.

72. *Economist,* July 18, 1987, p. 39.

73. *South African Digest,* March 11, 1961, p. 3; *Economist,* September 14, 1985, p. 56.

74. *Africa News,* September 23, 1985, p. 2.
75. *Businessweek,* September 23, 1985, p. 114.
76. Investor Responsibility Research Center, *Reporter* (September 1985):15.
77. International Council for Equality of Opportunity Principles, Inc., *Ninth Report on the Signatory Companies,* October 25, 1985 (Philadelphia, 1985). See also Investor Responsibility Research Center, South Africa Review Service, *Directory Update* (New York, May 1985), pp. 1–3.
78. Carole Cooper, ed., *Survey of Race Relations in South Africa, 1986* (Johannesburg, 1987). See also *South Africa/Namibia Update,* March 3, 1982, p. 4.
79. Investor Responsibility Research Center, *Reporter* (September 1985):13; Wayne G. Broehl, *John Deere's Company,* pp. 707–709. See also F. N. Robinson, ed., *General Electric Investor* 9, 3 (Fall 1978) Centennial Issue (Fairfield, 1978).
80. "South African Watchdog," *African Business* 89 (January 1986):14; *IBM Operations in South Africa* (Armonk, N.Y., April 1985); *The New York Times,* October 22, 1986, p. D-1.
81. Investor Responsibility Research Center, South Africa Review Service, "Divestment Roundup," (New York, October 1985).
82. Agency for International Development, *Congressional Presentation,* F. Y. 1989, Annex 1, Africa (Washington, D.C., 1988), pp. 401–15. See also African American Institute. *Annual Report, 1983* (New York, 1984), p. 12; International Executive Service Corps, "South Africa," *IESC News* 1, 1 (June 1987):1.
83. Barclays, *Business Briefs* (September 1985):1–2. See also *South Africa, 1984/85. Official Yearbook* (Pretoria: Govt. Printer, 1986), p. 377; "South Africa," *Economist Intelligence Unit* 1st quarter (London, 1986).
84. Nedbank Group, *Economic Unit* (Johannesburg, June, 1985), p. 2; *Businessweek,* September 23, 1985, p. 105.
85. *Africa Economic Digest,* March 22, 1986, p. 19; "Searching for Causes," Reserve Bank Supplement, *Financial Mail,* November 7, 1986, p. 33.
86. U.S. Department of Commerce, *List of U.S. Firms or Affiliates Operating in South Africa, November 1982* (Washington, D.C., 1983); *Fortune* September 30, 1985, pp. 18–26.
87. Rone Heyns, ed., *South Africa, 1986. Official Yearbook,* 12th ed., Department of of Foreign Affairs (Pretoria, 1986), p. 533. See also *Economist,* September 26, 1987, pp. 93–94.
88. *The Wall Street Journal,* June 20, 1986, p. 9.
89. Glenn S. Goldberg, *IRRC Directory of U.S. Corporations in South Africa,* passim. See also *Businessweek,* September 23, 1985, p. 44.
90. General Electric. *Update on South Africa,* November 1984 (Fairfield Ct., 1984), pp. 4–7. *Financial Mail,* August 23, 1985, p. 56. *New York Times,* September 18, 1986, p. D1.
91. *Comprehensive Anti-Apartheid Act of 1986,* 99th Cong., Public Law 99-

440, 1st session October 2, 1986 (Washington, D.C., 1986). See also *Anti-Apartheid Action Act* U.S. Senate, 99th Cong., 1st sess., June 28, 1985 (Washington, D.C., 1985).

92. Robert Shepard, *The 99th Congress and South Africa Sanctions,"* May 1987 (Washington, D.C., 1987). See also *Economist,* October 11, 1986, p. 76.

93. W. H. Cooper, "Sanctions Against South Africa," Congressional Research Service, April 1988 (Washington, D.C., 1988).

94. U.S. Department of State, *A U.S. Policy Toward South Africa,* Report of the Secretary of State's Advisory Committee on South Africa, January 1987 (Washington, D.C., 1987).

95. Brenda Branaman, *"South Africa: U.S. Policy After Sanctions,"* April 1988 (Washington, D.C., 1988). See also *Africa News,* November 10, 1986, p. 5.

96. John D. Battersby, "U.S. Goods in South Africa," *New York Times,* July 27, 1987, p. D1. See also Agency for International Development, Congressional Presentation, p. 402; "Gold, Sunny Skies Again?" *Financial Mail,* October 3, 1986, pp. 30–33.

97. "South Africa," *Economist Intelligence Unit,* 2nd quarter (London, 1988), pp. 17–26; Nedbank Group, *Executive Guide to the Economy* (February 1988), p. 3. For data on U.S. investments in South Africa in the 1984–1986 period see Carl Hartman, "Sanctions Have Cut U.S. Trade With South Africa," *The Washington Post,* October 12, 1988, p. 3. For the Ford disinvestment, see "Foreign Policy Cynicism," *Wall Street Journal,* January 5, 1988, p. 9.

98. "South Africa 1988," in Frost and Sullivan, *Country Reports* (1988), p. C3. *Africa Confidential,* September 2, 1987, p. 2.

99. "South Africa," *Economist Intelligence Unit* 3rd quarter (London, 1988), pp. 29–33. See also *Economist,* November 5, 1988, p. 76.

100. First National Bank, *Business Brief* (Johannesburg, December 1987), p. 5; Nedbank Group, *Executive Guide to the Economy, 1987,* p. 3.

101. Nedbank Group, *Executive Guide to the Economy* (November 1987). For more information on 1987 performance of the economy, see Katzen, "The Economy," *Africa South of the Sahara, 1988,* pp. 931–35.

102. Katzen, "The Economy," *Africa South of the Sahara, 1987.* See also Barclays, *Business Brief* (March 1987).

103. Ibid., p. 1.

104. *Washington Report on Africa,* December 15, 1987, p. 102.

105. "COSATU Congress," *Work in Progress* 54 (June–July 1988):3–25. See also Stanley B. Greenberg "Resistance and Hegemony in South Africa," in Wilmot James, ed., *The State of Apartheid* (Boulder, 1987), p. 57.

106. Meg Voorhes, "American Universities," p. 17.

107. American Committee on Africa, *Action News,* Spring 1987 (New York, 1987), pp. 2–5. See also "Building the Cultural Boycott," *Southern Africa,* 16, 1, (January–February 1983):3–6.

Appendix

TABLE 1

United States Exports
to Cape Town
(U.S. dollars)

Year	Amount
1796	33,325
1799	183,569
1802	240,286
1806	473,345
1808	12,390

Sources: Timothy Pritkin, *A Statistical View of the Commerce of the United States of America*, p. 213; George McCall Theal, *History of South Africa 1792–1872* (London, 1897), p. 240.

TABLE 2

Number of Ships Clearing Port
Elizabeth for the United States
(June 17 to September 14, 1863)

Destination	Number of Ships
Boston	37
New York	31
Baltimore	2
Philadelphia	1

Source: Alagoa Bay and the Trade Statistics of Port Elizabeth, pp. 11–12.

361

TABLE 3

Trade Between the United States and South Africa (U.S. dollars)

Year	U.S.–S.A.	S.A.–U.S.	% S.A. Imports	% S.A. Exports
1835	60,724	50,829	2.4	2.7
1840	87,892	27,247	1.2	.5
1845	102,014	53,405	2.3	2.3
1850	191,217	94,022	3.1	3.1
1855	232,480	189,878	4.1	3.7
1860	866,842	1,717,022	6.8	17.2
1865	251,044	825,489	2.5	7.5
1877	629,000	900,000		

Sources: Alan R. Booth, *The United States Experience in South Africa, 1784–1870,* p. 159; R. W. Schufeldt, *Report on Commerce and Navigation* (Washington, D.C., 1879), p. 7.

TABLE 4

South African Trade with the United States (in thousands of pounds sterling and including gold exports) Note: Bullion exports are not included after 1909.

Year	Imports	Exports
I. Cape colony only:		
1850	40	20
1855	48	40
1860	181	358
1865	52	172
1870	49	236
1875	130	169
1880	301	192
1885	133	84
1889	229	77
1890	282	101
1895	873	120
1896	1,739	88
II. Cape and Natal colonies:		
1900	2,311	22
1905	2,309	56

TABLE 4 (*Cont.*)

South African Trade with the United States (in thousands of pounds sterling and including gold exports) Note: Bullion exports are not included after 1909.

Year	Imports	Exports
III. The Union of South Africa:		
1910	2,731	411
1915	4,447	2,367
1920	18,408	3,990
1925	9,995	2,145
1930	9,288	1,261
1935	12,747	665
1940	23,556	2,657
1945	81,150	10,197
IV. The Union of South Africa (in millions of S.A. pounds):		
1950	49	21
1955	100	27
V. South Africa (in millions of S.A. rands):		
1965	215	54
1970	423	129
1975	986	377

Source: B. R. Mitchell, comp., *International Historical Statistics*, pp. 407–26.

TABLE 5

Value of U.S. Trade with the Cape Colony, 1865 (in thousands of pounds sterling)

Imports	Exports
52.3	171.9

Source: Cape of Good Hope Blue Book, 1865 (Cape Town, 1866), pp. AA 88–89.

TABLE 6a
South Africa's Imports
from the United States
(percentage share
of total)

Year	Percentage
1910	7.8
1920	18.0
1930	14.9
1938	19.1
1948	35.7
1950	15.2
1955	21.4
1958	17.5

TABLE 6b
South Africa's Exports
to the United States
(percentage share
of total)

Year	Percentage
1910	2.0
1920	7.9
1930	3.5
1938	2.4
1948	7.4
1955	8.0
1956	8.5
1958	7.2

Source: Our First Half Century 1910–1960 (Johannesburg, 1960), pp. 548–49.

TABLE 7
United States Trade with South Africa
General Merchandise
(in thousands of U.S. dollars)

Year	U.S. Exports	U.S. Imports
1902	25,789,000	460,000
1907	7,690,000	1,574,000
1911	12,842,000	2,160,000
1919	44,042,000	839,000
1920	60,939,000	6,640,000
1921	25,351,000	7,894,000
1922	20,910,000	8,203,000
1923	28,401,000	13,423,000
1924	36,020,000	7,727,000
1925	46,162,000	9,215,000
1928	59,013,000	9,179,000
1929	63,690,000	9,656,000
1933	22,050,000	3,895,000
1934	45,350,000	2,859,000
1935	52,860,000	3,850,000
1936	70,079,000	5,915,000
1937	88,723,000	14,402,000
1938	70,066,000	15,988,000
1939	69,145,000	28,721,000
1940	103,916,000	47,338,000
1941	186,980,000	66,181,000
1942	99,919,000	96,303,000
1943	152,036,000	88,443,000
1944	128,846,000	88,895,000
1945	131,130,000	103,893,000
1946	228,338,000	150,311,000
1947	413,938,000	111,119,000
1948	492,111,000	135,224,000
1949	266,049,000	116,351,000
1950	119,879,000	141,560,000
1951	247,200,000	138,000,000
1952	214,100,000	105,114,000
1953	207,381,000	91,774,000
1954	236,896,000	90,595,000
1955	267,643,000	95,561,000
1956	267,095,000	111,057,000
1957	284,824,000	100,968,000
1958	248,643,000	98,326,000

Source: U.S. Department of Commerce, *Statistical Abstracts of the United States* (1913–1959), nos. 35–80.

TABLE 8

Balance of Trade
with South Africa
(in millions of
U.S. dollars)

Year	Balance
1958	+41.8
1959	+11.3
1960	+76.3
1961	+19.2
1962	−35.6
1963	+18.9
1964	+153.0
1965	+207.3
1966	+138.0
1967	+185.5
1968	+199.8
1969	+262.5
1970	+274.7
1971	+335.9

Source: U.S. Department of State, *United States Trade with Africa* (Washington, D.C., 1972), November 7, 1972.

TABLE 9

United States–South Africa Trade Current
Account Transactions (in billions of U.S.
dollars)

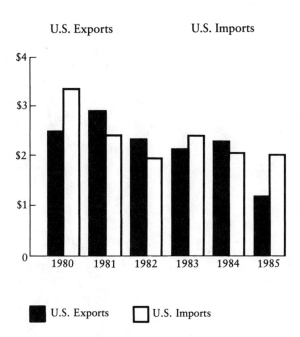

U.S. Exports   U.S. Imports

U.S. Exports   U.S. Imports

Source: U.S. Department of Commerce, *Statistical Abstracts of the United States* (1980–1985), nos. 101–106.

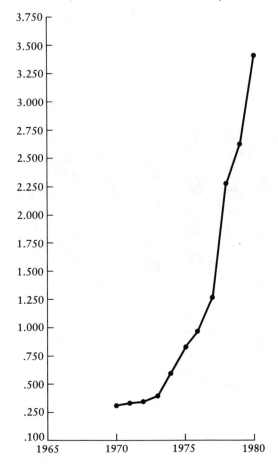

TABLE 10a
U.S. Imports from South Africa
(in millions of U.S. dollars)

TABLE 10b
U.S. Exports to South Africa (in millions of U.S. dollars)

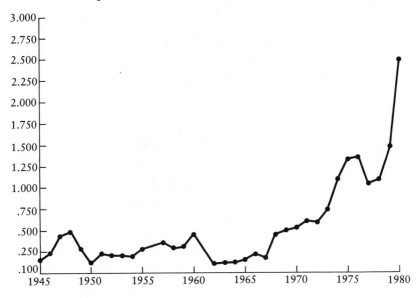

Source: U.S. Department of Commerce, *Statistical Abstracts of the United States* (1945–1980), nos. 66–101.

TABLE 11
Book Value of Private American Direct Dollar Investments in South Africa (U.S. dollars)

Year	Amount
1938	72.9 mn
1943	50.7 mn
1950	140.3 mn
1952	194.0 mn
1953	212.0 mn
1955	259.1 mn
1956	289.3 mn
1957	300.1 mn
1958	329.3 mn
1959	323.0 mn
1960	350.0 mn

TABLE 11 (Cont.)
Book Value of Private American Direct Dollar Investments in South Africa (U.S. dollars)

Year	Amount
1961	353.2 mn
1962	357.0 mn
1963	411.0 mn
1964	467.1 mn
1965	529.0 mn
1966	597.0 mn
1967	666.2 mn
1968	692.2 mn
1970	778.8 mn
1971	875.2 mn
1972	941.1 mn
1973	1.24 bn
1974	1.47 bn
1975	1.58 bn
1976	1.67 bn
1977	1.79 bn
1978	1.99 bn
1979	1.91 bn
1980	2.35 bn
1981	2.63 bn
1982	2.80 bn
1983	2.00 bn
1984	1.50 bn
1985	1.20 bn
1986	1.10 bn

Sources: Colin Legum, ed., *Africa: Contemporary Record: Annual Survey and Documents* (1972–77); *Africa South of the Sahara* (1980–85); *South Africa Year Book* (1957–71); "This is South Africa," *New York Times,* June 4, 1961, p. 9; Ann & Neva Seidman, *South Africa and United States Multinational Corporations,* U.S. Department of Commerce, p. 80; Bureau of Economic Analysis, Survey of Current Business (June 1987), p. 17.

TABLE 12

Percentage Rate of Return on United States Direct Investments in South Africa

Year	Rate of Return
1950	27.0
1960	17.5
1961	19.6
1962	19.9
1963	20.0
1964	18.6
1965	19.1
1966	20.6
1967	19.2
1968	17.3
1973	18.6
1974	17.9
1975	9.0
1979	18.0
1983	18.0

Sources: Colin Legum, ed., *Africa Contemporary Record* (1973–1979); Department of Political and Security Affairs, Unit of Apartheid, United Nations, *Foreign Investment in the Republic of South Africa* (New York, 1970), Annex, Table 18, p. 29.

TABLE 13
Top United States Employers in South Africa in 1987
(companies with majority ownership)

Company	Employees
Mobil Corporation	3,106
Goodyear Tire and Rubber Company	2,471
USG Corporation	2,239
RJR Nabisco	2,202
Steiner Corporation	2,000
Caltex Petroleum Corporation	2,140
Johnson & Johnson Company	1,376
Emhart Corporation	1,159
United Technologies Corporation	1,060
Minnesota Mining and Manufacturing Company	824
Xerox Corporation	824
Joy Manufacturing Company	800
Baker Hughes	771
Colgate-Palmolive Company	696
Crown Cork and Seal Company	693
Unisys Corporation	693
American Cyanamid Company	689
PepsiCo	688
Dresser Industries	665
Union Carbide Corporation	616

Source: Investor Responsibility Research Center, South Africa Review Service, *Divestment Action Roundup* (Washington, October 1985), p. 29; "Pullout Scheme," *The Wall Street Journal,* August 24, 1987, p. 18.

TABLE 14

Net Capital Outflows from South Africa
(in billions of U.S. dollars)

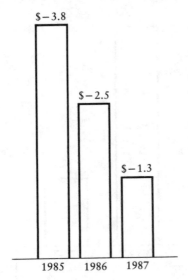

Sources: Barclays *Bank Business Brief* (Johannesburg, July
1986); p. 1; South African Reserve Bank, *Annual Report,*
1988, p. 40.

TABLE 15
South African Average Annual Change in Export Volumes (1975 prices)

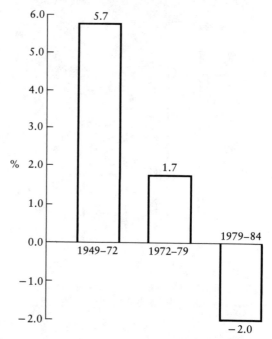

Source: Barclays Bank, *Business Brief* (Johannesburg, July 1986), p. 1.

TABLE 16
Annual Percentage
Growth of South
African GDP
(by volume)
at Market Prices

Year	Percentage
1964	9.5
1965	9.7
1966	8.5
1967	10.8
1968	7.4
1969	11.3
1970	8.9
1971	10.9
1972	12.2
1973	22.1
1974	19.5
1977	0.0
1978	3.2
1979	5.5
1980	8.0
1984	5.1
1985	−1.2
1986	0.9
1987	2.6

Sources: Republic of South Africa, Bureau of Statistics, *Statistical Data,* pp. 96–99. "South Africa Country Report," September 1, 1988, Frost & Sullivan (New York, 1988).

TABLE 17
South African Average Annual Growth
in Real GDP (1975 prices)

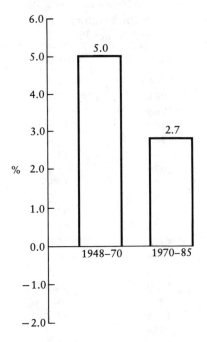

Source: Barclays Bank, *Business Brief*
(Johannesburg, July 1986), p. 1.

TABLE 18

Gold Production in South Africa

Year	Production kg.	Realized value (thousands of rands)
1900	10,852	2,964
1905	152,665	41,698
1910	234,252	63,983
1915	282,930	77,276
1920	253,756	91,212
1925	298,519	81,536
1930	333,316	91,040
1935	335,109	153,066
1940	436,895	235,981
1945	380,229	210,569
1950	361,849	289,552
1955	454,154	365,491
1960	665,085	536,019
1965	950,332	766,549
1970	1,000,417	831,223
1975	713,447	2,560,395
1979	703,473	5,842,003

Source: Chamber of Mines of South Africa, Annual Reports (1975–1976).

TABLE 19
International Price for
Gold per Fine Ounce
(annual average in
U.S. dollars)

Year	Price
pre-1972	21
1935–1972	35
1971	41
1972	58
1973	97
1974	159
1975	161
1976	125
1977	148
1978	193
1979	307
1980	613
1981	460
1982	376
1983	424
1984	360
1985	335

Sources: Intergold. International Gold Corporation, Ltd. (New York, 1985), p. 17; Louis du Boulay, *Gold 1984,* Consolidated Gold Fields PLC (London, 1984), p. 6.

TABLE 20

Krugerrands: Coins Sold and Revenue Earned in
U.S. Dollars

Year	Quantity (ounces)	Earnings
1970	211,018	7,958,000
1971	550,200	23,097,000
1972	543,700	32,097,000
1973	859,300	77,733,000
1974	3,203,675	533,812,000
1975	4,803,925	805,387,000
1976	3,004,945	394,317,000
1977	3,331,344	518,915,000
1978	6,012,293	1,201,290,000
1979	4,940,755	1,580,540,000
1980	3,142,500	1,909,580,000

Source: *Intergold.* International Gold Corporation, Ltd. (New York, 1985),
p. 19.

TABLE 21

Gold and Foreign Exchange Holdings in South Africa
(in millions of U.S. dollars)

Gold Holdings

1938	1947	1950	1953	1961	1963	1968
220	762	197	176	443	630	1,243

Foreign Exchange Holdings

1938	1947	1950	1953		1955	1961
38	249	279	116		302	248

1963	1968	1970	1980
96	168	346	726

Source: U.S. Department of Commerce, *Statistical Abstracts of the United States* 1965, no. 86 (Washington, D.C., 1965), p. 993; ibid., 1981, no. 102, p. 868.

TABLE 22
South Africa:
Average Annual
Rate of Inflation

Year	Rate
1945	3.5
1950	3.8
1960	3.5
1965	2.2
1970	3.3
1975	9.5
1979	12.1
1981	16.1
1983	12.6
1984	11.7
1985	16.2
1986	18.6
1987	16.1

Sources: Jill Nattrass *The South African Economy*, p. 253; Nedbank Group, *Guide to the Economy* (May 1986), p. 1; South Africa Country Report, September 1, 1988, Frost & Sullivan (New York, 1988).

TABLE 23

U.S. Supply of Ten Critical Materials
Import/Source as a Percentage of 1983–85 Average Consumption

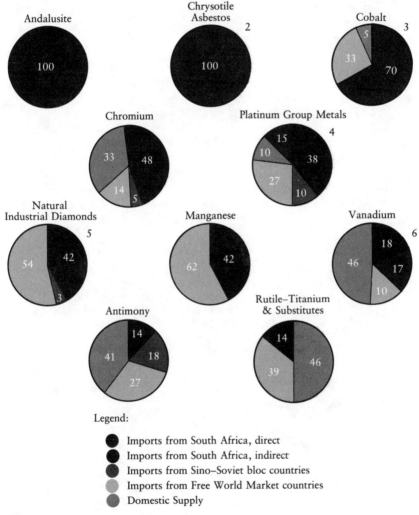

Legend:

- ● Imports from South Africa, direct
- ● Imports from South Africa, indirect
- ● Imports from Sino–Soviet bloc countries
- ● Imports from Free World Market countries
- ● Domestic Supply

Notes:

1. Percentages may not equal 100 due to stock adjustments, proprietary data, or fractional input.
2. Zimbabwe is the only source. Export through South Africa.
3. Sources, Zaire (49%) and Zambia (21%), export through South Africa.
4. 15% of supply is from U.K. where source of raw material is South Africa.
5. DeBeers Central Selling Organization, a South African Company, markets 80–85% of all Diamond Production.
6. 1984 data.

Source: Datasource; Bureau of Mines, December 1986.

Select Bibliography

MANUSCRIPT SOURCES

Occasionally source materials are available in a single location or in a very limited number of venues. In such cases I have identified the location with the following abbreviations:

GREAT BRITAIN

Rhodes House, Oxford University (RH)

UNITED STATES

Department of Commerce, Washington, D.C. (DOC)
Hoover Institution Library, Stanford (HIL)
National Archives, Washington, D.C. (NAW)
Sterling Library, Yale University (YUL)

SOUTH AFRICA

Cory Library, Rhodes University (CL)
Cullen Library, University of the Witwatersrand (CLW)
Killie Campbell Library, Durban (KCL)
Natal Archives Depot, Pietermaritzburg (NAD)
Strang Library, Johannesburg Public Library (JPL)
South African Library, Cape Town (SAL)
Transvaal Archives Depot, Pretoria (TAD)

ZIMBABWE

National Archives, Harare (NAZ)

SOUTH AFRICA

BIBLIOGRAPHIES

Any study of this nature must commence with an examination of key biblio-
graphical guides.
Duignan, Peter. *Handbook of American Resources for African Studies.* Stanford,
1967. An excellent guide to libraries with large collections of Africana.
Keto, C. Tsehloane. *American–South African Relations, 1794–1980, Review
and Select Bibliography.* Columbus, 1981. A useful work.
Mendelssohn, Sidney, ed. *Mendelssohn's South African Bibliography.* 2 vols.
London, 1968. Comprehensive catalog of works published in the 19th cen-
tury.
Witherell, Julian, comp. *The United States and Africa: Guide to U.S. Official
Documents, 1785–1975.* Washington, D.C., 1978. A source for government
publications on Africa.

BIOGRAPHICAL RESOURCES

REFERENCE WORKS

These include reasonably accurate and complete biographies.
De Kock, W. J., ed. *Dictionary of South African Biography.* 2 vols. Cape Town,
1972.
De Kock, W. J., ed. *South African Who's Who: Social, Business, and Farming
for 1921–1922.* Johannesburg, 1922.
Karis, Thomas, and Gwendolen M. Carter. *From Protest to Challenge: Docu-
mentary History of African Politics in South Africa, 1882–1964.* Vol. 4.
Stanford, 1972. A classic source.
Lipschutz, Mark, and R. Kent Rasmussen. *Dictionary of African Historical
Biography.* Berkeley, 1986.
Rosenthal, Eric, comp. *Southern African Dictionary of National Biography.*
London, 1966.
Rotberg, Robert I., and Miles F. Shore. *The Founder: Cecil Rhodes and the
Pursuit of Power.* New York, 1988.

MEMOIRS

These are not very reliable, and only a few were utilized.
Blake, J. Y. F. *A West Pointer with the Boers.* Boston, 1903.
Hammond, John Hays. *The Autobiography of John Hays Hammond.* 2 vols.
New York, 1935.
Kruger, Paul. *Memoirs of Paul Kruger.* New York, 1902.
Williams, Gardner F. *The Diamond Mines of South Africa.* New York, 1902.

GENERAL HISTORIES

Works that contain important information on the growth of the South African economy include:
Davenport, T. R. H. *South Africa: A Modern History.* Toronto, 1987.
Keppel-Jones, Arthur. *South Africa: A Short History.* London, 1975.
Oliver, Roland, ed. *Cambridge History of Africa.* Vol. 7. London, 1986.
Wilson, Monica, and Leonard M. Thompson, eds. *Oxford History of South Africa.* 2 vols. London, 1971.

POLITICAL ECONOMY

Several scholarly works offer able analyses of South African political economy:
Birmingham, David, and Phyllis M. Martin, eds. *History of Central Africa.* Vol. 2. New York, 1983.
Horwitz, R. *The Political Economy of South Africa.* London, 1968.
Magubane, Bernard M. *The Political Economy of Race and Class in South Africa.* New York, 1979.
Nyaggah, Mougo, and Agrippah Mugomba, eds. *Independence Without Freedom: The Political Economy of Colonial Education in Southern Africa.* Santa Barbara, 1980.
O'Meara, Dan. *Volkskapitalisme: Class, Capital and Ideology in the Development of Afrikaner Nationalism, 1934–1948.* Johannesburg, 1983.
Stadler, Alf. *The Political Economy of Modern South Africa.* New York, 1987.
Stultz, Newell. *Afrikaner Politics in South Africa, 1934–1948.* Berkeley, 1974.
Van Onselen, Charles. *Studies in the Social and Economic History of the Witwatersrand, 1886–1914.* 2 vols. Johannesburg, 1982.
Yudelman, David. *The Emergence of Modern South Africa.* Westport, Ct., 1983.

THE UNITED STATES AND SOUTH AFRICA

GENERAL HISTORIES

Of the limited number of major general works on this subject, the best are:
Chester, Edward. *Clash of Titans: Africa and U.S. Foreign Policy.* Maryknoll, N.Y., 1974.
Clendenen, Clarence, Robert Collins, and Peter Duignan. *Americans in Africa, 1865–1900.* Stanford, 1966.
Clendenen, Clarence, and Peter Duignan. *Americans in Black Africa up to 1865.* Stanford, 1964.
Duignan, Peter, and L. H. Gann. *The United States and Africa.* London, 1984.
Goldschmidt, Walter, ed. *The United States and Africa.* New York, 1958.
Hance, William, ed. *Southern Africa and the United States.* New York, 1968.

Howard, Lawrence Cabot. "American Involvement in Africa South of the Sahara, 1800–1860." Ph.D. dissertation. Harvard University, 1956.
Howe, Russell Warren. *Along the Afric Shore: A Historical Review of Two Centuries of U.S.–African Relations.* New York, 1975.
Minter, William. *King Solomon's Mines Revisited: Western Interests and the Burdened History of Southern Africa.* New York, 1986.
Noer, Thomas J. *Black Liberation: The U.S. and White Rule in Africa, 1948–1968.* St. Louis, 1985.

ECONOMIC HISTORY

There are very few good general surveys of the economic history of South Africa, and not one specifically examines the role of Americans in the Republic's economic development. Nevertheless, I found valuable information in the following:

Alford, B. W. E., and C. E. Harvey. "Copperbelt Merger: The Formation of the Rhokana Corporation, 1930–1932." *Business History Review* 54, 3 (Autumn 1980): 66–84.
Coleman, Francis, ed. *Economic History of South Africa.* Pretoria, 1981.
De Kiewiet, C. W. *A History of South Africa: Social and Economic.* London, 1957.
De Waal, Enid. "American Technology in South African Gold Mining Before 1899." *Optima* 33, 2 (1985):88–96.
First, Ruth, J. Steel, and C. Gurney. *The South African Connection: Western Investment in Apartheid.* New York, 1972.
Frankel, S. H. *Capital Investment in Africa: Its Course and Effects.* London, 1938.
Goodfellow, D. M. *A Modern Economic History of South Africa.* London, 1931.
Houghton, D. Hobart *The South African Economy.* London, 1973.
Houghton, D. Hobart, and Jenifer Dagut, eds. *Source Material on the South African Economy, 1860–1970.* 3 vols. Cape Town, 1972.
Kooy, Marcelle, ed. *Studies in Economics and Economic History.* Durham, N.C., 1972.
Lipton, Merle. *Capitalism and Apartheid, 1910–1984.* London, 1985.
Marais, G. "Structural Changes in Manufacturing Industry, 1916 to 1975." *South African Journal of Economics* 49, 1 (1981):11–32.
Nattrass, Jill. *The South African Economy.* Cape Town, 1982.
Schumann, C. G. W. *Structural Changes and Business Cycles in South Africa, 1806–1936.* London, 1938.
Spilhaus, M. Whiting. *South Africa in the Making, 1652 to 1806.* Cape Town, 1966.

AMERICAN PHILANTHROPIC ENTERPRISE

While there is a paucity of works that deal specifically with this topic, I was able to cull relevant information from the following:

Arnove, Robert F., ed. *Philanthropy and Cultural Imperialism.* Boston, 1980.

Berman, Edward H. *The Influence of the Carnegie, Ford, and Rockefeller Foundations on American Foreign Policy: The Ideology of Philanthropy.* Albany, 1983.

Bolling, Landrum R. *Private Foreign Aid: U.S. Philanthropy for Relief and Development.* Boulder, 1982.

Curti, Merle. *American Philanthropy Abroad.* New Brunswick, 1963.

Ferguson, Milton J. *Libraries in the Union of South Africa, Rhodesia and Kenya Colony.* New York, 1929.

Grosskopf. J. F. W., et al. *The Poor White Problem in South Africa: Report of the Carnegie Commission.* 5 vols. Stellenbosch, 1932.

Jones, Thomas Jesse. *Educational Adaptations: Report of Ten Years' Work of the Phelps-Stokes Fund, 1910–1920.* New York, 1921.

Jones, Thomas Jesse. *Education in East Africa: A Study of East, Central, and South Africa.* New York, 1924.

King, Kenneth James. *Pan-Africanism and Education: A Study of Race Philanthropy and Education in the Southern States of America and East Africa.* Oxford, 1971.

Kallaway, Peter, ed. *Apartheid and Education.* Johannesburg, 1984.

Kitchen, Helen, ed. *The Educated African: A Country by Country Survey of Educational Development in Africa.* New York, 1962.

Lewis, L. J. *Phelps-Stokes Reports on Education in Africa.* London, 1962.

Murphy, E. Jefferson. *Creative Philanthropy: Carnegie Corporation and Africa, 1953–1973.* New York, 1976.

Murray, A. Victor. *The School in the Bush: A Critical Study of the Theory and Practice of Native Education in Africa.* London, 1938.

Oldham, J. H. *White and Black in South Africa.* London, 1930.

Smith, Edwin. *Aggrey of Africa: A Study in Black and White.* Freeport, 1929.

Thomas, Franklin, et al. *South Africa: Time Running Out.* Berkeley, 1987.

MISSIONARY ENTERPRISE

This has been an extremely vital aspect of American activity in South Africa, and there is a vast body of literature on the subject, though as yet no comprehensive history. The most important works include:

Albert, Bill, and Adrian Graves, eds. *Crisis and Change in the International Sugar Economy, 1860–1914.* Boston, 1975.

American Board Mission. *Annual Reports of the Mission to the Board in Boston, 1848–1897.* Vol. 41. NAD.

Anonymous. "Frederick Brainerd Bridgman: A Modern Pioneer Missionary." The American Board, Envelope Series 29, 4. Boston, 1927. NAD.

Bird, John, ed. *The Annals of Natal, 1495–1848.* 2 vols. Pietermaritzburg, 1888. NAD.

Booth, Alan R., ed. *Journal of the Reverend George Champion.* Cape Town, 1967.

Brookes, Edgar, and Colin DeB. Webb, *A History of Natal.* Pietermaritzburg, 1965.

Christofersen, Arthur F. *Adventuring with God: The Story of the American Board Mission in South Africa.* Durban, 1968. KCL

Davies, Horton, and H. W. Shepard, eds. *South African Missions, 1800–1950.* New York, 1954.

Dhlomo, Oscar D. "A Survey of Some Aspects of the Educational Activities of the American Board of Commissioners for Foreign Missions in Natal as Reflected in the History of Amanzimtoti, 1835–1956." M.Ed. essay. University of Natal, 1975. KCL.

Elphick, Richard. "Africans and the Christian Campaign in South Africa." In Howard Lamar and Leonard Thompson, eds., *The Frontier in History: North America and Southern Africa Compared.* New Haven, 1981.

Etherington, Norman. *Preachers, Peasants and Politics in Southeast Africa, 1835 to 1880.* London, 1978.

Goodsell, Fred Field. *You Shall Be My Witness.* Boston, 1959.

Goodsell, Fred Field. *Among the Bantu in Africa: Story of the American Board of Commissioners for Foreign Missions South of the Equator, 1835–1960.* Waban, 1962. KCL.

Groves, C. P. *The Planting of Christianity in Africa.* Vol. 1. London, 1948.

Grout, Lewis. *Zulu-land: Or, Life Among the Zulu.* Philadelphia, 1864. KCL.

Hance, Gertrude R. *The Zulu Yesterday and Today: Twenty-Nine Years in South Africa.* New York, 1916. KCL

Hill, Patricia R. *The World Their Household: The American Women's Foreign Missionary Movement and Cultural Transformation, 1870–1920.* New York, 1985.

Kotzé, D. J. *Letters of the American Missionaries, 1835–1838.* Cape Town, 1950. SAL.

McCord, James Bennett. *My Patients Were Zulus.* New York, 1951.

MacKenzie, K. M. *The Robe and the Sword: The Methodist Church and the Rise of American Imperialism, 1865–1900.* Washington, D.C., 1961.

Mackeurton, Graham. *Cradle Days of Natal, 1492–1845.* Pietermaritzburg, 1948. NAD.

Mann, Robert James. *The Colony of Natal.* London, 1859.

Page, Carol A. "Colonial Reaction to African Methodist Episcopal Missionaries in South Africa." In Sylvia Jacobs, ed., *Black Americans and the Missionary Movement in Africa.* Westport, 1982.

Phillips, Ray E. *The Bantu Are Coming.* New York, 1930.

Phillips, Ray E. *The Bantu in the City.* Lovedale, South Africa, 1937.

Du Plessis, J. *A History of Christian Missions in South Africa.* London, 1911.

Ross, Andrew. *John Philip (1775–1851).* Aberdeen, 1986.

Smith, Edwin. *The Life and Times of Daniel Lindley, 1801–1880.* New York, 1962.

Tracy, Joseph. *History of the American Board of Commissioners for Foreign Missions.* New York, 1842.

Tyler, Josiah. *Forty Years Among the Zulus.* Boston, 1891.
Verbeek, Jennifer and Alistair. *Victorian and Edwardian Natal.* Pietermaritzburg, 1982.
Washington, James Melvin. *Frustrated Fellowship: The Black Quest for Social Power.* Macon, 1968.
Wood, Agnes. *Shine Where You Are: A History of Inanda Seminary, 1869–1969.* Lovedale, 1972. KCL.
Wilder, G. A. *White African.* Bloomfield N.J., 1933. KCL
Welsh, David. *The Roots of Segregation: Native Policy in Natal, 1845–1910.* Cape Town, 1971.

CULTURAL STUDIES

A number of books has been published touching upon the ways in which Americans and South Africans have interacted culturally and how American attitudes and perceptions of South Africa and its peoples have evolved. I found the following to be most useful for this study:

Barratt, John, and A. O. Hero, eds. *The American People and South Africa.* Lexington, Mass., 1980.
Bissell, Richard E. *South Africa and the United States: The Erosion of an Influence Relationship.* New York, 1982.
Beniger, James R. *The Control Revolution: Technological and Economic Origins of the Information Society.* Cambridge, 1986.
Bigelow, Poultney. *A White Man's Africa.* New York, 1898.
Brown, William Harvey. *On the South African Frontier: The Adventures and Observations of an American in Mashonaland and Matabeleland.* New York, 1899.
Cell, John W. *The Highest Stage of White Supremacy: The Origins of Segregation in South Africa and the American South.* New York, 1982.
Champion, George. "Letter to Professor Benjamin Silliman of Yale College on the Topography, Scenery, Geology, and Climate of the Cape of Good Hope." *American Journal of Science* 29 (1836): 67–80. YUL.
Coplan, David B. *In Township Tonight: South Africa's Black City Music and Theater.* New York, 1985.
Davis, Richard Harding. *With Boer Armies in South Africa.* New York, 1900.
Eltis, David, and James Walvin, eds. *The Abolition of the Atlantic Slave Trade: Origins and Effects in Europe, Africa, and the Americas.* Madison, 1981.
Fredrickson, George M. *White Supremacy: A Comparative Study in American and South African History.* New York, 1981.
Gutsche, Thelma. *The Historical and Social Significance of the Motion Picture in South Africa, 1895–1940.* Cape Town, 1977. JPL.
Herskovits, M. J. "The Image of Africa in the United States." *Journal of Human Relations* 10, 2 (1962):19–30.
Kitchen, Helen, ed. *Africa, From Mystery to Maze.* Lexington, 1976.

Jacobs, Sylvia. *The African Nexus: Black American Perspectives on the European Partitioning of Africa, 1880–1920.* Westport, Ct., 1981.

McCarthy, Michael. *Dark Continent: Africa as Seen by Americans.* Westport. Ct., 1983.

Marks, Shula. *The Ambiguities of Dependence in South Africa.* Baltimore, 1986.

Seitz, Donald C. *Joseph Pulitzer: His Life and Letters.* New York, 1924.

Smyth, Rosaleen. "Factors Inhibiting the Development of Feature Film Production in English-Speaking Africa." Paper read at African Studies Association of Australia and Pacific (ASAAP) meeting, Melbourne, August 27, 1986.

Thompson, Kristin. *Exporting Entertainment: America in the World Film Market, 1907–34.* London, 1985.

BLACK AMERICANS IN SOUTH AFRICA

Research on this subject, especially at the turn of the century, is particularly revealing. I found information in:

Chirenje, J. M. *Ethiopianism and Afro-Americans in Southern Africa, 1883–1916.* Baton Rouge, 1987.

De Waal, Enid. "American Black Residents and Visitors in the S.A.R. before 1899." *South African Historical Journal* 6 (November 1974): 52–56.

Fatton, Robert, Jr. *Black Consciousness in South Africa.* Albany, 1986.

Franklin, John Hope. *George Washington Williams.* Chicago, 1985.

Gatewood, William B. "Black Americans and the Boer War, 1899–1902." *South Atlantic Quarterly* 75 (1976):44–71.

Hill, Robert A., and G. A. Piro. "Africa for the Africans: The Garvey Movement in South Africa, 1920–1940." In Shula Marks and Stanley Trapido, eds., *The Politics of Race, Class, and Nationalism in Twentieth-Century South Africa.* London, 1987.

Kilson, Martin, and Adelaide Hill, eds. *Apropos of Africa: Sentiments of Negro Leaders of Africa, 1800s to 1950s.* London, 1969.

Jacobs, Sylvia. *Black Americans and the Missionary Movement in Africa.* Westport, Ct., 1982.

Martin, Tony. *The Pan-African Connection: From Slavery to Garvey.* Dover, 1983.

Williams, Walter Lee. "Black American Attitudes Toward Africa: The Missionary Movement, 1877–1900." Ph.D. dissertation. University of North Carolina, 1974.

AMERICAN MULTINATIONAL CORPORATIONS IN SOUTH AFRICA

While much has been written on the emergence of American MNCs, very few scholars have examined their activities in South Africa—how they got there and the role they played. For information on this topic I turned to the following:

Africa. The South African Market: 1960. New York, 1960.

Bailey, L. Scott. *General Motors: The First Seventy-Five Years of Transportation Products.* Detroit, 1983.

Booth, Alan R. *The United States Experience in South Africa, 1784–1870.* Cape Town, 1976.

Bradley, Kenneth. *Copper Venture: The Discovery and Development of Roan Antelope and Mufulira* London, 1952.

Broehl, Wayne G., Jr. *John Deere's Company.* New York, 1984.

Bursk, Edward C., Donald T. Clark, and Ralph W. Hidy, eds. *The World of Business.* Vol. 2. New York, 1962.

Chandler, Alfred D. "The Beginnings of Big Business in American Industry." *Business History Review* 33, 1 (1959):9–22.

Chandler, Alfred D. *Giant Enterprise: Ford, General Motors, and the Automobile Industry.* New York, 1964.

Clark, Victor S. *History of Manufactures in the United States, 1893–1928.* Vol. 3. New York, 1949.

Cleveland, Richard J. *Voyages and Commercial Enterprises of the Sons of New England.* New York, 1857.

Clough, Shepard B. *A Century of American Life Insurance: A History of the Mutual Life Insurance Company of New York, 1843–1943.* New York, 1946.

Cooper, Allen D. *U.S. Economic Power and Political Influence in Namibia, 1700–1982.* Boulder, 1985.

Davies, Robert Bruce. *Peacefully Working to Conquer the World: Singer Sewing Machines in Foreign Markets, 1854–1920.* New York, 1976.

Davis, Merle. *Modern Industry and the African.* New York, 1933.

Dunn, Robert W. *American Foreign Investments.* New York, 1926.

Dunning, John H. *American Investments in British Manufacturing Industry.* London, 1958.

Eysenbach, Mary Locke. *American Manufactured Exports, 1879–1914.* New York, 1976.

Gladwin, Thomas N., and Ingo Walter, eds. *Multinationals Under Fire.* New York, 1980.

Glover, John. ed., *The Development of American Industries.* New York: 1959.

Greenfield, Sidney M., ed. *Entrepreneurs in Cultural Context.* Albuquerque, 1979.

Hatch, Alden. *American Express: A Century of Service.* Garden City, N.Y., 1950.

Hidy, Ralph W., and Muriel E. Hidy. *History of the Standard Oil Company (New Jersey): Pioneering in Big Business, 1882–1911.* New York, 1952.

James, Barrie G. *The Future of the Multinational Pharmaceutical Industry.* New York, 1977.

Jenkin, T. Nicol. *Report on the General Trades of South Africa.* London, 1902.

Jenkins, Rhys. *Transnational Corporations and Uneven Development.* New York, 1987.

Kenwood, A. G., and A. L. Lougheed. *The Growth of the International Economy, 1820–1980.* London, 1983.

Keto, Clement Tsehloane. "American Involvement in South Africa, 1870–1915: The Role of Americans in the Creation of Modern South Africa." Ph.D. dissertation. Georgetown University, 1972.

Koether, George. *Ingersoll-Rand: The Building of Men, Machines, and a Company.* Woodcliff Lake, N.J., 1971.

Larson, Henrietta, Evelyn H. Knowlton, and Charles Popple. *History of the Standard Oil Company (New Jersey): New Horizons, 1927–1950.* New York, 1959.

Leape, Jonathan, Bo Baskin, and S. Underhill. *Business in the Shadow of Apartheid: A Survey of U.S. Companies.* Lexington 1984.

Leonard, Richard. *Computers in South Africa: A Survey of U.S. Companies.* New York, 1978.

Lewis, Cleona. *America's Stake in International Investments.* Washington, D.C., 1938.

Lewis, Cleona. *The United States and Foreign Investment Problems.* Washington, D.C., 1948.

Litvak, I. A., and C. J. Maule, eds. *Foreign Investment: The Experience of Host Countries.* New York, 1970.

Mackler, Ian. *Pattern for Profit in Southern Africa.* Toronto, 1972.

McHenry, Donald. *United States Firms in South Africa.* Bloomington, 1975.

McKenzie, F. A. *The American Invaders.* London, 1902.

Marquette, Arthur. *Brands, Trademarks, and Good Will: The Story of the Quaker Oats Company.* New York, 1967.

Marton, Katherine. *Multinationals, Technology, and Industrialization: Implications and Impact in Third World Countries.* Lexington, 1986.

Mobil Oil Corporation. *Mobil in South Africa.* New York, 1972.

Moolman, H. M., ed. *South African–American Survey.* New York, 1947.

Myers, Desaix. *U.S. Business in South Africa.* Bloomington, 1980.

Nelson, Theodore. "Republic of South Africa." In Bernard Blankheimer, ed., *A Special Report on African Sales Frontier for U.S. Business.* Department of Commerce Supplement. Washington, D.C., March 1963.

O'Reilly, Maurice. *The Goodyear Story.* Elmsford, N.Y., 1983.

Pound, Arthur. *The Turning Wheel: The Story of General Motors Through Twenty-Five Years, 1908–1933.* Garden City, 1934.

Pratt, Edmund, Jr. *Pfizer: Bringing Science to Life.* New York, 1985.

Price Waterhouse. "Doing Business in South Africa." New York, 1972.

Razis, Victor. *The American Connection: The Influence of United States Business on South Africa.* New York, 1986.

Rogers, Barbara. *White Wealth and Black Poverty: American Investments in Southern Africa.* Westport, Ct., 1976.

Rosenberg, Emily, *Spreading the American Dream: American Economic and Cultural Expansion, 1890–1945.* New York, 1982.

Rosenthal, Eric. *The Rolling Years: Fifty Years of General Motors in South Africa.* Johannesburg, 1976.

Seidman, Ann and Neva. *South Africa and United States Multinational Corporations.* Westport, Ct., 1977.

Sekaly, Raymond R. *Transnationalization of the Automotive Industry.* Ottawa, 1981.

Sklar, Richard. *Corporate Power in an African State.* Berkeley, 1975.

Smith, Stewart. *U.S. Neocolonialism in Africa.* New York, 1974. *South African Production.* Johannesburg, 1967.

Stackpole, Edouard. *Whales and Destiny: The Rivalry Between America, Britain, and France for Control of the Southern Whale Fishery, 1785–1825.* Amherst, 1972.

Starbuck, Alexander. *History of the American Whale Fishery.* Waltham, 1878.

Stead, W. T. *The Americanization of the World.* London, 1902.

Stopford, John M., and John H. Dunning. *The World Directory of Multinational Enterprises, 1982–83.* Detroit, 1983.

Wendel, C. H. *One Hundred and Fifty Years of International Harvester.* Sarasota, Fla., 1981.

Wilkins, Mira. *The Maturing of Multinational Enterprise: American Business Abroad, 1914–1970.* Cambridge, Mass., 1974.

Wilkins, Mira, and Frank E. Hill. *American Business Abroad: Ford on Six Continents.* Detroit, 1964.

AMERICAN INVESTMENTS

While tracking investments in South Africa is tedious and enormously time-consuming work, requiring careful scrutiny of mainly government publications, I was able to cull valuable information from the following:

GOVERNMENT PUBLICATIONS

Clark, Dick, et al. *U.S. Corporate Interests in South Africa, Report to the Committee on Foreign Relations.* U.S. Senate, 95th Cong., 2nd sess. Washington, D.C., 1978.

House Committee on Foreign Affairs. *Hearings on U.S.–South African Relations.* 89th Congress, 2nd session, House Report 2112. Washington, D.C., 1966.

Investment in the Union of South Africa: Conditions and Outlook for U.S. Investors, 1953–1961. New York, 1969.

Moolman, H. M., ed. *South African–American Survey, 1947.* New York, 1947.

Sammone, Robert L., to Director of Foreign Reporting Services. "American Capital Investment in South Africa," April 22, 1948, U.S. Department of Commerce Washington, D.C., 1948.

South African Industry and Trade, 1907–1957: Golden Jubilee Number. Vol. 53, no. 5. Pretoria, 1957.

U.S. Department of Commerce. *American Direct Investments in Foreign Countries.* Bulletin no. 731. Washington, D.C., 1930.

U.S. Department of Commerce. *American Direct Investments in Foreign Countries in 1936.* Washington, D.C., 1938.

U.S. Treasury Department. *Census of American-Owned Assets in Foreign Countries.* Washington, D.C., 1930.

OTHER SOURCES

Bhatt, U. D. "Relations of Governments and Private Interests with South Africa." *United Nations Unit on Apartheid* 42, 71, Notes and Documents. October 1971.

Goldberg, Glenn S. *IRRC Directory of U.S. Corporations in South Africa.* Washington, D.C., 1982.

Pillay, Vella. "The Role of Gold in the Economy of Apartheid South Africa." United Nations Centre Against Apartheid. *Notes and Documents* (March 1981). New York, 1981.

Walke, Roger, and Richard Knight. *Unified List of U.S. Companies with Investments or Loans in South Africa and Namibia.* New York, 1985.

AMERICAN ECONOMIC DIPLOMACY

There has been a number of worthwhile studies on this subject, which includes sanctions and disinvestment. The ones I used included:

Bevans, Charles I., comp. *Treaties and Other International Agreements of the United States, 1776–1949.* Vol. 10. Washington, D.C., 1972.

Branaman, Brenda. "South African Issues for U.S. Policy." Issue Brief no. IB 80032. Washington, D.C., 1984.

Brent, R. Stephen. "The Reagan Policy Toward South Africa." Paper read at the Roundtable, session no. 5, the Lehrman Institute. New York, March 5, 1985.

Carter, G. M., and Patrick O'Meara, eds. *Southern Africa: The Continuing Crisis.* Bloomington, 1979.

Clough, Michael. "Beyond Sanctions: Reorienting U.S. Policy on Southern Africa." *Critical Issues,* vol. 3. Council on Foreign Relations. New York, 1988.

Coker, Christopher. *The U.S. and South Africa, 1968–1985: Constructive Engagement and Its Critics.* Durham, N.C., 1986.

Danaher, Kevin. *The Political Economy of U.S. Policy Towards South Africa.* Boulder, 1985.

Doxey, Margaret. *Economic Sanctions and International Enforcement.* New York, 1980.

Ferguson, John H. *American Diplomacy and the Boer War.* Philadelphia, 1939.

Glennon, John P., ed. *Foreign Relations of the United States, 1952–1954.* Vol. 11. Washington, D.C., 1983.

Greenberg, Sanford D. "U.S. Policy Toward the Republic of South Africa, 1945–1964." Ph.D. dissertation. Harvard University, 1965.

International Economics Seminar. *South Africa: Myths and Realities of Divestiture.* New York, 1985.

Jackson, Henry F. *From the Congo to Soweto: U.S. Foreign Policy Toward Africa Since 1960.* New York, 1982.

The Kissinger Study of Southern Africa: National Security Study Memorandum 39. Westport, Ct., 1976.

Lemarchand, René, ed., *American Policy in South Africa: The Stakes and Stance.* Washington, D.C., 1976.

Noer, Thomas J. *Black Liberation: The U.S. and White Rule in Africa, 1948–1968.* St. Louis, 1985.

Oye, Kenneth, Robert Lieber, and Donald Rothchild. *Eagle Resurgent: The Reagan Era in American Foreign Policy.* Boston, 1983.

Parrini, Carl P. *Heir to Empire: U.S. Economic Diplomacy, 1916–1923.* Pittsburgh, 1969.

Pastor, Robert. *Congress and the Politics of U.S. Foreign Economic Policy: 1929–1976.* Berkeley, 1980.

Prinsloo, Daan. *United States Foreign Policy and the Republic of South Africa.* Pretoria, 1978.

Reynolds, J. N. *Voyage of the "Potomac", 1831–34.* New York, 1834.

Semmes, R. *Two Years in the Alabama.* London, 1869.

Slawecki, Leon M. S. "The Development of U.S. Foreign Policy Toward South Africa, 1948–1963." Ph.D. dissertation Yale University, 1964.

Trevelyan, G. M. *British History in the Nineteenth Century, 1782–1919.* New York, 1962.

U.S. Department of State. *Papers Relating to the Foreign Relations of the United States, 1929.* Vol. 3. Washington, D.C., 1944. NAW.

U.S. War Department. *Reports on Military Operations: South Africa.* Washington, D.C., 1901. NAW.

TRADE AND COMMERCE

This subject, which includes shipping, banking, and the general financing of trade between South Africa and the United States, is usually embedded in broader works. I found the most useful government publications in the library of the U.S. Department of Commerce (DOC) and the National Archives in Washington (NAW) as well as in the Sterling Library at Yale University (YUL). I drew upon:

GOVERNMENT SOURCES

Cutler, B. S., to W. C. Redfield. "Markets for Agricultural Machinery in South Africa." August 1, 1917. U.S. Bureau of Foreign Commerce. *Reports from the Consuls.* Washington, D.C., 1918. YUL.

Department of Agriculture (South Africa). *Handbook of Agricultural Statistics 1904–1950. Economics and Marketing.* Pretoria, 1960. TAD.

Dickens, Paul D. *American Direct Investments in Foreign Countries in 1936.* Bulletin no. 725. Washington, D.C., 1938. DOC.

General Agreement on Tariffs and Trade. *International Trade, 1981–82.* (Annual.) Geneva, 1982.

Hollis, George F. "Commerce and Agriculture in Cape Colony." U.S. Bureau of Manufactures. *Reports from the Consuls,* no. 134, November 1891. Washington, D.C., 1891. YUL.

Hollis, Stanley W. "American Trade with Natal." U.S. Bureau of Manufactures. *Reports from the Consuls,* no. 141, June 1892. Washington, D.C., 1892. YUL.

Mitchell, B. R., comp. *International Historical Statistics: Africa and Asia.* New York, 1981.

Siler, James W. "Mining Laws of the South African Republic." U.S. Bureau of Manufactures. *Reports from the Consuls,* no. 93, May 1888. Washington, D.C., 1888. NAW.

Stevenson, P. J., to Director, Bureau of Foreign Commerce. July 20, 1921. Washington, D.C., 1921. DOC.

Stevenson, P. J., to A. G. Goldsmith, Opportunities in South Africa. June 6, 1922. U.S. Department of Commerce. Washington, D.C., 1922. DOC.

U.S. Department of Commerce. *Statistical Abstracts of the United States,* nos. 35–102. Washington, D.C., 1913–1980. (Annual.)

U.S. Department of Commerce. *American Direct Investments in Foreign Countries in 1930.* Bulletin no. 731. Washington, D.C., 1930. DOC.

U.S. Department of Commerce. *Trade of the United States with the Union of South Africa., International Reference Service* 4, 58 (October 1947). Washington, D.C., 1947. DOC.

U.S. Department of Commerce. *Union of South Africa. Business Information Service.* World Trade Series, no. 40 (June 1951). Washington, D.C., 1951. DOC.

U.S. Department of Commerce. *Commercial Relations of the United States with Foreign Countries 1855–1902.* vol. 20, 1903. Special Agents Series no. 199. Washington, D.C., 1903. DOC.

U.S. Department of Commerce. *Exporters' Digest and International Trade Review* 19, 9 (September 1945). Washington, D.C., 1945. DOC.

U.S. Department of State. *Monthly Consular and Trade Reports* (November 1909). Washington, D.C., 1909. NAW.

U.S. Department of State. *Commerce and Manufactures. Consular Reports,* vol. 67 (September–December 1900). Washington, D.C., 1900. NAW.

U.S. Department of State. *Reports from the Consuls of the United States,* vol. 39 (May–August 1892). Washington, D.C., 1892. NAW.

U.S. Department of State. *Despatches from U.S. Consuls in Cape Town* (1799–1853), Document no. 205. Washington, D.C., 1870. Reel 1, RG 59 T191 YUL.

U.S. Department of State. *Despatches from U.S. Consuls in Pretoria (1898–1906).* Part 1: 1898–1899. Washington, D.C., 1907. NAW.

U.S. Department of State. *Despatches from U.S. Consuls in Pretoria (1898–1906)*. Part 2: 1900–1903. Washington, D.C., 1907. NAW.
U.S. Department of State. *The Trade Debate*. Special Report no. 147, Washington, D.C., 1978.

SECONDARY SOURCES

Albion, Robert Greenhalgh. *Seaports South of the Sahara*. New York, 1959.
Berridge, G. R. *The Politics of the South African Run: European Shipping and Pretoria*. Oxford, 1987.
Carosso, Vincent P. *Investment Banking in America*. Cambridge, Mass, 1970.
Carosso, Vincent P. *The Morgans: Private International Bankers, 1854–1913*. Cambridge, Mass., 1987.
Cleveland, Harold van B., and Thomas F. Huertas. *Citibank, 1812–1970*. Cambridge, Mass., 1985.
Eiteman, David, and Arthur I. Stonehill. *Multinational Business Finance*. Reading, Mass., 1985.
Houser, George M. *No One Can Stop The Rain*. New York, 1989.
Hughes, David. *In South African Waters: Passenger Lines Since 1930*. Cape Town, 1977.
Hutchins, John G. B. "The American Shipping Industry Since 1914." *Business History Review* 2 (June 1954): 79–88.
Jones, Charles A., *International Business in the Nineteenth Century*. New York, 1987.
Kim, S. H., and S. W. Miller. *Competitive Structures of the International Banking Industry*. Lexington, 1983.
Lary, Hal B. *Problems of the United States as World Trader and Banker*. New York, 1963.
Marais, George. "Foreign Trade of the Union of South Africa, 1926–1952." Ph.D. dissertation. University of Wisconsin, 1956.
Pan-Am/Farrell Lines. *African Marketing Guide, 1968*. New York, 1968.
Porter, Andrew. *Victorian Shipping, Business and Imperial Policy: Donald Currie, the Castle Line, and Southern Africa*. New York, 1986.
Reynolds, J. N. *Voyage of the Potomac During the Circumnavigation of the Globe, 1831–34*. New York, 1834.

MINERAL SOURCING

This dimension of United States–South African relations, especially the transfer of gold, diamonds, and strategic minerals, is a fascinating, little-explored, and misunderstood subject. Useful information can be found in these works:
Anderson, E. W., and G. H. Blake. *The Republic of South Africa as a Supplier of Strategic Minerals*. Braamfontein, 1984.
Bateman, Alan. "Wartime Dependence on Foreign Minerals." *Economic Geology* 41, 4 (1946):309–22.

Brobst, Donald, and Walden P. Pratt, eds. *United States Mineral Resources.* Washington, D.C., 1973.

Cartwright, A. P. *Golden Age: The Story of the Industrialization of South Africa and the Role Played by the Corner House Group of Companies, 1910–1967.* Cape Town, 1968.

Castle, Emery N., and Kent A. Price, eds. *United States Interests and Global Natural Resources.* Washington, D.C., 1983.

Cotman, Walton. "South African Strategic Minerals and U.S. Foreign Policy, 1961–1968." *The Review of Black Political Economy* 8, 3 (Spring 1978):277–300.

Davis, John H. *The Guggenheims: An American Epic.* New York, 1978.

Dumett, Raymond. "Africa's Strategic Minerals During the Second World War." *Journal of African History* 26, 4 (1985):381–408.

Elliott, William Y., ed. *International Control in the Non-Ferrous Metals.* New York, 1937.

Emeny, Brooks. *The Strategy of Raw Materials.* New York. 1934.

Frankel, S. H. *Investment and Return to Equity Capital in the South African Gold Mining Industry.* Cambridge, Mass., 1967.

Furness, J. W., and L. M. Jones. *Minerals Raw Materials. A Survey of Commerce and Sources in Major Industrial Countries,* Washington, D.C., 1929.

Hocking, Anthony. *Oppenheimer and Son.* New York, 1973.

Innes, Duncan. *Anglo-American and the Rise of Modern South Africa.* Johannesburg, 1984.

Katzen, Leo. *Gold and the South African Economy.* Cape Town, 1964.

Kemmerer, E. W., and G. Vissering. *Report on the Resumption of Gold Payments by the Union of South Africa.* Pretoria, 1925.

Krasner, Stephen D. *Defending the National Interest: Raw Materials Investments and U.S. Foreign Policy.* Princeton, 1978.

Leith, C. K., J. W. Furness, and Cleona Lewis. *World Minerals and World Peace.* Washington, D.C., 1943.

Lovering, T. S. *Minerals in World Affairs.* New York, 1943.

Lumby, A. B. "Tariffs and Gold in South Africa, 1886–1939." *South African Journal of Economics* 44, 2 (1976):139–51.

Ogunbadejo, Oye. *The International Politics of Africa's Strategic Minerals.* Westport, 1985.

Rosenthal, Eric. *Gold, Gold, Gold: The Johannesburg Gold Rush.* Johannesburg, 1970.

Salamon, Miklos. "Research in South Africa's Gold Mining Industry." *Optima* 34, 2 (June 1986): 44–70.

Tanzer, Michael. *Race for Resources.* New York, 1980.

U.S. Department of the Interior. Bureau of Mines. *Domestic Supply of Critical Minerals.* Bulletin no. 144. Washington, D.C., 1943.

U.S. Department of the Interior. Bureau of Mines. *Mineral Facts and Problems.* Bulletin no. 630. Washington, D.C., 1965.

U.S. Department of the Interior. Bureau of Mines. *Mineral Commodity Summaries.* Bulletin no. 60. Washington, D.C., 1983.
Van Rensberg, W. C. J. *Strategic Minerals: Major Mineral-Consuming Regions of the World.* Vol. 2. Englewood Cliffs, N.J., 1986.

STATISTICAL INFORMATION

A number of directories are especially helpful:
Alagoa Bay and the Trade Statistics of Port Elizabeth, 1864. Port Elizabeth, 1864.
Fleming, William. *Alagoa Bay: Trade and Statistics.* London, 1868.
Glanville, E., comp. *The South African Almanack and Reference Book, 1911–1912.* Cape Town, 1911.
Goldman's Atlas of the Witwatersrand and Other Gold Fields. Johannesburg, 1899.
Harrison, C. W. *Harrison's Business and General Year Book of South Africa, 1927–1928.* Pietermaritzburg, 1928.
Horsefield, J. Keith, ed. *The International Monetary Fund 1945–1965.* Vol. 2. Washington, D.C. 1969.
International Bank for Reconstruction and Development. *World Bank* Annual Reports. Washington, D.C., 1953–1987.
Jeppe, Fred. *Transvaal Book Almanack and Directory for 1877.* Pietermaritzburg, 1877.
Jeppe, Fred. *Jeppe's Transvaal Almanack and Directory.* Pretoria, 1889.
Laite, W. J., ed. *Laite's Commercial Blue Book for South Africa, 1914.* Cape Town, 1914.
Legum, Colin, ed. *Africa Contemporary Record, Annual Survey and Documents.* London, annually. *Africa South of the Sahara.* London, annually.
Longland, J. ed., *Longland's Johannesburg and District Directory, 1899.* Johannesburg, 1900.
Longland, J. ed., *Longland's Johannesburg and District Directory, 1897.* Johannesburg, 1898.
Mitchell, B. R., comp. *International Historical Statistics.* New York, 1982.
The Natal Directory, 1910. Pietermaritzburg, 1909.
Port Elizabeth Yearbook and Directory, 1905–1909. Port Elizabeth, 1910.
Pritkin, Timothy. *A Statistical View of the Commerce of the United States of America.* Hartford, 1816.
Rosenthal, Eric, ed. *Cape Directory, 1800.* Cape Town, 1969.
South African Agriculturalists' Almanac for 1893. Wynberg, 1893.

SOUTH AFRICAN GOVERNMENT PUBLICATIONS

Bureau of Statistics. *Union Statistics for Fifty Years.* Pretoria, 1960.
Department of Agriculture, Economics, and Marketing. *Handbook of Agricultural Statistics, 1904–1950.* Pretoria, 1960.

Official Yearbook of the Union and of Basutoland, Bechuanaland, Swaziland. No. 4. 1921.
State of the Union: Economic, Financial, and Statistical Yearbook for the Union of South Africa. Cape Town, 1957.
South Africa 1980/81, Official Yearbook. Johannesburg, 1981.
South Africa 1983, Official Yearbook. Johannesburg, 1983.
South Africa 1986, Official Yearbook. Pretoria, 1986.

PERIODICALS

SCHOLARLY JOURNALS

The best journals for a study like that of this book are:
African Affairs: The Journal of the Royal African Society. Oxford.
Business History Review. Chicago.
International Journal of African Historical Studies. Boston.
Journal of African History. London.
Leadership. Johannesburg.
Optima. Johannesburg.

NEWSPAPERS AND MAGAZINES

Information on American entrepreneurial activity in South Africa at various times can be found in the following:
Africa Confidential. London.
Africa Digest. London.
Africa Economic Digest. London.
Africa News. Durham, North Carolina.
Africa Report. Washington, D.C.
African Business. London.
American Metal Market. New York.
Cape Argus. Cape Town.
Business Day. Johannesburg.
Businessweek. New York.
Cape Times. Cape Town.
Cape Town Daily News. Cape Town.
Christian Science Monitor. Boston.
Corporate Examiner. Interfaith Center on Corporate Responsibility, New York.
Directory Update. Africa Review Service, Investor Responsibility Research Center, Washington, D.C.
Divestment Action Roundup. Africa Review Service, Investor Responsibility Research Center, Washington, D.C.
Economist. London.
Financial Mail. Johannesburg.
Financial Times. Johannesburg.

Fortune. New York.
Journal of Commerce. New York.
Monthly Journal of the Johannesburg Chamber of Commerce. Johannesburg.
National Geographic Magazine. Washington, D.C.
New York Times. New York.
Reporter. South Africa Review Service, Investor Responsibility Research Center, Washington, D.C. Extremely valuable in terms of evaluating the performance of American MNCs.
Wall Street Journal. New York.
Washington Post. Washington, D.C.

BANKING REPORTS AND DIGESTS

These are also quite helpful. Among the most useful are:
Barclays Bank. *Business Brief.* Johannesburg.
Nedbank. *Economic Roundup.* Johannesburg.
Nedbank. *Executive Guide to the Economy.* Johannesburg.
Standard Bank. *Standard Bank Review.* Johannesburg.
Trust Bank. *Economic Monitor.* Johannesburg.

Index

Date Due

JAN 0 4 1990			